AS IT WAS

FRED TRUEMAN (or to give him his Sunday name, Frederick Sewards Trueman) was born on 6 February 1931 at Scotch Springs in the village of Stainton, Yorkshire. Another 300 yards down the road and he would have been afforded Nottinghamshire citizenship and thus never have been able to play cricket for his beloved Yorkshire.

He joined Sheffield Cricket Club and quickly advanced to play for his county, making his Yorkshire debut against Cambridge University in May 1949. In addition to enjoying a phenomenally successful career as a player, he was a member of BBC radio's *Test Match Special* team from 1974 until 2000. For forty-three years he wrote a cricket column for the *People* and has earned renown as one of the most humorous and brilliantly entertaining speakers on the after-dinner circuit. He lives in the Yorkshire Dales and Spain with his wife, Veronica. They have been married for thirty-one years.

AS IT WAS

The Memoirs of

FRED TRUEMAN

PAN BOOKS

First published 2004 by Macmillan

This edition published 2005 by Pan Books
an imprint of Pan Macmillan Ltd
Pan Macmillan, 20 New Wharf Road, London N1 9RR
Basingstoke and Oxford
Associated companies throughout the world
www.panmacmillan.com

ISBN 978 0 230 76852 9

A CIP catalogue record for this book is available from
the British Library.

Typeset by SetSystems Ltd, Saffron Walden, Essex

My memoirs are dedicated

to my darling wife,

Veronica – the best thing

that has ever happened to me

began on the day we first met.

Acknowledgements

I would like to thank the following, who by way of expertise, access to memorabilia, friendship or detailed recollection where my own personal memory was sketchy have helped in the writing of my memoirs: Julian Alexander and all at Lucas Alexander Whitley; Trevor Bailey; Ken and Jean Bolam; Brian Close; Phill Dann; Terry and Machita Denny; Ray Illingworth; Stanley Jackson; Georgina Morley; Stuart Evers and all at Macmillan; Jane, Toni and Charley Morrell, Steve and Deb Waterall; Yorkshire CCC – and the respective families of Veronica and me.

I would particularly like to express my sincere thanks to my good friend Les Scott, who collaborated with me on my memoirs. Having worked with George Best, Sir Stanley Matthews, Gordon Banks, Jimmy Greaves and Peter Shilton on their respective books, Les' kudos and standing as a writer is well known in sporting circles.

He has written for press, television and radio and wrote the screenplay for *The Rose of Tralee*. Having been an admirer of his writing for some years, when I decided to write my memoirs it was to Les to whom I turned for a helping hand. Thanks for all your help, Les, it has been a joy to work with you and above all, great fun!

For Sal, Lauren and Ruby

Fred Trueman, 2004

Contents

CHAPTER ONE

MOTHER NATURE'S SON

I HAVE ALWAYS BEEN HONEST, upfront and forthright. I see things for what they are and tell it the way it is. Such an attitude has not always been to the benefit of yours truly, Frederick Sewards Trueman, to give me my Sunday name. I always offer respect for others and expect the same in return. Again, that has not always been to my benefit. Countless words have been written about me and numerous stories attributed to my name, Sunday or otherwise. Some of these stories are true, some are half-truths, others downright lies. There is also much about me that has not been told. Until now, that is. When I decided to write my memoirs, among other things I saw it as an opportunity to put the record straight. To denounce the lies and the half-truths and reveal the myriad untold stories, all true, that have made me who I am. In so doing I will be as I have always been: honest, upfront, forthright and respectful of my fellow man. Laudable qualities to my mind, though you wouldn't believe the trouble they have caused throughout the course of my life.

In the early sixties, following a Test match in Melbourne, I joined my England team mates for a post-match drink. The atmosphere was convivial and I was sharing a joke with my good pal and 'Roses' adversary, Lancashire's Brian Statham. The room was filled with the soft hum of conversation when I heard a plummy, Old Etonian voice elevate itself above all others.

'Trueman! Over here!'

I felt the hackles rise on the back of my neck. I turned to see where the voice was coming from and saw a knot of MCC selection committee members, seemingly doing their best to help the profits of Gordon's gin and Schweppes' tonic. 'Trueman!' repeated the plummy voice, the owner of which was now crooking a finger, beckoning me to join him.

'Excuse me, Brian,' I said to my England colleague before making my way across to the gentleman who was so rudely demanding my presence.

'With all due respect, who the hell do you think you're talking to?' I said as I joined them. 'My parents christened me Frederick Sewards Trueman. Now friends may call me Frederick, Fred or Freddie. I don't mind. But what I do not respond to is "Trueman!" Especially when beckoned. I have a dog, it comes to my side when I call its name. I'm not anybody's dog to beck and call by shouting "Trueman".'

By way of emphasis I gave a sharp nod of the head and watched the faces of those committee members fall like a cookbook cake. The Old Etonian in question was none other than the Duke of Norfolk. Credit to him, he never said such again. In fact, from that day on, we were to have nothing but the greatest respect for one another and became good friends. I was later to learn, however, that my forthright attitude hadn't gone down well with the other MCC selection committee members. In time stories got back to me of conversations and mumblings that had taken place within Lord's committee rooms and gentlemen's clubs.

'What's up with that Trueman fellow? Seems to have an almighty chip on his shoulder.'

'That Trueman, always seems to be upsetting the apple cart. Bit of a rebel if you ask me. Must keep an eye out for him, what?'

'Trouble with Trueman is, he won't listen to advice.'

Such comments would eventually make their way back to me and, though never one to go with hearsay, I was left in little doubt such comments were true. The truth of the matter is, I was never a rebel. Neither was I anti-establishment. On the contrary, I was wholly supportive of cricket's hierarchy. What I objected to was the attitude, snobbery and bigotry displayed by some who, by way of their heredity, money or social connections, beset cricket's establishment in my time as a player – and beyond.

I played sixty-seven Tests for England between 1952 and 1965, becoming the first player in the history of the game to take 300 Test wickets. Though far fewer International matches were played in my time as a player, my sixty-seven Tests were spread over a period of thirteen years. Irrespective of the fact I was at the top of my game for Yorkshire and frequently topped the county bowling averages I was often overlooked for England. To my mind the reason for this was personal. Quite simply, some of the selection committee did not like my forthright attitude, which they misinterpreted as being 'bolshy'. Rather than pick the best eleven players for the job, the selection committee would often choose someone because he was, in their eyes, a gentleman and a decent chap. Such attributes often took precedence over someone's ability to play International cricket.

For this reason, I was selected for far fewer Tests than I believe I should have been. To my mind, if I'd had the opportunity to play in those Tests, I'm sure I would have topped 400 Test wickets. But that was not to be – even though I was regularly taking 100-plus wickets a season for Yorkshire.

In all, I took 2,304 wickets – to date no other fast bowler in the history of the game can claim more – took 438 catches and scored 9,195 runs (981 for England) including three centuries – two for Yorkshire and one for England. Not a bad record for a player considered by many as simply a fast bowler!

Yet nowhere have I ever seen it written that Fred Trueman was an 'all-rounder'. I have no gripes with that. It all comes down to how one is perceived. To some I was a troublemaker and rebel; to others simply a fast bowler. Those with only a passing interest in the game recognize me through my career as a journalist, TV presenter and broadcaster. I don't mind how people perceive me in terms of my career as long as they recognize me as being honest, forthright and respectful of others.

I have put my name to several books. What I have not done up to now is write my memoirs. When I came to the decision that the time was right to commit my life to the written page, I also decided that I would need a little guidance. I asked my good friend, the writer and broadcaster Les Scott, to help. We discussed a possible title for my book. I told Les I didn't want any of the silly titles I had seen on other autobiographies.

'Dickie Bird's was called *My Autobiography*,' I told Les. 'What sort of title is that? It's an autobiography, who else's could it be? Victoria Beckham's was called *Learning to Fly*. Sounds like a training manual. I bet that confused a few would-be terrorists.'

Les said I should keep it simple. 'Why not just call your book *As It Was*?'

'Not bad, but how's about this for a title,' I suggested tongue in cheek, '*The Best Bloody English Fast Bowler That Ever Drew Bloody Breath*?'

Les knows a little more about writing and books than I do. He explained to me why his suggestion might be better. And so another misconception about me is exploded. I *do* listen to advice.

WHEN I CAME INTO this world on 6 February 1931, south Yorkshire was as white as the county's rose. Snow in winter was to be something I would grow accustomed to during my childhood in Yorkshire. Even now, when the Meteorological Office announces it has not been a white Christmas, I sit in my home in the Dales watching their broadcast whilst snowflakes the size of espresso saucers descend from a battleship-grey sky. The snow that falls in the country is different to that which falls in towns. Snow opens out the countryside and gives emphasis to distance. It creates a feeling of great light and spaciousness in the fields and a comforting softness and silence in the woods. There is no stillness in the world quite like the stillness of the countryside under snow. The silence of snow is absolute. Birdsong is frozen. Trees don't move. Wind is deadened. Footsteps muffled. In the distance the ice-cream hills and small bandaged towns are also silent. It is not an illusion. Moreover, it's a silence that is absolutely complete in itself. I love the country because I am, and always have been, a country person. My family were country people, though I was born into a house that formed a row of miners' cottages.

I've been told my birth that snowy night had a certain poignancy about it, as it was much in keeping with how I would make my name in life. When my mother, Ethel, realized she was about to give birth, my father ran out of the house to bring the doctor. But I was fast even then. Speed coupled with a rhythmical approach and a good follow-through saw me into the world before my father had even reached the doctor's home. My delivery was overseen by my grandmother, whose maiden name was Sewards, which gave her a good call when everyone sat down to think what my name should be. Apparently my birth was straightforward and without complication, though as I weighed in at 14lb 1oz, my mother might have taken issue with such a claim.

There were seven children in our family and I was the middle one. Home was 5 Scotch Springs in Stainton, which was so close to the Nottinghamshire county boundary, should I have been born 300 yards further south, I would never have been able to play for my beloved Yorkshire. Our home was one of a row of twelve terraced houses surrounded by open countryside. The houses were owned by a colliery, though when looking out from windows you would never know a colliery was nearby, as it was situated over a mile away and out of sight behind a hill. The other houses were occupied by miners' families, and though my father did work as a coalface worker at Maltby Main, we were country people who lived off the land.

My grandfather, Albert Trueman, had been a well-known horse dealer. During the First World War he had a contract with the government to buy horses on behalf of the Army, which were then shipped out to the Western Front. Grandfather was also a decent cricketer. Good enough to be invited to the Yorkshire nets in the late nineteenth century and offered professional terms. Grandfather turned down the offer from Yorkshire and for one simple reason. He earned more in one day from selling horses than Yorkshire were willing to pay him for a week of playing cricket.

Grandfather's knowledge and expertise with horses were passed on to my father, Alan. My father served his time at Earl Fitzwilliam's stables at Wentworth Woodhouse, and rode in the Earl's colours as both a steeplechase and point-to-point jockey. When his weight counted against him, my father worked for a time as a miner, then secured employment with the well-known race-horse owner Captain Adcock, whose estate and stables were situated in nearby Stainton Woodhouse.

My dad was what some might call a man's man. He was only five feet eight tall, but his upper body was very broad. He was physically strong, worked hard and loved sport. He was also a teetotaller, God-fearing and a real stickler for discipline. He worked impossibly long hours to put food on the table and heat in the hearth for all nine of us, and with so many mouths to feed, waste was anathema to him. My mother, too, worked long and hard. This being the 1930s and with our home being so far from shops, Mum's life at home was labour intensive. Every day she baked nine loaves of bread for her family and Dad made sure not one crumb was wasted. If you didn't eat your crusts at tea time, they would be there on your plate at breakfast the next morning. If you didn't eat them then, they would appear at lunch and then tea again, until you did eat them.

Dad instilled in all of us a sense of discipline – especially self-discipline. Even in my thirties I never dared answer Dad back, though admonishments from him were rarely needed. Such self-discipline would serve me well later in life when I became a professional sportsman.

Mum and Dad also encouraged us to be honest, respectful and forthright. As a small boy, I once found a ten-shilling note on the lane that led to our house. A ten-bob note was some find. The average take-home pay from the pit at the time was thirty-seven shillings. So that ten-shilling note represented nigh on one-third of a weekly wage for a miner. I handed the note to my mother, who then proceeded to knock on all doors of Scotch Springs asking if anyone had lost any money.

Honesty prevailed. Not one person laid claim to the note. Mum's quest to find the rightful owner didn't end there. Some two miles away there was post office and a general store. Mum made enquiries there, but still no one came forward claiming they had lost the ten-shilling note. The postmaster put a notice in the window. After a week had passed and still no one had come forward, then and only then did Mum decide to keep the money.

Though I knew better than to answer my father back, I was encouraged to speak my mind on any subject, or matter. Voltaire said language was invented to conceal one's thoughts. Where I grew up people were plain-speaking, and for a person to speak his or her mind was considered a mark of how open and upfront they were. An indication that they were not devious, deceitful or, to use modern-day parlance, had a hidden agenda. Having been brought up in an environment with such an attitude, little wonder such attributes became a part of my character in adulthood.

Sunday was church day. We would accompany Mum and

Dad to Stainton parish church sometimes twice, often three times, every Sunday to offer thanks for our lot. In truth we had much to be thankful for. The thirties were a time of extreme hardship for many working people. Every decade enjoys its own descriptive prefix. The Roaring Twenties. The Swinging Sixties. The Grabbing Eighties. The thirties were frugal. A decade of depression, though not for the Trueman family. Being country folk who lived off the land, we enjoyed a good and varied diet of fresh meat, vegetables and fruit, which changed according to the seasons. Food was plentiful. My father at one point had four allotments, where he grew fruit and vegetables as well as rearing pigs and hens. Everyone mucked in. My brothers, sisters and I had to help with feeding and cleaning, boiling up potato peelings and other scraps from mum's kitchen to feed to the pigs. As I've said, nothing went to waste in the Trueman household.

Dad's employer, Captain Adcock, valued my father's expertise and hard work with his horses. So much so the Captain allowed Dad to shoot across his land. Dad only ever shot to meet the needs of his family, never to sell on. As a result we Truemans often sat down to meals that would be alien to the vast majority of working families of the time. In addition to rabbit, a common meat of the day, we'd also enjoy pheasant, partridge, woodcock, wood pigeon, hare, duck and occasionally quail. Eating 'posh' we used to call it.

Another benefit we enjoyed was electricity. The colliery had installed electricity in every home in Scotch Springs, whereas most other homes in the area still ran on gas. Looking back, I was very fortunate indeed with regard to my upbringing and the home I lived in. There being nine of us, it was a bit crowded, but each of us had our own bed. My sisters slept in one bedroom, my brothers and myself in another. If you're wondering who had the fourth bedroom, that was occupied by my grandmother Sewards. So, in reality there were ten of us in the family!

My abiding memory of my mother is that of a loving woman, devoted to her family, who never seemed to stop working. She was a very placid lady, not given to saying too much. She didn't get out a lot, her life was spent attending to the needs of her family and so hard did she work I can recall, even as a small boy, feeling sorry for her.

Being country people, our lives were very much governed by the seasons. Boyhood life for me was cyclical. Summer and autumn fused into one another almost always imperceptibly. I could never remember the actual day summer turned into autumn, the point of fusion was invariably lost some time in mid-September. Autumn would come along slowly and, having arrived slowly, would depart in much the same way. So much so, the coat tails of autumn might still be present in December.

Autumn provided a bountiful harvest for the family, though it was a far different harvest to the one we gathered in late August. In September I would join my brothers and sisters in gathering blackberries, gooseberries and wild raspberries. We would gather countless shopping baskets full to overflowing with these raven multi-berried fruits that were so tender even though I handled them with the utmost care, at the end of picking my fingers would be indigo blue. Mum would make blackberry pies, and as we had no means of storing it for any period of time the remainder of the fruit she made into jam.

I was eight years old when war was declared. The war provided another source of income for us Truemans because Dad was awarded a contract to raise six pigs for the government twice a year. He would acquire them as piglets, rear them, then, when the time was right, they would be slaughtered and sold to a government official as rationed meat. Dad, however, always ran seven pigs, the last being for our own consumption. In addition to the pork and bacon they provided, Dad used to cure his own hams and make his own black puddings. More often than not every year Dad would kill two pigs for us, so we always had a bountiful supply of home-cured ham, bacon and gammon.

We kept in the region of sixteen hens and one cockerel. Another of my jobs was to collect the fresh eggs from the coop. The hens would flap and squawk when I reached into the nests, and I always felt a comforting satisfaction when delicately extricating the warm eggs, knowing that no other eggs could be as fresh as these.

Autumn also provided us with mushrooms. Tender, wild mushrooms, their gills tickled pink, were strewn across the meadows like miniature white parasols. They had a very distinctive taste, dewy and faintly fragrant of autumn earth – quite unlike the tasteless ones you now buy in supermarkets. Collecting blackberries was fairly routine, but one never knew what to expect in the way of mushrooms. One day we would collect in excess of twenty pounds, a couple of days later less than six pounds, only to return twenty-four hours later and reap another bountiful gathering.

Just about everybody I knew took a short holiday from their normal work in September, though holiday is something of a misnomer, as we all went potato picking. Even as a small boy I would join my mum, brothers and sisters picking potatoes from Monday to Friday and on a Saturday morning, for which we were collectively paid £2. That may seem a nominal amount of money for so much work from so many people, but in the late thirties and early forties, we considered it a very good wage. The bonus of potato picking was the farmer allowed us to fill a basket with potatoes on the Friday night and take it home. Needless to say we took along the largest basket we had, which, when filled to overflowing, was then carried home by my brothers and me. Once home, we stored the potatoes in a pile in an out-house at the bottom of the garden and they would see us through to Christmas and often into January.

I have fond recollections of my childhood Christmases. Ever at the mercy of the seasons, the clothing we wore in December was different to that of any of the preceding months. Python-like mufflers reminiscent of stage-coach days. Hand-knitted woollen gloves that could have been made for sloths. Balaclavas. Rasping vests. Worsted overcoats. Fair Isle sweaters. Heavy grey cotton shirts and wool socks thicker than pipe lagging would suddenly appear from their darkling sabbatical at the back of the wardrobe to engulf us young Truemans in a haze of mothballs and lavender.

I can still recall the wonderful mixture of excitement, anticipation and joy that swept through my body on awaking to find a large Christmas stocking hanging from the post at the end of my bed. The sock would bulge as if holding a leg suffering from the worst case of varicose veins and arthritic lumps imaginable.

'He's been!' I would cry at the top of my voice, much to the chagrin of my slumbering parents. In my stocking there would be toys in boxes on which was emblazoned CWS – the mark that they had come from the Co-operative Welfare Society. The toys varied in type from one Christmas to the next, as if Mum was adhering to an annual theme. One year an ambulance and fire engine. The next a clockwork train and coach. The following year a military tank and scout car similar to those produced by Dinky. Then farm vehicles, and the next Christmas, racing cars.

Also in my stocking there might be a colouring book and some coloured pencils, perhaps a rubber ball, a classic children's book such as *Treasure Island* and always an orange, apple or some nuts. The latter which I had helped to collect some months previously. Compared to what youngsters receive today, the contents of my Christmas stocking might appear frugal, though I never thought it to be. On the contrary, I was always overjoyed by what I received and a simple rubber tennis ball, colouring book and pencils would afford me countless hours of entertainment. They were simple presents that gave simple pleasures.

If there is one thing I miss about my childhood life, it's the simplicity. True, there was hardship for many, but I feel the uncomplicated, unaffected, quite often disengaged nature of life back then in some way compensated. What I received in my Christmas stocking was par for the course for every working-class child of the time.

Being a country boy, I had the advantage of knowing the identity of the nuts I received, and of even knowing what an orange was. I dare say there were many inner-city and town kids of the thirties who, on receiving a tennis ball and an orange in their Christmas stocking, didn't know what they were. On being told 'an orange to eat and tennis ball to play with', I can imagine there being more than one inner-city boy who nearly took his thumb off trying to peel a tennis ball.

Once our Christmas presents had been opened and breakfast taken, my job was to accompany Dad to one of his allotments, where we would spend a part of Christmas morning picking Brussels sprouts and Savoy cabbage for Christmas dinner. Dad always reckoned the best time to pick either sprouts or cabbage was immediately following a sharp frost. From my recollection of their taste I reckon he was right.

I can never recall having turkey or goose for Christmas dinner. Usually there would be pheasant and a rabbit. Occasionally rabbit would be replaced by a cockerel, either a Rhode Island Red or a Light Sussex. Meat was plentiful for us, though I never realized at the time how fortunate we were in this respect. Especially during the war years.

British weather is no more fickle than when winter begins to give way to spring. The weather in March and April is like a fitful beast. Inconsequent, unreliable, changing from warm to bitter like some jealous lover. This is where the resilience and fortitude of country people comes to the fore, for you never know what's coming next and must adapt and cope accordingly. In March, many was the time as a boy I saw purple and buttercup-yellow crocuses catching the first flakes of a snowfall in their orange hearts before closing, stiff and tight, imperishable and unearthly like plastic flowers. April, too, was equally unpredictable. In squally showers wallflowers would buckle and then be laid to rest, as would the first of the corn, while the petals of tulips were scattered across the still cold soil like colourful casino chips. Then suddenly all would change. I would awaken one shooting green morning in mid-April to find new life unfolding all around Stainton. The fields about Scotch Springs that had flowered and died would be in the process of renewing themselves. The nearby woods having been stripped, thinned and pillaged would be bud bursting into life. I would take off on a walk accompanied by the clap of the wings of wood pigeon, the squawk of blackbirds and scuttling rabbits. There would be little in the way of flowers other than chance bunches of primrose, and by the woods a few transparent cups of wood-sorrel. But the surrounding countryside would hold great optimism and expectancy for me, as only it can when in the throes of rebirth and on the point of breaking into the first flame of summer.

In the summer holidays, all we kids would go pea picking, when occasionally Mum would join us for a day. I received 2/6d for every hundredweight of peas picked. On a good day I would pick around two hundredweight of peas for which I was paid five bob. That may seem small change, but if you could do that five days a week the take-home pay of twenty-five shillings (£1.25p) was considered very good money for a child to earn. There being four or five Truemans pea picking, at the end of the week the family had an extra income in the region of £6, which would have taken a miner nigh on a month to earn.

These days many well-meaning folk would be up in arms at the thought of children working long hours in fields, five days a week, humping heavy sacks of peas. Back then no one gave it a thought. Such work in the summer was considered the norm by country people and we children loved it. Yes, it was hard work, but it was also educational: I learned much about country ways and the environment in which I lived. The pea picking also acted as a social glue. Most of the families in the area went pea picking, people would chat as they picked, recalling events and characters of the past.

Everyone knew each other. We knew the trials and tribulations of one another's families. We acquainted ourselves with the history of illnesses and operations, marriages, loves unfulfilled and, of course, deaths. All of which fostered a great sense of community. There were no secrets because it was impossible to be secretive in such a small community.

In this age of social displacement and the breakdown of nuclear families and communities, many people have taken to communicating via email, Internet or text. There is nothing wrong in that, but communicating via email is further evidence to me that we are increasingly fostering a curiously indoor culture, characterized by sofa-bound kids. What's more, this kind of communication means there's no eye contact – something you couldn't avoid while pea or potato picking.

Curiously, modern technology, the decline of traditional industries and the breakdown of families and communities as people travelled far and wide to work have broadened people's horizons. When I was a child, people found their marriage partner within a radius of ten miles, and the location of everyone's work was within walking distance of home. Because we all knew one another and the history of everyone's family, it meant we were familiar with our origins, which gave everyone a sense of identity. Even as a small boy I had a keen sense of who I was, what my roots were and where I belonged. Though I have travelled the world, this sense of knowing who I was as a child remains with me. I still live – and belong – in the Yorkshire countryside.

Today people are far more sophisticated than they were in the thirties. But I feel the price we have paid for this is that many people are unable to connect with themselves and enjoy a keen sense of their own identity, knowing who they are and where they have come from. I believe this is very important. Life made sense to me as a child. The notion that there was purpose to everything and that everything made sense offered me a great sense of security, a security that would be cemented when the whole life cycle of country life began again.

Come the end of a summer, the corn was cut and carted, the fields nothing more than stubble. In the farmyards, brown dusty sacks stood ready for threshing and there would be a fresh clean smell of straw on the air. And so the cycle would begin again, which for me meant blackberry picking. The poet Philip Larkin described his childhood as 'a forgotten boredom'. I was never bored as a child. In addition to my schooling and the jobs undertaken in Dad's allotments and on the nearby farms, I also had a paper round which produced an additional half crown for the family budget. People in Australia tend to live their lives outdoors, which goes some way to explaining why Australia produces so many top sports people.

As a boy most of my life was spent outdoors, either working or playing sport. Though I would later make my name as a cricketer, I enjoyed all sports. In addition to cricket I played football, rugby and in the summer was also a member of the school athletics team. My childhood is not forgotten and neither was it one of boredom.

When there was no pressing work to be done, we would all go for long walks together in the countryside. Though even on these walks our propensity for self-sufficiency would be evident and we would return with a few bags of whatever berry, fruit, mushroom or nut was in season.

Apart from newspapers, we didn't have much contact or communication with the outside world. When I was a small boy Dad listened to the news on a crystal set and headphones, until one day excitement such as I had never known gripped the whole family when Dad came home carrying a wireless. My sense of anticipation and joy was overwhelming as I impatiently watched Dad erect an aerial at the bottom of the garden. That done, he plugged in the radio and every single one of us sat listening to the BBC Home Service feeling as Columbus must have felt when realizing he hadn't sailed over the edge of the world.

The wireless brought news, and often commentary of major sporting events. For me this was absolutely fantastic. I could experience great sporting events and great sportsmen right there in our living room. I'd listen to the commentator setting the scene, picture it in my mind and there it would remain for the duration as events unfolded.

Among my earliest memories was hearing of the 1938 Test between England and Australia at the Oval when Len Hutton made a then record Test score of 364. In the same innings Maurice Leyland made 187 and Joe Hardstaff 169, helping England to declare on the unbelievable score of 903 for 7. Australia, minus the injured Don Bradman, were bowled out for 201 and 123 respectively, to give England an historic win by an innings and 579 runs. 'Hutton – Hero and History Maker' said the headline in the newspaper of the following day. Never in my wildest dreams could I have imagined that within a few years, my childhood hero and I would be teammates.

We had simple needs and pleasures. To see a car round our village was something of an event. The odd one would pass by on the road that was situated at the bottom of our lane and many was the time my pals and I would sit on the fence by the roadside with a notebook and pencil jotting down the numbers of the cars that passed by. The thrill to be had here was in seeing a car whose make and marque was unfamiliar to us. Such as the car of a travelling salesman from a faraway place such as Leeds or Rotherham! It might not compete with television, video players, music systems, DVDs, mobile phones, PCs or Internet chat rooms, but we had our friends and we made our own entertainment.

These were the days when cigarette smoking was fashionable. 'Grass' was mown, 'coke' kept in the coal house, and a 'joint' was a piece of meat we ate hot on Sundays, cold on Mondays, in sandwiches on Tuesdays and in toad-in-the-hole on Wednesdays. 'The dope' was Sheffield Wednesday's latest signing from a club in Division Three North, and a gay guy was the life and soul of a party. It was a time before house husbands, dual careers and computer dating. When a 'meaningful relationship' meant getting along with your cousins, and soul mates were two flatfish side by side on a fishmonger's slab. When the only thing in the kitchen that could whisk, stir and blend was a spoon, and the only fast food was stewed prunes. James Cagney was shot so many times in films we thought he was worth more to MGM as scrap than he was as an actor, and the only thing that promised people sex, drama, mystery and intrigue was a marriage licence.

Occasionally the outside world would penetrate Scotch Springs, however tenuously. I remember one evening there was a thunderstorm the like of which I had never experienced. It was as if Thor and Woden had taken to their anvils. The sound of a million boulders tumbling was followed by a sloe-coloured sky suddenly fizzing and cracking. In the intervals between thunder and lightning the whole family became aware of a droning sound from somewhere above. We all stepped outside and when I looked up into what was a racing, tempestuous sky, I was amazed to see a low-flying aeroplane circling our village. It was the first time I had ever seen an aeroplane and I dare say most of Scotch Springs hadn't seen one either, because the entire population of Stainton, some 250 people, left their homes to experience this unusual sight. The aeroplane flew lower and lower. I could see it was a Royal Dutch airliner and it was flying so low I could actually see the people inside illuminated by the cabin lights. People's curiosity turned to concern when Dad said he thought the aeroplane might be in trouble. The aeroplane circled our village a couple more times before breasting a hill and disappearing over the side. Dad and his pals looked at one another anxiously as if expecting the worst. But we didn't hear a thing with the exception of the aeroplane's engines becoming ever distant until we could hear them no more.

When Dad came home from working with Captain Adcock's horses he was always a source of news. The men had been talking about the aeroplane at the stables and Dad had learned, thankfully, that it had managed to regain altitude and fly away. That circling aeroplane was a major event in Stainton life, hence the entire population coming out to witness it.

I attended the village school in Stainton. I warmed to the two teachers, Miss Nelson and Miss Robinson. Teaching seemed to be the preserve of single women in those days, or spinsters as they were known – even if they were in their early twenties. With domestic life being labour intensive I suppose once single women who were teachers married and had children of their own, they no longer had the time or inclination to return to teaching. Even on a part-time basis.

At school I read everything I could get my hands on and was ahead of most of the other children when it came to literacy and arithmetic. The school had only one room with a thin partition across it to divide the juniors from the seniors. Away from the classroom, however, I'd begun to play – and fall in love with – cricket. I clearly remember one day hearing Miss Nelson through the partition, reprimanding one of the seniors for his lacklustre attitude during a school cricket match.

'Go and watch young Freddie Trueman play cricket if you want to know what determination and the right attitude is all about,' I heard her say. I was taken aback. It was the first time anyone had passed favourable comment about my ability as a cricketer, and I also felt a sense of pride in being cited as a good example to someone older than me.

Cricket was very much part of the way of life in any Yorkshire village. I suppose my interest in the game came from my dad, who played for Stainton every Saturday and from the age of five took me everywhere with him. He was the captain, a very good batsman and a decent left-arm spin bowler. Encouraged by Dad, I had been bowling since the age of four, first with a rubber ball then with a proper cricket ball. I bowled at the dustbin lid which had been propped up at the bottom of our garden. I graduated from that to bowling at an old wooden orange box. Once I became adept at that, the orange box was broken up and I practised bowling at two of its wooden slats, then just one. Eventually my line, length and accuracy was such that I was bowling to a stick.

By the time I was eight years old I could bowl out men on the village green, and I was the same age when I first played for Stainton. As usual I had gone along to watch, but when Dad and I arrived at the ground he discovered one of the players was unable to attend. It was too late to try to rustle up a replacement because, if my memory serves me well, Stainton were playing either Firbeck or Thrybergh from just outside Rotherham, so Dad included me in the team.

I remember going out to bat, and on seeing me walking to the wicket, the opposing captain saying to his bowler, 'Take it steady, he's nowt but a boy.'

'Tha'll bowl at him proper, or don't bother,' Dad replied.

I think I made a run that day, whatever, my performance was such that Dad started to take me along to the club's practice sessions on a Tuesday night. I didn't bat, but I would have a bowl at the players and run around the pitch fielding the ball for them while they were practising their batting.

My proudest moment when playing for Stainton came when Dad made a century and I was batting at the other end.

I was nine years old, and, again, was only playing because someone hadn't turned up. I can't recall my own score but that was of little consequence to me even then. The fact that I had been at the other end when Dad hit the runs that gave him a century was a tremendous thrill and a great source of pride.

I was brought up as a church-goer, sang in the church choir and attended Sunday School regularly. I remember having a small blue attendance book. Every time I went to Sunday School the teacher would stick a stamp in the book, the carrot here being that a certain number of stamps qualified you for the annual Sunday School outing. This was the only holiday I had as a boy. Albeit it was only a single day out to Cleethorpes or Skegness I, like every other kid, considered it to be a real treat.

As far as I was concerned, going to Cleethorpes or Skegness was like travelling to the other side of the world. I had never travelled beyond a twenty-mile radius of my home, and the journey to the east coast was in itself a source of wonderment to me. For all I loved the countryside, for weeks prior to the outing I would look forward with great anticipation and excitement to my day out at the seaside.

On the day of the Sunday School outing there was no need for me to be shouted down for breakfast. I'd be up at dawn, at the sink washing face, hands and arms like a miner. I'd drag a gap-tooth comb through my hair and descend the stairs two at a time. Breakfast would be eaten with a steam-hammer right hand. Mum would give me a brown paper parcel of 'snappin' and off I'd run with that astronaut bounce in the step that only brand new sandshoes worn for the first time can give.

On the charabanc bus to the seaside there would be Pontefract cakes, Liquorice Allsorts, gobstoppers, tiger nuts, bullseyes, acid drops and, invariably in the end, green faces. But queasy tummies and bursting bladders would be instantly forgotten with the first glimpse of the sea.

Irrespective of the weather we would head straight for the beach. Sandcastles sprung up like houses on a new estate. Holes were dug in an attempt to reach Australia. The waves would roll in and we kids would screech and squeal as we rolled out to meet them. Once in the chilled, choppy waters our hand-knitted costumes hung heavy with the North Sea, making a builder's bum, by comparison, the epitome of decorum.

The smell of the sea was different to that of the countryside. One of wet flesh, wet hair, seaweed, toffee apples, cockles, winkles, tumbled, tossed and well-trodden sand and somewhere on the air, the very faint hint of ammonia. The wind would throw pleading gulls across the sky, their cries competing with the sound of donkeys braying, toy trumpets, Punch pummelling Judy, soprano shrieks, fiendish laughter and the distant whirr and clatter of the fairground.

And what a fairground! It was jam-packed full of lolling and larking. Older boys would hang from the railings of the dodgems eyeing rows of passing girls who found a bravery from linking arms. Beneath the 'Test Your Strength' machine miners from Maltby and colliers from Castleford would spit into the palms of their hands, before heaving the heavy hammer above their heads and sending it crashing down onto the pulverized plate, every 'dong' greeted with cheers by everyone within earshot, not to mention much strutting and smug satisfaction from the men.

I would be in a tizzy as I walked among the coconut shies and hoop-la stalls, desperate to spend my few pennies, but dazzled by the sheer choice on offer. After a time I would be in a dream-like state, unable to make a decision, like a Christmas shopper lulled into a stupor from having gone looking for presents without a list.

Cries of 'Roll up! Roll up!' assailed my ears from every direction. There would be the thundering roll of the big dipper and the screams of its white-knuckled passengers. The rumbling roustabout melodies of a steam organ accompanying horses of every colour of the rainbow as they bobbed up and down in the futility of a perpetual circle. Mothers with hoary hats and hostile hatpins, toddlers clinging to their skirts like ice-cream-smeared limpets. Mining fathers in collar and tie, jackets draped over their arms, realizing only now that they are truly on holiday when spitting and seeing the colour of their spit on the ground is white. Little hands grasping balsawood sticks on top of which sits a cloud of pink candy floss like Marie Antoinette's wig. Billowing and withering bodies, pinheads and balloon heads in the Hall of Mirrors. Sand in sandwiches. Sand in towels. Sand in sandshoes. Sand everywhere. Shrieking everywhere. Laughter everywhere. The same every year. Or so I believed.

I was eight years old when war was declared. It would be an exaggeration to say the tranquillity of life around Stainton was shattered with the advent of war. In truth, war in all its horror didn't descend on Stainton, but it is equally true to say life was never the same again. There were no dog fights in blue skies strewn with the spaghetti of vapour trails. No wailing sirens. No need for us to take to the Anderson shelter every night. No barns or warehouses ablaze. No death and destruction. Not a stain on Stainton. But that is not to say I didn't experience war at first hand. I watched the reality of war unfold before my eyes ten miles away.

Even allowing for the Quixotic policies of the Luftwaffe, Stainton was never on their agenda. Sheffield, the city built on steel manufacture, however, was an entirely different matter. 'Sheffield came in for it,' as people were given to saying at the time. I can recall one particular Thursday night, when from our back garden I watched Sheffield suffer a horrendous pounding. The sky hummed to a frightening droning sound from which, ominously, there appeared no respite. Ack-ack guns thumped away in the dark distance. The sky flashed and flared. The sound of thunder beset Sheffield. Then the skyline immediately above the city took on a crimson aura. Within half an hour that thin layer of crimson had turned into a billowing fire of hedges that lit up the surrounding countryside for miles. Sheffield was ablaze. Only then did the ghostly droning sound in the darkness of the sky depart.

That horrific scenario was repeated often. Watching it unfold from some miles away I was gripped by the sense of being helpless. I was of course only a boy, but should I have been an adult, I am sure I would have experienced the same feeling. Most of the young men around Stainton were either miners or worked on the farms. These were considered to be 'essential occupations', so few men from our area were called up.

Dad joined the Home Guard. I can clearly remember accompanying him to one of the first meetings, where he and his pals discussed what plans they would put into action should the Nazis ever land in the Stainton area. In those early days of the Home Guard Dad and his mates had yet to be issued with uniforms and guns. They wore their civilian clothes and armbands, but unlike most of the other newly recruited Home Guard soldiers, being countrymen, Dad and his colleagues had shotguns. They were never to use them. As they would never have occasion to use the official arms they would later be issued with. Stainton was at war, though it was to remain at peace with itself.

Though the frequent bombing of nearby Sheffield was a constant reminder to me of the suffering and destruction of war, the fact that it did take place ten miles away meant the war for us was largely fought on the horizon and in the newspapers. Only later, when I was twelve or thirteen years of age and we had moved to Maltby, did I come into close proximity with the war itself.

In 1944 the Nazi's changed tack. The heavy bombing raids were replaced by another horror, the doodlebug. The Nazis launched them from mainland Europe, and once the lifespan of the rocket had expired the doodlebug and its deadly cargo simply plummeted to earth. Whereas conventional bombing was contained to certain strategic areas, there was no exactitude where doodlebugs were concerned. Once their rocket had cut out, they could land anywhere and to devastating effect.

The advent of doodlebugs was the only time throughout the entire war that I ever felt fear. In fact it was more than fear, they terrified me. I was told that when you heard their distinctive high-pitched drone in the sky you had to keep listening. If they kept going you were all right, but if they stopped you threw yourself on the floor and prayed. It meant they were coming down in your vicinity.

Doodlebugs apart, the only other time the war really came to our area was when a Nazi bomber was shot down. I suppose it was hit by one of the guns in Sheffield and made its way over to Stainton before the crew bailed out. I'm not sure but I think it was a Heinkel bomber. Whatever, it crash-landed a couple of miles from Scotch Springs and, of course, became an instant magnet to us schoolboys. As far as I know the crew survived and, following a transitory spell in the local police station, were then collected by soldiers and taken on to a POW camp.

Death never stalked me during the war. In fact the only real danger to my young life had occurred some years previously. When I was three years old I caught black measles, serious tick-borne illness, and for a while it was a bit touch and go. I can recall little of it, but I do remember my other brush with danger a few years later.

I'd gone scrumping for apples and rather than being content to scoop up windfalls, had climbed an apple tree. I was halfway up the tree when I slipped and a jagged branch pierced the back of my shirt, jerking the collar against my windpipe. Within seconds I had blacked out but fortunately my pals saw what had happened. They quickly climbed the tree and by means of a collective effort managed to free me and carry me back down to the ground. I woke up in the arms of my mother. According to Mum, when I regained consciousness I told her I had been talking to Jesus. So it must have been a close thing, not to mention the nearest thing to a public hanging Stainton had seen since the Middle Ages.

In 1943, when I was twelve years old, we moved house. Tennyson Road in Maltby was only three and a half miles from Scotch Springs, but very much a part of a mining town as opposed to being situated in the countryside. We moved because the house in Tennyson Road was bigger than the one in Scotch Springs, affording the Trueman siblings, who were growing up, more room and privacy. It was also to make life easier for Mum, as our new home was nearer the shops and local amenities. Number 10 Tennyson Road was a house of red brick and blue-grey tile situated across the road from a well-trodden football pitch. It was part of a concentrated group of houses inhabited by miners' families and was within walking distance of the colliery. At the centre of the neighbourhood was a crossroads flanked by the largest pub in the area, The Queens, the Grand cinema, a working men's club and a variety of small shops. It was a two storey-town, apart from the ambitious gesture of Millard's Emporium, which sold everything from clothing, kitchenware, cosmetics and stationery to furniture, carpets, curtains, lighting and, curiously, ironmongery. On the top floor of Millard's was a café which was a major selling point in their advertisements in the local newspaper. One such advert offered local folk a dubious opportunity to escape the dust and grime of living in a colliery environment with its bizarre claim: 'Be nearer the sun – take tea in our second-floor café'.

A visit to Millard's café with Mum was a rare treat for me. With so many mouths to feed money was tight and our rare visits to Millard's never extended beyond a cup of tea for Mum and soft drink, usually lemonade, for me. We were not unique in this. Most of the womenfolk only took tea in Millard's. The plates of freshly prepared sandwiches, the meagre rationing of cakes and scones forever strangers to us all, more decorations to the pseudo-metropolitan atmosphere Millard's café strived to create than feasible options for their breadline clientele. Sugar, like everything else, was rationed, so the cakes on offer were basic and limited in variety. But the rationing imposed by the government, strict though it was, was never as severe as the self-imposed rationing practised by the women of Maltby Main who practised 'make do and mend' out of sheer necessity.

I attended Maltby Secondary School, having to forget about my chances of going to the local grammar school. I was bright enough to pass the qualification exam for grammar school, the school said as much, but Mum and Dad simply couldn't afford the expense of the uniform, PE kit, books and the rest. I wasn't disappointed. I simply accepted the situation. Mum and Dad didn't have the money and that was that. Whether the fact Mum and Dad were unable to finance me at grammar school hung heavy with them I don't know. Though they didn't have much money, Mum and Dad gave me a lot of love. Even as a twelve-year-old I recognized that as being the most important thing of all.

At Maltby Secondary I discovered that there were two teachers, Dickie Harrison and Tommy Stubbs, who shared the same sort of enthusiasm for cricket as Dad. They watched me bowl and put me into the school cricket team straight away, where I found myself playing with, and against, lads who were often three years older than me. Dickie Harrison in particular gave me a lot of encouragement and spent countless hours after school supervising his young charges. One of Dickie's incentives was to place a penny on each off-stump and a two-bob bit on the middle stump. He would then invite us to bowl at him and anything you knocked off, you kept. After two or three sessions of this I'd earned another five bob for the family budget. It was a pity the cricket season at school was so short, otherwise I might have earned enough to finance myself at grammar school.

I was still only twelve and playing for Maltby School when I sustained the worst injury of my entire cricket career. I was playing for the school at Wickersley, near Rotherham – and batting, as did every boy then, without a protector – when I was hit in the groin by what passed in schoolboy cricket as a fast bowler. I was taken to hospital in Sheffield where I underwent an emergency operation. The injury was so serious I was virtually immobilized for nigh on twelve months and was unable to play cricket, or any other sport, for two years. This was a very worrying and depressing period in my young life. Messrs Stubbs and Harrison were very sympathetic and understanding of my plight. Both did what they could to sustain my enthusiasm for cricket by arranging for me to score or umpire in school matches until, at the age of fourteen and a half, I left school to work in a local newsagent's.

If I had been less than wholly committed to cricket, I think the injury and consequent inhibitions and lack of progress might have caused me to give up the game. But, encouraged by my dad, my brothers, sisters and mum, I took to cricket once again. Dad was of the mind I should play proper club cricket, so applied to Maltby Cricket Club to get playing membership for me. To Dad's disappointment and that of my own, Maltby said 'thanks but no thanks', intimating they already had 'plenty of my sort at the club'.

Unfazed by Maltby's rejection of my services, Dad turned to a small village club where he knew a lot of the committee and players. Roche Abbey is situated just a few miles from Maltby and, to my delight, the club welcomed me with open arms. Roche Abbey were very understanding. They were aware of the debilitating injury I had suffered at school and told me I was under no pressure to prove myself. I was told I was there to enjoy my cricket, and that they would do their best to help me and develop my game in general. I was not yet fifteen and playing alongside men, but they were a great bunch of lads who took me under their wing and my game blossomed right from the word 'go'.

After impressing in net practice I was pitched straight into the team and in my first four matches took 25 wickets at a total cost of 37 runs. As a club Roche Abbey did not have the stature of Maltby, and the standard of cricket we were playing was not as high as the league Maltby played in. However, within weeks the paths of the two clubs were to cross when Roche Abbey were drawn against Maltby in a knock-out cup competition. I had no gripe with Maltby for having rejected me. It is not in my character to bear grudges. I didn't think I had anything to prove when I took to the field; Roche Abbey had been good to me; though all older, my teammates had become friends. I went out to do my best for my club, as I always did, irrespective of the opposition. As it happened, I murdered the Maltby batting, taking 6 wickets for 9 runs to help Roche Abbey to a convincing victory over their more illustrious neighbours.

The Maltby club was run from the pit where Dad had gone to work, having left the employment of Captain Adcock. Following my performance against Maltby, their officials never left Dad alone. They turned up at his allotments offering him all manner of perks, even a better job at the pit if he would agree to letting me play for them. He even got a note to this effect from the colliery manager that was left on his Davy lamp. Dad politely rejected all their overtures. He was a very proud man, my dad. I was not only proud of dad for the stance he took but also pleased. I was enjoying my cricket with Roche Abbey and the fact they had taken me on when others had closed doors to me induced in me a strong sense of loyalty to the club.

However, such were my performances for Roche Abbey that it was evident to all that if my development was to progress, I would have to play in a higher grade of cricket. The club entered another cup competition and were once again drawn against a leading light in league cricket. We were playing at home and, having been put in to bat, were skittled out for 43. The opposition obviously believed they were a different class to Roche Abbey and that the outcome of the game was academic. During the tea interval a number of the opposition players began to get changed out of their flannels, convinced they wouldn't be called upon to bat. When Dad went to see them only three of their number were wearing whites. He advised them to get changed back again. They laughed at him, advising him that two of the men waiting to bat had both scored centuries in league cricket the week before.

'All right. That as maybe,' said Dad. 'But I feel I should point out that I've got a lad of fifteen here who might cause you a bit of trouble.'

Again they laughed.

'Fifteen?' one queried. 'That'll be the day when a fifteen-year-old rips through this batting.'

It was the day.

I took 6 wickets for one run. They were all out for 11.

To his credit, after the game the captain of the opposition came to Dad, offered his congratulations and told him I shouldn't be playing for a village side – that I was much too good. Dad, at first, wasn't in agreement. He told the captain I only had a few games under my belt and was too young and inexperienced to move into a higher grade of cricket. But the captain was insistent. He told Dad the news of his team being bowled out for 11 against a village team, for whom a fifteen-year-old had taken 6 for one, would spread like wildfire. That it would only be a matter of time before someone from a higher grade of cricket would take an interest in his son.

That captain was right. My performances for Roche Abbey brought me an invitation to go on a tour of the south of England with the Yorkshire Federation boys' team, which included another young player who had begun to make a name for himself in junior cricket – Brian Close.

I had now left the newsagent's and was working at Maltby main pit as a haulage hand pulling the tubs of coal. The work was hard and physical, but the long hours made me stronger than your average fifteen-year-old. My upper body in particular thickened out and became muscular. At this point Dad knew that I was now strong enough to cope with a better standard of cricket.

Word had spread of my achievements and reached the ears of Cyril Turner, the former Yorkshire player who had been appointed coach to the Sheffield United Cricket Club. Cyril came to watch me in action for Roche Abbey, came up to Dad and said, 'This lad, Trueman. Suppose he's yours, is he, Alan?' Dad said: 'Yes, he is. But he's only fifteen.' Dad's response being indicative to me now that he was still not wholly convinced I was ready for a higher grade of cricket. Cyril Turner, however, was in no doubt.

'I want him in my nets next week,' Cyril told Dad – and such was Cyril Turner, there was no arguing with him.

The whole family came along to watch me play for Roche Abbey on Saturday afternoons. When we got home at night, Dad would analyse my performance, sometimes in great detail. If I'd bowled well and taken a few wickets I could tell he was very happy and proud but never at any time did he say as much to me. If I had taken 6 wickets he'd tell me I'd been lucky to get more than 2 because the other 4 had come from poor deliveries. He'd spend a good part of a Saturday night analysing my game and offering his considered opinion. He'd say I'd have taken even more wickets but my left arm was in the wrong position, or my chest was opening too early, or my run-up was too quick for precise and accurate bowling.

I would listen to Dad's advice intently, taking on board what he'd said before indulging in a little self-analysis of my own. Never at any time during these talks did Dad ever say anything about the possibility of me becoming a professional cricketer or playing for Yorkshire, though I should imagine that secretly he nursed such a hope. To be honest, I never gave the matter a thought. I was the product of a working-class generation that possessed little in the way of expectation. I had been brought up in a family and a community where we were taught not to have great hopes, because invariably that would result in disappointment. In the main most men worked in the pits, in agriculture as farm hands, or in manual labour. No one I knew ever aspired to do anything different. Young people simply accepted that they too would embark upon such work for the rest of their lives. Which explains why, rather than being a cricketer for Yorkshire, my ambition was to become a bricklayer.

My ambition, however, was not to be realized. Oddly enough, I was never disappointed about that.

CHAPTER TWO

YORKSHIRE CALLING

SOME PEOPLE we never forget in life. Your first love. Your driving instructor. The person who was always top of the class. The couple who never returned the invitation to your party. Likewise there are some things we never forget. The multiplication tables, for example, that I was taught parrot-fashion at school. To this day should anyone ask me any multiplication from any table from one to twelve I answer in an instant. Another thing I will never forget is my first ever day at Bramall Lane, the home of Sheffield United Cricket Club and, of course, the football club of the same name.

When I first attended nets at Bramall Lane it was the first time I'd set foot inside a county cricket ground. Though in my mid-teens, I had not the faintest idea what league cricket was all about, let alone county cricket. What I knew about the top players of the day such as Len Hutton, Maurice Leyland, Walter Hammond and Herbert Sutcliffe I'd gleaned from reading newspapers on my delivery round. It was as if they lived in another world. As with the multiplication tables, my first impressions of Bramall Lane were to remain with me for ever.

Bramall Lane was originally constructed in 1854, when six local cricket clubs got together to rent the site from the Duke of Norfolk on a ninety-nine-year lease for the princely sum of £70 per annum. One of the stipulations laid down by the Duke was that 'every game of cricket should be conducted in a respectable manner' and at no time should players 'indulge in pigeon shooting, rabbit coursing or country pursuits of any kind'. It was just as well the old Duke had long since departed this earth and that that caveat had gone with him, otherwise we Truemans might never have been allowed to set foot in the place.

It was not surprising, then, that when I finally did I was somewhat in awe of the place. History and tradition seemed to seep from every brick. The ground had been host to some of the greatest matches in the history of cricket and had been graced by players of equal stature. I have to say, Bramall Lane, for all its glorious past and illustrious present was, to me, far removed from any cricket ground I had ever known. The grounds where I had watched games and played cricket had idyllic country settings. They were surrounded by trees, lush fields and sometimes rolling hills. Though excited to be attending nets at this famous venue, my first impressions of the ground itself were a little disappointing. There was not a single tree to be seen and rather than the chirping of birds or the distant drone of a mower or chug of a tractor, there was the constant sight and sound of the heavy industries on which the city had built its name. Outside the walls of the ground, tramcars clattered along cobbled streets and hissed like ganders as they stopped to pick up passengers. The ugly fingers of soot-blackened chimneys forever pointing at the sky belched great fugs of yellowy-brown smoke into the atmosphere. There was the bustle of a city whose industry lived cheek by jowl with the homes of its workforce. The sound of a thousand hammers echoing in cavernous corrugated-iron-roofed factories. The fiendish chatter of electric riveters. The sudden squeal of tortured metal. And in the air an acrid mix of fired coal, sulphur-tainted steam and human sweat fought for ascendancy with the yeasty odour of a nearby brewery. The old Duke of Norfolk could lie at ease in his final resting place. 'Country pursuits of any kind' would never again be perpetrated at Bramall Lane.

If Bramall Lane was an eye-opener to me, so too was the Sheffield United Cricket Club net practice. Cyril Turner proved himself a superb coach. He gave me any amount of good advice, as did many others connected with the club. Though I had enjoyed initial success in village cricket, some of it against league teams in cup competitions, under Cyril's tuition I was amazed to discover I had not been holding the ball properly. He was flabbergasted when he saw me holding the ball with my fingers across the seam. He couldn't understand how the hell I had managed to make the ball swing so much with a grip like that. Cyril taught me how to hold the ball properly and, as with all technique when learned, I was astonished by the improvement to my game. Similarly, when striving for extra pace, my delivery had become nothing more than a sling. As a result, I lost both length and direction. Cyril taught me how to make the ball swing both ways and how to follow through properly. Armed with even this basic knowledge I began to get seriously interested in cricket for the first time. The more I learned the more I realized how much there was to learn.

By now I had given up any desire to be a bricklayer. I was working in the bricking industry, spending long hours every day wheeling enormous barrowloads of bricks to the brickies. Not content at that, after a few weeks my boss told me he wanted me to load the bricks onto the barrow as well and then complained at the fact I was not delivering the same volume of bricks as previously. I explained that I couldn't because time was now taken up loading bricks as well as delivering them. He didn't accept that as an answer and became bombastic. I'm afraid I told him to 'bugger off' and I was promptly given my cards. I wasn't out of work for more than a day. I promptly got another job at Tinsley Wire Work making wall tiles on a machine. Like the brick carrying, this work was mentally undemanding, and though I quickly demonstrated myself as being competent at the job, the monotony of the work and the lack of mental stimulus prompted me to look for alternative employment.

Work was plentiful in Sheffield in the forties. I had heard about the good money to be had from doing 'piece work' at a glass works in Rotherham and promptly went down there to see their Works Manager. Though the basic wage was very low, decent money was to be had from the 'piece work', which paid a bonus for every bottle a worker made. The more bottles you produced, the more money you received. It was a good company to work for, the management were fair and my workmates industrious and friendly. But cricket was looming larger and larger in my life and in the summer months I found I couldn't wait for Saturdays to come round.

The improvement to my game was such that I was soon chosen for the Sheffield United second XI and in my first match I took 6 wickets for 11 runs. Following a handful of games in the Sheffield United second XI, I was selected for the club's Yorkshire Council team. I played the last five matches of the season for them and took 15 wickets.

All League cricket in Yorkshire was geared to supplying the needs of the County Cricket Club. Headingley kept in constant touch with clubs and coaches to see if they had any promising youngsters who might have the potential to develop to county standard. I was by now coming up to seventeen years of age. Though my development had been satisfactory, my perform-ances, as with all young players, were erratic. But I had honed a decent delivery and had the positive merit of speed. Cyril Turner transmitted that information to the county's cricket committee and during the winter I received a letter inviting me to Leeds for the indoor winter coaching classes under the super-vision of Bill Bowes and Arthur Mitchell. I was not yet seventeen and only a touch over five feet four and Cyril, I am given to understand, thought I would give a better demonstration of my potential when I had grown taller and thickened out. Headingley, however, were insistent and a date was fixed for me to travel to Leeds, all expenses paid.

As I say, I was still very green, but my game had improved in leaps and bounds thanks to Cyril Turner. I remember once playing in a second XI league match and a chap coming up to me and saying, 'You'll never make a bowler.' I asked him why. He said, 'Because you bowl at stumps too much, instead of bowling to your field.' This was a revelation to me. I'd never realized you could bowl at the stumps too much and his answer immediately set me thinking. I think that was the first time I realized quick bowling had as much to do with technique and brains as it did speed and brawn.

I had never been to Leeds before and was accompanied by Dad and Cyril Turner. I had every confidence in my own ability but was apprehensive about doing myself justice at Headingley. I'd been made aware of the big difference between the various standards of cricket in Yorkshire. The Sheffield United second team played in the Sheffield League and I found the quality of cricket in that competition was far higher than the village cricket of Roche Abbey. The Sheffield first XI played in the Yorkshire League, which proved a even higher grade of cricket than the Sheffield League. To graduate from the Sheffield League to the Yorkshire League was like moving from Minor Counties cricket to International cricket. Now I was leap-frogging the Yorkshire League – though I would play at that standard the following summer – to attend nets at the seat of county cricket. It was one hell of a jump for me and one I had undertaken within a very short period of time. Hence my apprehension.

When I saw the Headingley pitch I was stunned by the sheer size of it. The only field of that size I had seen had been full of turnips. The introductions over, I was taken to the nets and bowled just eleven balls, that's all. I didn't think anyone could judge my worth from just eleven deliveries but my efforts had been watched closely by one man in particular. After nets I was approached by an elderly man who introduced himself as George Herbert Hirst. His face was unfamiliar to me but his name was legend. George Hirst along with Wilfred Rhodes were unbeatable as all-rounders in the years leading up to the First World War. In 1906 George Hirst achieved the unique feat of scoring 2,000 runs (2,385 to be exact) at an average of 45.86 and taking 200 wickets (208 at 16.50) in a first-class season. That was one of fourteen doubles of 1,000 runs and 100 wickets in a single season. Those fourteen doubles included a record eleven in succession between 1903 and 1913. In 1906, when playing for Yorkshire against Somerset, he achieved a feat which remains unique in first-class cricket when he scored a century in each innings (111 and 117 not out, and also took 5 wickets in each of the Somerset innings (6 for 70 and 5 for 45). Hirst was a forceful right-handed middle-order batsman and a superb left-arm medium-fast in-swing bowler, and if that wasn't enough, he also proved himself to be a magnificent fielder. The man was an idol. That he deigned to speak to me made me weak at the knees.

I shall never forget my conversation with George Hirst. He asked me my name and then asked where I came from. I told the great man I lived in Maltby, but had been born in Scotch Springs in Stainton.

'Stainton. Forgive me for asking, but is that in Yorkshire?' he asked.

'Oh yes, Mr Hirst,' I replied, 'I'm Yorkshire born and bred all right.'

'Pleased to hear it.'

Hirst asked me if I was on my own and I told him I was with my dad and Cyril Turner. I pointed to where they were sitting and Hirst followed me over. When Dad looked up and saw me standing with this legend of cricket he immediately took to his feet and removed his cap.

'This is Mr Hirst, Dad,' I said, not knowing what else to say.

'Yes. Yes. Of course. I recognize you Mr Hirst,' said Dad. Until that moment, I had never seen Dad in awe of anyone, though typically he never said anything about it afterwards. Hirst talked to Dad for a few minutes, then called over Cyril Turner and all three had a quick chat then walked off together and disappeared. The nets took place in what to all intents and purposes was a large shed. Not dissimilar, albeit a much smaller version, of the type you see nowadays on what one Labour government minister fatuously described as being 'regenerative emplacements of commerce and culture for sustainable income displacement'. Do-It-All and B&Q to you and me.

I sat alone in that shed for an hour and a half wondering what on earth was going on. I feared the worst. They had only let me bowl eleven times and had not asked to see me bat or field. Why had they not asked me to show what I could do with a bat and in the field? Initially I thought they'd reached the conclusion that I was simply nowhere near the required standard. But I'd hit the stumps three times, which, given I had bowled only eleven balls, seemed a reasonable return to me. When Dad eventually returned he said nothing. We caught the bus home and still he remained tight-lipped. I was too scared to ask him what was occupying his mind. It was not until our bus approached the outskirts of Doncaster that he spoke up.

'It's going to cost me six pounds, but I don't care about that,' he said. 'You've been picked for the Federation tour and I'll find the money to make sure you go.'

The Federation team I suppose was the latterday equivalent of an academy side. Come the cricket season we embarked upon a short tour of the south of England. The team coach picked me up in Maltby and I felt very proud of Dad and Mum as I waved goodbye carrying a cricket bag and wearing a green sports jacket and grey flannel trousers. That night was the first night I had ever spent away from home. We broke our journey by staying overnight at Harrow school, by which time

I'd got to know most of my teammates. We all seemed to get on well, but I do remember feeling sorry for one young lad who suffered from travel sickness for most of the way. We all tried to comfort him as best we could, which was a sign of the camaraderie that existed among us even at this embryonic stage of the tour. Happily, once we reached Harrow school, the lad in question recovered quickly. Poor Ray Illingworth, though he would go on to travel the world as captain of England, he was never to overcome his travel sickness.

Another future Yorkshire and England player on this tour was Brian Close, who without a doubt was the star of the team. Brian was a big lad even as a teenager and he had oodles of personality. I kept pretty quiet since I had never experienced anything of this kind before and was not as familiar with the other lads as Brian was. Our first match was against Bucking-hamshire Colts, which, if my memory serves me right, we won. What I do remember clearly is the following day. After the game against Buckinghamshire we travelled down to the south coast to watch Sussex play Somerset. It was the first county match I had ever seen. All the other lads had attended county games at Headingley. The fact I felt inexperienced even when in the company of boys of the same age was another reason for my relatively low profile. I wasn't so much overawed as sussing it all out.

The Sussex–Somerset game proved to be highly memorable in that we saw Somerset's Harold Gimblett hit a triple century. Following our day at a county match it was back to the tour, though I can't recall it in any detail. I remember Brian Close scoring a century at Brighton against an equivalent side from Sussex County Cricket Club and my taking 4 wickets in a match, though the opposition escapes me.

The year 1948 proved a good one for me. Cyril Turner promoted me to the Sheffield first team in the Yorkshire League. Again, I felt happy with my efforts, in what at the time was a very high standard of cricket. Quite a number of players in the Yorkshire League had played for Yorkshire County second XI and a number of them for the county's first team. Sheffield had themselves a number of players who had knocked at the door of county cricket, some of whom had had it opened to them.

Charlie Lee had played a number of games for Yorkshire's second XI and a few games for the county team before moving to Derbyshire, where he ended captaining their county side. Ken Lee (no relation), and a slow left-arm bowler, Johnny Ashman, were other members of the Sheffield team who had played for the county's second string. I had by now set my sights on becoming a professional cricketer, though I found that there was money to be made even in the Yorkshire League. With my expenses added I was earning £6 a week playing for the Sheffield United first team. To me this was an unbelievable amount of money. When I worked shifting bricks on the building site, the most I had ever earned was 17/6d a week. To be paid so handsomely for playing the game I loved was simply fantastic.

My deeds on the pitch saw my name being bandied about in the circles of league cricket. A couple of clubs approached me saying they could offer me more money than I was making at Sheffield, but I declined their overtures. I told Cyril Turner about these approaches and assured him my loyalty at this level of cricket was to Sheffield United and him in particular.

Occasionally I would top up my £6 by earning a collection. If a batsman made over 50, or a bowler took 6 wickets for under 25 runs, they passed a collection bucket among the spectators. The spectators would contribute two bob or perhaps more depending on your achievement and what they thought of your performance. Such were the attendances at Yorkshire League matches in the late forties, a 6-wicket haul for me would earn me a collection in the region of £5–6. When added to the £6 I received from the club, this meant

I occasionally took home nigh on £12. An exceptional amount for an adult to earn in 1948, let alone a seventeen-year-old.

Towards the end of the season one of Dad's pals called at our house with a copy of the *Sheffield Telegraph*. The newspaper carried a report of an after-dinner speech given by the legendary Yorkshire and England batsman Herbert Sutcliffe. Like George Hirst, Sutcliffe was revered, not only in Yorkshire but throughout cricket. Always of immaculate appearance, he was a batsman of great renown. A commissioned 2nd Lieutenant in the First World War, he didn't make his first-class debut for Yorkshire until he was twenty-four but he quickly made up for lost time. He scored 1,839 runs in 1919, a record aggregate for a debut season. After which he kept the scoreboard clicking at a furious pace, scoring over 1,000 runs each season up to the Second World War including over 2,000 runs each season from 1922 to 1935, a feat he repeated in 1937. Included in that record were three seasons when he scored over 3,000 runs (1928, 1931 and 1932). He still has the best record of any English batsman against Australia, his 2,751 runs being made at an average of 66.85. As you would expect with a record like that, when Herbert Sutcliffe talked cricket, everyone listened. So what was he saying in the *Sheffield Telegraph*? Dad's pal read the article out loud.

'I am confident about the future well being of Yorkshire cricket,' read Dad's pal. 'There are a number of very promising youngsters in development. One such young man is called Freddie Trueman, whose talent is such I predict he will play for Yorkshire before he is nineteen, and for England before he is twenty-one.'

An unusual silence beset the Trueman household.

'Well, I'll be blowed,' I said.

'Language, Fred,' said Dad, mildly rebuking me for what was on my part an instinctive reaction to the greatest plaudit I had ever received.

'Yon Sutcliffe knows what he's talking about,' said Dad's pal.

'If he says . . .'

'Aye. If he says . . .'

Dad's voice trailed away. He turned his head to look at me. That look I shall never forget. It appeared to me a mixture of absolute wonder and complete surprise. As if he had just laid eyes on me for the very first time.

DURING THE WINTER of 1948–9 Yorkshire paid my travelling expenses to attend the indoor nets at Leeds, where I was coached by Bill Bowes and Arthur Mitchell. Bill Bowes was six feet four, fair-haired and cut an unmistakable figure on the pitch. He generally bowled at a fast-medium pace, though was eminently capable of bowling a genuinely fast ball when the occasion merited it. Off a short run he was extremely accurate, swung the ball either way and possessed a sharp break-back. Bill took over 100 wickets nine times in a season, and averaged under 20 runs per wicket in every one of his thirteen seasons with Yorkshire. Bill was every inch a bowler but never truly comfortable with a bat in his hand. Indeed, he was one of those rare cricketers who took more wickets in a first-class career than he scored runs. Oh, one other thing about Bill Bowes: he was one hell of a coach. As was his partner at indoor nets, Arthur Mitchell.

My weekly return journey from Maltby to Leeds I made by bus. I first travelled by bus to Doncaster, where I caught a South Yorkshire Transport bus into Leeds city centre. I would then catch a local bus out to Headingley, or if it was a fine night and time was on my side, I would embark on a brisk walk. On arriving at Headingley I'd report to Mr Nash, the secretary, and sign for expenses, which was always a brand new ten-shilling note. I would then get changed, practise in the nets, then change back into my civvies and commence the journey home. It being winter, some of those return journeys had more than a touch of adventure about them.

On one particularly snowy night I arrived in Doncaster too late to catch the last bus to Maltby. I had no alternative but to walk nine miles home in what had turned into a blizzard. I finally reached home at about three-thirty in the morning, went to bed, and got up as I always did at five a.m. to go to work. On the homeward journey making my connection in Doncaster was always a worry. Like the railways, bus services had been run into the ground during the war, and the quality of service was not as good as it had been in the pre-war years. That said, regarding both railway and bus services in Yorkshire in 1948–9, they were a damn sight better than they are now!

The shed is no longer. It was situated where the Yorkshire club offices are now to be found. Though the facilities were basic compared to those offered by counties today, in 1948 for a county to have an indoor training area was considered cutting-edge. We bowled and batted on wooden boards. That may not sound to be in keeping with cricket, but these boards were wonderful surfaces to play on. I see teams practising in the nets these days and occasionally see bowlers bowling bouncers and the batsmen ducking. If we had done that, Bill, Arthur or the other coach, Maurice Leyland, would have come over and said, 'Hey, what do you think you're playing at? Get-that-ball-pitched-up!'

They were absolutely right, of course. The whole idea of practice is for a bowler to find his line and length and get the ball up there, and for the batsman to play his shots and get into form. That's what it's all about, not ducking and diving. Pitch the ball up, perfect line and length. That's what I had to do. That's how it was and woe betide any youngster who tried anything different.

Bill Bowes, Arthur Mitchell and Maurice Leyland watched and studied me and seemed convinced that my delivery swing was so essentially fine that all else had to be built around it. I was told that the first thing they wanted me to concentrate on was control. I had to learn to bowl within myself. They taught me to use only as much pace as allowed me to maintain accurate line and length. At that age I tended to over-pitch the ball. My response to anything in a batsman that displeased me – an edged stroke, an effective stroke and, above all, a hook shot – was to deliver a bouncer. I was taught to threaten the bumper ball so convincingly that the batsman had to move onto the back foot to deal with it and then bowl him out with a yorker.

I also tended to drag my foot an inordinate distance. They decided that any attempt to cure that might destroy much of what went before. I was, however, subjected to some crucial alterations regarding the landing of my feet in the three strides of the actual delivery. I practised and practised until these new techniques were assimilated into my bowling style.

In later years Bill Bowes very kindly said that I was the ideal pupil. According to Bill, not only was I anxious to learn, but unquestioningly obedient and untiring in practice. The winter of 1948–9 was one of improvement for yours truly. I wasn't the only youngster to greatly benefit from the guidance of Bill and Arthur. Brian Close had also come on in leaps and bounds.

My development had obviously pleased the powers that be. Yorkshire asked me to get a job in a reserved occupation to avoid conscription for National Service. That meant only one thing where I lived – Maltby Main pit. When I told Dad I wanted a job at the colliery, he didn't know what to say – he had always said that no child of his would ever follow him down the mine. Earlier, my eldest brother, Arthur, had flown in the face of Dad's wish and secured a job down the pit, which upset Dad considerably. After much discussion he agreed to me working in the tally office, which meant I didn't have to work at the coalface with him. Though often was the time I did go underground and find the seam where he was working and spend fifteen minutes or so shovelling coal onto the belts to give him a helping hand.

I enjoyed my work at the pit and continued to work there all through the winter. I was, however, longing for spring and the advent of another cricket season. It was a Friday morning in early May. The wild flowering trees of the surrounding countryside were at their best. The sky had softened into a sea of white islands. Gorse and broom broke the sequence of pink and white of crab apple and cherry blossom. The fields were dotted with the full floppy lushness of primrose and in the woods there was a smattering of the delicate blue of the first bluebells. It was the sort of morning which in those days was said to turn a young man's fancy to thoughts of love. My love at this time was cricket.

For some reason I wasn't at work that day. There was a knock on the door and when I answered it I was confronted with a Post Office boy.

'Telegram for Mr F. Trueman.'

I'd never received a telegram before. Eager to see who could be sending me an urgent message, I ripped it open and read the message in the 'stop-start' fashion of telegrams: 'Frederick Trueman. Stop. Chosen for Yorkshire County Cricket Club first XI. Stop. Versus Cambridge University. Stop. Fenner's. Stop. Contact Headingley immediately. Stop. Nash. Secretary. Stop.'

I stopped all right. Dead in my tracks. I had been picked to play for the Yorkshire first team. Standing there in the hall, staring at the telegram in my hand, all manner of feelings swept through my body. I was excited. Gloriously happy. Mortified. Proud. Apparently Mum shouted through from the kitchen, asking me who had been knocking at the door. I didn't hear her for the sound of angels singing.

Dad didn't see the telegram until he came home from the pit. Typically, he didn't say anything and kept his emotions and thoughts to himself. Though the way he kept putting the telegram down only to pick it up minutes later and read it again suggested to me that he was very proud and wanted to savour and cherish the moment, relive it again and again, so that it would be imprinted in his memory for all time. He didn't say anything. But that was typical of working men at that time. In tight-knit working-class communities such as ours, it just wasn't the done thing for men to show their emotions. For a man to display his emotions was seen as a sign of weakness. The only time men gave vent to their emotions was at funerals and even then, it was restrained. Thus there existed a strange dichotomy among the working men of South York-shire, who would be forthright and speak their minds, yet would never be given to outward displays of emotion.

Dad had a day off from work on the Monday and took me into Doncaster to buy a complete set of new clothes for me. It set him back more than £20, which I knew was a considerable outlay on his part. Again, he never said anything, but for Dad to spend so much money shows how important he thought my call-up for Yorkshire. After my initial elation had tempered somewhat, it suddenly occurred to me that I didn't have any cricket equipment of my own. Playing for Sheffield I simply used the equipment that was provided by the club. But I knew that Yorkshire players were expected to supply their own equipment. Dad borrowed a bat, a big heavy thing, from the colliery cricket club. I had a pal who owned a decent pair of pads and batting gloves. I called on him and he was only too happy to lend them to me, pleased at the thought of his pads and gloves featuring in a Yorkshire match.

I mentioned earlier how I was naive in terms of professional cricket and the politics of the game. Regarding the latter, this was particularly so where Yorkshire was concerned. I, like my family, had taken the telegram at face value. We saw it for what it was, a call-up for Yorkshire, and took that to mean the club believed the young yours truly was very much in their thoughts regarding my potential as a future Yorkshire County player. I was later to learn, however, that such a notion was indeed naive on my part.

Yorkshire had no formal relations with young players. They were not contracted to play for the county and played only on an ad hoc basis. This situation enabled the county committee to be autocratic in its dealings with young players. The telegram I received summoning me to play against Cambridge University meant simply what it said, not what I had inferred from it. I was single-mindedly ambitious about a future in cricket and with Yorkshire in particular, but in making my county debut against Cambridge I did so without any experience whatsoever of second XI cricket. In fact, at this point, I hadn't even seen the Yorkshire first XI play.

Having been called up to play in the first XI, I harboured thoughts of being a part of Yorkshire's future plans. But this was far from being the case. It was Yorkshire policy to arrange three or four friendly matches against the Universities, the MCC or perhaps a touring side, as high-quality practice matches before engaging in the serious business of trying to win the County Championship. Yorkshire also used these friendly games as trials for young players who had been recommended to them. Indeed, if one looks at the details of these pre-season matches in the *Wisden* of the day, the Yorkshire line-ups contain names of young players who were often never heard of again. The county used these pre-season matches not so much to assess the worth and potential of youngsters but rather to satisfy themselves that the youngsters who had been recommended did not possess the necessary. It was a strange policy, one based on negativity rather than positive optimism. Welcome to the real world, Fred!

Yorkshire had, over the decades, possessed very few bowlers of real pace. The county had never been won over by sheer speed. They had always made accuracy their first demand and, as such, had generally preferred medium or fast-medium bowlers with their capacity for control, economy and their ability to bowl for long spells. Yorkshire saw fast bowlers as being less precise, less flexible in technique and because of the sheer physical effort exerted, capable of fewer overs. I, of course, was aware of none of this at the time. But such was my embryonic success, it forced the county committee to change their views about fast bowlers and, in particular, about myself.

Throughout their entire history Yorkshire had rarely blooded three youngsters in the same match, but they did so against Cambridge University. I joined the team coach at the Danum Hotel in Doncaster, and on boarding the bus discovered two other lads were also making their county debuts. Opening bat Frank Lowson and Brian Close, who was the only person I knew in the party.

Norman Yardley was the Yorkshire captain and I was delighted when, having put Cambridge in to bat, he asked me to open the bowling. My first ever ball for Yorkshire was in many respects an achievement given my experience of league cricket was cursory. Having bowled an over, I realized the Fenner's pitch was easy and leisurely, affording me little if any bounce. I tried to compensate by bowling quicker but only succeeded in losing my rhythm and, with it, most of my control and pace as well. It was not the start I'd hoped for and for a time it got worse. I was no-balled on two or three occasions for dragging my back foot over the line of the bowling crease. I quickly came to the conclusion that there was a hell of a lot more to bowling at county standard than meets the eye. To my complete and utter relief, after that shaky start I started to bowl nearer the point and pace I intended.

Cambridge began to clock up runs, in particular Hubert Doggart, who seemed set to make a decent score. I was bowling against a guy called Morris when Norman Yardley came over to me and asked if I could bowl a bouncer.

'Aye,' I told my captain.

'Then bowl this fella one. I've come across him before. That's the way to get him out.'

As Norman Yardley walked back to take up his position in the field, I too walked back, ready to bowl Morris the bouncer. The problem was the Fenner's pitch was as lifeless as a string of dead fish, as I would always find it to be throughout my career. When it came to the delivery I dug the ball in and managed to get enough lift to effect a decent bouncer. Morris fended it off short but straight into the hands of short leg to give me my first ever wicket for Yorkshire. Regarding the history of Yorkshire cricket, what I'd achieved was a minute drop in the ocean. But I felt pride and satisfaction at having taken my first wicket. I had made an indelible mark on the county's statistics, however small. Strangely, that first wicket also served to give me a greater sense of my own being. I felt my life had real purpose. I knew what I was cut out to do. Play professional cricket and, in particular, take wickets.

Hubert Doggart was on 94 when I clean bowled him. I was to take another wicket in the match, though I wasn't overly excited at having taken 3 wickets. It was only later that I discovered just what an achievement 3 wickets was for a young debutant at Fenner's. Just about every other young fast bowler had struggled to make any impression on the easy Fenner's wicket.

The game against Cambridge was a culture shock to me in more ways than one. I can remember at the end of the first day's play, joining my teammates for dinner at the University Arms. When I was handed the menu I was dumbfounded to see that the entire contents were written in French. I scanned the bottom of the menu in the hope that at least one dish was written in English, but all I found was the sentence 'Jeudi le douzième mai'. Again, I didn't have a clue what that meant. I was beginning to feel a little uncomfortable. Then I glanced across the table to where Brian Close and Frank Lowson were seated. To my complete and utter relief, Brian and Frank both offered me looks to indicate they too were at a complete loss as to what to order. Skipper Norman Yardley appeared to know what was what, so when the waiter turned to me after taking Norman's order, I simply said, 'I think I'll have the same, please.' I had worked up quite an appetite from my exertions but had no idea what dishes were to be presented before me. It appeared I wasn't the only Yorkshire player similarly disposed. When the first and main courses appeared on the table, just about every player had the same dishes placed before them. Seemingly I wasn't the only one to have placed faith in Norman Yardley's knowledge of the French language and cuisine.

The Cambridge University cricket team was the nation's future establishment at leisure. Their players were obviously well versed in matters of dining etiquette. Seated among their number, I was given to thinking I had come a lot further than simply the 120-mile journey from Doncaster. I felt a stranger in a strange land. Not that the Cambridge players had a leisurely time of it against us. Their world may have been alien to just about every member of that Yorkshire team, but the Cambridge students' discomfort was in playing us at cricket. We beat them easily.

When it came to social faux pas (in time I picked up the French!), dining at places such as Cambridge University was a potential minefield for working-class cricketers such as myself. County cricket was made of gentlemen players and professionals. The latter were by far in the majority. The division was in essence a simple one. The gentlemen players were amateurs who enjoyed an independent source of income and were therefore not reliant on cricket for a living. Players were professionals. They were paid by their counties and for them cricket was their living, in the summer anyway. There was, however, other, more subtle differences between gentlemen and players. Due to their upbringing and the circles they moved in, gentlemen players were more au fait (there's the French again) with the ways of the upper social strata that cricket often encompassed, such as Cambridge and Oxford

Universities, the gentlemen's clubs frequented by MCC committee members and what was called high society. For a young inexperienced working-class lad such as myself, playing county cricket opened up a whole new world of experience.

I never knew what an hors d'œuvre was. I had never heard of canapés and never come across consommé. For me playing for Yorkshire was both an education and a culture shock, not only in terms of the game itself but also socially. The cricketers' bible, *Wisden*, would later note, 'Against Cambridge University, Yorkshire gave a trial to three young players: Lowson, an opening batsman; Close, an all-rounder; and Trueman, a slow left-arm spin bowler.' Arguably the most monumental error to have occurred in the pages of cricket's annual encyclopaedia. The use of the word 'trial', however, was spot on. The selection committee apparently had no more hope of me establishing myself in the first team than they had of some three dozen other young hopefuls. I, however, had other ideas.

To my delight, I was chosen for Yorkshire's next match against 'the other student lot', Oxford University. The Parks pitch at Oxford was much livelier than the one at Fenner's. The Parks was much more to my liking, though Norman Yardley and other senior players in the team impressed upon me that I must not strain for pace, but concentrate on keeping a good line and length.

I felt comfortable with my rhythm and in two spells in the first innings took 4 wickets for 31 runs. I captured the key wicket of Clive van Rynefeld, who was in the process of building a decent score when he aimed to play me in the direction of mid-on. I, however, bowled him a late out-swinger, which ripped his off-stump out of the ground. I finished with match figures of 6 for 72. During the course of the match I heard Denis Hendren, the umpire, say to his colleague, 'If that lad Trueman doesn't end up playing for England, then I'm no umpire. In my first two senior matches I had taken 9 wickets.

Not bad, I thought, for a young rookie fast bowler. Denis

Hendren's words fuelled my confidence further, but I was to come down to earth with a mighty bump within twenty-four hours. When the team was announced for Yorkshire's next game, Frank Lowson and Brian Close were included, but there was no place for me.

Though disappointed, I can't say I was unduly worried. I was just happy to have played for Yorkshire. I hadn't disgraced myself, far from it and I believed I had the talent to eventually make a living from the game. My rise from village cricket had been meteoric. I was just eighteen and was content to bide my time, confident in the notion that if, to my mind when, I was given another crack at senior cricket I'd seize the opportunity with both hands. As I have said, Yorkshire were not enamoured by fast bowling. At this time their opening attack consisted of Alex Coxon, who was good enough to have been picked for England against Australia in 1948, and Ron Aspinall, a doughty and hard-working guy of whom many at the club harboured high hopes. Coxon and Aspinall were both fast-medium bowlers whose style adhered to Yorkshire's preferred bowling policy.

Yorkshire's bowling policy aside, I knew I would have a difficult job on my hands being a regular in the first team, for in addition to Coxon and Aspinall the county had the all-round ability of my contemporary Brian Close, and skipper Norman Yardley was a more than decent swing bowler.

As is so often the case in life, one man's misfortune proves to be another man's success. In 1949 Ron Aspinall appeared to be at the top of his game. Ron had taken 30 wickets in three matches and was picked for an England Test trial. Unfortunately for Ron, he then ruptured an Achilles tendon. Though he received the best treatment available, in 1949 the knowledge and expertise for treating injuries was nowhere near as good as it is today. So debilitating was his injury and rudimentary the treatment of it that he was out of the game for a long time, though he did eventually return to cricket.

I think it's fair to say he never again bowled with the same effectiveness. I had been playing in the second XI, though to my mind I was now very much a Yorkshire cricketer. Once you had played in the first team, the county automatically gave you your second XI cap and a club blazer, which in the eyes of any Yorkshire person was good enough to establish you as a professional cricketer with the county. Aspinall's injury threw the county's bowling policy into disarray and, though I never fully realized it at the time, changed my life. Yorkshire could call on the services of two other bowlers, John Whitehead and Bill Foord, but for reasons that now escape me, neither was available.

The player chosen to replace Ron Aspinall was Frank McHugh, a tall and lean bowler of slavish in-swing but one who could deliver at a decent pace when so inclined. From all this you may be given to thinking I featured some way down the pecking order at Yorkshire where bowlers were concerned, and you'd be right. But I had it in my head that I could make the breakthrough into the first XI and, should I be given that opportunity, had the talent stay there. All I wanted was a chance to prove my worth. As things were to turn out, I wouldn't have to wait long for that chance.

In three County Championship matches Frank McHugh failed to make any great impression on proceedings, while in the second XI I was sending wickets cartwheeling. The way I had applied myself to second XI matches was to pay off. I was called up to the first XI in place of Frank at Whitsun, for the 'Roses' clash against Lancashire at Old Trafford. I could have had an easier county debut, at Taunton against Somerset or Hampshire at home. The 'Roses' clash was the most eagerly awaited of all Yorkshire games. In terms of kudos, competitiveness and passion it was cricket's equivalent of a Merseyside or Manchester 'derby' in football.

Old Trafford was always packed to the rafters for the 'Roses' match, as was the corresponding fixture in Yorkshire at either Headingley or Bramall Lane. Rather than being overawed at the thought of making my first-class county debut for Yorkshire in such an important fixture, I relished the challenge. It would be the largest crowd I had ever encountered – a capacity crowd of some 20,000. As was always the case throughout my career, the bigger the occasion and the crowd, the better I liked it.

In the second XI and in net practice I had noticed that I wasn't bowling as straight as I should have been. I had come to the conclusion that this was because I had too much swing and not enough speed. That said, for someone of my pace I moved the ball a long way, often aiming at off and middle and missing the off-stump by anything up to a foot. I could also pitch at the leg-stump and catch the outside edge of the off. Brian Close once said I could swing like Glen Miller and I am firmly of the mind that it was my ability to swing the ball that contributed to my subsequent success in the game.

Ray Illingworth is on record as saying I moved the ball more than any other pace bowler in the history of the game. 'What's more,' said Ray, 'Fred could make the ball swing away from the bat. It was his ball that shifted even the greatest of batsmen.' It was my special delivery. A very good batsman, especially a great one, will invariably counteract, even punish, the in-swinger, but the out-swinger is the one most have difficulty playing effectively. In time, that delivery will always get even the most accomplished batsman in trouble, because I'd force them to adjust their bat at the risk of edging it to the wicket-keeper or slips.

I had by now started to pay particular attention to the batsman's footwork, to see if he was essentially a forward- or back-foot player. I started to commit idiosyncratic batting styles to memory. If I detected a batsman had a high back lift, I would make a mental note and resolve to bowl him the occasional yorker. I noticed some players had trouble counter-ing the short-pitched bouncer, so would send them a delivery

directed on a line of the middle- and off-stump, which, nine
times out of ten, rattled them if it didn't actually get them out.
I learned to be sparing in the use of this type of ball, as I knew
the effectiveness of the bouncer lay in its element of surprise.

Genuine speed is as much a gift as great batsmanship.
That's why not all aspiring fast bowlers can produce that extra
yard of pace that will elevate them from fast-medium into the
category of fast bowlers. To be a genuine fast bowler every
part of your body must move smoothly and rhythmically,
simply because after running full pelt for twenty paces or so,
then propelling the ball at ninety miles an hour, there is very
little margin for error. For fast bowlers there is no golden rule
as to the amount of paces your run-up should have. The key
thing is to devise a run-up that suits you, one that you feel
eminently comfortable with.

I had discovered mine simply through trial and error. I
never started my run as I would finish, at top pace. I began
with a trot and worked up a head of steam, so by the time I
reached the bowling crease I was perfectly balanced to use my
body and the speed of my run-up to release the ball at
optimum speed. While in the Yorkshire second XI, I had been
trying to perfect the smoothness of my run, the rhythmic
movement of my body and arms in the delivery stride to effect
the pace I desired. Speed is a fast bowler's main attacking
weapon, but speed alone doesn't rattle top batsmen. An opening batsman's job, apart from keeping his wicket intact, is to
take the shine off the new ball. Once he has achieved this, he's
able to gauge the speed of the wicket and, if you don't have
your wits about you, will then start using your speed off the
wicket to drive you through the covers.

Prior to making my bow in the County Championship
against Lancashire I had been working hard at my game.
Building my speed, improving my run-up while concentrating
on bowling straight and mastering my swing, as opposed to

letting it run wild. I was still far from the finished article, of course, but felt I had enough powder and ammunition to make my mark in the first XI.

What I remember about my county debut against Lancashire was the pitch. There was more life in a tramp's vest. Alex Coxon took one look at it and his face fell.

'This is gonna be hard work, Fred,' said Alex, 'knock bowling averages all t' buggery.'

It did. I laboured in vain, as did Alex. Our only consolation being so too did the Lancashire bowlers. Even the spearhead of the Lancashire attack, Dick Pollard, failed to take a wicket. I gave it my all at Old Trafford, but that cut no ice with the committee selecting the team for the next match against Surrey. I was back on second team duty.

My return to the second XI was fleeting though effective. One game and 8 wickets. Yorkshire's next fixture was against the Minor Counties. This fixture was outside the Championship, a friendly, though always keenly contested by the part-time professionals and amateurs who formed the representative team chosen from the best players of what was deemed to be England's second-string cricket competition. The selection committee saw the game as an opportunity to rest several senior players, so having returned to the second XI for one game, to my utter delight I found myself once again on first team duty.

Now with all due respect, a game against the Minor Counties was hardly the sort of fixture to set the pulse racing. But my pulse was in danger of snapping my watchstrap, because the game was to be played at the headquarters of cricket, where history was hung from every wall and was ingrained in every gnarled floorboard – Lord's. For me the thought of playing at Lord's was more than a dream come true. It was like going to heaven without all the bother and problem of dying.

For cricketers throughout the world Lord's has a special

significance. It is where laws are made and reformed. Where decisions are taken that affect all cricketers, whether they play for their county in the Championship or Championship Tyres in the Mid-County League. Lord's was where the feudalism and. it has to be said, pomposity of those charged with running the game rubbed shoulders with legends of cricket and those who paid hard-earned wages to watch their heroes in action. Where the Long Room enshrined the history of cricket and where formal dress was obligatory. Where membership of the MCC was denied to women for over a century – something I was totally against. Incompetence should not be confined to a single sex.

That most eminent of cricket writers, Neville Cardus, with his gift for an anecdote that painted a vivid picture with an economy of words, once told the story of two workmen at Lord's. The men in question turned up during the final game of 1939 to place a green baize cloth over the bust of W. G. Grace in some futile attempt to protect it from expected Nazi bombs. On seeing this, according to Cardus, one greying old MCC member turned to another and in hushed tones said, 'Did you see that, sir? It's an outrage. This means war!'

I had been to London just once, passing through when playing for the Yorkshire Federation team. I remember catching a glimpse of the Houses of Parliament but other than that I was as familiar with London as I was Timbuktu. The lure of our capital city meant nothing to me. Only the fact that I was to play at Lord's mattered to me.

When I received news of my call-up, the telegram from Headingley omitted one vital piece of information – where to join the team. I caught a bus into Doncaster and from there a train to King's Cross. I arrived at that terminal almost terminal myself. I had not the faintest idea where to go, all I knew was that I had to present myself at Lord's the following morning. I had £5 in my wallet to last me the duration of the game. That fiver being to cover my hotel bill, meals and travel around

London. I had been brought up with the notion that 'when in doubt, ask a policeman'. So I did. Only for the London bobby to inform me that, for all he had received intense training at Hendon Police School and was well versed in the ways of London life, his training 'unfortunately did not run to knowing the whereabouts of the Yorkshire cricket team'! Not knowing who to turn to next, I flagged down a London taxi. I explained my dilemma to the cabbie, who informed he that he 'thought' he knew where Yorkshire stayed on their visits to London and drove me to the Bonnington Hotel in Southampton Row. When I presented myself at the hotel reception I informed the clerk I was a member of the Yorkshire cricket team and had arrived a little late.

'You're telling me,' said the clerk, 'the Yorkshire cricket team hasn't stayed at this hotel since 1937!'

I returned to the only person I knew in London – the cabbie. We cruised around WC2 inquiring at one hotel after another with the meter ticking away at an alarming rate. Finally I decided to cut my losses and asked the cabbie to drive me back to the Bonnington, where I booked in for the night. The following morning I made sure I knew which bus to catch to Lord's – and it had to be a bus because my first ride in a London taxi cab had cost me thirty bob, little short of a third of my financial resources.

When I presented myself at Lord's, skipper Norman Yardley said, 'Oh, you've got here have you?' So I had to start a long and detailed explanation of what had happened to me since receiving the late telegram informing me of my call-up. My angst was further compounded when Norman asked me where I had ended up for the night.

'I booked into the Bonnington,' I said.

'We're only around the corner in the Great Western,' Norman said. For some reason, I wasn't too pleased to hear that.

'All right,' said Norman, 'you're here now and in good

time for the game. That's the main thing. Sit down, have a cup of tea and calm yourself.'

After a cup of tea I walked out onto the pavilion balcony and surveyed the headquarters of world cricket, the stage on which every player wants to perform. I was keen to commit everything to memory. 'After all,' I thought, 'you only make your debut at Lord's once.' In the build-up to the game and at every given opportunity during the three days of the match I made a point of exploring every corridor, room and staircase.

I can clearly remember the instructions I was given as regards clothes. 'A suit, or sports jacket and flannels, must be worn and when going to lunch at Lords, you will wear your blazer over your whites.' Yorkshire's secretary was seemingly not too concerned how I was to make my way to London, or where I would spend the night, but he was taking no chances of the rookie fast bowler being turned away from the 'home' of cricket for being improperly dressed.

Walking out to bowl for the first time was an experience like no other – and one that seems as though it could have happened yesterday. My body tingled with nerves. My mind focused. My heart swelling with pride. Initially the pitch seemed nothing to shout home about. It granted some turn and it was the spinners who took most of the wickets in the first three days, until, on the third day, with the Minor Counties needing 272 to win and with the weather having changed, the Lord's track came to life.

My most abiding memory of the match itself is of the Minor Counties' second innings. Norman Yardley bowled me right through and in my first nine overs before lunch, I had taken 5 for 30. Following the lunch interval, I continued to bowl and picked up a further 3 wickets. My legs started to wobble as my mind raced away and conjured up a vision of taking all 10 Minor Counties wickets on my first appearance at Lords. At the other end was Alan Mason, a slow left-arm bowler who for some time had been in competition for that essential and traditional role in the Yorkshire attack. The role at the time was up for grabs following the tragic loss of the sublime left-armer Hedley Verity, who had been killed in Sicily during the war, and also the sudden retirement of Arthur Booth. Alan was a super lad, who in terms of waiting for opportunities in the first XI had the patience of a cigar-store Indian. Unfortunately he never did make the role of our slow left-arm bowler his own, in the end losing out to the great Johnnie Wardle.

Alan was a great team player and I will never forget the ongoing encouragement he offered when I was on 8 wickets. 'Keep it going, Freddie, lad,' he said, 'I'll bowl wide of the off-stump to help you out. So give it all you've got for the last two wickets and make your Lord's debut one to remember.' The very next ball Alan did as promised. He bowled wide of the off-stump but the batsman, a tail-ender, decided to go for glory. He played an ambitious shot at Alan's wide ball and dragged it onto his wicket. As his stumps tumbled so did my dream of a unique and glorious debut at Lord's.

The initial disappointment I felt at not being able to take all 10 Minor Counties wickets was mirrored by Alan. 'Tough luck,' he said. 'Well, I suppose there's nothing left for me to do now but bowl properly.' He did just that. With his very next ball he clean bowled the last man. Alan was left stranded on a possible hat-trick that could never be, and I was left to reflect on what might have been.

My figures in the second innings were 8 for 70. *Wisden*, in recording the match, referred to me as being a 'young fast-medium bowler'. Seeing as their only other reference to me was as a 'slow left-arm bowler', regarding my quest to be a genuine fast bowler, according to *Wisden*, I was making progress! I was only eighteen and remained a fairly slight figure, something the Middlesex and England batsman Bill Edrich picked up when referring to Yorkshire's game against the Minor Counties in his newspaper column of the day. Wrote

Edrich, 'In young Fred Trueman England might now have a new fast bowling prospect to nurture. Though looking at the young prospect it appears to me this lean lad could benefit from a few helpings of roast beef and Yorkshire pudding.' Not the greatest epithet awarded to a Lord's debutant, but one that pleased me. As opposed to roast beef I was still very much in my salad days as a cricketer, but people whose opinions I respected were beginning to take notice of me. I took great heart from that.

I was in and out of the Yorkshire team until early July, when suddenly, to my surprise, I was peremptorily dropped following our game against Surrey at Park Avenue, Bradford. I was soon to learn that the selection committee at Yorkshire had a penchant for chilling confidence or self-satisfaction amongst their young up-and-coming players. I am sure there was an element of the aforementioned in my sudden exclusion from the first XI, but for all I was taking wickets I was also conceding runs, and perhaps that offended their traditional sense of economy where Yorkshire bowlers were concerned. I had taken 4 wickets against a very strong and talented Surrey side, but had conceded 5 runs an over. Obviously a situation which the selectors deemed intolerable in their opening bowler. Bill Foord and John Whitehead were back on duty, and their ability to bowl accurately and tactically had endeared them to the powers that be at Headingley.

All I wanted to do was play first XI cricket for Yorkshire. To give my all for the team and my native county. The fact I was dropped to the second XI was a great disappointment to me; nevertheless, my appetite and enthusiasm for the game and Yorkshire in particular waned not one jot. I didn't go away and brood, I didn't sulk out in the field when on duty with the second XI. That wasn't and never has been me. I was happy enough. I was earning what I considered to be very good money for playing the game I loved.

After the matches against Cambridge and Oxford Universities, Yorkshire gave me £40. More cash than I had ever seen in my life. I paid Dad what I owed him, gave some to Mum, put some in the bank, bought a decent pipe and a good brand of tobacco. As I keep saying, I am a man of simple pleasures.

When I wasn't on duty with Yorkshire, any number of league clubs were keen for my services. They were prepared to pay me anything between £10 and £15 a match, and I could pick up more with a bucket collection if I did well. Invariably I did, frightening a few batsmen in the process.

I began to expand my wardrobe. I wasn't a slave to fashion. You couldn't be in 1949. Youth culture was still some eight years from evolving with the advent of the beat culture. As an eighteen-year-old in 1949, like any other teenager, I wore clothes not dissimilar from my dad's generation. The new items of clothing I treated myself to were stylish for the day, but what you might call standard, even formal. That didn't stop the first crop of ridiculous stories circulating about me. Word got back to me that certain people were saying I was courting the displeasure of the Yorkshire committee by turning up at nets wearing 'loud clothes'. One story even had me wearing a tie on which was a picture of a naked woman. Such stories were, of course, totally untrue. It was the first time I'd been subjected to rubbish stories about my character and behaviour, but it was far from being the last.

I have no idea where the story of me wearing that tie came from. Let me tell you, if ever I'd worn such a thing Dad would have pulled it so tight I would never have breathed again let alone played cricket. Dad had standards, and the one he was most particular about was being properly and appropriately dressed.

Not long after my seventeenth birthday I started smoking a pipe. I had only been smoking it a few weeks and one day I absentmindedly walked into our house smoking it. I stepped into the lounge, Dad looked up from his newspaper and I immediately saw that something was up. Then it suddenly dawned on me. I was still puffing on my pipe.

'How long you been smoking a pipe?' Dad asked.

'Oh, er, just a few weeks. Thought I'd give it a try.'

His face studied me for a moment and I was very wary about what his next words might be.

'Areet lad, suppose you won't go far wrong smoking a pipe. But not in the house,' said Dad, and then took to reading his newspaper again.

I can remember clearly the relief. I was eighteen, fit and strong for my age, but still in awe of, and full of respect for, my father. I think most teenagers were respectful in those days. I had been brought up to respect not only my parents, who, again, I emphasize were loving to me, but also to respect my fellow man, irrespective of colour, race, creed or financial status, and to respect other people's property, in particular their homes. As a teenager I was far from being alone in adhering to this edict. The noiseless and inaudible foot of time moves on. Society is far different now to what it was in 1949, but I am firmly of the mind that if more young people had been brought up like that in recent years, society would not have many of the problems that beset it now. I hear young people talking, and R&B singers singing, about 'respect'. All well and dandy. But what some people these days forget is, in order to gain someone's respect, you must, in turn, show respect to others.

Though I was totally unaware at the time, the powers that be at Headingley didn't rate my chances of becoming a regular in the Yorkshire first team as highly as I did. In fact, I have since been given to believe, some didn't rate my chances at all. Bill Foord was contemplating giving up, or at least taking a sabbatical from, his career as a teacher and trying his luck as a full-time professional with Yorkshire. Something Yorkshire were very interested in him doing. John Whitehead was still attending university but, college vacations being what they are, was available for the meat of the cricket season. Foord, Whitehead and Alex Coxon were all preferred to me, but I was still to be given opportunities when the aforementioned were unavailable or resting.

Such an opportunity came in Yorkshire's match against the touring New Zealanders at Bramall Lane that summer of 1949. For all the game was against the tourists, Yorkshire's priority was always the County Championship. The selection committee rested both Coxon and Foord, while I was recalled from second XI duty to open the bowling in collaboration and competition with John Whitehead.

To show the selection committee just exactly what I was capable of, I was hell bent on blasting to smithereens not only the New Zealand batting order, but also the competition for the position of opening bowler. The occasion had the added impetus of having my dad, mum, brothers and sisters in the crowd. I was very keen to do well. Too keen, as it turned out. I had only bowled a few overs when I wrenched a thigh muscle and was ignominiously carried off the field. Not only did I take no further part in the match, my injury was such I didn't play cricket again that season.

Unlike the other sixteen senior cricketing counties, Yorkshire, with their numerous venues, had no official home for players. Headingley in Leeds was the hub, the administrative side of the club, but there wasn't one place where the players regularly gathered or had permanent lockers. So not having a home ground to call in to every day where I might collect and reply to mail and see teammates on a daily basis, while injured I had no alternative but to recuperate at home. I felt miserably forgotten. No official from the club telephoned to see how I was. No one called to keep me in touch with events. My only contact with the fortunes of Yorkshire was through the newspapers, from which I learned John Whitehead occasionally replaced Bill Foord in the bowling position I had so eagerly aspired to fill. Yorkshire enjoyed a tremendous run in the latter part of the season, winning seven of the last eight games, a sequence of results that saw the team rise from mid-table to share the County Championship with Middlesex. Not only had Yorkshire done it without me, they had done it without word and, as far as I knew, a thought to me. In this, my first season in senior cricket, I had played eight matches for my county, bowled 233.3 overs and taken 31 wickets at an average of 23.19. I knew I hadn't covered myself in glory but I believe I had shown a degree of promise worthy of encouragement. But none had been forthcoming from those charged with running the club and team affairs. That experience was to have a profound effect on my thinking. It changed me.

The self-belief that I could make the grade as a top-class fast bowler never wavered. I knew I had a lot to learn, was confident that I would learn and achieve my goal. The total lack of contact from Yorkshire resulted in me looking to Dad for constant reassurance. Dad, of course, was there for me. He offered encouragement, reaffirmed in me that I had a talent for fast bowling and lifted my spirits whenever I felt down or frustrated because of my debilitating injury.

'Circumstances form character,' Dad told me one day.

It would only be much later that I would come to realize the wisdom of his words. Being young, that spell out of the game, in particular the circumstances surrounding it, was character-forming.

My treatment by the powers that be at Yorkshire instilled in me a wariness of those charged with authority in the game. A feeling that, if I didn't watch them, 'they' might do me some injustice. Let me say now that I didn't have a chip on my shoulder, but when I recovered from my injury, should the Yorkshire selection committee have told me, 'We're right behind you,' I would have told them, 'I'd prefer it if you were in front of me, where I can see you.'

Throughout my life whenever I have met youngsters (and I

have met countless thousands at schools, youth centres, sporting academies, creative workshops and so on) and they have told me what they would like to do in life, I have always offered words of encouragement. Whatever a youngster's ambition, goal or dream I tell them to work hard, to ride any disappointment that comes their way, to keep at it. 'It's a tough road,' I tell them, 'but by doing that, you can be what you want to be.' Youngsters who have a talent and an ambition shouldn't be mollycoddled. What they do need, however, is encouragement. I, however, received nothing of the sort.

Those who had helped and encouraged me in my short time at Yorkshire, such as Cyril Turner, Bill Bowes, Maurice Leyland and Arthur Mitchell, I responded to with respect, loyalty and affection. Dad, of course, was my mentor and bedrock. But the way the Yorkshire hierarchy had ignored me would forever make me wary of figures of authority in cricket. What's more, I sensed these people didn't believe I had it in me to become a top-class fast bowler. I was determined to prove them wrong.

CHAPTER THREE

TO CAP IT ALL

WHEN I EVENTUALLY recovered from my wrenched thigh muscle I returned to the winter coaching classes at Leeds. Arthur, Bill and Maurice welcomed me back with open arms, and in no time at all set about giving me the benefit of their considerable experience and expertise. Each had their own idiosyncratic style, but in the final analysis what all three were adamant about me doing was finding good line and length. This, more often than not, followed by the instruction, 'And get that ball pitched up.'

Arthur Mitchell was, to my mind, one of the best coaches there has ever been. He was a dour man who I can never recall smiling, let alone laughing. The type of man who, if he went riding with the four horsemen of the Apocalypse, would not noticeably enliven the party. But talk to Arthur about cricket and his knowledge was second to none. What's more, he devoted himself to his young charges and nothing was ever too much trouble for him, though given his general demeanour, no one would have noticed if it was. Suffice it to say, I owe Arthur Mitchell a massive debt. I still occasionally see Arthur Mitchell's son. I once asked him, 'What would your father have made of today's Test cricketers hugging and kissing one another when a wicket falls?' He replied, 'I don't know. Put it this way, I can't ever recall him hugging or kissing my mother.'

Maurice Leyland was a completely different character, a happy-go-lucky man who loved a joke and a funny story.

Maurice was an outstanding left-handed middle-order batsman, who scored over 1,000 runs in seventeen successive seasons between 1923 and 1939. His unorthodox slow left-arm bowling was as useful to Yorkshire as his prowess with the bat. An invaluable member of the England team throughout the 1930s, he produced his best batting against the Australians, scoring 137 and 53 in his first Test against them. His Test average against Australia was a highly laudable 68.28 in 1934 and included three centuries. In all he played in forty-one Tests for England, scoring 2,764 runs at an average of 46.06 – not bad for a middle-order batsman!

Following his retirement as a player in 1948, Maurice coached at Yorkshire until 1963. In these days, when many sports people display all the characteristics of a dog except its loyalty, Maurice was loyal to Yorkshire through and through. He and Arthur Mitchell were forever telling me, 'Freddie, will you please try and bat. Because you can bat if you put your mind to it. You're capable of playing shots, so do it.' My priority was bowling and I only played lip service to Maurice's and Arthur's pleas but, looking back, I wish I'd taken their advice more seriously.

As I've said before, Bill Bowes enjoyed a very successful playing career. Following his retirement as a player in 1947, he not only coached at Yorkshire but became an eminent writer on the game, contributing to numerous newspapers, most notably the *Yorkshire Evening Post*. During his time as a cricket writer the word was Bill was earning more from writing about cricket than he did from playing the game. Rumour had it that he was paid a shilling a word for his articles. One day Bill received a letter from a Yorkshire supporter. In his letter the supporter referred to this so called 'fact', saying, 'I hear that your cricket writing is so prized by editors, they are willing to pay you a shilling a word. I enclose in this correspondence, one shilling, and would be most grateful to receive one of your prized words.' Bill's reply was a single word: 'Thanks!'

I owe a great debt to all three, but if I had to choose the best coach, it would be Arthur Mitchell, who, though a fine cricketer in his own right, never scaled the lofty heights achieved by Maurice and Bill. In the winter of 1949–50, Arthur, Maurice and Bill worked hard to enhance my development as a fast bowler – and so did I. But after my injury, my former boyish cheerfulness and naive optimism had been replaced by an altogether grimmer determination.

I spent the 1950 cricket season as somewhat of a transient young cricketer, shuttling between first and second XIs and, when not required by the second team, playing for any number of league teams. Now nineteen, I wreaked havoc in Yorkshire league cricket, where I was appreciably faster than any other bowler at that level. I was still somewhat wayward when it came to line and length, but the sheer pace of my bowling somewhat compensated, and I found myself amongst the wickets in no uncertain fashion. In one game I returned figures of 9 for 12, in another, 8 for 13. The collection bucket was passed around as much as if the pavilion had caught fire.

During the summer of 1950 I played fourteen first XI matches for Yorkshire. While my loyalty to my county was as strong as ever, my hunger for cricket insatiable and my determination to succeed resolute, I was never truly happy in the first XI. It was not a happy dressing room. That summer Yorkshire possessed arguably the strongest batting of any county team, but failed to win the Championship because they lacked the services of a true fast bowler and a second finger spinner. I was frustrated. I could see my chance but the selection committee would only allow me 'a bit part' in the first team.

I felt I was being treated as a commodity to be utilized and cast aside as they thought fit. The Yorkshire committee behaved like lords of the manor, and I was made to feel like I was some kind of serf. Seemingly I wasn't the only player to feel that way.

There was a lot of discontent in the dressing room which eventually resulted in something of an exodus. Johnnie Wardle was dismissed for what officially was put as being 'unsatisfactory behaviour' – a grey and woolly charge if ever there was one. Alex Coxon also departed because 'his face did not fit'. Frank Lowson retired early when he still had a number of years as a top-class player left in him. That superb dual-sportsman Willie Watson, who played football for Sunderland, left to play cricket for Leicestershire.

These departures were indicative of the unrest in the Yorkshire dressing room. Norman Yardley was a superb captain on the field whose tactical nous and ability were respected by every player. Norman was, however, a laid-back guy and by no means always in control of the senior players, nor able to quell the rancours or reconcile the strong antipathies that existed in the dressing room. I think the disharmony got to Norman and also to Len Hutton. If a happy and harmonious atmosphere had existed at the club, both Norman and Len might have continued playing for longer than they did. As elder statesmen they could have contributed much to the team by way of knowledge, skill and advice. But the 'them and us' situation that existed between players and committee, and the niggling unrest in the dressing room, I believe contributed to both Norman and Len bowing out before their time. In the event, the two players who were to prove the most durable were the youngest members of that Yorkshire team – Brian Close and myself.

It was Norman Yardley who came up with the epithet 'Fiery Fred'. I was the junior member of the team and uncapped by my county, but that didn't stop me asserting myself in matches. When bowling I would occasionally further unrest a taut batsman with some well-chosen words. Likewise a batsman I had just removed for a duck. Every opposing batsman that took to the field was a potential victim, and I let him know it. Even at this early stage I had supreme confidence in my own ability and would use any tactic at my disposal to remove a batsman. That was my job. Trouble was, as far as some people at the club were concerned, it wasn't, and, should they have their way, never would be.

I was omitted from the first XI for the first two matches of the 1950 season but received a call-up for the game against Cambridge University. At nine o'clock on the morning of the first day a dim sun peered over Fenner's, less day realized than day potential. By about a quarter to ten the sun had retreated behind clouds that were as black and unwelcoming as a coal shaft. The rain didn't fall in droplets then increase in intensity. It descended on Cambridge as if someone in the heavens had opened the sluice gates – and kept on falling for three days.

The game was abandoned without a ball being bowled. I was disappointed at not having the opportunity to show what I could do, but remained hopeful that I would be retained for our following game courtesy of the club's policy of making County Championship matches their priority. Yorkshire's next match was against the touring West Indies, always a draw for spectators, but, as I say, touring teams were always down on the list of priorities for the selection committee.

True to form they selected me for Yorkshire's match against the Windies, though such was my contribution in terms of overs I might have been better employed in the second XI. Our match against the tourists turned out to be a very low-scoring match. Mindful of the fact I could be a little expensive, skipper Norman Yardley erred on the side of caution and bowled me for only four overs in the West Indies' first innings and only one in their second. Hardly the opportunity I had been so eagerly awaiting.

Having bowled a total of only five overs in the two previous matches I feared the worst when the team sheet was pinned up for our next game against Gloucestershire. To my delight I found I was retained, and spurred by a combination of the confidence that had seemingly been placed in me and my desire to establish myself in the team, I got stuck into the upper order of the Gloucestershire batting taking 6 wickets in the match.

I was oozing with confidence and optimistic but even in my most extravagant hopes never anticipated what was to happen next. My performance against Gloucestershire earned me good reports in the press. The *Daily Graphic* describing me as 'a young greenhorn but with genuine pace, the like of which has not been seen on the County circuit for some years'. The favourable write-ups in the press must have made their mark with the England selection committee, because to my complete and utter surprise – and no doubt that of the Yorkshire selection committee also – I was picked for 'The Rest' against England in the Test trial at the end of May. I was astounded. In truth I had no sustained figures or performances to justify my selection, but the fact I did receive a call-up I put down to two things. First, I would like to think the selectors – Leslie Ames, Tom Pearce, Brian Sellars and R. E. S. Wyatt – recognized my potential and were willing to give an up-and-coming youngster a fillip and an opportunity to show his mettle. Second, mindful of the repeated downfall of the English batsman against Australia when faced with Keith Miller and Ray Lindwall, perhaps the selectors were keen to give the England batsmen practice against pace. At the time there was also a national desire for England to boast a bowler of genuine pace. I was not known to many, but to my mind no one else had given comparable evidence or even promise of genuine pace. True, Brian Statham was emerging but at this stage had yet to play a first-team game for Lancashire.

I was still an uncapped Yorkshire player when I played in the 1950 Test trial at Park Avenue in Bradford. The game was played on a turning wicket, which suited Surrey's Jim Laker, who returned sensational figures of 8 wickets for 2 runs. To my chagrin 'The Rest' were all out for a miserly 27, the lowest total ever recorded in a representative match and indicative of the quality of some of the batting chosen for this supposedly prestigious fixture. I batted at number eleven and at least escaped a duck. With one run to my name, I was stumped by Godfrey Evans off the bowling of Alec Bedser when going for glory!

When England batted I was sorely disappointed not to be given the new ball. Our captain, Hubert Doggart, placed his faith in Derbyshire's Les Jackson and Surrey's Eric Bedser, the twin brother of Alec, the latter bowling off-breaks from the end Jim Laker had used to such devastating effect. Two spinners, Jenkins and Berry, were also tried before Hubert Doggart turned to me. I had nine overs in which to make an impact, and to my immense pride clean bowled my Yorkshire teammate Len Hutton. To keep the Yorkshire connection going, I then caught Norman Yardley. I hadn't made the impact I had hoped in the Test trial. How could I? That said, I left the ground believing that, having been instrumental in the dismissals of Len Hutton and Norman Yardley, I had done my interests no harm.

I was still some way off bowling tight and straight on batsmen's wickets. On my return to the Yorkshire fold my haul of 10 wickets in four games was reasonable but did not compensate for the fact I had conceded 3.5 runs an over. When John Whitehead announced his availability for Yorkshire I feared the worst, and the worst was realized. I was out of the first team and John was in.

At first John Whitehead appeared to have seized his chance, in his second match against Essex taking 5 wickets for 50 runs, an average that was more in keeping with the demands of the committee. In the following three weeks I made but one first team appearance, against Derbyshire at Chesterfield, when I was given second use of the new ball after Alex Coxon and John. I was a little wayward in my bowling, but in the end John Whitehead and I returned similar analyses. John picked up a niggling injury and I was chosen to replace him in the side to play Nottinghamshire at Trent Bridge.

The Trent Bridge pitch, as usual, favoured the batsmen. That dreadnought of Nottinghamshire batting, Charles Harris – always keen to seize the verbal and psychological advantage over a young bowler, especially one from Yorkshire – and his cohort, Walter Keenan, set about plundering my bowling. Norman Yardley resorted to the spin of Johnnie Wardle and it brought dividends. The Nottinghamshire batting crumbled, not once but twice, and Yorkshire won handsomely by an innings and 124 runs.

I had bowled nine overs in Nottinghamshire's first innings but was not called upon to bowl in their second, partly due to the effect the spinners were having on the home side's batting, partly because I was suffering from a strained muscle in my side which left me unable to bowl at all. The injury proved worse than I had first feared and put me out of the game for six weeks. Once again I found myself recuperating at home in Maltby with not one word of communication from Yorkshire. For the second time, it was left to my family, in particular my dad, to lift my spirits and offer words of encouragement.

Dad was at pains to tell me that those weeks of silence from Yorkshire did not mean they were rejecting me. 'That's how it is with them up there,' he told me, 'they have a very loose arrangement with uncapped players. Always have done. That arrangement being no retaining fee, no contract, no contact, until they feel you can be of use to them again. It's not how we treat people, but it's their way.'

I did a lot of thinking during those six weeks at home. Especially when I received news of tentative interest in my services from Lancashire, Surrey and Sussex. I received no official approach but the very fact that word had reached my ears that counties of such esteem as Surrey and Lancashire were keen on me pepped me up. Who knows, if such interest had taken firmer shape, I may well have thrown in my lot with one of those teams. As it was, for all I found the atmosphere and policy of the club not to my liking, I was devoted to

Yorkshire Cricket Club. Those charged with running affairs were not the club or county of my birth. They were, as far as I was concerned, temporarily in charge. Just 'passing through'. When their time was up, Yorkshire Cricket Club would still be there – and, hopefully, so would I.

I may not have been the most popular player at Yorkshire, but experience had taught me Yorkshire's players and committee were not popular in the eyes of the other counties. They provoked at best indifference, at worst hostility. I was a gregarious lad, keen to make friends with all I met. I would walk into an opponent's dressing room eager to chat about the game in general, but very quickly realized I was not a welcome figure. At first I thought this had something to do with me, but Brian Close received similar treatment. Brian and I couldn't work out why opposing teams were so unfriendly to us, especially when we knew they welcomed the friendship of players from other opposing teams. That's when it dawned on us. It was a legacy of the way Yorkshire had treated other teams of the inter-war period.

The Yorkshire team of the thirties were an outstanding side. They beat everyone out of sight, but were far from gracious in victory. As far as I can make out, they often chided opposing players, casting aspersions on their worth as cricketers and telling home teams, 'We've only booked into our hotel for two days. That's how long it's going to take us to beat you lot.' Needless to say, such posturing and boastful talk went down like a bag of spanners with opponents.

The players who had faced Yorkshire before the war had never forgiven the county for its arrogance, and neither had those who were now coaches or committee members of their respective counties. I also knew that my obsession with pace was endangering my career as a bowler. During my enforced sabbatical I resolved to concentrate on accuracy and line and length with a view to becoming more economical, rather than the fastest pace bowler in the world.

My avowed intention and my desire to hold down a regular place in the Yorkshire attack was given a lift by the performances of both John Whitehead and Bill Foord. On one hand, I wanted John and Bill to do well. On the other hand, should they not do well, my instincts of self-preservation told me that this was good for me. Anyone who has played any team sport at any level will know what I mean. When you are out of the team you are torn between wanting your side to do well, and not so well, so that the chances of you being recalled are greater. That's how it is in sport, in life. Anyone who says they have never felt that way when sidelined through injury is lying.

John Whitehead had walked into the vacant place in the Yorkshire attack with seemingly an open invitation to make it his own. Unfortunately for John, his fine performance against Essex apart, he failed to do so. Though he had less incentive and opportunity, so too did Bill Foord. I knew then and there that, once fully fit, I could make that place in the team my own. I turned all this over and over in my mind during those six weeks. Towards the end of the period I felt fit enough to accept a number of invitations to play league cricket. Still the call did not come from Yorkshire, not even to play for their second XI. I have to say some innocent and rather apprehensive club batsmen bore the brunt of my smouldering frustration and displeasure.

My performances in league cricket and the fact that both John Whitehead and Bill Foord had failed to grasp the nettle saw me earn a recall to Yorkshire a few games before the end of the Championship season. If any of the committee expected to see a repentant prodigal gingerly walk through the gates of Headingley, they were going to be in for a surprise. Following my lay-off, I returned to Yorkshire still confident of my own ability to succeed but now even more determined to 'bloody well show 'em'.

Initially I was once again frustrated, as our game against Glamorgan was washed out by rain. In our next game, Yorkshire prevailed against Hampshire, winning by an innings. Again I was used sparingly by Norman Yardley, but even so took three key Hampshire wickets and, more importantly, exercised far better control in my bowling.

I was not invited to play in the end of season 'beano' against the MCC in the Scarborough Festival, so my season of fits and starts was finally over. My tally of 30 wickets was exactly the same as it had been in 1949, though in 1950 I bowled more overs, 290.1 as opposed to 233 the season before. My final average, however, was not as good as the summer of 1949: 28.25 runs per wicket as opposed to 23.19. 'Right, Fred, me lad,' I thought to myself, 'this coming winter, you really have some hard work to do.'

During the winter of 1950–1 I regularly attended indoor practice at the 'shed' and worked on control rather than sheer pace. Being an uncapped player, I had no source of income in the winter, so returned to working at Maltby pit. I kept myself fit by playing football, the occasional game of rugby and indulged in some solitary road running. That winter I gained a couple of inches in height and developed physically. When the 1951 cricket season got under way, I felt better equipped, more technically adept, fitter and stronger than ever before. Not to mention more worldly wise in the ways of Yorkshire cricket.

In the close season Alex Coxon had announced his retirement from first-class cricket. This came as a surprise not only to me, but to all who knew him. Alex's retirement could not have been on the grounds of performance. He had finished seventh in the national averages, having taken 131 wickets at the economical rate of 18.6. Inevitably, rumours were rife as to the real reason behind Alex's decision to call it a day . . .

Even in the light of Alex's retirement I didn't think I was automatically certain of a place in the first team. Bob Appleyard, who had been 'blooded' the previous season, was being widely touted to win a regular place in the first XI. In the event, Bob dominated not only the Yorkshire bowling, but the bowling figures for the entire County Championship with 200 wickets at 14.14. In addition to Bob, I also knew that Bill Foord was still on the fringes and that once John Whitehead had completed his degree course at university in London, he too would figure in the competition.

I was picked for four of our first six important matches. Bill Foord on the other hand played three games, each one of those being non-Championship fixtures. I felt I did reasonably well in those four matches, whereas Bill failed to pull up any trees. Three indifferent performances with the ball against non-Championship opposition contrived to make up Bill's mind. He was, he said, 'going to put a career in teaching before first-class cricket'.

Yorkshire lost heavily against the MCC, a match in which I wasn't the only player not to play to his full potential. In our game against the touring South Africans, however, I found good line and length and to some effect. On what began as a spinner's wicket I made little impact against what to all intents and purposes was South Africa's preferred Test side. In their seconds innings, however, with the pitch more to my liking I came into my own, taking 5 South African wickets for only 19 runs.

My early-season bowling figures were testimony to my hard work over the winter months. Following our match against South Africa, in subsequent games I returned figures of 3 for 16, 3 for 23 and 5 for 93. When one of the mainstays of the opening attack did not play for whatever reason, Norman Yardley gave me the new ball in tandem with the in-form Bob Appleyard.

When Yorkshire hosted Nottinghamshire at Sheffield's Bramall Lane I was hell bent on putting old ghosts to rest. Though Bramall Lane had been the setting for my induction into league cricket in Yorkshire, it had not been a happy hunting ground for me since. It had been the ground where I had picked up my injury against New Zealand in 1949 and where I had endured a disastrous match the season before. With Dad in attendance. I was determined this time, however, that neither anxiety, any sense of being badly done to, nor over-straining in my attempts to do well would impair my performance.

In the first innings, John Whitehead, fresh from university, was given the new ball with Bob Appleyard. John did well, taking 2 for 25. When Norman Yardley said, 'I think the situation now calls for some Fiery Fred,' I rallied to his call, taking 3 wickets for 26 runs. When Nottinghamshire batted again, needing 164 to prevent an innings defeat, rain intervened. I sat in the pavilion twiddling my thumbs, keen to finish the job. When the skies eventually cleared, we were left with just the last session after tea to tie up the game. Time was against us, but the pitch was now soft on top and hard underneath and when I opened the bowling with John Whitehead, to my delight I made the ball rise angrily and often enough to rattle the Nottinghamshire batsmen.

Previously the sight of the ball flying so spectacularly would have incited me to drum up every inch of pace I could muster. But now I was more methodical and calculating. Accuracy and control were uppermost in my mind and I used the wickedly lifting ball only as a variation of my tactics. I was bowling straight. Straight enough to clean bowl five Nottinghamshire batsmen. When our opponents were all out I enjoyed second-innings figures of 8 wickets for 68 in 20.8 overs, providing me with match figures of 11 for 94. Yorkshire won by an innings. It had been a race against time, but I had kept my cool and was delighted with my haul of 8 wickets in the second innings that effectively gave us victory.

My teammates were also delighted with my performance. I felt a mixture of pride and humility as they stood to one side and applauded me as I ascended the steps of the pavilion, where, unbeknown to me, a big shock was awaiting me. As I entered our dressing room I felt not only on top of my game, but on top of the world. Against the clock I had taken 8 wickets at an average of 8.5. 'At last,' I thought, 'I've shown "them" what I am capable of.' To my horror, as I walked into our dressing room I was immediately to come to terms with what 'they' were capable of.

I happened to glance at the notice board, on which were printed the first and second XI teams for the next matches. My name was not there in the first XI. To my complete and utter astonishment, and anger, I was down for the second XI fixture against Lincolnshire at Grimsby. What's more, I wasn't even playing. I was twelfth man! When skipper Norman Yardley entered the dressing room he was full of the fruits of victory. His face was beaming but when he caught sight of me, it soon lost its lustre.

'Skipper, could I have a word, please?' I said barely able to control my anger and disgust. We stepped outside, out of earshot of the other players.

'What the hell is going on, skipper?' I asked.

'What d'you mean, Fred?'

'What do I mean? That nonsense in there,' I said pointing back to the dressing room. 'I've just bowled my bloody guts out for the team and this club. I come back to find, not only I am not playing in the next game, I'm not even considered worthy of a starting place int' second XI – at bloody Grimsby.'

'Oh, aye, that,' said Norman sheepishly.

'Oh, aye. THAT!' I reiterated.

'You see, Fred, it's like this,' said Norman, and proceeded to tell me how 'like this' was.

According to Norman, the press boys were keen to solicit from the selection committee the team for our next match before their deadlines. This in mind, the selection committee had picked the team earlier that day, in so doing incorporating the three lads who had been on Test duty with England (two batsmen and a spinner!) while we had been in action against Nottinghamshire. Also, according to Norman, John White-head was once again available and was favoured above me, a decision the selection committee had made prior to my 8-wicket haul and in light of my previous performances which, to their mind, had been 'somewhat indifferent'.

'Somewhat indifferent?' I queried, 'The scorebook might beg to differ. Saying as it does, 3 for 16, 3 for 23, 5 for 93. I didn't bowl particularly well in the game that followed against Middlesex. Fair enough. But, that match apart . . . well, to now be twelfth man for the second team against Lincolnshire. It's a bloody joke, and a cruel one at that.'

'Well that's the explanation I've been asked to . . .' Norman's voice trailed away. 'That's the reason behind you not being chosen for the first team. Your performance today was terrific, it just came a little too late. The selection committee had to choose the team for the press before that second innings.'

'Well, it's an explanation of sorts, skipper,' I said. 'But I tell you now, it isn't acceptable to me. What's the criterion for picking this team? Performances or adhering to press deadlines?'

To this day I am convinced Norman Yardley played patsy in all this. The executioner's face is always well hidden. I travelled to Grimsby with the second XI and fulfilled my duties as twelfth man to the best of my ability. I've never been one to sulk, but deep down I felt bitter disappointment and anger. Earlier in my story I made mention of the Quixotic policies of the Luftwaffe; I was increasingly of the mind those of the Luftwaffe had nothing on those of the Yorkshire selection committee. As if to prove my point, having ferried drinks for the second XI against Lincolnshire, little over a fortnight later I was recalled to the first team!

In a run of four matches I took 18 wickets and kept my place for our game against Nottinghamshire at Trent Bridge. On the morning of the game Norman Yardley inspected the pitch and on returning to the pavilion said, 'Hazy morning and the pitch's green.'

'Suits me,' I told him. And it did.

Making the ball swing late and with some pace, I removed the off-stumps of both Reggie Simpson and Alan Armitage in successive balls. I was on a hat-trick and next man in was Peter Harvey. My teammates closed in for the kill as I walked about prior to commencing my run-up. The ball I delivered swung away from Harvey's timed stroke at the last moment. I heard the click of contact between ball and bat before the ball carried through to wicket-keeper Don Brennan, who characteristically gathered the chance into his gloves. My first hat-trick in senior cricket and the first by any Yorkshire player for five years. As good as I felt, I wasn't done yet. Ten minutes later, Nottinghamshire weren't just on the back foot, they were reeling at 18 for 6, and I had taken 4 of their wickets. We won at a canter and my final figures of 8 for 53 were the best of my career to date.

With my improved control and buoyed by success, I was beginning to bowl to Norman Yardley's direction with method as well as pace. In our next game against Derbyshire, on what was a good batting wicket at Harrogate, I took all 5 first wickets ending with figures of 6 for 59. Though Derbyshire rallied to make 339, I believed this to be a penetrative and frugal spell of bowling on my part. My wickets against Derbyshire came from a continuous spell of bowling that lasted for twenty-seven overs. I not only felt strong and fit, I felt I was giving ample evidence of my developing tactical perception and ability with the ball.

Word was getting around and articles were being written in the press that Yorkshire had, as the *Daily Sketch* put it, 'come up with a genuine fast bowler of class'. Following my success against Derbyshire, I called into our local newsagent's for a morning paper.

'Ye showed them, Fred lad,' said the newsagent, 'show'd them reet enough.'

'Aye,' I said, 'and God willing, I'm show them more.'

I'm not too sure my success went down with my teammates as well as it had done with our newsagent. Looking back, there was dichotomy to my game. A part of me was totally dedicated to the team and the Yorkshire cause, but another part of me was playing for myself, to further my own career. I can only put this down to the dressing room disharmony. The team was split into cliques, with the senior players like Norman Yardley and Len Hutton along with the 'gentlemen' players keeping much to themselves. Occasionally, they even made their own way to away games and stayed at different hotels, needless to say more salubrious hotels than I and the other young pros were booked to stay in. I detected the senior pros and gentlemen were even at times jealous of the success of us up-and-coming players.

On one occasion Ray Illingworth sought the company of Len Hutton as Ray wanted the benefit of his advice on a certain aspect of his game. Ray returned from that consultation, such as it was, not only crestfallen but so browbeaten he was in a state of distress. Seemingly Len had been less than complimentary about Ray's ability as a young player.

During this era in cricket, even at International level, promising young players would often find themselves crucified by their seniors. It happened to Brian Close when he went on his first tour of Australia with England at the age of nineteen. I was told one of the golden boys of English cricket, Denis Compton, gave Brian a torrid time and was forever on his case. Seemingly Brian could nothing right and on one occasion when the England team attended a party, Brian spent the night alone in his hotel room nigh-on heartbroken. On one occasion Denis Compton allegedly pushed Brian too far. Seemingly Brian lost his cool and responded to Denis's taunts with a combination of punches that Lennox Lewis would have been proud of. I was told he was wise enough never to give Brian a hard time again. But Denis seemingly didn't learn from this experience.

Some time earlier, during a Festival match at Kingston, it is alleged that Denis continually lambasted my Yorkshire teammate and good pal Alex Coxon. Again Denis went too far. Eventually Alex saw the red mist and the call, once again, was one for smelling salts. Following that incident. Alex never played for Yorkshire again. Now then, whether that incident had anything to do with Alex's unexpected departure, I shall never know.

Skipper Norman Yardley, his vice captain, Geoffrey Keighley, and wicket-keeper Don Brennan were the 'gentleman' players in that Yorkshire team. For a time Brian Close and I were the youngest of the juniors. Yorkshire didn't have as many amateurs as other clubs did and for all the back-biting and disharmony that prevailed in the dressing room, by and large we at Yorkshire stayed together as a unit. At some counties the opposing captain and the amateurs would have lunch and dinner in the committee room, whereas their professionals joined the entire Yorkshire team in the players' dining room. At some county grounds, most notably Lord's and the Oval, there were even separate changing rooms for amateurs and professionals. Though again, credit to Norman, Geoffrey and Don, they always refused to utilize this facility.

In the late forties and early fifties I never considered a train journey to be travelling. That's how cricketers got around the country from one county match to the other, but it wasn't travel. We were 'sent' to a place and it was little different from being a parcel. Trains in the late forties and early fifties were like women, or money, or happiness. If you wanted to catch them, the chances are you wouldn't. Should you be indifferent, however, they'd very often alight on your shoulder. In which case, happiness is, of course, more preferable to a 100-ton steam engine.

County games were three days in duration with play concluding at five-thirty on the final day. There was not time to hang about, especially if we had just completed a game in

Leeds and were due to play one of the southern counties the very next day. All our kit, jumpers, shirts, flannels, boots, bats, gloves and pads was loaded into cricket bags and it was the job of the junior players, usually Brian Close and me, to lug that about from station to station. No easy task, especially when we played the likes of Sussex or Hampshire, which involved humping the bags across London from King's Cross to Victoria or Waterloo. The team travelled across London by taxi, and again it was the responsibility of junior players, such as Brian and me, to summon the taxis and pay the fares. On one occasion at King's Cross I flagged down a passing taxi.

'Waterloo, please,' I said to the cab driver.

'The station?' he enquired.

'Well, I'm too bloody late for the battle!' I said.

As one of the junior players I'd have to pay for our taxis, then reclaim the money from the senior players. Players had to pay their own travel, hotel and food bills when on the road, and once expenses had been met, there wasn't much in the way of money to take home to their families. Uncapped county players, such as myself, were paid £12 for a home game and £20 for an away match. At Yorkshire we were also on a £2 bonus per man for a victory. In relation to what the average working person earned in a week, that may appear to be a very decent wage, especially as we were often involved in playing two games a week. However, once travel, hotel and food expenses had been met, because professional cricketers could only work five months a year, in the final analysis they were only marginally better off financially than the average working person. That's why the vast majority of professionals sought work during the autumn and winter months. In the case of myself, in the tally office at Maltby pit.

Cricket at this time was burdened by many dictums and rules that were simply preposterous. For example, amateur players were allowed to travel to away games by car should they so wish, but not the professionals, a rule that didn't directly affect me, or the vast majority of professionals, who didn't have cars. Whilst any number of amateurs with other counties took advantage of this ruling, to the further credit of Norman Yardley, Geoffrey Keighley and Don Brennan, they never did. Regarding travel to and from home matches, again I relied on trains. During this period, Yorkshire played home matches at seven venues throughout the county. Should we be playing at Park Avenue in Bradford, I would get up at half-past six, travel to Bradford, which involved a change of train at Leeds, play in the game, journey back and arrive home in Maltby at around nine-thirty p.m. I'd have a little supper, retire to bed at around ten-fifteen, and repeat the whole process the following day.

Leaving one venue in the evening to reach another later that night was often perilous. We were dependent on connecting trains and sometimes we just didn't make it. I remember one trip from Leeds to Bournemouth. Our game at Headingley had run the full course, concluding at five-thirty p.m. Having loaded the bags with fellow junior Eddie Leadbetter, we set off for Leeds station in double quick time with the rest of the team to catch a train to King's Cross. Our London-bound train suffered a series of delays and by the time we arrived in the capital, we were cutting it very short. We managed to make Waterloo but missed the last train to Bournemouth and had to be content with catching a train that only went as far as Christchurch. Again, there were delays.

We eventually arrived in Christchurch at four in the morning but managed to find a hotel that would put us up for a few hours. There was a strict rule that all teams must report to a ground by ten-thirty a.m. on the first day of play. We snatched a few hours' sleep, wolfed down some toast and tea at nine a.m. and caught a train from Christchurch for the remainder of our journey to Bournemouth.

As one of the junior professionals I was responsible for the bags and along with Eddie, lugged them from Bournemouth station to Hampshire's ground. We lost the toss, Hampshire chose to bat so we took to the field. Norman Yardley asked me to open the bowling. When I took the new ball, the indentations made by the handles of the heavy bags were still clearly visible on my fingers and the palms of my hands. It was the mark of that Yorkshire team that for all we were exhausted, we beat Hampshire within two of the allotted three days.

The juniors kept a notebook in which we jotted down all expenses and who owed what. Quite often some of the senior pros didn't settle their accounts for a fortnight. On more than one occasion I went to Norman Yardley and said, 'Skipper, I'm sorry but so and so and what's his name, their bags are going to stop int' dressing room because they haven't paid what they owe.' To his credit, Norman would go to the players in question and tell them to settle their account immediately. If they didn't, he'd stop it out of their wages and reimburse me accordingly.

On the first morning of an away game, Norman Yardley would go to a bank and withdraw the players' wages from the Yorkshire account. He'd then place the money in brown envelopes and lay them out on a table in the dressing room for collection when the team arrived. For home matches, this duty was performed by the club secretary, John Nash. I find it amazing that in those days, in addition to being responsible for conducting affairs during the course of a game, the role of captain also involved collecting and paying players' wages for away games. But that's how it was back then.

Yorkshire is the largest county in England. Such is its size even home games necessitated staying overnight. Because all expenses came out of our match fees, when we played at places such as Scarborough or Middlesbrough the players would opt to stay in bed and breakfast guest houses. This cost around 17/6d per night. By and large these guest houses were perfectly adequate, though oddly, they all appeared to share certain common characteristics you never came across in hotels. No matter how small the room it would boast a wardrobe large enough to hold the costumes from the stage production of *Oklahoma.* There would be a burn mark on the lampshade of the bedside light and the strip light above the washbasin never worked. As opposed to a posh hotel, which would provide a bar of soap the thickness of a box of Swan Vestas, guest houses offered a bar of soap the size of a house brick. As for the beds, for years these establishments must have kept the wheels of the pink candlewick bedspread industry spinning like those of a fruit machine.

I remember in 1950, Len Hutton's benefit year at the club, being asked by Len if I would play in a one-day benefit match on Teesside. For all our differences as people, we respected one another as players. Len was one of the greatest players ever to grace English cricket; my admiration and respect for him as a batsman was absolute. So when asked to play in this benefit game at Middlesbrough, I readily agreed to his request. The game took place on a Saturday as Yorkshire were not involved in a county match that day. I travelled up to Teesside with Len in his car. It being one of his benefit matches, we stayed on at the Middlesbrough ground for far longer than we would for a county match, chatting with supporters, signing autographs and what have you. On the return journey, to my complete and utter surprise, Len swung his car onto the forecourt of Leeds station and wished me goodnight before heading off home to Pudsey. It was 10.40 p.m. and I still had to get back to Maltby. I caught a train to Rotherham but got no further. I had missed both the last train and last bus and had no option but to walk home with my kit bag slung over my shoulder. Even as a nineteen-year-old in awe of Len, I can remember thinking it a bit rich he hadn't given me a lift all the way home.

Len understood me as a bowler but not as a man. I felt the same way about him, I understood him as a cricketer but not as a man. As people we were like chalk and cheese. Nowhere was this more evident than with regard to our sense of humour. Len had a strange sense of humour. I say that because it was not only me that didn't share it but many others as well. On one occasion on a train journey to Bristol, where Yorkshire were due to play Gloucestershire, I decided to go to the buffet for a cup of tea.

'Does anybody want owt while I'm down there?' I asked.

Len asked me to get him twenty Senior Service.

On my return I sat down with my cup of tea and handed the cigarettes to Len who said 'thanks' but made no effort to pay me the 2/6d they'd cost. Years later, in 1988, I was the guest speaker at a sporting dinner held in honour of Len. Just before I was about to stand and speak, Len took to his feet. For the benefit of the audience he recalled the story of the train journey to Bristol some thirty-eight years previously and that of the unpaid cigarettes.

'No doubt, Fred, you believed I had forgotten this and that you would never be paid the money I owe you,' said Len.

He then counted out thirteen brand new shining one-pence pieces and placed them on the table before me.

'See, I didn't forget,' said Len, 'by my reckoning twelve shillings and sixpence in current money is twelve and a half pence. There's thirteen pence there. So, Fred, you've made a half-pence profit from that errand for me.' Len thought this hilarious. Even when he sat down again he was still chuckling to himself, while the audience sat there like Peter Sutcliffe's jury.

There was most definitely a pecking order in the dressing room, one that was perpetuated by the Yorkshire committee. If a senior player decided that he wanted some net practice at, say, nine-thirty the following morning, the club ruling was a junior member of the team such as myself had to be in attendance to ensure his kit was laid out and ready on his arrival.

I can remember one occasion when we were playing at

Headingley. The match had finished and we were dashing like mad to get everything and everyone together in order for us to catch a train from Leeds to London, as we had a match against Surrey the following day. Bob Appleyard and Eddie Leadbetter were packing the bags as both were junior to me by virtue of a year or so. Suddenly a member of the Yorkshire committee appeared on the scene, somewhat irate.

'Bob can't take the bags!' said the committee man. 'Trueman and Leadbetter. Get on with it!' (Note how Bob Appleyard was referred to by his Christian name but Eddie and me by our surnames.)

'It's a nonsense to expect Bob to take the bags,' the committee man reiterated, 'he's been bowling all afternoon.'

'And what do you think Freddie's been doing all afternoon?' asked skipper Norman Yardley. 'Bob and Eddie are the junior players, it's their job to take the bags.'

Confronted with the captain, the committee man bit his lip before storming out of the dressing room.

That incident was not only typical of how committee members viewed players, in particular the junior pros, it was also indicative of the attitude of many to me as a fast bowler. As I have said, for years the policy of the committee was not to have a fast bowler playing for Yorkshire. Though I had made my mark in the first XI as a fast bowler – in the minds of many with some distinction – the majority of the committee saw me as raw-boned and lacking in finesse. As John Arlott was later to write,

> That the Yorkshire committee of the day were too dim to appreciate the worth of the emerging young Trueman, had much to do with their being entrenched in the past as it was their inability to recognize rare talent and the fact that the game of cricket was changing rapidly as a new decade got under way. Whilst England as a nation cried out for a fast bowler to rival the Australians Miller

and Lindwall, the minds of the Headingley committee still happily dwelt with the pre-war Yorkshire teams of the thirties where searing pace was considered both uncouth and anathema to success.

In 1951 I was being touted as the fastest bowler in English cricket. I felt I was, though to be honest there were no other English fast bowlers of genuine pace around, with the possible exception of Derbyshire's Les Jackson, in my opinion one of the most underrated fast bowlers ever to have played cricket. I played a total of thirty matches for Yorkshire in the summer of 1951. I bowled 737.4 overs and took 90 wickets at an average of 20.57, my best analysis to date. That summer I took 5 or more wickets in a match on six occasions. I was making headlines in the press. The Yorkshire supporters had taken to me, but not so many of my opponents and, it was to turn out, neither had some of my teammates.

Prior to my arrival on the scene opening batsmen had it relatively easy. Such was the pace of the bowling they faced they were able to play off the front foot with relative comfort. I changed that. If an opponent started playing forward to me before I'd even delivered the ball there was every chance I'd send it whistling past his ears, and they didn't like it. I wasn't trying to hurt them, I was just trying to force them onto their back foot to play a little and hopefully afford my teammates the opportunity of a catch. Inevitably such was the technique one or two did get hit. I was also upset when this happened, but never allowed myself to show it. If I had done, batsmen would have seen that as a weakness and I would have been on the receiving end.

Some opposing batsmen took to calling me names. Now that didn't bother me one iota. Sticks and stones and what have you. The more they indulged in verbal attacks on my personage, the more the ball bounced. By and large the confrontations I had with opposing batsmen was heat-of-the-moment stuff. Once the game was over, it was forgotten and we'd enjoy a drink in the bar together. Leicestershire's Maurice Hallam once said on seeing me enter the bar, 'Fred, I'd willingly put my hand in my pocket and buy you a drink, but I think you've broken my wrist!'

The occasional trouble I had with opposing batsmen was, however, nothing compared to what I encountered at Yorkshire. Cricket to my mind is the greatest game in the world, but I also found it to be the most vicious, two-faced, backstabbing sport you could ever encounter.

During that summer of 1951 I was soothing my aches and pains in the bath after taking 7 wickets on a batter's wicket at Park Avenue, Bradford. Suddenly I was aware of a big rumpus in the dressing room. I wrapped a towel around myself and went out to see what all the fuss was about. Seemingly one of our senior players, Johnnie Wardle, had been saying, 'Trueman was bloody lucky to get all those wickets today. Falls on feet every time.' John Whitehead had taken exception to this and stuck up for me. Words were exchanged, it all got rather heated and allegedly John made a grab for Johnnie. That type of incident was par for the course. The junior players in the side would be run down if we performed well. When the team hadn't performed well, it was our fault and we got it in the neck. Even when Brian Close or Ray Illingworth made a good score, afterwards there would be no congratulations or words of encouragement. On the contrary, the player would be berated for having played for himself and not for the benefit of the team.

'Even when we win, *we* can't win,' remarked Brian one day, referring to yet another bout of criticism from the senior players. Usually with men, when they have their differences they say their piece and it's over and done with there and then. Not so in that Yorkshire dressing room.

On one occasion there was a mix-up between Len Hutton and young Frank Lowson when they were running between the wicket. Frank got in a muddle and ran Len out. At the club this was a crime tantamount to murder. Not only did the inquest and castigation of Frank take place after the game, it dragged into the next day and the day after that, eventually going on for nigh-on three weeks as not only senior players but committee members and the press all stuck their oar in. Poor Frank, it's a wonder he ever played cricket again, let alone gave sterling service to Yorkshire.

The senior pros were crafty so-and-sos. They had scores to settle with certain opposing players and, being naive, it took me a while before I realized that, having made the bullets, they then used me to fire them. For example, there was a lot of rivalry and bitterness between Yorkshire and Middlesex which dated back to the pre-war years. When I came on the scene, against certain Middlesex batsmen I was encouraged to 'let one fly' or 'shave his ears'. The senior pros of both clubs were jealous as hell of each other, but it didn't take me long to realize I was being used. When I did, I simply ignored the overtures of my seniors in the Yorkshire team to 'rattle' so-and-so in the Middlesex team. When I cottoned on to what was happening I told them to do their own dirty work and started to stay out of everyone's way and tried to avoid trouble.

The feud between Yorkshire and Middlesex eventually came to an end as senior players retired and were replaced by younger men who would have no truck with this nonsense. As emerging young players such as Brian Close, Ray Illingworth, Frank Lowson and myself asserted our influence in the York-shire team so did our counterparts at Middlesex. Though highly competitive on the field we became good friends with the likes of Peter Parfitt, John Murray and Freddie Titmus in the Middlesex team.

Though by now I had established myself in the team I virtually had to ask for my county cap. Word had got round that I wasn't overly happy playing for Yorkshire – who was, in that set up? Both Lancashire and Surrey made overtures, and I began to think that if I was to make any progress in the game my career would be better served at a more friendly and convivial club.

The very thought of leaving the club and playing for another county was anathema to me. I knew it would be a great wrench, but for a time I felt it in my best interests to seek pastures new. I went to see Norman Yardley and told him how I was feeling.

'I'm not happy here, skipper,' I told Norman, 'basically because I haven't been made to feel happy here. I've given my all for this club, my teammates and you as captain. I mean I still haven't been awarded my county cap! Other counties are interested in my services. I don't want to leave this club, but I'm going to have to.'

My meeting with Norman took place on Thursday, 9 August 1951. The following Monday I was awarded my Yorkshire county cap. No one told me it was to be awarded and there was no ceremony. We were playing at Bradford when Norman Yardley told Bob Appleyard and me to report to the club office. Neither Bob nor I knew what was up and when we presented ourselves before Norman he simply handed over our caps.

I felt the award of county caps to Bob and me was fully merited and long overdue. Bob was already mature in terms of being a cricketer when he made his debut for Yorkshire at the age of twenty-six in 1950. In 1951 Bob enjoyed an exceptional season when replacing the departed Alex Coxon and Brian Close, who was on National Service in the Army. Over six feet tall, Bob bowled medium-paced swingers with the new ball. On a turning pitch, or when the ball had lost its shine, he deployed slow to slow-medium off-spin and cut, with variations of flight and pace. In his first full season he took 200 wickets, more than anyone else in county cricket, at an average of 14.4, to top the first-class bowling averages. He was not physically strong but was so confident about his bowling, Norman

Yardley frequently found it difficult to take him off. He bowled for long spells, making up in stamina what he lacked in physical strength.

Bob, however, never enjoyed the best of health. In 1951 he suffered an attack of pleurisy when he was on 99 wickets. He missed our next three matches, consequently missing the chance of becoming the first player that summer to reach 100 wickets. Bob played only one match in 1952 and none at all the following summer. He returned to the fold in 1954 but missed half of the 1955 season and eventually retired from the game in 1958. Nevertheless, in barely five full seasons his record was exemplary – over 700 wickets for an average of 15.0. I sometimes wonder what Bob might have gone on to achieve in the game had it not been for ill health and injuries.

I greatly admired Bob as a player and believe the feeling was mutual. Though it has to be said, though we respected one another on a professional basis, we weren't the best of friends. But that happens in any team sport, particularly cricket. Eleven guys from widely differing backgrounds and often of contrasting personalities are brought together as a team. Ask yourself, how many of your work colleagues can you number as being very good friends? How many do you get on with, as opposed to simply tolerating? In a cricket team the chances of all players becoming bosom friends with one another is unlikely. Though it has happened. When eleven players with their own personalities, idiosyncratic ways, characters, opinions and egos are thrust together, the best that can be hoped is that they do form friendships, at worst, that they will respect one another as professionals.

After the 'pomp and ceremony' of receiving my Yorkshire county cap from Norman Yardley I couldn't wait to get home. Though I had received my county cap in circumstances that were far from in keeping with the kudos and importance of the award itself, this couldn't detract from my joy. I had no car, so travelled by train and bus from Bradford to Maltby. For reasons that are now lost to me the journey took longer than usual and I didn't arrive home until ten p.m. When I walked into our house I was surprised to see Dad sitting there in his armchair, as I knew he was due on night-shift at the pit. News of my award had already reached Maltby via the newspapers and so Dad had swapped shifts so that he'd be at home when I got in. When I walked into our lounge with a big, broad smile on my face, Dad's face puckered up. I thought, 'Good God! He's going to cry.' Dad then pulled himself together.

'Well, lad, on a night like this in a Yorkshireman's life, he doesn't go to work,' said Dad. 'Come on, then, lad, where is't?' I took my cap out of my kit bag and handed it to him. Again I thought he was going cry. Dad studied the cap and gently ran his coarse fingers over the material, pausing at the county's white rose emblem before emitting a sigh of satisfaction. I'll never be able to describe exactly what that cap meant to Dad. Only Yorkshire people of a certain age will know.

'Go on, then, let's see it on, lad,' he said.

I placed the cap on my head. Dad stood staring at me, his face a mixture of pride and wonder.

I never wore the cap again. As far as I was concerned it was his. He'd worked and sacrificed for it. He had been my bedrock and encouragement during the times when I was down. Mum was watching all this from the kitchen. I turned to her and saw that she too was greatly moved.

'Now, Mum, don't you worry. You can have my first England cap,' I told her. 'And I will get one. We're gonna be areet. So neither of you worry.' On hearing my words, Mum also burst into tears.

I kept that promise. When I was chosen for England, once the game was over, the first thing I did was go straight home and give her my cap. Dad wasn't all that bothered. That Yorkshire cap was everything to him. It was all he wanted and he still has it. When Dad died, I placed it in his coffin so that he'd never be separated from it.

CHAPTER FOUR

SERVING MY COUNTRY

JUST BEFORE I RECEIVED my county cap, the Yorkshire committee made a ruling (they loved their rules) that any capped players called up for National Service would be paid £5 a week. As I was just beginning to establish myself in the team and make a name for myself in the game in general, I didn't want to stop playing for Yorkshire. I knew, however, that I would be called up for National Service sooner rather than later. My winter job in the tally office at Maltby pit was soon to be declassified and I would therefore be liable for call-up. With this in mind I decided to get my National Service over and done with. At the same time taking advantage of the Yorkshire committee's offer of a fiver a week.

I am patriotic through and through. I had no qualms about being called up for National Service and serving my country, though I have to be honest and say, just for the sheer hell of it, I tried to pull a flanker at the medical. After receiving my call-up papers I attended a medical on the afternoon of the day we had just beaten Essex before lunch. When the medic asked me if I had any 'medical deficiencies' he should be aware of I told him, 'I think I may be slightly colour blind.'

To my complete and utter amazement the medic roared with laughter.

'I was told you had a great sense of humour. By Jove they were right. Wonderfully funny. A good one that!' said the medic when he pulled himself together.

I purported to be laughing too. Though I had no idea as to why I was pretending to laugh. The joke was lost on me.

'Yes, very funny,' reiterated the medic. 'I was at the game against Essex today. I saw you take a brilliant catch at leg slip. In poor light at that. Now here's a joke for you, Mr Trueman. What's the connection between you and the main road that runs through Yorkshire and up through Durham and Northumberland to Scotland?'

'Don't know, sir,' I informed him in all honesty.

'You're both categorized as A1,' said the medic. 'Report in two weeks.'

I was assigned to the Royal Air Force, and after basic training was posted to Hemswell in Lincolnshire. Being only thirty-two miles from home, it was not only handily placed, but it was also commanded by a marvellous man called Jim Warfield, a group captain and a real cricket enthusiast. I was willing to serve my country in whatever capacity I was ordered. With my sporting background, Jim Warfield felt I would be best employed in the sports section, looking after equipment and the playing fields.

My two years in the RAF were not wasted on me. I thoroughly enjoyed my service days, in which I made any number of lasting friendships. I also matured physically, putting on a little under three vital inches in height and even more around the chest. One of my RAF pals likened me to a Spanish fighting bull, which was just about right. I shot up to a little over five feet ten, weighed thirteen and half a stone, measured 46 inches round the chest and hips and almost 20 inches round the thighs. That all happened during my two years in the RAF, and I didn't alter much during my entire playing career. And I had the confidence to match my strength. Self-appraisal is no guarantee of merit, I know, but I was confident of becoming the best fast bowler Yorkshire had ever produced. I was also confident that one day I would play for England.

Australia had dominated recent 'Ashes' series, primarily

because they possessed two great fast bowlers in Ray Lindwall and Keith Miller. But we had none worth speaking of and the need to find fast bowlers who could retaliate by rattling the Aussies was uppermost in the minds of just about every cricket writer of the day. They went on about it as if it was a national emergency which, in some ways, I suppose it was. They say cometh the hour cometh the man and my confidence in my own ability was such, I knew that man would be me. I also knew it would not be easy.

I began my service in the RAF as an AC2 eventually rising to the dizzy heights of AC1. My duties in the sports section consisted of looking after the sports equipment store and being groundsman to the cricket and football pitches. In the summer I played cricket for the station, the RAF and the Combined Services, and kept fit in the winter by playing football. In the summer of 1952 I remember reading a lengthy article in one of the broadsheet newspapers which said that if the answer to England's fast bowling problem was in the forces, then arrangements must be made for his release. Though I was not mentioned by name, I thought this might be an oblique reference to me but kept quiet, carried out my RAF duties to the best of my ability and hoped that one day the call would come.

Not long after that article appeared in the press, Yorkshire applied to have me released for two weeks prior to the start of a Test match against India. Looking back now, I'm of the mind that this application for my release and the subsequent compliance was probably instigated by the England selectors at Lord's so that they could have a look at me. If not exactly establishment figures themselves, the England selectors certainly rubbed shoulders with the establishment and major figures in the armed forces.

Both the press and the public were calling for my inclusion in the England team. Though, of course, I didn't realize this then, in 1952 I was seen as a symbol of the times. Rightly or wrongly many people saw me as being not only a genuine fast bowler but also dramatic, comic, downright earthy, nostalgic and in some ways epic and heroic. In short, I embodied exactly the demand of the day. Many of those who returned to an everyday peace-time existence in Britain after the war saw cricket as confirmation that life had returned to normal. Cricket, and Test matches in particular, were seen as evidence that all was again well, whereby men could busy themselves with and talk seriously, sometimes gravely, about unimportant matters. Cricket was once again English life's greatest irrelevancy and a lot of people took great comfort in that fact.

The golden summer of 1947 had been lit by the genius of the Middlesex pair Bill Edrich and Denis Compton. The former scored 3,539 runs at an average of 80.43 while also taking 67 wickets at 22.58. Denis Compton, a brilliant right-handed batsman and unorthodox slow left-arm bowler, hit a record 3,816 runs that summer at an average of 90.85. He scored an amazing eighteen centuries, four of them in the Test series against South Africa. Denis thrilled the large crowds of 1947 with his dashing and cavalier strokeplay but it was not only at cricket that he excelled. Denis was also a top-quality footballer. In 1947–8 he helped his club, Arsenal, win the First Division Championship and, in 1950, the FA Cup. A highly gifted dual-sportsman he brought colour and sparkle to cricket and football in the austere post-war years of rationing.

After the heroics of Edrich and Compton in 1948 came Donald Bradman's Australians, personified by the searing pace of Ray Lindwall and Keith Miller. Two contrasting fast bowlers who destroyed English batting with the sweeping inevitability of an uncontrollable forest fire. When Lindwall or Miller took the new ball – and in 1948 under the sixty-five-over rule such moments were not far apart – even a packed Lord's or Old Trafford fell as silent as a country churchyard.

The quest to produce a genuine English fast bowler to match Lindwall and Miller was undertaken more in hope than certainty. There were my two competitors and friends in the Yorkshire team, John Whitehead and Bill Foord. Les Jackson of Derbyshire and his teammate Tom Hall, who joined Somerset. For a time Ken Preston of Essex came into the reckoning until tragedy struck and he broke a leg. P. A. Whitcombe, formerly of Oxford University, was another, if unlikely, candidate to fill the breach until his bowling was murdered one day at Lord's by Bill Brown. Though all fine bowlers in their own right they were all, in truth, fast-medium-pacers. With all due respect, I doubt if any of them could have made an impact on the top Australian batsmen of the day.

It had been four seasons since the pace of the Australian attack had wreaked havoc throughout English cricket, but the Holy Grail of a home-grown fast bowler had remained elusive. But in my heart of hearts, I knew I had it in me to be that bowler. All I wanted was the opportunity to prove it.

My leave of absence was two weeks prior to the start of the Test series with India. I was fit and ready and keen to show everyone what I was capable of. Yorkshire were embarking upon a sequence of four successive home matches, the first against Somerset at Huddersfield. It was the first time that summer that I had bowled a ball in earnest and quite literally, I hit the ground running, bowling Gimblett and having Stephenson caught at the wicket. Somerset 2 for 2 and I felt I was just getting warmed up. I took 6 for 45 in Somerset's first innings, but hampered by cramp and stiffness due to lack of match practice, returned figures of 2 for 44 in the second innings. We beat Somerset by an innings and 32 runs within two days. At the end of the match a Yorkshire supporter approached me and said, 'You made light work of them Fred, 'specially int' first innings.'

Cricket wasn't work to me, neither did I feel it was a vocation. It was simply bubbling out of me. At Park Avenue in Bradford, Yorkshire demonstrated the excellence of the pitch for batting when making 399 on the first day against Worcestershire. That was a good total to make, but Worcestershire had a fine batting line-up themselves and many believed they would get somewhere near that total if not actually exceed it. I, however, had other ideas. I was pumped up, motivated, determined and, more to the point, bowling with control, accuracy and speed. Not forty-five minutes had registered on the clock of the first session of the second day's play and I had Worcestershire reeling. Their top five batsmen – Don Kenyon, Peter Richardson, Laddie Outschoorn, Bob Broadbent and Ronnie Bird – were all back in the pavilion courtesy of yours truly – four of them clean bowled. I had taken 5 wickets in nineteen balls for 5 runs. What's more, I went on to take another 3 wickets and the 2 wickets I didn't take, I was instrumental, as I caught both. Yorkshire won again without needing to bat for a second time and with more than a day to spare.

Against Derbyshire at Sheffield the Bramall Lane pitch was slow and more suitable for spinners. Nevertheless, I once again gave it my all and in what was a third successive Yorkshire victory finished with match figures of 5 for 107. 'All in all,' I thought to myself, 'not a bad effort over three games considering my lack of match practice.'

A bumper Whitsun holiday crowd turned up at Headingley for our 'Roses' match with Lancashire. In a closely contested game that ended in a draw I returned figures of 4 for 86. In my four-match return for Yorkshire I had taken 32 wickets at an average of 14.2 runs each. I was satisfied with those statistics and felt I had proved a point. If not England, then certainly Yorkshire now had a genuine fast bowler capable of getting amongst the wickets with an economy of bowling to boot. My return to Yorkshire had gone better than even I had dared hope. The newspapers were singing my praises, the Yorkshire supporters were delighted with my efforts and there was even grudging appreciation from some of the Yorkshire selection committee –'Bowled very well in those four games, yes. But raw, you know, probably never come to anything' being typical of the sort of comment that reached my ears.

I returned to my duties in the sports store at RAF Hemswell satisfied that I may have proved something at last, but convinced I was still some way off gaining a call-up for England because I wasn't, after all, playing regularly in first-class cricket. I was working in the sports store when I was summoned to the telephone.

'How do you feel about having been picked to play for England in the next Test?' the voice asked.

Before replying I gathered my thoughts.

'Bollocks to you, mate,' I said convinced it was a wind-up from a fellow erk – 'erk' being the common RAF term for those on National Service. A few moments later the telephone rang again, the voice was the same.

'Mr Trueman, you have been picked to play for England against India. How does it feel to be an International cricketer?' the voice asked.

My fellow erks and I were forever playing practical jokes on one another, but this was one joke I wasn't falling for.

'Listen, you're not going to catch me on this one. So bugger off,' I said and slammed the phone down.

Two minutes later another call.

A warrant officer picked up the phone and informed that a man called Bill Bowes wanted to speak to me. I was still incredulous until the voice spoke and I recognized the voice. It was indeed Bill Bowes calling from Leeds.

When Bill told me I had been picked to play for England I was, initially, still disbelieving but after a minute or so the news sank in. The person who had made the original calls turned out to be John Bapty, who covered Yorkshire games for the *Yorkshire Post*. Having got nowhere with me, John had brought Bill to the phone to convince me that my Test call-up was no hoax. Having spoken to Bill and then made suitable apologies to John Bapty, I then went to see my Group Captain, Jim Warfield. I didn't march to his office. I floated on air.

I told him of my news and asked if it would be possible for him to release me. Though I had just returned from two weeks' leave of absence I was hopeful of being released for the Test match. To have International players of any sport in their ranks was a great PR exercise in the eyes of all three senior services. In addition to the prestige and publicity, having an International sportsman in the ranks was considered a great fillip to recruitment and, of course, there was more than a hint of one-upmanship. Not only between the three senior services themselves, but within the commands of the RAF. To my delight Jim Warfield informed me that he would approve my release, but on one condition.

'That you get me a couple of tickets for my wife and me,' said Jim partly in jest.

Of course I arranged for those tickets to be waiting for him on the first day of the Test match. The game against India was to take place at Headingley. No scriptwriter could have written it better. I was to make my International debut for my country in front of my home crowd. I knew it would be a packed house and I also knew I was ready.

It was a bit nerve-racking turning up at the Prince of Wales Hotel in Harrogate on the night before the Test for the traditional pre-match dinner. In addition to my Yorkshire teammate Len Hutton the team also included Bill Edrich and Denis Compton, all three of whom had been scoring centuries for England when I was nowt but a lad. The first thing I noticed was that there was a hierarchy in the England team similar to the one that existed in the Yorkshire dressing room. And being the young debutant I was at the bottom of the pecking order. I was made aware of that by the fact that Bill Edrich, Denis Compton and even my club teammate Len Hutton kept themselves to themselves all evening, only recognizing my presence by way of a nod of the head when I was initially introduced to them. I felt as if I had gained entry to a small and elitist club, which, in many ways, I had.

Though still only twenty-one I felt mentally and physically ready for the task ahead. The couple of inches I had gained in height while in the RAF provided me with the fresh and crucial advantage of being able to dig the ball in, as opposed to skidding through. I possessed a well-hidden slower ball, command of a menacing bumper when the occasion demanded, and given the right conditions could make my out-swinger 'go' very late indeed. If need be, again given responsive conditions, I could also bowl a good in-swinger. I felt I possessed the armoury to make my mark at Test level, though was aware that certain people, Len Hutton being one, still considered me 'raw and immature in bowling terms'.

I suppose this was true in certain respects, but my bowling was acquiring subtlety and finesse on a daily basis. I was happy with my run-up, which consisted of twenty-two measured paces with three or four walking steps thrown in for launching purposes. I moved up in a measured curve, swerving slightly out and round the umpire. Though one or two may have seen me as 'raw', Arthur Mitchell and Bill Bowes thought my run-up to be, as Bill put it, 'as natural as it was splendid'. Needless to say it was the comments of Arthur and Bill of which I took notice. If they had not been happy with my run-up and delivery, I would have listened to what they had to say and taken their advice.

Bill told me I was now hitting the ground with the ball in the constant manner of the Australian bowlers. In an interview for the *Daily Graphic* Bill said, 'In addition to his natural outswing – often late and from the line of middle stump – which is his deadliest weapon, Fred Trueman can make the most of a green wicket with movement off the seam. He bowls a tremendous yorker and has proved himself to be a genuine fast bowler of style and finesse.' I now find it odd that coaches such as Bill Bowes and Arthur Mitchell had a view of me seemingly at odds with that of people such as Len Hutton. That's cricket. A game of differing opinions – as the guy standing next to you in the pub would no doubt disagree.

England's game against India was the first of a four-match Test series and turned out to be one of some moment. Not only the Headingley crowd but all of Yorkshire was deeply conscious and proud of the fact that Lord's had, for the first time in the history of English cricket, appointed a professional as captain of England and that the man chosen was our own Len Hutton, recognized from Middlesbrough to Sheffield and from Huddersfield to Hull and all points in between as being not only the best batsman in England, but the world.

As a batsman Len was touched with genius. He was *the* complete batsman on all types of wicket. That he was a truly great batsman was all the more remarkable for the fact that during the war he was involved in an accident which resulted in his left arm being shortened by two inches.

Like me, Len Hutton first played for England at the age of twenty-one, though his Test debut was ignominious when set against what he would go on to achieve. Len made his International debut against New Zealand in 1937 and made a duck in his first innings and one solitary run in the second. He more than made up for that disappointing start by then making a century in his second Test and the rest, as they say, is history – and of the most glorious kind. Less than twelve months after his first Test, he created cricket history when scoring 364 against Australia at the Oval. From 1937 to 1953 he averaged just under 50 in every English season, his most prolific season being that of 1949 when he scored 3,429 runs at 68.58 and created another record by scoring 1,294 runs in June, the most runs ever scored in a single month.

His genius with the bat was most evident during England's 1950–51 winter tour of Australia, when he scored 533 runs in Test matches at an average of 88.83. To place this feat into true perspective, the next-best average to that of Len in that Test series was 38.77. All in all he played in seventy-nine Tests for England in which he scored 6,971 runs at 56.67, which included nineteen centuries. But lest we forget, he also captained England twenty-three times, winning eleven of those Tests and losing just four.

For any young Yorkshire lad of the time, Len was true hero – and I include myself in that number. Now Len was to become the first professional to captain England. The fact that he would do so on his home ground of Headingley was a story straight from the pages of a *Boy's Own* adventure story. It was not only poignant but highly appropriate, for in the eyes of many, Len Hutton appeared to have jumped straight from the pages of an adventure story for boys. He was charismatic, heroic, dashing, daring and formidable when faced with adversity.

The Indian captain Hazare won the toss and elected to bat on what was a typical Headingley pitch of amiable batting pace. Right from the start the ball ran away quickly over the close-cut grass of the outfield, a sure sign that bowlers could be in for a hard time. Sure enough, my opening spell against Gaekwad and Roy failed to trouble either batsman unduly and Len Hutton asked me to take a rest, only to quickly bring me back once Gaekwad was out so I could bowl at Umrigar. Umrigar was a consistently high scorer against medium-pace and spin bowling, but Len believed him to be vulnerable to pace – especially my pace. I had been a little disappointed when the Kirkstall Lane end with its downhill run had been given to Alec Bedser. That was usually mine, Len knew that; what's more, he also knew that I was highly effective when bowling from that end down the slope. With my normal rhythmical approach and speed and accuracy when bowling down the slope I reckon I could have made serious inroads into the Indian batting even on a Headingley wicket that was favouring the batsman. I remember desperately wanting to make cricket history by getting a wicket with the first ever ball I bowled in a Test, but that was one record I had to do without.

Polly Umrigar was a super batsman, but Len Hutton's notion that he didn't like pace proved to be spot-on. The previously confident and unruffled Umrigar looked uncomfortable at the very first ball I bowled. Minutes later he jabbed at a delivery and edged it into the gloves of Godfrey Evans behind the wicket. I had claimed my first ever wicket at Test level. I didn't run up to Polly Umrigar and wave a fist at him. I didn't do a lap of honour. Nor did my teammates run to me arms aloft expecting a 'high-five'. And I didn't look over the members enclosure and place a finger to pursed lips. That wasn't how it was back then. I simply nodded in the direction of Umrigar to acknowledge his efforts with the bat, and he reciprocated by nodding his head in my direction as he began his walk back to the pavilion. On the outside I was calm and collected, but inside my emotions were roller-coasting; excitement coursed through my veins and I was consumed with pride. I knew I'd arrived.

India rallied. There was a major stand of 222 between Hazare and the precocious talent of young Manjrekar, who was outstanding in making 133. That pairing brought India back to 264 for 3. After having seized the initiative at the outset we were now chasing the game. Len Hutton had given Alec Bedser and me a good rest, but with an hour of play remaining brought us both back to bowl. Len's ploy worked. Alec Bedser had Hazare caught by Godfrey Evans and before another run had been scored I bowled an out-swinger to Manjrekar, who edged it low but into the hands of Watkins at second slip. Two deliveries later I bowled Gopinath. Three Test wickets to my name and the initiative was back with England. India ended the day on 272 for 6. In less than ten minutes the whole shape of the game had changed, which for me is the beauty and intrigue of cricket.

It rained during the night, and though the grey clouds had long since passed over when we commenced play, the dampness in the air made the pitch difficult. The conditions, however, suited Jim Laker, who worked his way through the tail end of the Indian batting without undue discomfort and they were all out for 293. I was delighted to have taken 3 wickets on my first appearance for my country, though the professional in me was annoyed at the fact they had come at a price: 89 runs.

When England batted everyone in Headingley realized how well matched the two sides were. A closely fought encounter seemed in store. The Indian medium-pace bowlers Ramchand, Hazare and Phadkar bowled accurately and well while their off-spinner Ghulam Ahmed weaved his own particular brand of magic. England progressed thanks in the main to some thoughtful and determined batting from Graveney, Watkins and Jenkins and swashbuckling 66 from wicket-keeper Godfrey Evans. England declared on 347 for 9 on the Saturday morning, a first-innings lead of 41, which many believed was insufficient to herald victory, given we'd have to bat again in what would be the fourth innings of the game.

The first two days of the Test took place on Thursday and Friday. But the great day of a Test, especially at Headingley, was a Saturday when all those who had been working on the first two days made the annual pilgrimage to see England in action. There was no saturation coverage of Test matches on television, besides which in 1952 very few homes possessed a TV set. The only way Yorkshire folk could see England in action was at the annual Test at Headingley.

Accordingly, the Saturday crowd at a Headingley Test was different to any of the other four days. Legions of schoolboys thronged the perimeter of the pitch six deep behind the boundary rope, in the hope of having the opportunity to field the ball back to one of their heroes. People came from the North, East and West Ridings, the Dales, the mill towns of

Halifax, Huddersfield and Bradford, from Sheffield's city of steel and from mining communities of Rotherham, Pontefract, Castleford and my own Maltby. There were fishing folk from Hull, railwaymen from York and brewery lads from Barnsley. They came equipped for the day with their thermos flasks, snappin' tins of sandwiches of luncheon meat, corned beef or spam, their black plastic macs furled like a pack of pedal bin liners in their jacket pockets. Tell these people cricket is nowt but one side trying to get t'other out so they can go in, and one might as well say the Bible is only so much paper and ink, a Stradivarius simply wood and catgut.

Headingley was heaving. There was not a vacant seat in the whole of the ground. There was the unique rustle and hum of a capacity Test crowd. Such was the setting when India batted for the second time on the Saturday just before three. The atmosphere that day is unforgettable for me. When Len Hutton led us out through the usual corridor of autograph-hungry boys, it was as if all of Yorkshire recognized and shared his distinction of being the first professional captain of England and one of their number to boot. Deep, sustained applause greeted Len when he first appeared on the pavilion steps and it remained with him until he reached the square on the middle. I was astounded and overwhelmed when I too received deep, warm applause when asked by Len to open the bowling from my favoured Kirkstall Lane end.

The pitch had been easy on the first day, difficult on the second morning, but had been helpful to spin until the end. Now it was lively, but true and honest. As I paced out my twenty-two-yard run everyone inside the ground settled down, the crowd being more meticulous about this at Headingley than any other English ground. Being one of their own, I knew all eyes were on me. I hoped and prayed I wouldn't let them down.

My first ball to Pankaj Roy was outside the line of the off-stump and Roy allowed it to go through to wicket-keeper

Godfrey Evans. My second delivery was a bumper. Roy moved inside it, attempted a hook but the pace of the delivery beat him and he skied it off the top edge. That ball went so high I thought it was going to come down with ice on it. It appeared to be in the air for an eternity. Eventually it obeyed Newton's law of gravity and dropped into the grateful cupped hands of Denis Compton at second slip. A roar of triumph rang around Headingley. India were none for 1.

In the following over Alec Bedser bowled the one ball of the day that behaved unpredictably. It lifted off a length to the right-handed Gaekwad, who couldn't move his feet quick enough to avoid it. The ball ran across the angled shoulder of Gaekwad's bat and he was caught by Jim Laker in the gully. Headingley once again resounded with applause. India none for 2. When I had dispatched Pankaj Roy the Indian skipper, Hazare, sent in Mantri, their wicket-keeper, as stoic and defensive a batsman as it was possible to be. Mantri had carried his bat in the first innings and was obviously there for damage limitation. The occasion and the atmosphere had me firing on all cylinders and our tremendous start had adrenalin racing through my brain like a formula one car.

I strode back to my run marker, turned, jogged three or four paces then took to my toes and sprinted along my curving run. I decided to vary things by giving him a slower delivery. I wasn't the best at concealing this type of delivery but I could do it. It's said that to disguise this delivery you should bowl at the same pace but release the ball behind the crease. But I had worked out my own way for a slower delivery, as usual. My idea was to make the batsman play early, and that delivery to Mantri is one I shall never forget.

It pitched on his middle-stump, then straightened out. Mantri's off-stump was ripped from the ground and cart-wheeled across Headingley's sward towards Godfrey Evans behind the wicket. Headingley erupted. The tumultuous hunt-ing call of a crowd sensing the kill swept up, then out of

Headingley, and across the rooftops of sooty grey Victorian terraced houses which appeared to be straining to get a view of the fantastic happenings taking place in the normally quiet and sedate confines of the cricket ground. India none for 3.

Manjrekar had top-scored for India in their first innings with 133. Along with skipper Hazare he was as good a player of fast bowling as there was in cricket at that time. It was largely due to Manjrekar's fluid batting style that I had conceded 89 runs during the first innings when taking 3 wickets. I stood on my run marker and gathered myself together and was suddenly aware of a very strange thing. There were 34,000 people inside Headingley and it was as silent as a tomb.

The uncommon silence of the crowd didn't get to me. I was totally focused as I commenced my run. When I hit the crease I let fly another straight delivery of full length. To my surprise Manjrekar attempted a cover drive. Yet again the pace of the delivery was too much for the batsman. Manjrekar's off-stump leapt out of the ground and yet again cartwheeled across the pitch in a futile quest for freedom. The killer cry went up with increased intensity. A roar that would not have welt the Wrekin but rather split it asunder swept down from the stands. Fourteen balls in total had been bowled. India none for 4 and I had taken three of their wickets.

There was pandemonium in the stands. I couldn't believe what was happening to India, to England, to me. I happened to glance across to Len Hutton. For a brief moment our eyes met. Then Len's head fell, he sighed and shook his head from side to side as if saying, 'I don't believe it, Fred.' I was having trouble believing it myself. My first Test match. India, second innings, 4 for no runs. Trueman 3 for none. Dad was somewhere in that crowd. The man who had sacrificed so that I could have the opportunities he was denied. The man who had stuck by me when I had been injured and Yorkshire had not given a thought to my welfare or well-being. Who, when my spirits were low, had been the man who had offered me constant encouragement and had instilled in me confidence and self-belief. I wondered how Dad was feeling.

The Indian skipper Hazare was next in. He was an officer in the army of the Gaekwar of Baroda. A lean, resolute man who stood as erect as a Grecian pillar. As I was on a hat-trick, Len summoned up a close field of eight men behind the bat. In the prickling silence I swept along my running curve and attempted a yorker. Hazare moved into line, bat close to pad and the ball missed the edge by a fag paper's width. Headingley collectively sighed, as if dropping from ecstasy to exhaustion.

Given the extraordinary nature of events thus far, I consoled myself that it would be asking too much to achieve a hat-trick as well. None for 4 wickets had never been seen on a Test match scoreboard before. That Headingley scoreboard became the most photographed scoreboard in cricket. The sports editor of the *Yorkshire Evening Post* telephoned the sports reporter he had covering the match to confirm that the figure hadn't been given the wrong way round, that India weren't, in fact, 4 for no wicket, and received the insistence on none for 4 wickets incredulously.

It had been very heady stuff. The adrenalin rushes served to tire me quickly and Len, sensing this, rested me after I'd bowled only four overs. I returned in the session immediately after tea but found, like my fellow England bowlers, I couldn't break a gritty stand between Hazare and Phadkar. With about fifteen minutes of play remaining in the day, Len Hutton displayed his tactical nous. Len asked me if I had rested sufficiently to have another crack at Hazare and I told him to give me the ball. I sent down a delivery of some velocity and accuracy. The sheer pace of the delivery beat Hazare and his off-stump was off on its travels again.

We mopped up the remaining Indian batting the next morning thanks in the main to the bowling of Bedser and Jenkins. England needed just 18 runs for victory. The press went overboard about my performance. I was headline news in all the sports pages, not only because of my achievements in my debut Test but also because the consensus of opinion was England had at last produced a fast bowler who could turn a Test match. I was, as the saying goes, 'good press'. The newspapers saw me as heroic, humorous, athletic and, as the *Daily Sketch* put it, 'a fearsome fast bowler exuding controlled aggression in the name of England and in the quest for victory of the most glorious kind'. Gossip, stories – some true, many of them false – followed. I've seen it written that I gloried in all this attention. Heard it said that in the week following the Headingley Test I swaggered up and down the streets of Leeds city centre revelling in the praise that was being bestowed upon me. The truth being, immediately following the Headingley Test, I was back at RAF Hemswell dishing out sports equipment, sewing straps back onto pads and mowing and marking out the cricket pitch as per my orders!

Over the years, various arguments have raged about fast bowlers of every generation. Pace bowlers have been electronically timed, photographed in sequence of movement, filmed in slow-motion. All in the quest to find out who was quicker than who. But when you come right down t'it, fast bowling and the effectiveness of it is all down to who is on the receiving end. The batsman is the only man who can say who was quicker or more effective 'to him'. It can depend on the pace of the pitch, the age of the ball, the bounce, the light, the moisture in the atmosphere, the state of the game even. But in the final analysis it's all about how that ball arrives at the batsman's end. Upon that depends whether, when sitting his grandchildren on his knee, he waxes lyrical about the demon pace of Lillee and Thomson, or Hall and Griffith, Holding and Roberts, Trueman and Statham, Lindwall and Miller, Malcolm Marshall, Joel Garner or Andy Roberts. Then someone who never faced a bowler quicker than Ashley Giles will leap in and say, 'But what about Harold Larwood?'

And you can turn round and reply, 'Tell thee what, lad,

there was an underarm bowler called Smith who played for Surrey. He once sent down one so fast it not only beat the batsman, but the wicket-keeper and long stop as well, and killed a dog that happened t' be passing byt' boundary rope.'

It's all relative. India had not encountered anyone like me and it gave me the edge over them. My job was to bowl people out and I made no major effort to disguise the fact. If I came up against sublime technique, stubborn resistance or both in a batsman, I used what technique I had at my disposal to send him on his way. Some people said at times I was ruthless. You have to be at that level of cricket.

Ten days after the Headingley Test I was released from a tour of Holland and Germany with the RAF to play in the second Test at Lord's. I arrived at the team hotel tired after a long, drawn-out journey where I had travelled first by bus, then train, caught a ferry across the North Sea, a taxi to the station before catching a London-bound train, whereupon I jumped in another taxi that took me to the hotel where the England team were staying. Europe had yet to 'open up' in terms of access and travel. My journey from Germany began at four in the morning and I arrived at our team hotel at a quarter-past eight in the evening. For the life of me I can't imagine a player of today embarking on such a journey two days before a Test match! Especially when he might be expected to bowl for a lengthy session on the first day. Len was sympathetic to my plight and the fact I looked shattered, so allowed me to sleep long and be called late to ensure I had adequate rest in advance of net practice on the day before the match.

The India team of 1952 were formidable opponents on their home turf but found it difficult to play against England on our pitches. In Vinoo Mankad, India possessed a world class all-rounder, but he was contracted to play league cricket for Haslingden as their pro. His commitments to Haslingden restricted his appearances for his country that summer. He was available only for this Test at Lord's and the two subsequent Tests. Again, a situation one would never come across today whereby playing for a league club, never mind a county side, took preference over International cricket.

At Lord's Mankad gave ample evidence that he was a real class act. In terms of sheer stamina and fortitude his performance had seldom been matched. He scored 72 and 184, opening the Indian batting despite having bowled seventy-three overs of slow left-arm spin in England's first innings for a return of 5 for 196. England made 537 in reply to India's first innings total of 235 and from that you may deduce we were very much in command of the game. Len Hutton was certainly 'on trial' as England captain but he offered ample evidence that he was more than up for the job in this match. In addition to having skippered the side well – as he had done at Headingley – Len scored 150 in our first innings before being caught by Mantri off the bowling of Hazare. Other notable contributions with the bat came from Godfrey Evans, who also made a century (104), Surrey's Peter May (74) and R. T. Simpson (53). Even yours truly batting at number eleven chipped in with what the *Daily Mirror* described as being 'a breezy seventeen'.

In India's first innings I had taken the prized wicket of Mankad and also those of Umrigar, Ramchand and Mantri to finish with figures of 4 for 72. In India's second innings Mankad set about our bowling with some determination and style. Mankad gave more than could be expected of a man during an innings that lasted four hours and twenty-five minutes. His 184 was the backbone of an Indian total of 378.

The *Daily Mirror* hailed him 'Mankad the Marvel' but his marvellous heroics were to be in vain. Though Hazare (49) and Ramchand (42) offered doughty resistance, Jim Laker and I found good form in taking 4 wickets apiece, with the other 2 falling to Alec Bedser. Roly Jenkins took just the one wicket in the game and came in for some severe punishment from Mankad, seemingly to the lasting disapproval of the England selectors, who never picked Roly for a Test again. Roly Jenkins' omission from subsequent Tests was to have an effect on me. His absence meant I could not be nursed in the team. I would form the spearhead of the bowling with Alec Bedser. Usually a young bowler who had played only two Tests would be used sparingly. A ploy to 'protect' him from the higher standard of batting than he had been previously used to. With Roly Jenkins out of the picture I was thrown in at the deep end. Fortunately, I've always been a bloody good swimmer.

England polished off the runs needed for victory against India without too much of a problem to win by 8 wickets. My performances in the two Tests resulted in me being the subject of many an article in the newspapers. I was making the headline news in the sports pages, one national newspaper even going as far as to call me 'The New Larwood' – after 'The Second Bradman', the most potentially career-threatening of all epithets.

I found the transition from young England cricketer to RAF AC1 a smooth one. Once I was back at camp and had donned my RAF uniform I not only played the part but felt the part, though my deeds on the cricket pitch and the subsequent press coverage I received didn't go down well with everyone. There was also some resentment at the fact I was readily awarded leave to play for my country. The officers never gave me a hard time over this, but some of the NCOs treated me in a terse manner when they weren't being down-right spiteful. I managed to avoid any nasty situations by letting their words go in one ear and out the other but there was one occasion when it did get a bit nasty. Though the instigator of this incident was not in the RAF.

I had joined a group of my fellow conscripts for a night out in Lincoln. We went to the pictures, after which we downed a quick drink in a pub before catching a bus back to camp. On its route back to the camp, the bus stopped for about five minutes at a particular stop where there were a number of shops including a fish and chip shop. My mates and I were just sitting chatting. When I noticed this particular stop looming I asked if any of them would like some fish and chips, and volunteered to nip into the shop to get our order. The bus was nigh-on full and when I returned with our fish and chip suppers I found my mates in an argument with a chap who had just boarded the bus. My pals were saving my seat for me and this guy had taken exception to this. When I appeared on the scene, sat down and he realized who the seat had being saved for, he turned really nasty.

'Who the hell do you think you are?' he asked menacingly, knowing fine well who I was, of course, which I suppose was what this was really all about. I tried to placate him and calm him down as did my pals, but he was having none of it.

'Mr Big Time England cricketer,' he taunted, following that with a few ill-chosen expletives. There were women on the bus. Again I tried to placate him, which only served to make him more hostile

'Listen, mate. Nobody wants any trouble. Now there's ladies on this bus and your language . . .'

I didn't get any further because he then swung a punch at me. That did it for me. I jumped up and pushed him away. He reeled back but once he regained his balance looked ready to come back for more. Fortunately my pals jumped to their feet and kept us apart. Which was just as well because I'd got so mad at some of the things he'd been saying I would have hospitalized him.

Given that you are unlikely to find a current England player catching a late-night bus (and in the RAF at that), that incident is another indication of just how much not only cricket, but the reporting of top sport in Britain, has changed over the years. Should any current International, be he a cricketer, footballer or rugby player, be involved in a fracas such as the one I experienced, it would be front-page news in the tabloids. It was different back in 1952. English sport had its heroes such as Len Hutton, Denis Compton, Stan Matthews and Tom Finney, but there was not the hyperbole from PR agencies to make those top sportsmen cult celebrities. Top-quality cricketers and footballers were paid not a great deal more than the people who came to watch them play. Though they lived comfortably in one of the more desirable areas of town, they lived cheek by jowl with the supporters who paid their wages. Players got to know supporters and vice versa.

This contact, often on a daily basis when you might pop into the newsagent's for a morning paper before catching the bus to the ground, fostered trust between players and support-ers. Many of today's top sports people are wary of supporters. This is especially the case with Premiership footballers, who now enjoy the status of the top movie stars of the fifties. The fact that many of our top sports people now have little or no real contact with their supporters I find sad.

Many of these so-called sports stars have nothing meaning-ful to say, but every word and antic is slavishly covered by certain elements of the media. This is particularly so where top footballers are concerned. In 1999–2000 Manchester United did not enter the FA Cup because of their involvement in the ill-fated World Club Championship in Brazil. Two national tabloid newspapers devoted their front page to the fact that United's first training session in Brazil had passed without a hitch. The story was a non-story, unbefitting of a filler column let alone a front-page story.

The point I am making is this. When even banal utterances from top sports people are reported with gusto and when footballers see a nondescript training session make front-page headlines in some national newspapers, little wonder our top sports stars become instilled with a warped sense of their importance. Having slavishly reported the minutiae and incon-sequential happenings in the lives of top sports people, should one of these stars do something untoward, as we have seen in recent years, the press go on a feeding frenzy, In so doing taking the moral high ground.

The confrontation I had with that passenger on the late bus back to RAF Hemswell never made news in the press for two main reasons. Firstly, irrespective of whether you played for the England cricket or football team, you were not considered a celebrity. You may have been a hero to some, but you were a working-class hero. You moved in circles similar to, if not the same as, the game's supporters. Because the lives and lifestyle of top sporting people were in essence the same as those of supporters, unlike today, there was no fascination as to how we lived our lives and conducted ourselves. People knew. Therefore, there was no prying on the part of the press.

Secondly, though the Second World War had been over for seven years, it was still fresh in everyone's minds. The war had touched every adult's life profoundly, in some cases tragically. Having been through a World War and been witness to death and tragedy on a monumental scale, people found an exchange of punches on a late-night bus a matter of inconsequence, even when it involved a current member of the England cricket team.

To my great delight, and expectation I might add, I retained my place in the England team for the third Test against India at Old Trafford. Len Hutton won the toss, opted to bat and in a first innings that was frequently interrupted because of bad light and rain, we made 347 for 9 when Len declared on the Saturday morning. By saying 'we' I am overstating the case because, when the ninth wicket fell, Len issued the declaration, which meant, as last man, I didn't bat.

Our score was decent enough but the clock was now against us. In essence we were halfway through the game and only one side had batted. Many of the press believed a result from this Test would be unlikely. But what makes cricket the great game it is is the way a match can change very quickly.

Due to the inclement weather of the previous two days, the Old Trafford pitch was wet through, and although no Indian bowler was fast enough to exploit it, I believed I could. Alec Bedser opened the bowling from the City end and Vinoo Mankad let Alec know he was there by driving his first ball through the covers for 4. The last ball of the over, Mankad leg-glanced Alec for what at first looked as if it would be another boundary. But there was our debutant, Surrey's Tony Lock, throwing himself forward at short leg to take the catch. 'Right,' I thought, 'there's still nine of them left, get to work, Fred.'

Bowling from the Stretford end with a stiff breeze blowing in over my right shoulder, I managed to bring the ball off the pitch at some speed, making it rear up in an intimidating manner. Len Hutton set a close field of three slips, three gullies, a silly point and two short legs, and I adapted my bowling accordingly. With a shiny new ball in my hand, an out-and-out attacking field waiting for chances, and armed with the knowledge that India must be apprehensive about facing my bowling after the first two Tests, I was raring to go and brimming with confidence.

I effected my usual run-up and then, as the square-on position of the approach gave way to the sideways-on of delivery, left side poised, right arm towering high in an arc and down, I let them have it.

In my first spell of four overs I had Pankaj Roy and Adhikari caught at slip and Phadkar in the gulley. The England catching was superb. Every time the ball was edged, or lifted, it went to hand and everyone held on. When Polly Umrigar came to the wicket he said, 'Bowling's not bad today, Fred.'

'It's not meant to be, Polly,' I told him.

Though satisfied with 3 wickets courtesy of the excellent catching by my teammates, I wanted to see the stumps go down. As I walked back to the starting point of my run, Tony Lock, at leg slip, called out to Polly.

'Polly. D'you mind moving back a bit? I can't see the bowler coming in.'

Polly did move – but in the other direction, because as I ran in I could see Tony between the stumps and the batsman! Whenever I saw a gap like that between a batsman and his wicket, I knew I had him rattled.

India were in a panic. A little earlier Dattu Phadkar actually charged towards me, swinging his bat from way outside the line and carved a catch to David Sheppard. Once panic sets in to a team it spreads like wildfire and the faster I bowled the quicker it spread throughout the Indian batting. Polly Umrigar wasn't at the crease for long. I knocked over his stumps to such devastating effect one of the bails broke and a piece of it carried to just short of the boundary at the City end.

When the broken piece had been retrieved and a new bail brought to the wicket, the umpire, Dai Davies, handed it to me. I kept the broken bail in my pocket until lunch then handed it to my brother Arthur, who was sitting with Dad in front of the pavilion. Arthur was taken with his souvenir. He had it mounted in a little showcase and was never to part with it. India were 17 for 5. Hazare and Manjrekar held us up a bit with a stand of 28 before, soon after lunch, Alex Bedser bowled Hazare. Not long after I delivered a pig of a ball to Manjrekar. The ball reared up off the pitch too quick to be avoided, Manjrekar held his bat up, mainly for protection, and the ball shot away into the hands of short leg. I followed that with the wicket of Divecha, who was clean bowled, then saw off both Ramchand and Sen in the space of two overs. India were all out for 58 and I had returned figures of 8 for 31 in 8.4 overs. The cricket writers in the press box scribbled away. My bowling analysis, I was later to be told, was the best ever recorded by a fast bowler in a Test match.

I was, of course, absolutely delighted with my 8 wickets. The Indian batsmen were intimidated by my pace and hadn't got into line. Much later, when playing for the Yorkshire side that won seven County Championships between 1959 and 1968, I remember teammate Doug Padgett saying to me, 'I go into bat prepared to be hit in the ribs. It doesn't matter who's bowling and how fast he is. If he gets one through it's going to hit you – if you're in line! The upside to that being – you're not out.' I guess the difference between the attitude of the India team of '52 and that of Doug Padgett, who personified the attitude of that Yorkshire side, is also one of the differences between winning and losing at cricket.

Perhaps that morning at Old Trafford, and a lot of other occasions when a fast bowler had skittled out a side, is best summed up by Herbert Sutcliffe, to me *the* master, and one of the best players of fast bowling of all time. Herbert once sat talking to me in my garden and told me, 'Some batsmen can play fast bowling, Fred, some can't. But if the truth be known, no one *likes* to play fast bowling. Remember, you will always have that on your side.'

When India followed on at Old Trafford, I picked up the same script. I inflicted a 'duck' on Pankaj Roy for the third time in consecutive Test innings and he was followed to the pavilion by Adhikari. Only Adhikari didn't walk, he was carried. The pitch was lively and somewhat unpredictable. I bowled a really quick delivery to Adhikari which suddenly lifted. He couldn't readjust his position or protect himself and the ball hit him in the mouth. That wasn't my intention, of course, I felt bad about it, but never showed it. Happily Adhikari later returned to the crease and can't have been that badly injured because he went on to top-score for India in their second innings.

I sustained an attack of stitch which resulted in me taking a rest from bowling. While I was out in the field, Alec Bedser and Tony Lock polished off the remaining Indian wickets. India were all out for 82 at half-past five, thus becoming only the second team to be bowled out twice in a single day's play of a Test match. Those who believed the clock would be against England achieving a result when Len Hutton had declared our first innings before lunch on this the third day were left to eat their words.

I was ecstatically happy with my figures of 9 for 40 in 16.4 overs, particularly my haul of 8 wickets in the first innings. The newspapers once again went overboard in their praise of my efforts, and messages of congratulations arrived in some number at our team hotel. Though not every telegram delighted me. I received one from my commanding officer at RAF Hemswell, Group Captain Jim Warfield. I thought he had taken the trouble to convey his congratulations and best wishes, but I was in for a surprise. The telegram read: 'Test match over. Stop. Do not stop. Stop. Report back to unit 8am Sunday.' It suddenly occurred to me that my efforts in the Test match had done me out of two days' leave!

The truth of the matter is, I did receive privileges whilst in the RAF. I was granted more leave than other erks in order that I represented my country at cricket. The ease with which I obtained this leave of absence, however, resulted in questions in Parliament. Thus I became the first ever cricketer to merit a mention in the official record of Parliamentary affairs, *Hansard*. A lady, whose name now escapes me, had written to her local MP complaining that whilst I seemingly had no trouble in being granted leave to play cricket for England, her son, also in the RAF, had his request for leave turned down. The MP raised her question in Parliament.

Apparently there were wry smiles all round when the MP detailed the reason for this lady's son's request for leave. He was stationed in the Far East, and had asked to be granted leave and flown home so that he might compete in the British Banjo-Playing Championships at the Albert Hall. I suppose you had to admire his pluck!

CHAPTER FIVE

AC1 TRUEMAN – OVER AND OUT

NO DOUBT TO THE CHAGRIN of the mother with the banjo-playing son, the RAF granted me leave to play for Yorkshire in the 'Roses' match at Old Trafford. The pitch had been subjected to rain in the previous days but was drying out when I set about the Lancashire batting in no uncertain manner. Myself and Eric Burgin – a medium-pace in-swing bowler with whom I had played league cricket at Sheffield United – ripped through the Lancashire batting in no time at all. The home side were all out for just 65 and I returned figures of 5 for 26. Not only was I continuing to take plenty of wickets, I was now conceding fewer runs. As Norman Yardley told the *Manchester Guardian*, 'It would appear that Fiery Fred, is indeed on fire.'

Near the end of the game I was called back to bowl in Lancashire's second innings with the new ball when Yorkshire were pressing for victory. I took two wickets, but the Lancashire tail-end pairing of Frank Parr and Bob Berry put up dogged resistance. We couldn't get them out, time ran out and the match ended in a draw.

The changeable weather remained for the fourth Test against India at the Oval. England batted through the first day and until lunchtime on the second, when the sky turned as black as Hitler's heart. Up in the heavens it was as if someone was ripping up the lino. Lighting flashed and cracked.

Rain lashed against the pavilion windows as if propelled by a youth on work experience in the special effects department of BBC Drama. It was at this juncture that Len Hutton issued the declaration. Some England players sat reading newspapers, others played cards. I sat kicking my heels, knowing that in the opposition dressing room the Indian team waited in trepidation of another onslaught from Alec Bedser and yours truly.

When play resumed with India batting, Alec Bedser got play under way with a maiden over bowling to Mankad. I opened my account by bowling to Pankaj Roy. With my very first delivery I dropped the ball short and it reared up menacingly. Roy raised his bat in double-quick time to prevent the ball rapping his ribs but only succeeded in presenting Tony Lock with a chance that he gratefully received.

In Alec Bedser's second over Adhikari pushed down on an in-swinger and the ball shot to me in the leg trap. The ball was travelling low and didn't look as if it would make it to me without bouncing. It is amazing what goes through your mind in a split second. I flung myself forward and managed to scoop the ball in my hands before it hit the ground. Next to go was Mankad, who mistimed a hook shot off a bumper from Alec Bedser. The ball skied so high, wicket-keeper Godfrey Evans had time to walk behind the slips before taking the catch. Off the next ball Manjrekar was dropped at slip, but in his next over Alec continued to keep the ball up to the bat and it paid off. Manjrekar was caught at short leg. Alec was bowling superbly, with pace and intelligence. He then yorked Umrigar to make India 6 for 5.

Annoyingly from England's point of view, with India well and truly on the rack, the weather once again took a turn for the worse. The rest of the day's play was truncated as we dodged in and out of the pavilion in the intervals between showers. Come the drawing of stumps Hazare and Phadkar were still there and India were on 49 for 5. Even the column fillers in the newspapers were read on the Saturday. There wasn't much else to do as we sat around and waited for the rain to cease. But it never did.

In a single over on the Monday morning I was no-balled three times, conceded a run but took the wickets of both Hazare and Phadkar. For good measure I also took the last wicket, that of the plucky Sen. India were all out for 98 and I had an analysis of 5 for 48 from sixteen overs. As I sat in the pavilion I couldn't help but think how everything had changed so dramatically for me in a relatively short period of time. In little over two years I had gone from being twelfth man for Yorkshire second XI against Lincolnshire at Grimsby to being a part of England's spearhead attack. I had achieved my goal of making it into the England team through a combination of self-belief, gritty determination, application and talent. Of course I owed much to the support of my family, in particular Dad. Also my coaches. But coaches can only teach you so much, they can't put in what God left out, and I felt I had a natural talent for fast bowling. That said, I knew I would have to work hard, to hone and develop that talent.

Len Hutton dearly wanted to win all four Tests in his first captaincy of England, so invited India to follow on. Unfortunately for Len nature denied him his dream. The rain returned and the rest of the match was washed out.

English cricket at this time was forever looking to replace the great names of the inter-war years. Any talented cricketer of my generation would be assigned an epithet to this effect. It was as if those charged with administrating or writing about the game couldn't accept us young players as being cricketers in our own right. We had to be recreations, or clones, of the greats of the thirties. I had been labelled 'The New Harold Larwood' and for his troubles Tony Lock had been referred to as being 'The New Hedley Verity'.

I suppose the Second World War played a part in all this.

It had denied English cricket the services of some great players who had been killed in action. Or in the case of those who had survived, the war had denied them their prime years as cricketers. This created a number of voids in English cricket. Such was the keenness to fill these voids, a number of my generation found themselves assigned labels they didn't want or, in the majority of cases, aspire to.

From time immemorial the actions of fast bowlers had been queried, but what gave the story of Tony's alleged throwing legs, and added controversy, was the fact he was a slow left-hander. Tony had in fact been no-balled for throwing before. When playing for Surrey against India at the Oval in 1951. Earlier that summer Cuan McCarthy, the South African Test bowler in residence at Cambridge, had been called for throwing when playing for the University at Worcester. These were the first two incidents of alleged throwing in English cricket for forty-four years. In calling Tony Lock, umpire Fred Price believed his faster ball was more than suspect. Tony's bowling, at times, was an open reproach to many, but given he was a slow bowler, the alleged throwing posed little or no threat to batsmen. That being the case, I felt he was really badly done to considering his livelihood was in jeopardy.

The newspapers had a field day. The debate raged for days before suddenly burning itself out. There was no official decision as to whether Tony's bowling action was legitimate or not. Some believed it was OK, others didn't. There was no conclusive proof forthcoming from those who had questioned his action. But when Tony subsequently modified his bowling action, the doubters receded into the background. The selectors did choose Tony for England again, on many occasions, though the belief that his bowling action was, at times, not legitimate would be raised again when he was no-balled on a number of occasions during England's (the MCC's) tour of the West Indies in 1953–4.

The impact I had made in my first Test series had proved

many of my doubters wrong. I had taken 29 wickets, which was a new record for an English bowler in a series against India. Despite my appearances for Yorkshire being restricted due to my service in the RAF, I ended the season topping the county's bowling averages. I was also second to Roly Thompson (who only had 18 wickets to his name) in the national averages, my 61 wickets being at a cost of 13.78. I was more than pleased with my efforts, feeling I had proved my worth at the highest level. I received a lot of very favourable press, but one or two in the Yorkshire camp were at pains to rein me in. When interviewed by the press after the Oval Test and asked for his opinion of me, Len Hutton joined the praise while at the same time offering a caveat: 'I think Fred Trueman will eventually be as fine a bowler as Lindwall,' said Len, 'though at the moment, he is a little on the colt side.'

For my part, I couldn't have been happier. That winter of 1952–3 I was voted the Cricket Writers' Club's 'Outstanding Young Cricketer of the Year'. In the spring of 1953 I would see myself in *Wisden* as being one of the 'Five Cricketers of the Year'. I was very proud and grateful of these awards. But I wasn't going to rest on my laurels. Far from it. I wanted to prove to everyone that I could be even better.

It came at me from all sides after that first Test series. I appeared to receive praise and criticism in equal proportion. By and large the press were delighted with my efforts for both England and Yorkshire. I was hailed as being a fast bowler of true quality. But I also had my critics and dissenters.

Some people began saying that my rise to fame had been too rapid. That the praise I was receiving from the press was undeserving of one with such little experience of International cricket. Some even went as far as to say I needed 'cutting down to size'. Though only twenty-one I had a sensible head on my shoulders. I didn't take as gospel all the good things that were written about me. I was supremely confident in my own ability, but even at this tender age knew how fickle some in the press could be. Their praise didn't warp my self-confidence to the point where I believed it would all be easy. That I would just have to turn up and bowl to get wickets. Neither did I take the criticism to heart.

What I did find difficult to accept was the sudden loss of privacy. It took me years to get used to that. Seemingly overnight I found I couldn't pop into a pub for a social drink or to a restaurant with family or friends without someone being provocative. Unflattering opinions would be voiced within earshot of me. Or else someone would come up to me and tell me his mate would have made a far better and faster bowler than me if only he had taken his cricket seriously, or, a terrible knee injury hadn't put an end to his fledgling career.

I was always ready to sign autographs for people, but sometimes the way in which this was demanded angered me. I would be in a restaurant having a meal and chatting with a friend when someone would come up, push an autograph book – or, more often, a scrap of paper – at me and say, 'Here, sign this!' Such people showed no consideration for not only me, but my friend who may have been talking at the time. These impolite and downright rude interruptions from people with seemingly no manners or social skills whatsoever would prompt the same response from me. 'Do you mind?' I would say. 'Firstly, I am having a meal with a friend whose conversation you have just so rudely interrupted. Secondly, in the humble home I come from I was brought up to say excuse me, please and thank you. You have been rude and impolite, so I will be the same. Bugger off!'

So amongst certain people I began to acquire a reputation for rudeness, though, I hasten to add, not amongst those who exercised common courtesy when asking for an autograph, or simply wanting to say 'hello' and 'well done'.

I was not alone in adopting this attitude. I remember once in 1952 during a Test match I was in the restaurant of a

London hotel with Len Hutton and Willie Watson talking to the entertainer Arthur Askey when a guy came up with five autograph books, slapped them down on the table in front of Arthur and said: 'Here, Askey, sign these!'

Without looking at the man or breaking from his conversation with Willie and me, Arthur with one stroke of an arm swept the books to the floor. It came as a big relief to me to find other people much more experienced at being in the public eye resented such rude interruptions.

Arthur Askey and I became good pals. No matter what impression that boorish autograph hunter may have gained, Arthur lived up to his nickname of 'Big-hearted Arthur'. He was only a small guy but he did have a big heart and was naturally funny. He used to boast that he was the only person in Britain to have a full-length photograph of himself in a passport. He had forged a successful career encompassing radio, films, plays, musicals and what in the early to mid-fifties was fledgling television. He was warm, full of bonhomie, at times silly but always friendly. To have lunch with Arthur was to spend an hour in sparkling and witty company. He also liked his cricket and, when commitments allowed, loved to attend Test matches or watch Lancashire.

Back in the RAF for the winter of 1952–3 I decided to concentrate totally on cricket. I loved nearly every minute of my two years' National Service in the RAF. I was proud to be a part of that great service. I made a lot of friends, real friends, and I played a lot of sport too.

It was while I was playing football for RAF Hemswell that I was spotted by the Lincoln City manager, Bill Anderson. Bill invited me to play for the Lincoln City third team and I must have impressed one or two people at the club because I soon found myself playing in City's reserve team. I was what, in those days, might be described as a 'bustling centre forward', but because of my speed I also occasionally played on the wing.

Anyway, either at centre forward or as an outside right I could usually manage to get in the thick of things and that was fine by me. I didn't mind putting myself about and gave as good as I got. As I was a Yorkshire and England cricketer there was a certain amount of interest for people in seeing how I fared on the football field. Attendances for Lincoln City reserve games soared, so much so that on occasions they were little different to those for the first team.

My inclusion on the Lincoln City reserve team resulted in quite a lot of publicity for the club, which I don't suppose did Lincoln City, or Bill Anderson, the manager, any harm. Bill was manager of Lincoln City from 1946 to 1965 and served as their general manager after that. When he handed over team management to Roy Chapman in 1965 Bill was, at the time, second only to Matt Busby as the longest-serving manager at one Football League club.

Bill Anderson was suitably impressed with my performances at Sincil Bank to offer me professional terms. But the publicity I had generated when playing for Lincoln reached all quarters, and one or two people whose opinion I respected pointed out to me the risks to my cricket career should I be injured. I told Bill Anderson that I was hanging up my football boots for good, and explained why. He was saddened to hear my news, but understanding. I was sorry to have to do it, but at the same time I was not exactly sorry I had decided to concentrate on cricket.

When compared with the heady events of 1952 the summer of 1953 was somewhat of an anti-climax for me. Due to my service with the RAF I only played intermittently for Yorkshire, and when I did, the wet weather of that summer didn't aid my bowling. The summer of 1952 produced a number of lively wickets, whereas the wickets I encountered in 1953 were often wet and dead. Yorkshire never hit a consistent run of form that summer, as evidenced by the club's final placing in the County

Championship of twelfth. Effectively one of the worst Championship seasons in the history of the club.

Because I was only playing intermittently, I was unable to reproduce the form of the previous summer. The England team that Len Hutton had envisaged was approaching maturity. The team boasted a variety of bowling strengths. Tony Lock or Johnnie Wardle was the slow left-arm bowler, though for some years neither was ever chosen for a Test at Lord's, where the selectors always opted for an extra seamer. The spearhead attack was never really settled. Candidates included the emerging Brian Statham of Lancashire, Northamptonshire's Frank Tyson and yours truly, with the slower Alan Moss and Peter Loader knocking on the door. Alec Bedser was still an automatic choice with his fast-medium deliveries and Trevor Bailey of Essex, a genuine all-rounder, often took the second seamer's place in order that another specialist batsman could be brought into the side.

Len Hutton appeared to be torn between the economical, fast-medium precision of Bedser, Bailey and the spin of Lock, Wardle and Laker on the one hand the pace of Brian Statham and myself on the other. The time had yet to come when England would be happy to play a Test match with two fast bowlers in tandem. It would be a while before the names 'Trueman and Statham' would be linked together in people's minds. In the summer of 1953, though Brian and I were on occasions both called up for Tests, we found one of us would be relegated to twelfth man.

I didn't play my first game for Yorkshire until the last week of May. I had picked up an ankle injury which had immobilized me for ten days. When I was granted leave from the RAF to play my first match of the season for Yorkshire in the 'Roses' match against Lancashire, although the ankle wasn't 100 per cent, I took a flyer and declared myself fit to play.

Though not fully fit, I felt I could still make a telling

contribution to the team. As it turned out I managed to take 3 good wickets in Lancashire's first innings. I was hopeful of developing matters from there, but the inclement weather was to have its say and my season never really got going. Due to rain, Yorkshire were unable to finish any of the five matches I'd been granted leave to play in. The matches were all disjointed affairs, with the players spending much time sitting in the pavilion waiting for breaks in the weather. It was a wholly unsatisfactory situation from my point of view as it denied me the cohesive platform I desired to show my worth. I did, however, bowl sufficiently well to be called up for England, but only played in one match against the touring Australians, which was the last match of the series at the Oval.

I had been called up by England for the Old Trafford Test but was named as twelfth man. As was the case in those days, the England twelfth man would be present at the Test for the first two days, but returned to play for his county on the Saturday. It was a curious situation that lasted well into the seventies. Once the designated twelfth man had returned to his respective county, after having sat in the pavilion for two days twiddling his thumbs, invariably sod's law was invoked and someone would get injured.

With the England twelfth man having returned to his county, a young member of the ground staff of the county at whose home the Test was being staged would be called up for duty. Many was the time a young unknown found himself pitched into a Test. He was unable to bat or bowl (not that he would have been called upon to do so); the sole role he was able to fulfil was in the field. On more than one occasion the young unknown fleetingly covered himself in glory by taking a catch, though his name was never to appear in the record books. The statistics of his achievement simply recorded as 'caught twelfth man'.

In this era of consummate professionalism, it is mind-

1. In my days as 'Fiery Fred'.

2. *Left.* My father, the batsman and left-arm spin bowler.

3. *Below.* I am a countryman at heart and learned a lot from my father. He is pictured here on one of Captain Adcock's horses.

4. *Right*. As a child with my mother and eldest brother, Arthur. Running a house of seven was hard work, but she managed it with aplomb.

5. *Below left*. Two Truemans in whites.

6. *Below right*. Practising, as an eighteen-year-old.

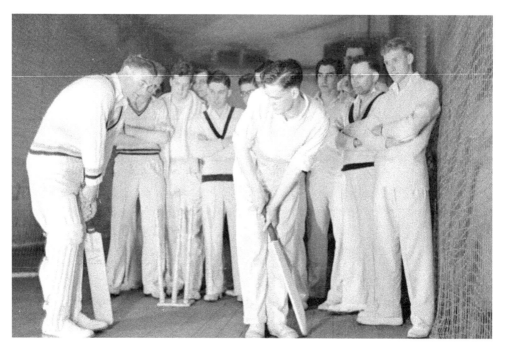

7. In the shed. Good pal Brian Close hones his batting stance with Gerald Smithson. I am third from right.

8. Bowling against Essex in 1951. I remain a strong advocate of side-on bowling.

9. *Right.* Len Hutton. The best batsman I have ever seen, though we never really saw eye to eye.

10. *Below.* The great Yorkshire side. The pre-war team had a reputation for excellence and arrogance. The inset picture is of Bill Bowes, who was a major influence on my development as a cricketer.

11. With Bob Appleyard after being presented with my Yorkshire cap by Norman Yardley. It is difficult to describe just what that meant to a Yorkshireman. When I saw my father later that day, it was the closest I ever saw him to tears.

12. *Left.* Me in action for Lincoln City reserves. The attendance on this day was 8,500, a very healthy crowd for a Lincoln reserve team game!

13. *Below, left.* On duty during my national service.

14. *Below, right.* Signing an autograph on the day of the presentation of the illuminated address paid for by the people of Maltby.

15. My twenty-first-birthday party. The cake I'm cutting I had to pay for myself!

16. Besieged by autograph hunters in Scunthorpe. Cricket had a much higher profile then and scenes such as this were not uncommon.

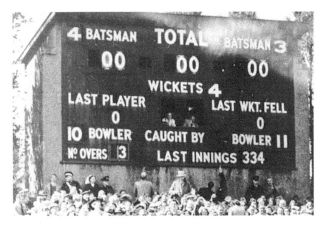

17. The first Test v. India at Headingley in 1952: the most photographed scoreboard in cricket history.

18. *Above, left.* My contract with the MCC for the tour of the West Indies. On the field, it was a successful trip, but away from cricket I was often the victim of scurrilous – and untrue – stories.

19. *Above, right.* On the plane on the way to the West Indies – via Alaska!

20. Playing on matting, such as we did in the West Indies, was not helpful to my bowling. However, I was very pleased with my performance.

boggling to think that in a Test match an unknown member of a county's ground staff could be called upon to play for England, albeit just in the field. I think there's a little TV documentary there . . .

The weary, wet summer of 1953 provided the slow pitches I hated but I battled on. I took 8 for 120 when playing for the RAF against a Pakistan XI, which in terms of winning me a place in the England team didn't add up to much. I took 4 for 93 against a strong Surrey side and at the end of July, the England selectors applied to the Air Ministry for my release in order that they could watch me in action against Kent at Scarborough to assess my current value as a Test player.

The Scarborough wicket was much more to my liking and I found myself feeling I was back to something like the form I had displayed the previous summer. In Kent's first innings I took the wickets of their first four batsmen and finished with figures of 6 for 47 in the second. Oddly, although there was another week or so before the England team for the Oval Test against Australia was to be announced, immediately following my performance against Kent and Scarborough I received notification that I had been selected for England's winter tour of the West Indies!

Naturally I was thrilled and delighted at this news. It was to be my first overseas tour with England. My inclusion put a bounce in my step and gave an edge to my game, though I do recall thinking it rather odd that I had been chosen for England's winter tour when I had yet to play for England that summer. The MCC had chosen ten players for the West Indies with the remainder of the squad to be announced at a later date. Again, an odd way to go about things in my mind, but that was the MCC for you.

I suppose my early inclusion for the winter tour to the West Indies had very much to do with the venue itself. England would come up against some fiery pace bowling out there. I should imagine it was thought my pace would not only be suited to the wickets we would come across but could also counteract, in some ways be a retort to, the fiery bowling of the Windies.

In announcing my early selection and that of nine other players for the winter tour, I suppose the MCC were doing us a favour. I was soon to be demobbed from the RAF and the fact I knew I was going on tour meant I knew where I stood and could plan accordingly. This wasn't always the case for players. Those hopeful of being included in the remainder of the squad would have to sweat it out, not knowing if they should apply for gainful employment over the winter months or not. This uncertainty was always a bone of contention amongst players anxious to provide an income for their families. Many was the player who, expecting to be chosen for England on a winter tour, didn't seek employment only to find, come October, he would be spending the winter at home.

Conversely there were also players for whom selection came as a surprise. They then had to diplomatically tell the employer who had given them winter work they were packing it in to go off and play cricket for England. International players are now contracted to play for their country and enjoy the security that entails. But for decades life for those players on the fringe of the England team was riddled with financial anxiety.

The fact that I had been told I would be touring injected me with confidence. What had been a frustrating summer up to that point suddenly blossomed for me. I took 6 for 139 against Lancashire at Bramall Lane and 3 for 23 against Leicestershire. Those performances earned me a call-up for the final Test against Australia. I was confident I wouldn't be named twelfth man again, as the named twelve included Tony Lock and Johnny Wardle and the odds on England opting for two spinners at the Oval were very long indeed. So it proved.

When the team was eventually announced, I was in and Johnny Wardle was named twelfth man.

The Oval Test had taken on extra significance. The previous four Tests had all been drawn, so everything hinged on this match. Len Hutton lost the toss for the fifth time, Australia opted to bat, so Alec Bedser and I were called into action straight away. The pitch was relatively easy going as Surrey, whose home ground the Oval is, had at this time a liking for spin.

I was back on the Test stage, where, deep down, I believed I ought to be. When I was called on to bowl a great cheer resounded around the ground, and that was topped by the Oval's reaction to my second ball. Lindsay Hassett had pushed my first delivery for a single, which had brought Morris to the strike. My second delivery was a bouncer. Arthur Morris ducked out of its way and a tremendous cheer resounded around the ground. The memory of the carnage Lindwall and Miller had inflicted on English batting lingered in the mind and for the spectators to see me give the Aussies a little taste of their own medicine went down rather well.

I sensed Morris was uneasy. I had an appeal for a catch at mid-wicket off my fifth delivery turned down by the umpire. With my next delivery Morris leg-glanced the ball to Denis Compton at slip, who uncharacteristically failed to hold the chance. I twice had Morris hastily repositioning his feet at my slower ball, but the break remained elusive. After five overs bowled in sultry, stamina-sapping conditions, Len Hutton replaced me with Trevor Bailey. Though I hadn't taken a wicket, those five overs had only cost 12 runs. Alec Bedser and Trevor Bailey accounted for the wickets of Morris and Miller, and though I returned to bowl three overs, I was frustrated at not achieving any reward for my efforts.

A short shower during the lunch interval livened the pitch sufficiently for me to effect more lift in the second session of play. Alec Bedser had Hassett caught short leg before I found myself bowling to Neil Harvey. I went over to Len Hutton and told him I was going to bowl a bouncer to Harvey, who I knew favoured the hook shot. My plan brought dividends. Harvey wheeled on to the bouncer, didn't quite time it right and the ball sailed over mid-wicket. Len, running away from the wicket and with his back to it, executed the perfect catch.

There was another short break for rain, after which de Courcy went fishing at a ball that lifted late and Godfrey Evans landed the catch behind the wicket. Len Hutton's reaction to the next man in, Archer, was to deploy six slips in an arc. Six slips for an Australian facing an English bowler was unheard of and once again the Oval crowd roared their delight at seeing this rare scene.

It was hard going in such humid conditions, but Len Hutton had the good sense of captaincy to use me sparingly, in short bursts. After another rest down by the boundary Len recalled me to the fray to bowl to Hole. I bowled an out-swinger of full length, a little outside the line of the off-stump. Hole went to play a cover drive but only succeeded in nicking the ball, which carried through to Godfrey Evans behind the timbers. My figures of 3 for 23 since lunch had helped England reduce Australia to 160 for 6. At this stage of proceedings an England victory looked a distinct possibility.

However, the Australian tail wagged like a dog with the proverbial two appendages. Ray Lindwall and Alan Davidson moved the score along and when Davidson was eventually out, 'Lanky' Langley picked up a similar cudgel to smack the English bowling. I looked on virtually helpless in the field wondering if Len Hutton was going to recall me at all. With about forty-five minutes' play remaining Len did invite me to have another crack. 'And about bloody time too, Len,' I muttered to myself as he called me over.

In no time at all, with Langley having been removed, I

then had Johnson in a muddle. He edged what was a decent chance to slips, but though the sultry weather had contrived to make my shirt stick to my back, the ball didn't stick in the hands, and the opportunity to remove Johnson went begging. Needless to say I was far from happy at having two catches dropped off my bowling. The Aussie tail end knew they were living dangerously but, unaware of the anger welling up inside me at having chances put down, they weren't to know just how dangerously they were living.

With Ray Lindwall back on strike I thought to myself, 'Time for a little retribution for what you did to English batting.' I dug the ball in at some speed, it lifted considerably, Lindwall flapped his bat, got an edge and the ball shot through to Godfrey Evans, who didn't disappoint me. Given I hadn't played much cricket that summer and was now up against Australia, I derived a certain satisfaction from the fact my final figures of 4 for 86 were the best analysis of all the England bowlers.

The story goes that following that particular day's play Godfrey Evans was chatting to a selector.

'I think, having seen Trueman's performance today, it shows that we selectors know what we're doing,' boasted the MCC official.

'More to the point, I think it shows Freddie knows what he's doing,' Godfrey is said to have replied.

I can imagine that of Godfrey Evans. Godfrey was a really colourful character, not afraid to speak his mind. He was a jack-in-the-box showman of a wicket-keeper who was so far ahead of his rivals they say that for over a decade his name was the first down on the England team sheet. When this ceased to be, he retired from cricket. Godfrey had a tremendous keeper's eye and a sublime technique which, coupled with natural athleticism, made him an outstanding wicket-keeper. He brimmed with confidence and this had a marked effect on his teammates. Such was his artistry and technique behind the stumps he made good bowlers look very good and helped very good bowlers live out their dreams.

In 1953 England stayed at the Great Western Hotel in Paddington. On the final day of the Test I came out of the hotel with Len Hutton and saw the newsvendor who had a stand near the hotel. On one of his boards he had sketched a fair approximation of the Ashes urn, underneath which was written, 'They're Ours!' As Len and I passed he looked up, recognized us and shouted, 'Good luck, lads!' He might have been a little premature but in the event he was proved correct.

I contributed 10 of the 69 runs by which the England tail wagged to give us a lead of 31. Len only bowled me for two overs in the Australian second innings. The pitch had changed again and in true Surrey fashion was taking spin. I helped myself to two catches as Tony Lock and Jim Laker worked their way through the Australian batting. Australia were all out for 162. In the end we won the match by 8 wickets and the series by virtue of this single victory. The Ashes had been regained after nineteen years. At the end a wildly enthusiastic and emotional crowd swamped the pitch calling for the England players to take a bow. I joined my teammates standing in the brightest sunshine any England player can know. After nigh-on two decades England had beaten Australia in a series to win the Ashes. I stood waving to the sizeable crowd that had gathered below the balcony of our dressing room. It was a wonderful, warm, ecstatic feeling. A glorious day in more ways than one. A day that for me, was destined never to die.

I wish I could have gone back to see our newsvendor supporter's little tribute officially on display, but given the circumstances, a certain amount of celebration was called for. Nevertheless, that is one of the little touches that I have never forgotten. The Japanese have a saying, 'Little fish are sweet', and that newsvendor's display of optimism and faith touched me. It is the sort of thing which is the very essence of cricket, the sort of minute moment which enables me to look back across the years and smile.

That's cricket. Life itself is often less kind. My grandmother, who had delivered me into this world and from whom I had derived my middle name, heard the news of my involvement in England's victory on the wireless. When the broadcast finished she told my mum and dad, 'I'm going to bed. I'm tired, but I had to see us win back the Ashes. I'm very proud of Freddie and his contribution.' And with that she retired to her bed and passed away in her sleep.

There are two footnotes to our victory over Australia. One concerns that dropped catch by Denis Compton. A bookmaker had offered odds of a hundred to one against my getting a wicket in my first two overs. Someone had faith in me because he placed a £1 bet. Which meant this punter stood to make £100, which was a dickens of a lot of money back in 1953. In the wake of our victory Denis gave an interview for BBC radio. As he departed, the interviewer's outwords were, 'Denis Compton, everyone in England loves him for the way he plays his cricket.' I remember thinking, 'Well, right now, I can think of someone who doesn't.'

The second footnote is really a shoulder note. In helping England to a first innings lead of 31, I weighed in with 10 runs. While I was batting, Ray Lindwall violated the longstanding gentlemen's agreement between fast bowlers that, not being recognized batsmen, our fraternity would never bowl bouncers at one another. Ray bowled me a wicked bouncer which, as I tried to avoid it, hit me so hard in the shoulder blade I thought someone had stuck a carving knife in it. It hurt like hell, but I didn't let him know he'd hurt me. Ray scowled and said, 'I suppose you're making a mental note to get back at me. Don't make a threat to me.'

'It's not a threat, Ray,' I said, 'it's a bloody promise.'

I had to wait five years before I carried out that promise.

Ray faced up to me in the fifth Test at Melbourne in the 1958–9 winter series. I gave him one which reared up like a wild stallion, struck the handle of his bat, and flew up in the air to give a straightforward catch. Ray came to me after that match to complain about the delivery, asking, 'What's going off?'

'Listen, Ray,' I told him. 'I'd played next to bugger all in the way of cricket in the summer of '53, when I came up against you at the Oval. You bowled me a bouncer then, but I didn't squeal or moan about it.'

'Christ!' said Ray, 'You remember that?' I assured him I did and also reminded him that I always keep a promise.

'So do I,' said Ray. 'I made a promise to myself to buy you a beer after that Test but never got round to it. What says you keep me to that promise now?' I did. We went off to the bar together and enjoyed a beer, or three, in each other's company. Again, that's cricket.

I was paid £238 for two years' work and cricket in the RAF. Of course, I was also earning money on those occasions when I was given leave to play for Yorkshire and England. In addition to which there was the fiver a week I received from my county as a capped player on National Service. I was doing all right where money was concerned and because of my earnings from cricket hadn't drawn my RAF wage for some time. I decided to go on pay parade to receive the money that was owing to me and so queued up with my RAF mates. I snapped off a salute, shouted my number and a young officer pushed eighteen shillings across the table at me. When he saw me looking at it somewhat askance, he asked, 'What's the matter, Trueman? Not enough?'

I answered, 'It will have to be sir,' and made a beeline for the pay office, where I discovered I was owed in the region of nine months' wages. I arranged with the Pay Master to receive my outstanding pay in a lump sum when I was due to be demobbed in September 1953. And there was a very good reason for me doing this. I was going to get mobile.

For some time I had courted the idea of buying myself a little motor car. I'd been scanning the local newspapers for some weeks and eventually saw one that caught my eye. It was for sale on the other side of Maltby, a little 1932 MG with a fabric-covered body and bumble-bee backside. A man and his son were asking £75 for it. I didn't think of trying to knock them down. I liked the car so much, I gave them their money there and then. I eased myself into the driving seat and said, 'Right, what do I do?'

Their jaws dropped onto their chins and the father said, 'Bloody 'ell, are't tellin' me tha canna drive?'

I said I couldn't, and since they were canny Yorkshire folk and didn't want to give me my money back, they showed me what was what and how to work the clutch and the gears. And off I went, vaguely in the direction of camp.

I drove the car thirty-four miles back to RAF Hemswell without trouble, incident or insurance. When I got back to camp, I was feeling pretty pleased with myself, but a good pal of mine, Peter Varley, blew his top and gave me a right bollocking. In those days you could drive unassisted as long as you displayed 'L' plates, but I didn't even have those. So I went out and bought some 'L' plates and Pete taught me to drive, and when he was unable to sit with me, I used to practise round the perimeter of the airfield when the planes were grounded. Six weeks later I took my driving test and passed it first time.

My final bow in the summer of 1953 was to play for the Combined Services against Australia at Kingston. Prior to the Oval Test against Australia I had helped the RAF to beat the Royal Navy by taking 10 wickets at Lord's. Against the Army I took 5 for 16 in their first innings and 2 for 16 in their second. So, even without my performance in helping

England win back the Ashes at the Oval, I believed my pedi-gree as a bowler would be known to the forces. It was, but what I hadn't reckoned with was my prowess as a bowler not going down well with some. Particularly with some of my sup-posed teammates in Forces' representative games.

In September 1953 I played for the RAF in a one-day game at Ealing and was then selected for Combined Services against Australia at Kingston. I had experienced irrationality, conceit, resentment and priggishness from some of the York-shire committee. Some England selectors would, in time, exer-cise similar traits, but I never expected such from senior officers in the services. How wrong I was. On arriving at Kingston for the game against Australia I discovered that the Combined Services were to be captained by Mike Ainsworth of the Royal Navy. I had expected my usual captain, Alan Shirreff – also of the RAF – to be skipper. I never thought anything untoward about this, but a sign that all might not be hunky-dory came when Jim Pressdee, a fellow aircraftsman and a very good cricketer, was omitted from the team in favour of someone from the Royal Navy who I had never heard of.

Australia won the toss and decided to bat. We took to the field and I began to pace out my run-up, only for Mike Ainsworth to come up to me and say, 'And what do you think you're doing?' I informed the skipper that I was 'marking my run-up'.

'Oh, really. And who says you're bowling?' said Ainsworth.

I didn't know what to say at first. As I was gathering my thoughts Alan Shirreff came onto the scene.

'Excuse me,' Alan said to Ainsworth, 'he's England's number one fast bowler. He's just played against Australia and we won the Ashes back.'

'Oh, really. Well he may well be England's number one fast bowler, but I say who's bowling and who isn't,' said Ainsworth.

Mike Ainsworth then called on Terry Spencer, a medium-fast bowler from Leicestershire.

'Spencer! Over here!' beckoned Ainsworth.

Now Terry Spencer was a good bowler. He had been listening to this conversation and wasn't happy.

'This is bloody stupid,' said Terry, 'Fred has to open the bowling.' Mike Ainsworth was having none of our protestations. He threw the ball to Terry and told him he was opening the bowling. Terry went to mark his run-up at the far end of the wicket and as he passed me said, 'I'm going down this end so you can bowl with the wind, Fred.'

I could tell from the look on his face that Ainsworth didn't like what Terry was doing, but thought better of ordering him back to the other end of the wicket. I had been rated as one of the top four leg slip fielders in the world, so as Terry marked his run-up I walked over to the slips to take up my specialist position in the field.

'And what do you think you're doing now?' Ainsworth asked.

'Fielding leg slip, skipper,' I replied.

'You can't,' intoned Ainsworth. 'An officer from the Army, Parnaby, is leg slip. Fielded there all his life. Go down to third man. You will field there until called upon to bowl.'

I wasn't angry. I was laughing at the absurdity of it all. I had just helped England regain the Ashes, and here I was not chosen to bowl for the Combined Services XI, what's more denied the opportunity to play at leg slip, where I fielded for both Yorkshire and England.

From my distant vantage point at third man I watched as Australia piled on the runs. Eventually I was called on to bowl. Now, given the circumstances, you may feel my heart wasn't exactly in this game – and you'd be right. Australia were in the process of compiling a sizeable total and no one, myself included, could stop them.

During an over from Terry Spencer, Keith Miller edged the ball straight to Parnaby at leg slip. It was a straightforward catch, but the ball evaded Parnaby's hands, went in between his legs and ran down past fine leg for 4. Keith Miller made us pay for that. He went on to make 262 not out and following the edged opportunity to Parnaby, never offered another chance to get him out. My agony became even more pronounced when, with me expecting a recall, Ainsworth threw the ball to Parnaby and asked him to bowl.

I thought to myself, 'Well this is it. I've seen the lot now.' The ball crossed the boundary so many times I thought the rope would end up threadbare at the finish. I was so cheesed off, I sat down on the sight screen and watched as Miller and Jimmy de Courcy whacked the bowling to all corners of the ground. Jimmy de Courcy also made a double-century (204), and when Australia finally put us out of our misery by declaring, they had made two million for 4. Their actual total was 592 for 4, but it felt like they'd made two million! The gulf in class between the two sides can be evidenced by the fact that Australia skittled out the Combined Services twice to win by an innings, and all this happened within two days.

In the dressing room after the game Ainsworth was not a happy man, far from it. He stormed across to me and said, 'And what do you think you were doing out there? Sitting on the sight screen! I can tell you, Trueman, that you will not play for the Combined Services again!'

'Well, you're right there,' I said. 'I was demobbed two days ago. I only agreed to play in this game because it was raising money for the Combined Services charity!'

As I left the dressing room I turned to Ainsworth.

'I understand you have played a little for Worcestershire,' I said.

'I have indeed one or two first team appearances to my name,' he haughtily informed me.

'Well I bloody well hope you get a game for them when they play Yorkshire,' I told him. He never did.

I went back home to Maltby to spend some time with my family. While I was there the people of the town paid me a great honour. They had organized a collection on my behalf to purchase a gift to be presented to me in recognition of my efforts and achievements in cricket. I was deeply touched, especially when I was presented with a new, suitably lettered cricket bag. The presentation was made by the Chairman of Maltby Urban District Council and on receiving these awards, I thanked everyone from the bottom of my heart. It was a great honour to be recognized in such a way by such marvellous people. In my acceptance speech I told them the cricket bag would serve me admirably on the imminent England tour of the West Indies, and assured them I would do my best for not only my country, but also the town and people of Maltby.

I had no idea what lay ahead of me in the West Indies. I was twenty-one and a tad concerned that a lot of people seemed to think I was going to murder the West Indies on their own turf. I had, after all, yet to play a full season in county cricket. I hadn't been able to train properly while in the RAF and though strong and full of vim and vigour, knew my two years of National Service meant I wasn't as fit as an International fast bowler should be. My knowledge of the West Indies was at best sketchy. What I did know, however, was that the wickets were paradise for batsmen and often not helpful to fast bowlers. The first triple-century in cricket history had been scored in Jamaica around 1912 and they had gone on from there, accumulating massive totals season after season. As I prepared for my first overseas tour I exercised caution. I was becoming more of a realist.

I was a little upset prior to leaving for the West Indies. A few days before the England party were due to fly out we had dinner with Lennox-Boyd, who was the Colonial Secretary in the government at the time. Lennox-Boyd told all the players that we had to be careful while out in the West Indies. The political situation was delicate to the point of being a tinder box, he explained, and we were told not to say or do anything that might inflame it. We were to be diplomats at all times.

Well, I already knew I was going out there to sweat my guts out in the blazing sun on wickets that would be unhelpful to me and all for £750. So I upped and said, with all due respect, that if I was expected to be a member of Her Majesty's Diplomatic Service, I should like to be paid like one and also receive the privileges associated with such a position. That googlie threw Lennox-Boyd. He blustered through a reply the gist of which was, when he said we had to be diplomats, he, of course, was not speaking literally.

'So we will not be paid accordingly, or receive privileges,' I affirmed.

'No,' he replied.

'Bloody hell,' said Godfrey Evans. 'A direct answer from someone in government. Fred, my boy, I think you may have created history tonight.'

Another odd piece of advice to come our way that night came from Len Hutton. On the night of the dinner prior to us flying out to the West Indies it was made clear by Len that we should not fraternize with the home players. I was really taken aback to hear Len say this, especially as he offered no reason for this stance. I really objected to what Len had said and I wasn't the only England player to do so. In my days playing League cricket I had come across West Indies players such as Everton Weekes, Frank Worrell and Clyde Walcott, and we had become good friends. There was no way I was going to ignore them and there was no way anyone was going to dictate who I could be friends with and who I couldn't.

To this day I don't know whether what Len said was of his own making, or something he had been told to say by someone in the hierarchy of Lord's. Whatever, I certainly wasn't going to pay heed to it. Given Len's instruction and that of Lennox-Boyd, I left that dinner thinking our tour of the West Indies might not be plain sailing either on or off the field. I would not be proved wrong in either assumption.

CHAPTER SIX

YOU WHITE ENGLISH
BASTARD

FOR ALL WE HAD received two curious and, to my mind, unacceptable requests prior to flying out to the West Indies I was looking forward to the tour with great anticipation. I knew those who believed the tour would be a cakewalk for me had it wrong. I was young, had still much to learn but was confident I could make a telling contribution to the tour and hoped I would return a better player for the experience.

The England party set off in high spirits. Everyone was upbeat about touring the West Indies. Fabulous cricket apart, those who had visited the islands before waxed lyrical about the friendly people, the lifestyle, the beaches, the social life and the music. In 1953 the popular music on most of the islands was calypso and what was known as R'n'B swing. The trend in ghettos, however, was for smaller, more exciting bands with a tougher sound, that of bop and rhythm and blues. This music was bright, optimistic, upbeat, sure of itself and had a hard edge. I was to discover why it was popular. It reflected the people – and their cricket team!

Though winter had set in at home, the vast majority of England players boarded the plane dressed for their destination. Most were wearing short-sleeved shirts, summer blazers and thin cotton slacks. We were flying on what was called a Boeing Stratocruiser and it was some aeroplane. It had two levels, the lower level little more than a small basement that contained a small lounge bar. And this bar was really small. So small we had to take it in turns to go for a drink. Three or four would go for twenty minutes, and when their time was up another quartet of players or tour officials would have their turn. By modern-day standards of air travel this little bar area appears laughable, but in 1953 it was considered state of the art and luxurious.

Everyone was enjoying the flight, but then the captain came on over the intercom and said, 'Though there is no cause for alarm, I have to inform you we are past the point of no return and are experiencing electrical trouble.' Well, that stopped people arguing about whose turn next it was in the bar, I can tell you. The captain went on to say that he would have to head for Newfoundland in Canada, where 'the electrical trouble may be addressed and rectified'.

So we headed for Newfoundland with the jovial, happy party spirit that had been present when we left London noticeably absent. Our original destination was Bermuda, from where we were due to fly to the West Indies. When the plane landed in Newfoundland, I looked out of the window to see the place covered in snow and the airport ground crew on the runway dressed in furs. The airport ground crew enjoyed a right good laugh at our expense as we gingerly made our way across the runway to the terminal building, with the temperature touching minus 30 and us dressed in short-sleeved shirts, summer blazers and thin cotton slacks!

We were taken into a canteen and given hot drinks and breakfast to warm us up. As we queued in the canteen I was taken aback to find myself standing behind the Duke of Gloucester, who apparently was also a passenger on the plane.

The chef said to the Duke of Gloucester, 'How'd you like your eggs, bud? Sunny side up?' It was the first time I had ever heard this phrase and from the look on the Duke's face, he wasn't familiar with it either. Then someone stepped in and said, 'Do you realize you're talking to the Duke of Gloucester?'

'Gee, a real live Dook?' said the chef. 'Like John Wayne?'

We ended up having to stay the night in log cabins. To the relief of all the electrical problem was sorted and, with the weather clear and bright, we were able to fly down to Bermuda the following morning.

We spent ten days in Bermuda. We practised in the nets, played a few practice games against local opposition and generally relaxed. We were a happy and optimistic bunch which, in addition to Len Hutton, included the likes of Denis Compton, wicket-keepers Godfrey Evans and Dick Spooner (The latter of Warwickshire), Brian Statham, Trevor Bailey, Alan Moss (Middlesex), Tom Graveney (then Gloucestershire), Jim Laker, Tony Lock and Johnnie Wardle. The team manager was Charlie Palmer, no mean cricketer himself, but whose days as an International cricketer were believed to be over ...

From Bermuda we few down to the Caribbean. We had only been there a matter of days when I realized it would be tough going for me on this tour. A number of the wickets we were to encounter were matting wickets. That is matting stretched over concrete. I found bowling on this type of wicket difficult because of the painful impact of my left foot on the concrete base. In an attempt to overcome this difficulty I ran wide of the strip, which served to impair my direction, and in the effort to correct it, I continually broke the rhythm of my run-up. In the very first match of the tour against a Combined Parishes XI in Jamaica Len Hutton was out off the very first ball, bowled by a guy called Mulder. Mulder's namesake was never to encounter anything more strange in the *X-Files*. The world's greatest batsman out to the first ball of the tour! It was Mulder's only ever claim. To the best of my knowledge he disappeared from cricket and was never heard of again. Though I wouldn't mind betting he dined out a few times on the story of getting the great Len Hutton out first ball.

My first ball against the Parishes was edged by Michael Frederick to Alan Moss, who failed to take the chance. Michael

Frederick, who had enjoyed a spell at Derbyshire, went on to score 84 and on the strength of that innings won a place in the West Indies team for the first Test. I keep saying it, but that's cricket!

The Parishes side also included George Headley. George was the greatest player in the history of Jamaican cricket. He was idolized by the entire population of the island. George had spent some time playing in England as a professional in the Birmingham League, which boasted a very high standard of cricket. He played for the West Indies in the home series against England in 1947–8 and against India in 1948–9. In the latter series George had failed to do himself justice and it was the generally held view that his career was over and he would wind down playing league cricket in the Midlands, as he was coming up to forty-five years of age.

The people of Jamaica, however, refused to subscribe to this view. What they did subscribe to was a fund to bring their hero back to his roots. Jamaican people raised over £1,000 to bring George back to the West Indies so that he could play against England in this Test series. When George returned to his homeland there were thousands there to cheer him at the airport. Though he was in his mid-forties, it was a matter of political certainty that he would play against England in at least the Jamaica Test. The Chairman of the 'Bring George Headley Back To Jamaica' campaign said it had been very hard for people who had little in the way of money to raise £1,000 for George's return, but that it would be worth the sacrifice everyone had made just to see the island's most famous son play in a Test against England. So you can imagine their reaction to me when I broke his arm in that first game against the Parishes!

George had been made captain of the Parishes team. In their second innings he was settling in rather well, so I tried to unnerve him. I bowled him a bouncer. George was particularly strong as a back-foot player; he timed his hook to perfection and hit the ball out of the ground! A few overs later I tried the same again. Only this time George made a complete hash of his attempted hook shot. He missed the ball completely and it broke his arm. George went down and the crowd went up. The anger and animosity of the crowd were so intense I had to be given a police escort when I left the pitch. For the rest of our stay in Jamaica I was simply referred to as 'Mr Bumper Man' or, more commonly, 'You White English Bastard'. Oddly, I never considered the latter to be a racist remark and I don't think it was ever intended as such. The people of Jamaica were very upset and angry that I had denied their hero the opportunity of playing against England.

There had been no intention to hurt George on my part, and he was the first to acknowledge this. I love Jamaica and the Jamaican people and have been back to the island many times. Following the incident with George, I was public enemy number one – but it had nothing at all to do with race, colour or the perception that I had been born out of wedlock.

George recovered sufficiently to play in a Test, though the circumstances surrounding his selection were somewhat fortuitous. George's broken arm kept him out of a number of Jamaica games. But when we later played Jamaica he was passed fit. In this game I bowled George a sequence of good-length balls then delivered the bouncer. I knew it would not go down well with the locals, but I had a job to do – to remove batsmen – and no amount of animosity or intimidation would ever stop me doing that job.

George Headley hooked the ball high but his timing again wasn't spot-on. Ken Suttle caught it on the run at long leg and Jamaica's hero was out for 5.

'They ain't gonna like that, man,' said George as he made his way past me to the pavilion.

'Not here. I'll give you that. But back home it'll go down a storm,' I replied. A remark which brought a broad grin to George's face.

'Yeah, guess so, 'specially round Sheffield way, Fred,' he said.

George went on to make 53 in Jamaica's second innings but his half-century took him four hours. However, his stand with Holt saved Jamaica from defeat and such was the strength of local feeling one local newspaper went as far as to say, 'It was the master's greatest innings.' There were threats to boycott the Test and dig up the pitch should George not be selected for the Test. In the event, Frank Worrell was injured and the West Indies selectors, with some relief, had justification to include him against England.

I was having a real set-to with West Indies' batsmen, but I was bowling really fast and well. The home players, on their own true wickets, were invariably strong hookers. So it all made for some intriguing and hostile encounters. The reaction of the crowds to a short-pitched ball that flew past the bats-man's head was nothing short of red rage. I became the England player they loved to hate. But just as I had respect for this knowledgeable crowd, deep down they also had respect for me. I became not only the subject of conversation, but song. One Jamaican songwriter penned a calypso number loosely based on the traditional song 'What Shall We Do with a Drunken Sailor'. The song received airtime on local radio and was often heard played by resident bands in hotels, restaurants and bars. The lyric went as follows:

> What shall we do with that Freddie Trueman?
> What shall we do with that Freddie Trueman?
> What shall we do with that Freddie Trueman?
> The guy who bowls them bumpers.
> Head down and up he rises
> Head down and up he rises
> Head down and up he rises
> He's a bowling bumpers.
> Four hundred on the scoreboard rises

> Four hundred on the scoreboard rises
> Watch that head it'll be two sizes
> Fred he bowls them bumpers.

For the first Test Len Hutton decided to rely on pace. He and the selectors omitted Jim Laker and opted for Brian Statham, Alan Moss, Trevor Bailey and myself as bowlers. However, a typically dead and bare wicket at Sabina Park gave us neither help nor encouragement. I was still having trouble with my run-up, so concentrated on bowling a good line and length. I was satisfied with the economy of my bowling, only 32 runs coming from my sixteen overs as the West Indies laboured to 168 for 2 on the first day.

Now the following is a mark of just how much the game of cricket has changed over the years. In the pre-match meeting it was agreed that, as a tribute to George Headley's eminence and service to West Indies cricket, he would be given 'one off the mark', that is, he would be allowed to make a single so that he would not have to suffer the ignominy of being out for a duck should fate conspire it. When George Headley came into bat on the second morning, Len ordered the field to move deep in order to accommodate George making a single. Brian Statham's first delivery to George Headley was less than medium pace; he pushed it away to the leg side and, as he trotted between the wickets, raised his cap. Come the lunch interval George took me aback. As he walked off the pitch he turned to me and said, 'Man, this ain't cricket any more. This is war!'

At first I couldn't understand why such a sporting and benevolent man should talk in such a way. But during the lunch interval it came to me. George was in his mid-forties and simply wasn't up for a fight any more. His reactions were not what they used to be and he had lost his appetite for playing the bouncer.

Everton Weekes hadn't. After tea, Everton hooked me so

hard that when the ball hit the concrete wall it rebounded more than a pitch length back onto the field. Sadly, George's time was up. After over an hour at the crease and having made just 16, he attempted a sweep shot and was caught by Tom Graveney at short leg. Though he was an icon of Jamaican cricket and a superb batsman, George had failed to recognize the 'tipping moment' in his career and had gone on too long. That happens with some players. They never stop loving cricket, but there comes a point in everyone's career when cricket doesn't love you any more. The trick is to recognize that.

The West Indies were 331 for 6 after tea the next day when Len Hutton took the new ball and asked Brian Statham and me to 'get to work'. It was agonizing. Gomes and McWatt put on 60, almost all off the edge of the bat. Chances abounded, but we didn't take one. McWatt had the lives of a cat. He was dropped twice off the bowling of Brian Statham and, to my intense disappointment, three times off my bowling. As you can imagine, I was not happy with my fellow England players! In International cricket for bowlers to have one batsman dropped five times is, to my mind, appalling fielding.

At the end of that day's play the West Indies were 408 for 7. I had bowled thirty-two overs and returned figures of none for 100. I was cheesed off. As far as I was concerned I'd had McWatt three times and Brian Statham had him out twice. Butter fingers didn't come into it. The following morning I went through the tail end, but it had been a chastening experience.

We made a disappointing score in our first innings and the West Indies captain, Jeffrey Stollmeyer, incurred the wrath of the crowd by not enforcing the follow-on. Stollmeyer decided to bat again with his side 247 ahead. The West Indies eventually declared, we flattered to deceive when batting, and the home side ended up winning the first Test at somewhat of a canter.

However, the game was not without controversy. Tony Lock bowled to George Headley with his highly suspect faster ball. The local umpire called Tony for throwing, and the debate about his bowling style erupted once again. The tour had been well planned, but it was far from going to plan.

For the second and third Tests it was thought the need was for us to be stronger in the batting department. Alan Moss and I were dropped, Brian Statham and Trevor Bailey formed the spearhead attack with at first Jim Laker then Johnnie Wardle supporting Tony Lock with spin. By the time of the second Test the atmosphere of the series had turned from being amiable and friendly to downright unpleasant. Stories were circulating about the bad behaviour of the England players – how we were unsporting in contesting umpiring decisions and that we had upset a number of local officials.

Let me address the latter first. We were on the receiving end of some gratuitously offensive behaviour on the part of local officials. Second, it is true there were disgruntled comments in the England camp about some absolutely diabolical umpiring decisions. In one match after having four good appeals turned down by the same umpire I eventually yorked this batsman. As the wickets went cart-wheeling my frustration was so great I turned to the umpire and said, 'That must have been very close.' Looking back now, I think the roots of the bitterness and dissent lay less in cricket than in the political mood of the Caribbean. The desire for independence was growing, and as the England cricket team we were seen as being representative of the imperialistic mother country.

We were there to play cricket. None of us wanted to get involved with politics and we didn't. But wherever we went the instability of the political situation was omnipresent, and there was always an undercurrent of resentment and dissension.

Overseas tours tend to be like the little girl with the curl. They are either very, very good, or very, very bad. This tour, however, fell between the two. Sometimes team spirit was very good, at other times the cliques in the dressing room were all too apparent. A curate's egg of a tour. At times things became fractious. Umpiring decisions gave rise to consternation, on occasions annoyance. There were disagreements within our camp, but the tour also had its lighter moments. There were the card schools, the fancy dress parties. The players attended cocktail receptions thrown by ex-pats, British Consular officials and local dignitaries that, for all their staid atmosphere, always produced a memorable moment.

During one party a British diplomat was most undiplomatic when remarking how folically challenged Tony Lock had become since the last time he had seen him.

'I lost my hair three years ago,' replied Tony. 'What a game of cards that was!'

Players live cheek by jowl on tour. It is great for engendering team spirit and a sense of 'togetherness', but problems can fester. Unlike today, players didn't benefit from an array of commercial deals, but we did have one promotional perk. As a team we promoted Coca-Cola, a product previous teams had signed up to promote when on tour. The arrangement with Coca-Cola was dealt with by a senior and prominent member of the team who had negotiated an all-inclusive fee of £500 to be split between the members of the squad. The fee had been the same for a couple of years. So when a representative of Coca-Cola turned up to supervise a promotional photo session, one of the lads indulged in a little jocularity, saying, 'Isn't it about time Coke reviewed the fee? £500 doesn't go far amongst the squad these days.'

'£500? You mean £1,000. That's what this company pays you as a squad to promote our drink,' replied the Coca-Cola representative.

As you can imagine, this came as a big shock to all the players – bar one, though I should imagine he was shocked to hear the true fee being revealed to the squad. This revelation, of course, did nothing to engender 'togetherness and team spirit'. On the contrary . . .

As the tour progressed this was not the only cause of disagreement within the England dressing room. Some of the more senior players thought Len Hutton too negative in his approach. After the second Test defeat the whiff of rebellion was in the air. One evening, following a team dinner, there was a discussion about what could be done to bring the team closer together. Players such as Godfrey Evans, Tony Lock, Trevor Bailey and I wanted everyone united – and united behind Len. Now I may not have warmed to Len as a person, but he was our skipper, and I felt it was the professional thing to do to get behind him. Len listened to what people had to say and accepted that he should adopt a more aggressive strategy. We improved as a result, but overall trouble still abounded and Len displayed his weakness once again as a man manager.

During the game against Guyana in Georgetown, one of the umpires complained to Len that he had been called a 'black bastard'. Len stormed into the dressing room and gave me a right old dressing down. He was livid, so I just sat there and took it all, though I had said no such thing to the umpire in question. The following morning I met the umpire at the top of the pavilion steps and asked him why he'd told Len I'd insulted him. The umpire was taken aback and said, 'I didn't say it was you, Fred. I said it was one of the Yorkshiremen on the field, but I know it wasn't you.' I asked the umpire if he would accompany me to our dressing room, which he did. I confronted Len, who said words to the effect that the incident was closed.

'It bloody well isn't, skipper,' I told him.

I made Len listen to what the umpire had to say. When the umpire left our dressing room the mood was not good. My teammates were mad with Len for having given me an unjustified bollocking. They thought it was bad captaincy for Len to assume it was me. As Godfrey Evans said, 'Assumption is the mother of all cock-ups.'

But that was nothing to the row that followed. I was doing some stock, fast-medium bowling in a minor match against some President's XI. I bowled one just short of length to a batsman. His response was to shout, 'You white English bastard.'

Now I knew various spectators at games referred to me in such a way, but it was all out of earshot and besides, we are talking spectators. Just about every cricketer has been called something disparaging at one time or another. It's not right or proper, but you learn to ignore it. But, because it was another player saying this to me down the track, it was much more personal than a lone distant voice in a crowd.

'No need for that type of talk,' I told him. 'Say it again to me, and I'll bloody well do you.'

A couple of overs later he did say it again, and with some venom.

'I did ask you not to say that again,' I told him and commenced to walk back to my run-up marker.

I had been bowling off a shortened run. It was a minor match, there was nothing at stake and even if there had been, such an insulting remark was totally uncalled for. I was so angry I delivered next ball more or less off my normal run-up and it was a bouncer. The ball reared up and he reeled back. His first port of call when he left the pitch was the hospital with a broken jaw. The trip to the dentist to replace his missing teeth had to wait.

I was twenty-one, and that's how I reacted to direct insults in those days. I was so angry, I didn't go up to the guy to see how he was or apologize. Instead, I walked back to my run-up and sat down as a doctor attended to him. I refused to apologize to him unless he apologized to me. I never enjoyed hurting anybody and I took no satisfaction from having hurt this guy. Hurting him was not my intention, but nobody was going insult me like that, twice, and get away with it. Of course, there was a mighty row about the incident and Len Hutton again failed to take a stand and come out in support of his players. I was young and headstrong. If Len had disagreed with my behaviour he should have rollicked me in private and taken a strong diplomatic stance in public. But he did neither.

Len was having problems, not specifically with me, but with the so-called established stars such as Denis Compton, nearly all of whom played for southern counties. I believe they resented him not just because he was a better player than them, but because he was the first professional captain of England and from Yorkshire. Leadership is action, not position. As the tour progressed and the problems mounted, rather than being proactive, Len became more insular. He scarcely seemed to talk to anyone for any length of time and went his own way.

Team selection became a bit of a joke. A batting place became open for the Barbados Test. I believed, as did several of my teammates, that Ken Suttle would be recalled as he was in a good vein of form, but when Len announced the team the vacant batting place had been given to Charlie Palmer, our tour manager. We were gobsmacked. Charlie Palmer had played for Worcestershire and Leicestershire, but had not come to the West Indies in any other capacity than tour manager. For him to be included in the team for the Barbados Test was a nonsense. He made 22 in his first innings and was out for a duck in his second. Though supposedly in the team as a batsman, he also came on to bowl, his five overs resulting in figures of none for 15.

To this day I believe that Ken Suttle should have played for his country and been the proud owner of an England cap. Ken was deserving of such, but Len denied him that honour. At the time I didn't hesitate to voice my opinions about Charlie's inclusion. Of course, this only served to make Len more withdrawn and anxious about his status as England captain. He was aware that a considerable body of opinion in cricket's establishment had not given their blessing to him being made England captain. Len wasn't the best at dealing with problems of a confrontational nature, even complaints about horseplay. I think Len believed his inability to conduct the disciplinary and diplomatic side of his duties would be seen by some in the cricket establishment as proof that a 'working-class' professional lacked qualities of leadership. Perhaps the inclusion of tour manager Charlie Palmer, an amateur as a player and a popular figure with Lord's, was an attempt on his part to endear himself to those who opposed him. Whatever, the Charlie Palmer affair was but one in a catalogue of incidents that brokered discontent amongst the players.

I never warmed to Charlie Palmer. I remember once playing for Yorkshire against Leicestershire, who had a young New Zealand batsman who kept putting forward before I'd delivered. I thought to myself, 'You'll have to stop that, Frederick.' So I flashed a couple past his nose. Never hit him, mind you, just a couple of warning shots across the bow. Charlie Palmer was at the non-striking end and took exception to this.

'I say, steady on, Trueman, will you? He's only a boy,' said Charlie.

'Well, tell him it's a man's game,' I replied.

Charlie didn't say anything, but I could see from the look on his face a certain contempt for yours truly. I never hesitated to voice my opinion on matters and I know that didn't go down well with Charlie Palmer, nor Len. Len was really a quiet and withdrawn guy who, when he did react to problems, never took the time to become familiar with the facts or think matters through. For all he was very thoughtful on the pitch both as a batsman and captain, when dealing with disciplinary matters his reaction was almost always of the knee-jerk variety.

I roomed with Tony Lock on the tour, and I recall Len coming to see us one Sunday morning in Barbados. Len was very vexed.

'I have received a serious complaint about you two and your behaviour,' he told us.

Apparently the wife of an MCC member had complained that in the early hours of the morning Tony and I had disturbed her and other residents by racing up and down outside their rooms on a food trolley and had then tried to push the trolley along the corridor and into an open lift. What's more, the lady in question claimed she had been 'jostled' when she had thought fit to complain about the rowdy behaviour.

This was news to Tony and me. We hadn't done any such thing. We had spent the previous night with the rest of team celebrating my birthday on the traditional – Saturday – 'club night' of MCC touring teams. Tony and I had both had a few drinks, after which we had gone straight to our room and taken to our beds at a reasonable hour.

Tony and I denied having anything to do with this horse-play whatsoever. For his part Len said that in order to smooth matters over quickly, would Tony and I go see this woman and apologize. Tony and I had nothing to apologize for, but for the sake of avoiding any ill feeling and to help Len assert his position as captain, we agreed to his request. After we apologized for disturbing the sleep of this lady, who had been adamant that the miscreants had been 'Trueman and Lock', Len said to me, 'She gave you a real dressing down and I thought you took it rather well.'

'So do I,' I replied, 'since it weren't us.'

It later transpired that the culprits were Denis Compton and Godfrey Evans. Though neither Denis nor Godfrey were asked to apologize to the lady, and no apology was forthcoming for Tony and me. The fact Len and certain members of the MCC were too quick to jump to conclusions and lay the blame at my door for indiscretions annoyed me. I found myself earning a totally undeserved reputation for being a trouble-maker and was constantly being told 'to watch my step'.

I had ignored the directive Len had issued prior to us leaving England that we should not 'fraternize with the opposition'. Jerry Gomes, Frank Worrell, Jeffrey Stollmeyer and Everton Weekes were old pals and I was invited to their homes to meet their families. On rest days they might take me to one of the local beauty spots for a day out, or simply get together for a Red Stripe and chat about cricket. The fact that I did 'fraternize' with the opposition was seen by certain people as openly flouting an official ruling.

The tour took place at a time when Britain was just beginning to come out of rationing. Cigarettes in particular weren't as readily available as they would be later in the fifties. Tony Lock and I had fallen into conversation with a guy in a Jamaican hotel. This chap's business happened to be in tobacco and at one juncture in the conversation he asked me, 'How do you go on for getting hold of cigarettes?'

I told him that it wasn't an issue with me as I didn't smoke cigarettes, I smoked a pipe. The chap asked if I would like some pipe tobacco as he had plenty of samples with him. I replied, 'Well, if it would be no trouble.'

He gave me about a dozen tins of a flake pipe tobacco called 'Mick McQuaide' and asked if the team would like some complimentary cigarettes. Tony Lock told him that that would go down well. Later that day, this guy dropped off a complimentary pack of 200 for every member of the squad. I gave my cigarettes to Tony and the rest we passed on to Len Hutton for distribution to the squad. Tony and I agreed with Len that it was pointless giving complimentary cigarettes to those who didn't smoke and agreed they would be divided up amongst those who did. However, it was later alleged that Len didn't do this and kept the remainder to himself. It was a minor incident really, but one that further served to fuel the growing discontent amongst the players. Before individual sponsorship deals a complimentary box of cigarettes was considered a real perk.

The tour continued to Trinidad. Apart from Jamaica, at the opposite end of the Caribbean, Trinidad is the largest of the West Indian islands. It was also the most cosmopolitan, with French, Portuguese, Dutch, Indian and German amongst its ethnic influences. This boiling pot of ethnicity produces a vibrant society, a rather laid-back attitude to life and many strikingly handsome and beautiful people. It also provided a major contribution to cricket terminology.

Ellis Achong, the Test spinner of the 1930s, was of Chinese descent. He made his debut at the Queen's Park Oval, and his first Test wicket was that of Patsy Hendren, bowled for 77. Patsy's innings saved a rather tricky situation for England, but this did not lessen his self-reproach at being clean bowled by an unorthodox delivery from a Test debutant. Patsy returned to the dressing room muttering, 'Can't believe it. Bowled by a bloody Chinaman!' Thus cricket acquired a new technical term.

In terms of cricket Trinidad has its own pronounced characteristics. It rarely, if ever, produces cavalier batsmen of the ilk one comes across in Antigua or Barbados, and its bowlers are not of the firebrand variety of Jamaica and other islands. Just as a European influence is present in Trinidadian batting, as instanced in 1953 by Stollmeyer and Gomes, so we find oriental wisdom and guile more often present in the island's bowling.

While this is in part due to the cosmopolitan nature of the population, the heart-breaking slow wickets are also an influence. Modern touring bowlers watching the ball bounce no more than shin high and nursing sore spinning fingers might do well to reflect on what life was like for us back in the fifties. The wicket we played on was one of jute matting, a surface so unhelpful to touring bowlers it would bring a tear to a glass eye.

The West Indies had gone two up in the series, having won the first Test at Sabina Park, Kingston, by 140 runs and the second at the Kensington Oval in Barbados by 181 runs. At the Bourda in Guyana, Len Hutton produced a marvellous performance with the bat, scoring 169 – an innings that was the cornerstone to a nine-wicket victory for England. With the series now more balanced, the next test was crucial. Jeffrey Stollmeyer won the toss in Trinidad and decided to bat. It was a hell of a toss to win because come the end of the West Indies' innings we needed 532 just to save the follow-on! Credit to the lads, we made it with five runs to spare, which led me to believe the West Indies' bowlers were no more keen on the jute matting wicket than I was.

Stollmeyer and J. K. Holt opened the batting in the second innings for the West Indies, and their scores of 41 and 40 respectively represented failure in relation to what was to come. The three Ws, Everton Weekes, Frank Worrell and Clyde Walcott, put England's bowling to the sword with, it has to be said, more than a little help from some very controversial umpiring decisions.

Everton Weekes and I were, as I say, great friends – and still are. Everton was the relatively unsung member of the three Ws. Everton was not born into an upper-middle-class family like Clyde Walcott, nor was he able to pick up academic qualifications like Frank Worrell. Cricket was all Everton knew. He had been superb during the tour of England in 1950 when the West Indies made history by winning the series. In his pomp he could slaughter any bowling, playing all the orthodox shots with power and panache and many more of his own improvisation with equal zeal. He was also brilliant in the field and very much a player for the big occasion – he averaged more in International matches than he did in first-class games.

Everton is a very warm and friendly guy with a tremendous sense of humour. He has a profundity of cricket stories; one of my favourite concerns that great West Indian fast bowler Joel Garner. Joel once guested in a Sunday charity match in Surrey. During the tea interval Everton joined Joel in queuing for a plate of sandwiches as prepared by the club's tea ladies. On seeing him, one lady enthusiastically remarked, 'Oh my, you're a tall fellow, aren't you?'

When asked how tall he was, Joel replied, 'Six feet three, ma'am.'

'Oooh,' coo-ed the tea lady, nudging her colleague, 'and are you all in proportion?'

'No, ma'am,' replied Joel. 'If I was, I'd be eleven feet six!'

On the occasion of the Trinidad Test, Everton had made about 10 when he edged one through to wicket-keeper Dick Spooner, who was deputizing for Godfrey Evans, who was sidelined with a nasty boil on his neck. Again, the sign of another era. When was the last time you ever heard of anyone with a boil? Dick took the 'catch', we all went up with the appeal, but to our chagrin the umpire ruled 'not out'. A little later, Everton got another touch to Dick Spooner and again we offered a vociferous appeal. To my amazement and incredulity the umpire simply shook his head. Later, Trevor Bailey got Everton to edge one through to the slips and again the verdict of the umpire was 'not out'. I couldn't believe what was happening. Eventually Everton reached 206, when he was caught by Trevor Bailey off the bowling of Tony Lock. As Everton walked past me on the way back to the pavilion I grinned at him.

'Well done, Everton, lad,' I said. 'Not bad, 206 from four innings.'

Everton grinned back.

'Five!' he said. 'I got a nick when I was in the sixties but none of you guys appealed.'

When Frank Worrell had come to the wicket after I had

taken the wicket of J. K. Holt, Denis Compton told me, 'Don't worry about Frankie, Fred. You'll see him off soon enough. He's right out of form.' Given Frank Worrell went on to make 167 and put on a stand of 338 with Everton, I would have hated to have come across Worrell when he was in form! And whether in form or out of form, there was still Clyde Walcott to come!

I couldn't make my mind up if Clyde was on top of his game or not, as he 'only' made 124. Umpiring decisions and the matting wicket apart, it was a marvellous achievement. Though all three were Barbadians, and despite the intense rivalry which exists between various teams within the West Indies, a collection was organized amongst the crowd for the benefit of this great trio.

The West Indies number six, Bruce Pairaudeau, was to run foul of my arm in the field. Bruce had just come in to bat and was at the non-strike end when Walcott pushed one away to the boundary. They were going for a third run when I seized on the ball before it reached the rope and from over seventy yards went for the run-out. I produced a flat throw at some pace and right over the top of stumps to run out Pairaudeau. He was gobsmacked and I dare say somewhat aggrieved to be out for a duck when those who preceded him had run up such gargantuan scores. In some small way that run-out helped ease the frustration I was feeling for having sweated and laboured on the matting wicket, and all for a return of one for 131.

During the match Denis Compton was bowling and got a 'Chinaman' to turn, and it was nicked by Holt to Tom Graveney at slip. Even after some of the decisions we had been subjected to, we were nonplussed as to why J. K. Holt was given not out. In a cruel twist of irony, the umpire in question was none other than Ellis Achong, Patsy Hendren's 'Chinaman' of nigh-on a quarter of a century previously. Maybe it was a case of Ellis taking umbrage at Denis for adopting a bowling technique he felt was the preserve of him alone. Whatever, Ellis Achong's decision to give Holt not out angered England. Tom Graveney hurled the ball down in disgust and here we come to one of those incidences of 'giving a dog a bad name'.

That evening, at a cocktail party, the wife of a diplomate remarked 'how disgusting it was of Trueman to have thrown down the ball in a rage because a batsman had been given not out'. Tom Graveney heard this, stepped in and said, 'Hold on a minute. What are you talking about? That wasn't Freddie, it were me.'

Stories about my supposed irresponsible behaviour abounded. I was later accused of insulting the wife of the Governor General, who, in fact, I had never met. When news of this reached the ears of the lady in question she said she would like to meet with me and apologize for this story, which she subsequently described as 'a slur against my character' and 'totally untrue'. I can only think that some person, or group of individuals on that tour, had it in for me. In truth I have no idea why I was the subject of so many scurrilous stories. I only know that I was.

The fourth Test at Port of Spain, Trinidad, lasted for six days. No Test had ever produced a result on Queen's Park jute since it had been laid more than twenty years earlier and we didn't spoil that record. The match produced an astonishing 1,528 runs and just 25 wickets to peter out in a draw.

The fifth Test in Kingston, Jamaica, produced a tour de force from Trevor Bailey, whose performance was largely instrumental in England winning the match. Again, Jeffrey Stollmeyer won the toss and decided to bat. Trevor bowled magnificently, taking 7 for 34, figures all but unheard of in a Test in the West Indies on a wicket as dry as old parchment. I felt I produced my best bowling of the tour in taking 2 wickets, which I followed by taking the key wickets of Stollmeyer, Holt and Worrell in the West Indies' second innings. Len Hutton made an outstanding 205, helping us to defeat the West Indies by 9 wickets. Given all our problems both on and off the field, to tie the series was a remarkable turnaround of events, given we had contrived to lose the first two Tests.

Only Tony Lock – by virtue of a single wicket – took more wickets than I did on that tour. My final tally was 27 and believe me I sweated for every single one of them, bowling as I did in intense heat. Should one go by the record books, my tour of the West Indies was a successful one. However, when we returned to England, my faceless antagonists had one last shot to fire. I was the only member of the squad not to receive his good conduct bonus.

People say, 'It's not the money, it's the principle of the thing.' In my experience it's always about the money. I resented not being given what I knew I was entitled to but, moreover, I was angered at being singled out for such unfair treatment. I asked Len Hutton for the reasons but received no explanation. Characteristically Len skirted the issue, muttering on about circumstances beyond his control and how it depends on how individuals interpret matters. Whether he meant himself, MCC committee members or myself, to this day I still don't know.

Having got nowhere with Len, I took the matter up with the MCC. I made an official and respectful request as to the reason why my good conduct bonus had been withheld. The reply I received could have come straight from a Kafka novel. I was informed that players could not question such decisions and, as such, no explanation could be forthcoming.

This really angered me. In fact, it rankled with me for years. So much so that in 1964 during a BBC TV programme I 'bowled a Chinaman' to Len Hutton by asking him for the true reasons. All Len would say was, 'They are in the official papers at Lord's. That's all I can tell you.'

Cabinet and secret government papers are available after thirty years to the public via the Public Records Office.

Seemingly not so the official papers of past meetings of the MCC's inner sanctum!

To this day I believe I was badly done by and ill-used on the West Indies tour of 1953–4. Despite all my achievements and my constant good form, my England career post-1953–4 was sketchy. Top players such as Brian Close, Godfrey Evans, Peter Parfitt, Ray Illingworth, Tom Graveney and Brian Statham have, over the years, all said I was unjustly treated by England selectors. I believe the reason why I didn't play many more Tests had its roots in that winter tour. Though Len Hutton and I were teammates, Len never offered any words of sympathy regarding the non-payment of my good conduct bonus. Nor did he ever offer words of consolation when I was omitted from subsequent England teams. I'm not saying Len had any say in me being left out of the England team. However, it does appear odd that following that tour of the West Indies, Len was to captain England on eleven occasions and I wasn't picked to play in one of those games . . .

Many years later, Len admitted to a mutual friend, David Brookes, that one of the biggest mistakes of his career was not taking me on the tour of Australia in 1954–5. On returning from the West Indies, the word was Len Hutton couldn't control me. I heard, on good authority, that the big guns of the MCC – Freddie Brown and Gubby Allen, along with Brian Sellars, the chairman of Yorkshire – decided they were going to sort me out and bring me to heel. Bill Bowes, whose word, in addition to his expertise as a coach, I always trusted, told me that an MCC committee member had approached him and said, 'My word, this Trueman's a bad-tempered devil, isn't he? What a troublemaker, and totally uncontrollable.'

Bill replied, 'If it's Fred Trueman you're talking about, I've coached him since he were a lad, and my answer to you is, "No he isn't" – have you ever met him?' The MCC member admitted that he hadn't, so Bill asked him how he could form such an opinion.

During the summer of 1954 I took 134 wickets for under 16 runs apiece. The press believed my inclusion in the England team to Australia was a formality. But England took five pace bowlers on that tour and I wasn't one of them. Len admitting his mistake is of little consolation to me. In my opinion, I was treated abysmally by Len in his role as England captain, and by the MCC. The career of a top-class cricketer is short. I was overlooked when in the prime of my career and over the years have often been given to ponder 'what might have been'.

CHAPTER SEVEN

THE CHANGING GAME

THE SUMMER OF 1954 was bitter-sweet for me. Food rationing finally ended in July and shops began to display on their shelves certain items of food we hadn't seen for years – such as grapefruits and bananas. New, modern consumer goods such as electric washing machines, kettles, vacuum cleaners and televisions became more readily available and, more importantly, more affordable.

There was a feel-good factor throughout British society. Major cities and towns resembled massive construction sites as the nation rebuilt following the destruction of the Second World War, and it was not only bomb-damaged buildings that were being swept away. Many early Victorian streets in our inner cities that were little more than slums were demolished as part of the government's plan to upgrade the quality of urban housing across the nation.

The singer Johnnie Ray captivated the hearts of a million and more young girls and became what in those days was termed 'a heart throb'. Doris Day topped the charts (which had only begun in 1952) for eight weeks with 'Secret Love', only to be replaced by David Whitfield's 'Cara Mia', which lorded it at the number one spot for ten weeks.

Generally people were imbued with optimism. If the pain and memory of the Second World War still lingered in the memory, for most it was not as pronounced. Britain was at last rebuilding, and Roger Bannister's achievement in running the world's first sub-four-minute mile helped reinforce the notion that Great Britain was, indeed, still great.

In the pre-season I worked hard to smooth out the last minor unevenness in my run-up. When the new cricket season got under way, I felt fit, strong and confident that I was going to have my best season with Yorkshire to date. The fact that it would be my first full county season was a great encouragement to me. There would be no interruptions. I wouldn't be playing two matches only to miss the next four. I felt I would benefit greatly from a consistent run in the Yorkshire team – and wasn't wrong on that score.

I knew there would be stiff competition for bowlers in the England team. This was a golden period for English fast bowling. Apart from myself there was Brian Statham (Lancashire), Frank Tyson (Northants), Les Jackson (Derbyshire) and Alan Moss (Middlesex). Then there were Loader and Ridgway, and at a lesser pace Alec Bedser and Trevor Bailey. All were superb bowlers, but I felt sufficiently confident in my ability that I would hold down a regular place in the England team.

Yorkshire were involved in some super games that summer. Every game against Northants became somewhat of a personal battle between Frank Tyson and myself, a contest fuelled by much hype in the newspapers. Everyone was keen to see which one of us could take the most wickets – and bowl the fastest.

We first played Northants at Bradford in June. In the event it was not Frank Tyson who bowled Yorkshire out but the Northants left-arm spinner George Tribe. For the record, George took 9 for 54. When Northants batted, first blood went to me. I had Dennis Brookes caught in the gully. Minutes later I delivered one short to Eddie Davis. Eddie played and missed, the ball struck him on the head and he retired hurt. Frank Tyson proved he was not just a great bowler but also more than handy with the bat. Frank made 70 in that innings and for a time it looked as if Northants were going to bat to a decent score. However, I took 4 of their remaining 5 wickets – including that of Frank – while conceding just 11 runs.

Frank made his presence known in our first innings, taking 2 early wickets and finishing with figures of 3 for 36. When Northants batted again I had Davis caught at slip before rain made a pitch for Brian Close and Ray Illingworth, who weaved their own particular brand of magic to bowl out Northants and give victory to Yorkshire. All of which served to prove absolutely nothing regarding who was the better bowler between me and Frank Tyson.

The return match with Northants was played at the County Ground in Northampton a week later. Again the press focused on the competition between Frank Tyson and myself. One newspaper going as far as to say, 'This will be not so much a match between Northants and Yorkshire as between Trueman and Tyson.' That sort of hyperbole brought a very good crowd into the County ground and what they saw was Frank on the top of his form.

Frank was bowling at a tremendous pace and took the wickets of Frank Lowson, Ray Illingworth and Billy Sutcliffe, who made a fine 105. When Frank returned to the fray in the afternoon you got the impression that earlier in the day, for all his searing pace, he had just been working up a head of steam. Frank was living up to his nickname of Typhoon Tyson. Johnnie Wardle was down the other end. Nothing ever frightened Johnnie, but such was Tyson's pace that afternoon, Johnnie became increasingly apprehensive. When Johnnie finally succumbed, it was my turn to take to the crease.

As Johnnie and I passed one another, I said, 'What kind of bloody stroke was that to play?'

Maybe the hype in the press had got to Frank. As we were potential rivals for a place in the England team, perhaps Frank wanted to try to gain some kind of psychological advantage over me. Whatever, he broke the unwritten rule amongst fast bowlers that we would never bowl bouncers at one another.

Now, whenever a fellow fast bowler delivered a bouncer or beamer at me, it never worried me unduly. I had enough confidence in my technique as a batsman to deal with such deliveries. Besides which, I knew a bowler would only do that to me once. Because when it was my turn to bowl and he was at the other end, I would make him pay for his folly – and some more.

The first ball I received from Frank was a wicked bouncer. I saw it coming and ducked. The evasive action I took was swift and I was never in danger of being clobbered, but it rankled with me. Frank's next ball was a straight half-volley and it was a 'good-un'. I was bowled on the retreat. When I walked back into the dressing room, Johnnie Wardle had a big grin on his face.

'What kind of bloody stroke was that to play?' Johnnie quipped.

'Aye,' I said, 'I slipped on that pile of shit you dropped on the crease.' The dressing room erupted into laughter. That remark did the rounds, I can tell you.

Frank Tyson finished with figures of 4 for 63. Overnight rain turned the wicket green and the outfield was very wet. I had trouble gaining a good foothold on my run-up, which served to make me do a little more slipping. That aside, I was bowling well and I soon had the Northants batsmen jumping about. Dennis Brookes was first to go, caught at the wicket off a lifter for a duck. He was followed by Peter Arnold, yorked, also for a duck. I then bowled Des Barrick with a ball that pitched middle-and-leg before ripping out his off-stump. When Vince Broderick fell to Bob Appleyard, Northants were reeling at 8 for 4 and they never recovered. Our spinners then seized the day and we celebrated a 'double' victory over Northants in the space of little over a week.

I was hitting a great vein of form. Wickets were tumbling, but I found myself out of the England team for the series against Pakistan. England opted for Brian Statham, Frank

Tyson and Peter Loader as their pace bowlers for the series, with Alec Bedser and Trevor Bailey chipping in with their brand of fast-medium. As the summer of 1954 progressed, the England squad for the winter tour of Australia took shape in the minds of Len Hutton and the MCC selectors. However, Len had come in for some criticism after the tour of the West Indies and for a time it was touch and go whether he'd retain the captaincy. In the end he was kept on as England captain, but only by virtue of a single vote over David Sheppard.

Knowing there were members of the MCC's hierarchy who were opposed to him being England captain must have been a source of anxiety to Len. That summer he missed quite a number of Yorkshire matches due to, we were told, mental stress. Nowadays, the England squad for an overseas winter tour is announced after the cricket season has ended and players have been afforded the opportunity of a whole cricket season to prove their worth. That summer the England squad for the winter tour of Australia was announced in August. The bowlers chosen to go on tour were Tyson, Statham, Loader, Bedser, McConnon, Bailey, Appleyard and Wardle. I wasn't even placed on stand-by.

I heard the news of the squad on the wireless at home in Maltby. I wasn't disappointed. I was totally gutted and devastated. Dad was so angry that I had been overlooked. In a pique he suggested he would be happy if I told the selectors 'where to get off' should they ever pick me for England again. A sports reporter visited me at home to gauge my reaction at not being selected for Australia. The reporter dutifully noted my response and quoted it in the article he was writing. The quote being, 'I am so disappointed not to have been chosen for the winter tour, at the moment I feel as if I could never play for England again.' Of course, in the time-honoured way in which things I have said became distorted, even though the reporter had quoted me correctly, word soon got round that what I had told him was, 'I will never play for England again.' Not the same thing, I think you'll agree.

My frustration and anger were compounded by the fact that following the announcement of the touring side in July, what up to that point had been a very good season for me turned into a great one. In the very next match I skittled out Derbyshire at Headingley, taking their first 3 wickets in just seven balls. Against Kent at the Crabble Ground in Dover I was bowling a good line and length and at some pace. Kent were all out for 76 before lunch and I returned figures of 8 for 28. As Kent's Arthur Phebey said to me during lunch, 'Fred, if there is a better fast bowler than you playing on the county scene at the moment, I haven't come across him. Those daft buggers at Lord's, eh?'

Against Surrey, the reigning county champions, at Bramall Lane, I reduced them to 13 for 3 in the first innings and 5 for 2 in their second innings. Bob Appleyard, with his accurate medium pace, and I formed a highly effective partnership throughout August and into September. Hampshire were bowled out for 72 and 89 at Bradford; Somerset for 48 at Taunton; Essex for 106 at Scarborough; and at the same venue an MCC team containing several players bound for Australia that winter were bowled out for 143.

My total of wickets that season was 134 at an average of 15.5 with a strike rate of a wicket every six overs. I took 5 wickets in a match on ten occasions, took 32 catches in the field and took great pleasure in scoring my first half-century when making 50 against Gloucestershire. A number of newspapers said my omission from the squad to tour Australia was a mistake, the *Daily Graphic* saying, 'Trueman has enjoyed his best season to date. He has bowled intelligently, with considerable pace and to devastating effect. His form this summer merited inclusion and it leaves one wondering just why he has not been selected.'

Away from cricket, my personal life was looking rosy. I became engaged to a lovely girl, Enid Chapman, who I had met at a reception given by her father, the then Mayor of Scarborough, at the Festival of 1950. Enid and I had been courting for four years. We were in love with each other and our engagement made us joyously happy.

With the season over, a national newspaper approached me and asked if I would fly out to Australia to comment on the Test series. The money on offer was very good. With Enid and I soon to be married I was keen to take the newspaper up on their generous offer, but when I referred it to the Yorkshire committee they refused me permission. Aware that I would be at a loose end over the winter, the Lincoln City manager, Bill Anderson, offered me professional terms. But mindful that I could pick up an injury playing football that would curtail my career in cricket, I told Bill 'thanks, but no thanks'. I found work that winter as a furniture salesman, and in March 1955 married Enid. We set up home in West Ayton, which is just outside her home town – Scarborough – and were initially very happy.

Cricket in the fifties enjoyed a golden period. By and large attendances for county games were good, though not what they had been in the thirties. A 'Roses' match between York-shire and Lancashire could still attract a full house and our games against Middlesex and Surrey also attracted sizeable crowds. The standard of cricket was very high at county level, and very good in the higher echelons of league cricket. Though the cricket and football seasons overlapped at both ends, there was a clear distinction between the two. From mid-May to mid-August there was no football, so cricket enjoyed centre stage for the rump of its season. As we know, there is virtually no close season in football these days. In the fifties, however, many was the schoolboy – and adult male – who once the FA Cup Final was over, focused totally on matters of cricket.

Cricketers enjoyed a profile on a par with that of the top footballers.

There was no saturation coverage of sport on television, besides which, even in 1955, the majority of people didn't own a TV set. The most exposure came from cigarette cards, passed on by fathers or uncles. To excited schoolboys these cards were highly collectable and also helped enhance the profile of cricketers. This trend was further exploited by companies such as A&BC (American and British Chewing Gum Company) and Chix Bubble Gum of Slough, who produced sets of cards featuring cricketers. Unlikely as it may seem nowadays, these bubble gum and cigarette cards enhanced the profile of cricket. Which, given football all but disappeared from the sports pages of newspapers for three months, was already very high in the fifties. These days you'd be lucky to see an attendance of 1,000 at a 'Roses' match. In the fifties, depending on the venue, attendances of 15–24,000 were commonplace for this fixture.

The 1955 season was somewhat of a relief to me. England regained the Ashes in Australia, which was some achievement, as they had lost the first Test in Brisbane by an innings and 154 runs. Len Hutton and his team came fighting back, however, to win the next three Tests, and so the Ashes were retained. Following such success, and given I had not been included in an England squad since the tour of the West Indies, I was delighted to be recalled to the International scene in 1955. I played just one Test in the series against South Africa, but was also called up as a replacement. My relief was not so much being back in the England fold as knowing I hadn't been permanently black-listed by the selectors.

On the domestic front, Yorkshire again finished as runners-up to Surrey in the County Championship. It was a repeat of the 1954 season, but to finish as runners-up in consecutive seasons was a marked improvement on 1953, when we'd finished thirteenth. Len Hutton played in only ten matches;

Bob Appleyard again succumbed to illness and was rarely seen on a team sheet after June, and so the main weight of the Yorkshire bowling rested on Johnnie Wardle and yours truly, with Brian Close as back-up.

Though runners-up in the Championship was satisfactory, I feel we would have won the title had it not been for our old problem. The dressing room remained as divided and bitchy as ever. Norman Yardley hung on to the captaincy, though Len Hutton was the national captain. When Len returned from his success in Australia the MCC took the unprecedented step of making him an honorary member. This was some gesture, as no one could ever recall anybody being given such an accolade whilst still an active professional. The selectors also broke with tradition when they named Len the England captain for the entire series against South Africa. Len's star was really in the ascendant. The establishment loved him. His fellow players respected him. The press were in awe of him and schoolboys worshipped him. So it must have been galling for him to take orders from Norman Yardley.

I'm certain that Len, for all his achievements, craved the captaincy of Yorkshire most of all – and I am equally certain that Norman had no intention of allowing that to happen. Norman was tactically adept and read a game very well. He was also good to me, being helpful and friendly, and used me judiciously as a bowler, never bowling me into the ground as some captains would have done. But I don't think Norman was the strong character Yorkshire needed at the helm. Johnnie Wardle and Bob Appleyard were fine players, but to my mind he let them dominate him. They wanted to bowl all the time and seemed able to talk him out of making a change even when it was clear to everyone else in the side that one was required.

At the end of the 1955 season, Norman retired and was replaced by Billy Sutcliffe. Billy was a great guy and a wonderful batsman. He was the son of the legendary Herbert Sutcliffe, and although Billy never scaled such lofty heights, he was a fine player in his own right. Whenever Billy failed with the bat he was taunted with insults like 'Give it up! You'll never be as good as your old man.' I fell out with some of the Yorkshire supporters over this. They seemed to be on to Billy all the time and I let them know what I thought about that!

But whatever the supporters said, it was incomparable to what happened later in his captaincy. What Billy endured was a slur on Yorkshire cricket. Billy, like Norman Yardley, also failed to cope with the assertive behaviour of Johnnie Wardle. Eventually, in 1957, a group of players demanded his resignation. I refused to have any part of it, but Billy, knowing he didn't have the full support of the team, tendered his resignation. It was the mark of the man that he did so with grace and dignity, because it must have broken his heart.

Credit to Johnnie Wardle, in 1955 he bowled magnificently, taking 195 wickets, second only to my good pal Tony Lock, at Surrey, who enjoyed a phenomenal season, taking 216 wickets. I bowled 3.2 overs short of a 1,000 that summer and took 153 wickets – the highest tally of my career to date. Those wickets were taken at an average of 16.0. I took 5 wickets in match on eight occasions and 10 wickets on three occasions. I also chipped in with 26 catches and had a batting average in double figures with a top score of 70.

I believe, however, I would have done even better if I'd had a regular fast bowling partner. As it was, the burden for pace lay squarely on my shoulders. When Mick Cowan, a lively medium-pace bowler, could obtain release from his National Service with the RAF, we formed a highly effective, if somewhat contrasting, spearhead attack. Our opening spell on a lively Headingley track reduced champions elect Surrey to 27 for 7 at the end of the second day. We went on to beat Surrey and end their winning run that stretched back for eighteen games. Mick Cowan was a ready wit and good enough to be chosen for the England 'A' tour of Pakistan. Unfortunately, he sustained a bad back injury on that tour and was never again fit enough to play a full season of cricket.

Frank Tyson, who had enjoyed considerable success on the winter tour of Australia, pulled out of the Lord's Test against South Africa with a badly blistered heel. I was called up as his replacement and needless to say was delighted to be back on the International scene. I made an immediate impact, not with the ball, but with the bat. England were struggling when I came to the crease but I played a sensible innings in supporting Johnnie Wardle. I didn't attempt anything flash, but concentrated on keeping my wicket intact. Johnnie and I shared a stand of 22, which doesn't seem a lot, but it helped England to a final total of 133.

When South Africa batted I opened the bowling with Brian Statham and to say our initial fortunes contrasted is putting it mildly. In his first over Brian took the wicket of McGlew, who was caught behind by Godfrey Evans. Looking back now I was too keen and eager to impress. As I ran up to bowl my first delivery I tripped and fell, much to the amusement of the crowd. My second delivery was called a 'no-ball'.

'Now then Frederick,' I told myself, 'calm down and get your bloody act together.' I did. My next ball moved away from Goddard, who fished, got an edge, and Godfrey Evans diving wide to his right at full stretch took a marvellous catch. My next delivery was another no-ball. Then Godfrey Evans, having taken a superbly athletic catch, contrived to put down an easy one when he dropped Cheetham. My next delivery went down at some pace. It lifted, Cheetham raised his bat and the ball created a crack in his bat just below the handle some three inches in length. What you might call an eventful first over. Later in the day I took the wicket of John Waite, but it was me who would had to wait – for another wicket.

England beat South Africa by 71 runs. Brian Statham took 7 for 39 in the second innings but my return to the Test side was not what I'd hoped. My second innings figures of none for 39 failed to impress the selectors, and for the remaining three Tests the seam bowling was shared by Brain Statham, Peter Loader, Alec Bedser, Trevor Bailey and Frank Tyson.

I returned to county cricket with Yorkshire and immediately found form, taking 25 wickets in three matches. I sustained that level of performance until the end of the season, taking a hat-trick for the second time in my career – oddly, against the same opposition, Nottinghamshire. In terms of county cricket it was a good season for me. But though happy to have been recalled by England, the fact I had not done myself justice at Lord's was a source of some frustration.

In January 1956, Len Hutton announced his retirement. The troublesome back that had plagued him for three years finally put paid to his career. He could have continued playing, but he wouldn't have been the player he once was. A few weeks later Norman Yardley also announced his retirement. It was almost as if Norman had been hanging on, waiting for Len to depart from the game and thus deprive him of that one honour he so sorely wanted – the Yorkshire captaincy.

One of the advantages I possessed as a fast bowler was my ability to bowl out-swingers consistently. Very few fast bowlers in the history of the game have been able to bowl a genuine out-swinger and mean it. I'd been bowling them naturally since about the age of eight, when I didn't even know what they were. I never forget my early days in the Yorkshire nets and the great Maurice Leyland saying to me, 'Freddie, keep bowling those out-swingers, lad, and thee'll be areet. That's the one that gets the great batsmen out!'

Ray Lindwall could bowl them, and so too could that great West Indian bowler Wes Hall, but the other English fast bowlers of my generation couldn't. Brian Statham could make the ball come back in off the wicket, but was the first to admit he couldn't intentionally swing the ball, making it curve wickedly in the air. Frank Tyson had tremendous pace but he bowled straight and to the best of my knowledge never intentionally bowled an out-swinger.

The out-swinger is a delivery bowled basically from close to the stumps and aimed to pitch around leg and middle then move towards the off-stump. Only sideways-on bowlers, of which I was one, are able to make the ball swing away. As you deliver it, your left elbow must point towards fine leg, which serves to bring your left shoulder in line with the batsman and the wicket. As your left foot goes across, you must swivel from the hips and the ball of your left foot as it hits the floor so that your whole body comes round as the ball is released. It is also essential to drag your back foot instead of picking it up to help you get round. It sounds complicated. You might wonder how you remember to do so many things with your body and how you can be comfortable and flexible in doing so. But as I say, I had been bowling out-swingers since I was eight – it was natural to me.

I see so many fast bowlers of today landing on their heel, which probably explains why so many suffer from leg injuries. I bowled for twenty years, often bowling 1,000 overs or more in a season, and never pulled a muscle, which I put down to my correct action. The in-swinger, which moves from off to leg, is a different bowling action altogether. I was never a natural at the in-swinger, but could move the ball back off the seam to leg by simply opening up my chest a touch. But most natural in-swingers of my time and subsequent generations bowl pretty well chest-on. The best exponent I ever came across was Yorkshire's Bob Platt, who adopted a stiff-legged run-up and bowled chest-on. Instead of looking outside the left elbow as he delivered, Bob looked inside, which meant his left arm finished on the outside of his left leg instead of the inside. Of course, an out-swinger becomes an in-swinger to a left-handed batsman. Lancashire's Jack Ikin, a very good left-hander who played for England, often told me that many people were incredulous when he told them I could pitch the ball to him six to eight inches outside his off-stump and make him defend leg and middle. But that's what I did. I always derived a great deal of pleasure from playing against a really good left-hander such as Jack, because there was much more satisfaction in getting a good batsman out. It was a real challenge and I relished such combat. The Old Trafford crowd would play merry hell with me when I put one around Jack's ears. But should I do that at Old Trafford in a Test against Australia or the West Indies, they cheered like mad. As we say in Yorkshire, 'There's nowt as queer as folk.'

In the fifties Yorkshire were the team to beat. We always drew larger crowds than any other county when on our travels, and on those rare occasions when a team such as Somerset or Sussex beat us, their supporters would stand on their seats shouting and clapping because we had come off second best. Even Australia and the West Indies feared us. County sides often triumphed over tourists, but invariably their success was over what in rugby they would call 'the Wednesday team', not the Test side. Whenever we played a touring team it was always their first-choice Test XI that we came up against. Whenever one of my teammates complained about this, I'd say, 'Oh, quit your moaning and be proud. It's the biggest compliment they could pay us.'

In my early career the ludicrous distinction between gentlemen and players still existed. Apart from the many privileges the gentlemen enjoyed, many of those so-called amateurs were drawing up to £1,000 in expenses, while we professionals earned around £750. I often referred to them as 'those bloody shamamateurs' and made myself somewhat unpopular with establishment figures as a result. That bothered me. So much so that, after a game, I would eat a hearty meal, perhaps watch some TV then enjoy a solid eight hours' sleep. That's how much it bothered me.

Snobbery was rife in cricket in my early days. Some of

those so-called gentlemen players who had come straight from Oxbridge into a county side would say to me, 'I believe you're an ex-miner,' with a sort of haughty disgust in their voices. I used to snap back at them, 'Aye, and what are you? An ex-schoolboy?' because I never let anybody get away with anything when it came to a question of personal pride. Now don't get me wrong, I'm proud of my roots and the fact I worked down Maltby pit, but I am a countryman and have always believed I am better than no one and no one is better than me.

If any of the MCC hierarchy strutted by, these former public school types would practically snap to attention. I used to think, 'Some people have no pride.' There was also a lot of nonsense talked about who should be called 'sir'. I refused to call anybody 'sir', with the exception of the Duke of Edinburgh. The snobbery perpetuated by many of cricket's establishment beggared belief. The story goes that one member of the MCC hierarchy, an ex-gentleman player who actually became manager of a Test tour, once got into a taxi outside Lord's. The cab driver looked in his rear-view mirror and asked, 'Where to, then, Guv?', only for this MCC member to say, 'You don't really expect me to give my address to the likes of you?'

I can remember cocktail parties where there were several titled people in attendance and some cricketers were forever edging up trying to talk to 'sir'. When they did eventually engage 'sir' in conversation they would laugh too loudly at his jokes and enthusiastically nod in agreement with every point that was made. I preferred the company of those who I felt had actually contributed something worthwhile to cricket, such as Jack Hobbs or Wally Hammond. As far as I was concerned they were giants of the game and deserving of respect.

By this time I had changed my sleeping habits. I found that getting up at half-five in the morning was no good to me as a professional cricketer. When a match started at 11.30 a.m. I felt I wasn't at my best mentally. I found it a positive advantage to go to bed later and get up late – late being around eight-thirty. If Yorkshire were playing in London and there was a play or cabaret show I fancied seeing, I'd go to a theatre or club. The floor show at a cabaret club finished much later than a play or a movie, but even taking to my bed at one in the morning didn't affect my performance on the field the following day. Contrary to common belief I have never been a big drinker, and other than the odd glass of wine with a meal do not drink alcohol now. When I attended a cabaret show I might be in the club for three hours but would make two pints of beer last all that time. Going to bed after midnight never affected my performance but I knew a hangover would . . .

One visit to a cabaret club really landed me in a spot of bother. I had gone to this club to see the comedian and drag artiste Danny La Rue, who I'd heard had a terrific act. A drag artiste in the fifties was somewhat of a novelty. I wanted to see for myself what all the fuss was about, especially as I had been told Danny's act was very funny. I was sitting puffing on my pipe when two guys asked if they could share my table. I had no objection to this, so invited them to sit down. It transpired that one was an Irishman and the other originated from the West Indies. We didn't exchange much conversation other than pleasantries until Danny La Rue took to the stage. Why these guys had come to see Danny I don't know, because throughout his act they began to hurl insults in his direction. I was there to see the show and these constant cat-calls were spoiling the atmosphere and no doubt making life difficult for Danny. I told them to shut up but they were having none of it.

They continued to shout insults, so I really told them where to get off. The next thing I know the Irish lad is on his feet and taking a swing at me. I jumped to my feet and hit the Irish lad and hard. Then the black guy thought he would get in on the action and rushed me. All hell broke loose as the black guy and I grappled with one another – the Irish lad was out of the equation as he had slipped into the arms of Morpheus. Fortunately, waiters and bouncers were quick on the scene and pulled us apart. The manger of the club arrived at the scene and asked, 'Are you all right, Mr Trueman?' On hearing this the black guy stood back and said, 'Hey man. It's not Freddie Trueman, is it?' I told him I was indeed Freddie Trueman. To my utter astonishment this guy laughed and whooped. 'Hey man, I'm from Jamaica,' he said, 'I'm your biggest fan out there. What's this with us fighting, eh?' As the waiters restored order to the table we shook hands and I invited him to sit down and talk cricket – but when Danny's act had finished. When the cabaret was over we did talk cricket. I ordered a bottle of champagne and we put the cricket world to right, while his Irish pal lay slumped in a seat still unconscious.

At least I was actually there when that fracas took place. There were any number of stories circulating about me that were totally untrue. According to legend I was supposed to be a real hell-raiser, partying until the wee small hours, but it was all nonsense. I found myself the subject of dozens of scurrilous tales, all of which were urban myths and damaging to my character and professionalism as an International cricketer. The following are but two examples.

A hotel in Bristol made an official complaint about me to the Yorkshire committee and I was hauled before them to explain my 'bad language and disgusting behaviour' at the hotel in question. The hotel management had demanded a full apology from me or else I would never be welcome in the hotel again. I sat in front of the committee while they ran through the accusations. Eventually, I was allowed to put my case.

'Well, if it wasn't for the set-up which exists at this club, I wouldn't be sitting here now,' I told them.

Sir William Worsley, the Yorkshire president and one of the few in the committee with a fairness of mind, common sense and a genuine appreciation of my efforts on behalf of the club, asked me what I meant. So I told them that I had not committed any of the despicable acts that allegedly took place in the hotel as I was somewhere else at the time.

'And have you any witnesses to that effect?' a committee member asked.

'Well, at least 20,000,' I replied.

Again, I was asked what I meant.

'I am given to believe that was the attendance at Lord's that day,' I said, 'and that's where I was when Yorkshire stayed at this hotel in Bristol. I was playing for England at Lord's on one and the same day. And if someone amongst you had taken the trouble to check the fixture list and the team for the Gloucestershire game, this pantomime could have been easily avoided.'

Sir William checked the fixtures and team for the Gloucestershire game and blew his top, demanding to know who was responsible for me having been brought before the disciplinary committee. He also insisted that the hotel must withdraw its complaint and make a full apology to me forthwith.

I was the subject of any number of untrue stories concerning wild and boisterous behaviour, all of which added to the 'terrible Trueman' tag. I hate to disappoint you but the vast majority of these stories were rubbish. If I'd done only half of the things I was said to have done, I'd have had a lifestyle to make George Best's seem like that of Steve Davis.

Unbelievably, I am the subject of such stories to this day. In 2002 I was the guest speaker at a sporting dinner and was signing autographs when someone told me that in the fifties his father ran a pub across the road from Bramall Lane.

'My father told me that as soon as the lunch interval came in a game, you'd run across the road and into his pub,' said the diner. 'You'd spend the lunch interval downing eight pints. And when you went back to play in the afternoon, my dad had to ensure you had a constant supply of pints. You used to mark your run-up with the pint glass and take a drink from it before every delivery.'

'I've never heard such a load of bloody rubbish in my life,' I told the diner, much to his astonishment. 'For heaven's sake,

I was a professional sportsman who played cricket at International level.'

The diner looked somewhat disappointed.

'So, it isn't true, then?'

'Of course it's not true!' I told him.

I signed for this chap and asked for the next autograph hunter in the queue to come forward.

'I heard what tha telt that bloke,' said diner number two. 'I knows all that about you 'n' that pub were rubbish.'

'Thank you,' I said as I signed his menu.

'I knows it were rubbish,' diner two continued, 'cos I know you used t' spend t' lunch interval having three women on t' go in different rooms int' pavilion!'

For all these stories about me being a hell-raiser are utter nonsense, there are times, even now, when I have to restrain myself from thumping somebody in the gob!

Apart from taking holy orders and entering a monastery, as a player I could think of no effective way of stopping these kind of stories. For a time I did begin to act like a monk. I stopped going to cabaret shows or theatres when in London and increasingly went my own way, whether travelling with Yorkshire or England. When my teammates were out on the town or attending a party, I would slope off and quietly enjoy a steak dinner in a restaurant. I gave up going to bed at midnight or one in the morning; instead I retired to my room between nine and nine-thirty p.m. The sheer physical and mental demands of being a fast bowler ensured that, though I was going to bed early, I went straight to sleep. I was bowling, in total, over 1,000 overs a season, which was unheard of for a man of my pace. I had become a bit of a folk hero to some, but one that was increasingly conspicuous by his absence from the rest of the team. I had no agent, no advisers and by keeping myself to myself, hoped to put an end to the scurrilous tales that were circulating about me. Some hope!

The summer of 1956 was one of the wettest on record.

Many county games suffered as a result, and in those that did go the distance the wet weather made it a season for the spinners. I took 59 wickets that summer, which, given I had taken 153 and 134 in the previous two seasons, was a disappointment. On the upside, I was recalled for England, playing two Tests against Australia, though I was not to feel I shared in the triumph as I had done in 1953. In the first innings of the Lord's Test I took 2 for 54. In the tourists' second innings I was troubled by a burst blister on my heel, but bowled with sufficient pace and precision and at one point had figures of 4 for 38 with Australia on 79 for 5. That helped give England the advantage but a superb innings of 97 from Richie Benaud the following day tipped the game back in favour of the Aussies. I eventually removed Richie, but the damage had been done. Keith Miller ripped through England batting and Australia enjoyed what was to be their only Test success of that summer.

Against Australia at Leeds I was to take 1 for 19 and 1 for 21, figures the selectors felt were not good enough for me to retain my place for Old Trafford Test – what a one to miss! As I have said, the weather that summer favoured spinners, but that must not detract from what was a truly remarkable performance by Jim Laker at Old Trafford.

Jim Laker was actually a Yorkshireman and had played in the Bradford League. However, at the end of his war service he was billeted to Catford in South London, which led to him being signed by Surrey. Jim was a modest, laconic, sometimes dour guy, but I got on well with him. At Old Trafford in Australia's first innings, on a pitch which was uncommonly dry and dusty and accordingly helpful to Jim's style, he returned amazing figures of 9 for 37 from 16.4 overs. In itself that would have been enough to ensure his immortality in Test cricket, but, amazingly, even better was to come.

Australia's first innings total of 84 in reply to an England score of 459 ensured the follow-on. And Jim Laker followed on from his feat in the first innings, only going one better, taking all 10 Australian wickets. Australia were all out for 205. Jim produced figures of 10 for 53 off 51.2 overs. It is not very often that an individual player becomes as important as the game, but Jim became the toast of cricket following his unique feat.

The mark of just how self-effacing Jim Laker was could be seen in the photograph of him that appeared in newspapers across the world the following day. Jim was seen leaving the Old Trafford pitch with David Sheppard and Brian Statham a few paces behind and offering formal applause. Jim isn't even smiling in the wake of his unique and historic achievement. He strolls towards the pavilion, sweater over his shoulder, as though returning from net practice.

Jim, of course, made back-page headlines in every newspaper the following day, but by contemporary standards the headlines were reserved and restrained. 'Laker Takes 19 Wickets,' said the *Daily Sketch*. The *Daily Herald* ran with 'England Congratulates Laker on Unique Feat'. In the unlikely event of an English bowler ever matching Jim's accomplishment against Australia, I shudder to think how some of today's tabloids would cover the story. No doubt there would be screaming headlines, not so much in praise of the bowler as insulting to Australians. In the fifties – and sixties – press coverage of a major sporting achievement such as Jim's focused on the feat itself, and did so with reverence and respect to the perpetrator. Such an achievement was never seen by the press as an opportunity for jingoistic posturing of the most unsavoury type. The game of cricket has changed irrevocably since Jim made history at Old Trafford, and so too has the way the game is reported in the press.

Jim Laker's feat helped further the renaissance of English cricket in the fifties. The game had produced a number of top-quality players after the war, of which I was considered to be one. Until my generation of players made their mark, English cricket had relied on pre-war players. This was all well and dandy against India and South Africa, but in the immediate post-war years the failings of this policy had been highlighted in home defeats to both Australia and the West Indies.

This new generation of players was responsible for not only winning but retaining the Ashes, for coming from two down to square the series in the West Indies and winning subsequent series against other nations. All of which enabled England to be declared unofficial world champions. England's success in the period was mainly due to a powerful and well-balanced attack, of which I was proud to be a part. This attack enabled us to dismiss even the best opponents twice on all types of pitch. In addition to myself England could call upon Frank Tyson, who, believe me, hadn't acquired his nickname of 'Typhoon Tyson' for nothing; Brian Statham, whose accuracy was unbelievable; and Alec Bedser, who had proved himself the best fast-medium bowler since the thirties. Then there was Peter Loader, who unfailingly supplied excellent back-up when called upon to do so.

England also had an embarrassment of riches regarding spinners. In addition to Jim Laker, there was Tony Lock, Bob Appleyard, Johnnie Wardle and Roy Tattersall. All of whom were being hard pressed by two up-and-coming spinners, Fred Titmus and Ray Illingworth. Regarding the batting when the great Len Hutton called it a day England could still boast the likes of Tom Graveney, Peter May, Colin Cowdrey, David Sheppard and, later, Ken Barrington.

To play for England meant something totally different to my generation: it was the ultimate accolade. We wore the three lions with immense pride because we knew we were representing the country for which many of our fellow professionals, and the vast majority of supporters, had fought a war. To play for England had not so much to do with recognition as a player as the honour of representing a great people. It was an accolade, but it was also seen to be a great responsibility and we conducted ourselves accordingly.

The fifties was a super era for county cricket. Attendances

were at worst reasonable, at best very good, and the highlight of the summer was the visiting tourists. For many supporters the enthusiasm with which they greeted a new season had much to do with who was touring. The big draw was Australia, closely followed by the West Indies. When they toured, the cricket season had an extra edge to it, not just because of the tradition of great rivalry between England and these two cricketing nations, but rather, with all due respect to other tourists, because the quality of their cricket was higher and therefore they posed the greater challenge.

It was, of course, not all sweetness and light in the fifties. Sport reflects society. British society was changing, people wanted a better way of life. In the Second World War everyone had to 'muck in'. With the exception of certain occupations such as mining, women had taken on jobs normally the preserve of men and had shown they could do them just as well. Working people had been given hitherto unknown responsibility and had demonstrated they could rise to the occasion. People's attitudes were changing in the fifties. They believed they were not inferior to their supposed betters in the establishment and challenged a lot of the mores and ways of the 'old guard'.

This was very much the case in cricket. My generation of professional player reflected the changing attitude of society. The cricketing establishment was riddled with snobbery and nepotism, which was anathema to myself and many of my fellow pros. I have already mentioned how the bitter hatred between Yorkshire and Middlesex players petered out in the fifties as the jealousy between public school and university types in the thirties fizzled out. The new generation of pro quickly began to question cricket's establishment.

The game itself was also changing. Many of the pre-war ideas on the game were challenged. It was believed that England should always take a wrist spinner to Australia simply because they had one. But players began to ask, 'Would it be better to take an off-spinner if he is the better bowler?' Tactics and field placings were also subject to a radical change of thinking. Australia had scored 721 runs while batting to a field that never changed, and so we began to see the strictures of the traditional set field as a handicap. Though captains preferred to opt for an attacking field, increasingly they reverted to the defensive should batsmen threaten to dominate a game. Field placings became more imaginative, changing in accordance with the idiosyncratic style of each batsman. Captains also began to appreciate that a run-saving field was a counter-attack, as it encouraged batsmen to take risks.

But these subtle shifts in both the way the game was played and the people who played it did not go down well with cricket's establishment. In every change they saw a threat to their power and position. Perhaps this was why the England selectors often picked a player because they thought him a decent chap who deserved a chance – even if someone else, for example yours truly, was top of the season's bowling.

In 1956 Yorkshire played what was in essence Australia's Test side at Bramall Lane. I bowled Rutherford with the first ball of the match, dismissed Burke with the second ball of my second over and when Bob Appleyard trapped Neil Harvey lbw Australia were 3 for 3. I was in good form in that match and carried on in our game against Northants. I was bowling as fast and as accurately as ever I had done. I was constantly beating the bat and to my chagrin on three occasions when I did manage to make the batsmen offer a chance, all three catches were dropped. One Northants batsman led a charmed life. He had already twice, unwittingly, deflected me between pad and leg-stump, made an on-side push and scored 4 to third man off the outside of the bat. My next delivery came off the edge of his bat. Initially he had no idea where the ball had gone but ran a single. That did it for me. I finished my follow-through and hands on hips turned to face him.

'Talk about luck,' I said. 'You've got more bloody edges than a broken pisspot!'

Northants took a first innings lead of 9. In their second innings, spurred on by my misfortune in the first, I yorked Arnold for 0. Mick Cowan then caught Denis Brookes when he was on 3. Mick then took the wicket of Jock Livingston before I had Reynolds caught in the slips. Northants were 23 for 4. Minutes later, a lifter hit Desmond Barrick on the hand and he retired hurt. I finished the innings with figures of 5 for 34. The newspapers were full of praise for my performances against both Australia and Northants. Whilst I had not enjoyed the best of seasons, in the main due to the weather – I had bowled 588 overs as opposed to 1,000 the previous season – I finished on top form and with a flourish. It was all to no avail. When the England squad was chosen for the 1956–7 tour of South Africa, my name wasn't in it.

CHAPTER EIGHT

THE INJUSTICE OF IT ALL

I SPENT PART OF the winter of 1956–7 playing in India. I had been picked to play for what today we would call England 'A', who were touring to commemorate the Silver Jubilee of the Bengal Cricket Association. It was my first visit to India and, like so many before me and since, I was struck by the sheer size and diversity of a country that can boast newspapers printed in nigh-on a hundred different languages or dialects.

There is extreme poverty and deprivation in India today, but in the fifties it was even more pronounced. As a cricketer I was staying in what passed for the best hotels. I travelled to and from games either by car or coach, but some of the sights I saw on those short trips were an eye-opener – I had never seen such squalor and it came as a real cultural shock. Whilst there is still abject poverty and suffering in India today, thankfully they have not been beset by the famines of the fifties and sixties.

Regarding the cricket, I took 8 wickets in two matches on wickets that were so dry and dusty David Lean could have filmed *Lawrence of Arabia* on them. I even top-scored in one innings, coming in at number ten and giving the bat the benefit of some fresh air to finish on 46 not out. Whilst ever mindful that the hotels I stayed in were a world away from the lifestyle many Indian people were subjected to, they were not what I was used to. The rooms were basic, sometimes a cast-iron bed, and in those days especially, you had to be very careful about what you consumed in the way of food and water. Those who had toured India before told mind-numbing stories of various intestinal tempests, described as 'Delhi Belly', 'Bombay Spray', 'The Madras Pebbledash' and 'Calcutta Splutter'. Teams did not have personal chefs or dieticians; the emphasis on what should or should not be eaten or drunk lay firmly with individual players. Away from cricket the players were encouraged to stay in the hotel. There was no TV or radio in some hotels, so it made for some very boring evenings. One hotel I stayed at had extensive gardens. Our guide informed us we were welcome to walk around these gardens but that we should be very alert about coming across a certain type of snake.

'This snake is easily recognized,' the guide informed us. 'It is vivid lime-green in colour and about twelve inches in length. Should you come across one, under no circumstances should you approach it. Inform the authorities. Because if this snake were to bite a man, so poisonous is it, he would be dead within thirty seconds.'

After three days in that hotel, I was on the point of going out and looking for the buggers.

The tedium of hotel living apart, India was a fantastic experience. The sheer diversity of the country is mind-boggling. There is a vibrancy and verve to India that, to this day, I have not experienced anywhere else. It's impossible in just a few words to sum up this incredible country. Such a diverse people, culture and lifestyle defies an all-encompassing description. Suffice it to say, many writers eminently more gifted than I have tried to describe the many facets of India and failed to do it justice.

On my return to England I was to receive a little fillip to my bowling technique courtesy of the introduction of some new regulations to prevent time-wasting. Due to the leisureliness of my walk-back – partly so I could recharge my body before the next delivery, partly to unnerve the batsman as he worried what the next delivery might bring – I had come in for some criticism for slowing down opponents' run rates.

Umpires were now set to clock watch between deliveries and so I decided to cut down my run-up to an exact eighteen-yard approach. It was, in fact, a minor alteration which did away with what I referred to as the scuffling and shuffling start by which I fell into step. Whether this slight adjustment to my run-up had any marked effect on my actual bowling I doubt very much, but I did feel more comfortable and at ease. From the very start of the 1957 season I was off to a flyer with 27 wickets in the first four games. It turned out to be a very successful season for yours truly but, surprise, surprise, a very turbulent one inside Yorkshire cricket club.

That season I took 135 wickets at an average of 17.05. Almost a quarter of the overs I bowled were maidens. I took 5 wickets in a match on nine occasions and 10 wickets in a game twice. I helped our quest by taking 36 catches and ended the season with a batting average of exactly 15.0, with a top score of 63. My success brought me to the attention of the England selectors yet again, only this time I was determined not to give them any opportunity or excuse to leave me out. In the event I played in all five Tests against the West Indies.

In the first Test at Edgbaston, England were all out for a modest 186, most having succumbed to the wiles of Sonny Ramadhin, who took 7 for 49. The wicket was slow and it was heavy going for me. That said, I still managed to york Bruce Pairaudeau and the following morning bowled Everton Weekes.

It was during this game that both Worrell and Walcott, who made 161 and 90 respectively, suffered muscle pulls. Bruce Pairaudeau came back out to act as a runner for Clyde Walcott for forty-five minutes, then Frank Worrell for over five hours. Bruce wasn't the tallest of people, and so for the best part of Friday and Saturday there were two 'batsmen' – one very tall and the other very short – at one end of the pitch. After the Saturday tea interval, Charlie Elliot and Emrys Davies in their white coats walked out through the dining room where both sets of players were having tea. Charlie was immediately followed by a white-coated pavilion attendant who was no more than four feet ten inches tall. I couldn't resist.

'I see you've got your runner with you, Charlie,' I remarked. The room went up as both sets of players howled with laughter.

When England batted again, Sonny Ramadhin looked set to wreak more havoc until, with 3 wickets down, Peter May and Colin Cowdrey got to grips with him by simply treating him as an off-spinner. Unable to spot for certain which way the ball would turn, May and Cowdrey thrust forward the left leg, bat and pad together to every ball from Ramadhin that pitched outside the off-stump. Umpires in those days were even more reluctant than now to give an lbw decision to an off-break if the leg is well forward. It was highly effective,

May and Cowdrey put on 411 for the fourth wicket, ostensibly destroying Sonny's hitherto unfathomable magic. Sonny Ramadhin bowled ninety-eight overs, the largest number ever bowled in an innings. It was a herculean effort from Sonny, but given he was being put to the sword, I think one has to question the wisdom of the West Indian captain, John Goddard, for playing him for so long. Sadly, Sonny Ramadhin was never quite the same bowler again.

England's second innings total of 583 broke the West Indies' cool and so I did my best to capitalize on May's and Cowdrey's fine batting performances. I had Rohan Kanhai caught at slip then bowled Pairaudeau before handing over to the spinners. Tony Lock took 3 for 32 and Jim Laker 2 for 13. At the close of play the West Indies were 72 for 7, leaving the match drawn. England felt this was a moral victory, as we believed, rightly as it was to turn out, that the initiative had swung our way. We beat the West Indies by an innings at Lord's in a game where I returned figures of 4 for 103 and enjoyed a whirlwind experience hitting three sixes off one over.

The Trent Bride Test proved highly significant for me and

England. The press considered my performance at Nottingham to be, as the *Daily Telegraph* put it, 'the finest sustained bowling performance of his career to date'. It was also the Test that saw the beginning of the somewhat famed bowling partnership of Trueman and Statham.

England began the Trent Bridge Test with a four-bowler attack of Brian Statham, myself, Trevor Bailey and Jim Laker. It was an attack of true Test quality backed by an extra seamer, Don Smith of Sussex. Unfortunately, Trevor Bailey was to tear a muscle in his back quite early in proceedings, leaving Brian, Jim, Don and myself to shoulder the burden of the bowling in what was sweltering weather.

Peter May won the toss, decided to bat, and it proved to be a good call. England made 619 for 6 with Tom Graveney's 258 being the highlight before Peter issued the declaration. The glorious weather lasted until the Sunday, when there was a little rain, but Frank Worrell remained as evidence that the covered pitch had not suffered in the least from the short showers. Frank Worrell earned the distinction of being the first West Indian player ever to carry his bat through an innings when making 191 not out. It was a superb effort from Frank, but I don't think I did too badly either. In my very first over of the morning I dropped a ball short to Everton Weekes. Everton, as I expected, attempted to hook but he was past the ball before it arrived and it ricocheted off his gloves and onto the stumps. That struck the spark. I gave it my all, excited at the fact I was bowling well and getting results. Frank Worrell apart, the West Indies batsmen had no answer. My opening spell of ten overs was physically demanding, especially with the temperature touching ninety, but my figures made for pretty reading: ten overs, six maidens, 5 for 20. Sonny Ramadhin offered good support to Worrell, their partnership in no small way contributing to a final West Indies' total of 372.

Peter May enforced the follow-on. At one point we had the West Indies at 89 for 5 and an England victory looked the likely outcome. But the jovial and talented Collie Smith settled in to play arguably one of the finest innings of his sadly all too short life. Collie made 168 and received dogged support from Atkinson and Goddard. On the Tuesday afternoon, the final day of play, the West Indies were still holding out. The heat was blistering. Having bowled for much of the day, I was feeling tired and weary when the England skipper, Peter May, asked me for another flat-out spell while there was still time to win the game.

My weariness must have been registering on my face because when I held out my hand to take the ball from Peter he said, 'Come on, Fred, England is expecting.'

'Is she really, skipper?' I replied. 'Is that why they call her the mother country?'

I was tired, but I removed Collie Smith and Sonny Ramadhin. Brian Statham took the last West Indies wicket and England were left to make 121 to win the match in an hour. The rate of two runs a minute was never on and the game petered out into a draw.

The game had been played in a heat wave. The pitch was a Trent Bridge classic, prepared for batsmen. England's depleted bowling resources had resulted in Brian Statham and me bowling for longer and more often than was good for us. But I think the measure of our strength, skill and application can be gauged by our final bowling figures, which read as follows:

	First Innings				*Second Innings*			
	O	M	R	W	O	M	R	W
Trueman	30	8	63	5	35	5	80	4
Statham	28.4	9	78	1	41.2	12	118	5

For much of the Test the temperature was in the high eighties fahrenheit. Fast bowling in such conditions was arduous. I think the mark of how well Brian and I applied ourselves to the task can be measured by our level of success when compared to that of the West Indies spearhead attack of Worrell and Gilchrist.

	First Innings				Second Innings			
	O	M	R	W	O	M	R	W
Worrell	21	4	79	1	7	1	27	0
Gilchrist	29	3	118	0	7	0	21	1

It is also worth noting that Worrell and Gilchrist enjoyed a decent rest between their spells of bowling. The West Indies used a total of nine bowlers in this Test, which meant Worrell and Gilchrist bowled in short, sparky spells. Not so Brian and I, who due to circumstances found ourselves called upon to bowl when really we should have been 'resting' out in the field to conserve energy.

England won all three of the remaining Tests by an innings. It was a convincing series victory over a good West Indies team, who some considered to be better than the side that had defeated England on their previous tour. I finished the series with 22 wickets to my name, which was more than any other seam bowler.

I'd bowled 173.3 overs in the series and my 22 wickets produced a wicket to run ratio of 20.68. I was proud of my achievements with the ball and also enjoyed a cheeky batting average in that series of 89.0! That Hutton-like batting average came courtesy of four innings in which I was not out on three occasions, with a top score of 36 not out. I never topped that series' batting average of 89.0, but given it was against the West Indies, I should imagine even Geoff Boycott eyes that one with envy!

On the domestic front I took 135 wickets at an average of 17.05, taking 5 wickets in an innings on nine occasions and twice taking 10 wickets in a match. I was developing as specialist slip fielder and helped the Yorkshire cause by taking 32 catches. My batting also continued to improve. I finished the season with an average of 15.0, was not out fourteen times and enjoyed a top score of 63. Coming in to bat at number ten I was officially referred to as being a 'tail-ender'. My growing contribution with the bat not only served to earn me a reputation as a decent lower-order batsman, but my aggressive and attacking style endeared me to Yorkshire supporters. As one female supporter remarked, 'Watching you bat, is like making love with my husband. It may not last long, but by heck while it does the sparks really fly.'

I remember doing particularly well that summer against Surrey at the Oval. Surrey won the toss and batted and, in a temperature of over 90 and high humidity, our skipper Billy Sutcliffe led out a Yorkshire team in which I was the only bowler faster than medium pace. The Oval pitch favoured batsmen and I sweated my guts out in helping Surrey to a first innings total of 365. I literally did sweat buckets. Despite the heat and humidity I bowled twenty-two genuinely fast overs and took 5 wickets – including four of the first six Surrey batsmen – for 67 runs. When my stint with the ball was over I was sweating so much my shirt and flannels were literally clinging to my body.

Another match from the summer of 1957 that I can readily recall was the Gentlemen versus Players match that was played at Scarborough. Godfrey Evans captained the Players, lost the toss, and the Gentlemen opted to bat. There was a south-westerly gale blowing across the ground with such force it rattled the windows of the pavilion. I formed the spearhead attack for the Players with Northamptonshire's Frank Tyson and before a ball was bowled I was at loggerheads with Godfrey.

'Fred, I want you to open the bowling,' said Godfrey and threw me the ball.

I started to walk towards the Trafalgar Square end only for Godfrey to call me back.

'No, not from that end, Fred,' he said, 'From the pavilion end against the wind.' I was mortified.

'If you think I'm going to bowl in a wind like this bugger after the season's work I've put in, you can bloody well think again. I've bowled a thousand overs this summer, I'm not going to be the one bowling into Hurricane Hilda!'

I stood there hands on hips, determined not to be the patsy.

'But I want Frank to bowl with this wind,' opined Godfrey. 'He's faster and he might knock down one or two early doors.'

'Don't talk daft, skipper. He's only faster than me if he's bowling with this sodden gale and I'm against it.'

'Fred, I'm skipper and I insist,' said Godfrey.

Johnnie Wardle, who had wandered into the scene, on hearing this last remark started laughing.

'Well you've done it now, skipper. He won't bowl now,' remarked Johnnie.

'If you don't bowl, Fred,' said Godfrey quietly but firmly, 'we shall all have to leave the field. I'm not having my authority as captain . . .'

Hearing this ultimatum I had no alternative but to bow to his wishes as, for all there was a gale blowing, the ground was nigh-on full.

'Don't be bloody daft, skipper. Gimme t' damn ball.'

I called on all my skills as a bowler in bowling into that gale. I used the wind to my advantage, using it to hold up my out-swinger. I could have been the one to 'knock down some early doors', only the two chances I contrived to create were both dropped. Frank Tyson, on the other hand, clean bowled Billy Sutcliffe for one.

After three overs Godfrey Evans said, 'Thanks very much, Fred, get your sweater. Good effort.'

'Nay, it's all reet. I'll carry on, we're doing well,' I told him. And I did carry on bowling.

Godfrey Evans initially stood up to me. But when I didn't want to take my sweater he saw the common sense of that because we were doing well and agreed to me continuing to bowl.

Godfrey and I had a great deal of respect for one another both as players and men. We became very good friends, roomed together on tours and would often take ourselves off to a restaurant and over a meal put the cricket world to rights. I liked Godfrey. He was a decent guy whose fairness extended to his appeals on the cricket pitch. Following his retirement in 1959 he continued to play cricket well into the sixties as captain of the Rothman's Cavaliers, who ostensibly were the pioneers of one-day cricket in this country. Peter Dimmock, who was in charge of sport at BBC Television, dubbed the Cavaliers 'the eighteenth county' and there was even talk of the Cavaliers joining the first-class counties, though cricket's establishment being what it was, this was never on from the start. When the John Player Sunday League started in 1969 the television rights to Sunday cricket were transferred from Rothman's to John Player. That marked the end of the Cavaliers, and the cricket career of Godfrey Evans.

Godfrey and I were real good pals, but that didn't stop me once breaking three of his ribs during a Yorkshire–Kent game. The delivery in question was a beamer, for which I immediately apologized to Godfrey.

'Sorry about the ribs, Godders,' I said with all sincerity. 'I didn't mean to do that. It was a beamer, I was intending to skull you. Anyway, you're an International cricketer, why the hell didn't you put your bloody bat there?'

'Exactly,' said Godfrey as he was helped off the field. 'Should know better.'

'Put it down to experience,' I told him.

'Experience!' grimaced Godfrey. 'That's what we cricketers call our mistakes.'

Godfrey Evans' mistakes as a cricketer were few. He illuminated the game of cricket in an irrepressible, joyous way. Sadly, the light he cast throughout the game was extinguished in 1999 when Godfrey died of a heart attack aged seventy-eight. Cricket was all the poorer for his passing.

I felt I had reached a high plateau of skill as a bowler in the summer of 1957. I was the most successful bowler in English cricket and had enjoyed what in the minds of many was a tremendous series against the West Indies, but never felt secure about my place in the England team.

Even when I was chosen, I felt the MCC selectors never wanted to pick me to play for England. My inclusion was often a result of pressure from the press and public opinion. I enjoyed a good relationship with both the press and cricket supporters of whatever hue, and had it not been for the pressure they exerted on the MCC, I am sure they would have happily chosen lesser bowlers for International recognition more often than they did. Which, believe me, was often.

It came to light that, when the squad for the 1954 tour of Australia was being chosen, three players had informed the MCC that they wouldn't go if I was chosen. This story was revealed in the *Sunday People* but as the newspaper didn't reveal the names of the three players in question I was left to wonder if it was fact or fiction – though it did have a twist in the tail. Following the piece, the Yorkshire secretary, John Nash, came to me and confessed that the MCC had in fact asked if I was available for that tour, but that he had forgotten to tell me. To this day I find the notion of a county secretary forgetting to ask a player if he is available for an England tour to be unbelievable, especially as John Nash hadn't forgotten to ask my teammates Len Hutton and Johnnie Wardle! Likewise, I also find it unbelievable that the MCC, having enquired about my availability, never put another call in to Yorkshire when John Nash didn't get back to them.

When I did make it into the England team I felt the selectors were keen to seize on any opportunity they could to omit me for the next Test. I reckon that I missed at least thirty Tests because the MCC found an excuse that to their minds justified their dropping me. One reason given for my non-inclusion was that I had been bowling extremely well but hard and they didn't want me to suffer burn-out. I wasn't rested, of course, I simply contrived to bowl extremely well 'but hard' for Yorkshire while England got on without me.

Now at the risk of citing a south versus north prejudice, there was no doubt in my mind that the MCC would opt for a southern player if possible, a northerner when pushed and a Yorkshire pro only when they couldn't possibly avoid it. In the fifties a northern player could burst onto the scene, as I had done, by first of all playing well so that the selectors couldn't ignore me. When they did ignore me, I kicked up a fuss, as this was the only way I was going to have my talent recognized. Taking 100-plus wickets a season, picking up a lot of catches and doing well with the bat obviously wasn't enough. In 1963 Cassius Clay entered boxing and was forced to do exactly the same thing. The boxing world, being what it is, saw Clay's outbursts as showmanship. Cricket's establishment viewed my extolling of self-belief with all the contempt they would reserve for a pile of dog poo on the carpet in the Long Room at Lord's.

I was so frustrated at being overlooked for the England team that it turned me into someone I didn't want to be, and in my heart knew I never was: an arrogant bastard. I began to take this attitude onto the field. Frustrated with a system that was preventing me achieving my goals, I became resentful of a number of players whose selection for England was, to my mind, unmerited. I started to use any device I could think of to vent my frustration and exert dominance over such players.

Every time I came up against a batsman with a big reputation I would go after him with every ounce of strength in my body, and use every psychological device I could think of to frighten him into submission. Many believed I had a personal grudge against them, but I never did. They were simply vehicles by which to prove a point to the selectors. I can honestly say during my entire career there was never a player I resented personally. But by reacting in this way, though it wasn't in my character, I acquired my reputation in the game.

For all I felt I received a really raw deal from the England selectors, other Yorkshire players received even worse. Brian Close is the strongest, hardest and most fearless man I have ever known. He used to field so close to a batsman that he was only a matter of a couple feet away from him. Even when Brian got hit at some pace with the ball, it never deterred him. Such bravery prompted the great comedian Eric Morcambe to once remark: 'You don't have to consult a newspaper to know when a new cricket season has started, you just listen out for the sound of Brian Close being hit with a cricket ball!'

But more importantly, he was the best left-handed batsmen of his generation, and his form was such he should have played in about seventy Tests; but he was picked for less than a third of that number. He was a super captain with a great tactical brain, unsurpassed in the field, a very good batsman and a better bowler than most. That many a lesser player was chosen ahead of him for England is a disgrace and indicative of a selection system that was rotten to the core. Brian should be a legend of International cricket, but the small-minded prejudices of those who ran the game denied him his rightful status.

In 1959 against India Brian returned bowling figures of 4 for 35, held 4 catches, scored 27 runs and wasn't picked for another Test for two years. When he returned to International cricket in 1961 it was against the Australians at Old Trafford. In the first innings Brian had bad luck, given out lbw off the bowling of Graham McKenzie when his bat had connected with the ball. In England's second innings they required 72 runs an hour to seal victory. Richie Benaud started to bowl around the wicket into the rough to slow down the England run rate. The two England batsmen at the wicket were Ted Dexter and Raman Subba Row. Brian was seated on the balcony next to the England captain, Peter May, and said to him, 'Skipper, don't get two left-handers in together, that's asking for trouble. If we are to stand any chance of winning this one, keep a right-hander and left-hander together.' Brian's advice went unheeded. When the time came for him to bat he gave it a go but threw his wicket away when going all-out for victory.

If Brian's advice had been taken, Richie Benaud would have had to consider going back to bowling over the wicket and pitching on the good part, which was playable. When it was apparent that England were not going to reach their target, if Brian had been captain, he would have issued the order to go on the defensive in the hope of making a draw.

England lost that Test and the finger of blame was pointed at Brian rather than Peter May. Following that Test Brian found himself out of favour with the England selectors for another two years.

In 1976 Brian was what you might call a veteran. He was forty-five but was recalled to the England team to face the express bowling of the West Indies. He was not found wanting. At Old Trafford the wicket was a nightmare for batsmen. The faster the West Indies bowled the more the wicket crumbled. Prior to the game the England skipper, Tony Greig, asked Brian to open the batting. Brian was slackjawed.

'I haven't opened the batting since 1955!' Brian informed his skipper. 'We have Bob Woolmer. He's a specialist opener. I've pulled this team out of the mire in the previous two Tests. You need someone in the middle order to anchor the innings if the upper order don't produce the goods.' Tony Greig's reply left Brian stupefied. Greig told Brian the selectors believed Bob Woolmer was one for the future and they didn't want him killed off!

Brian opened the England batting with John Edrich and together they made a stand of over 50, which was the highest for England in that Test. Typically, both Brian and John were dropped for the next game.

Arguably, the Yorkshire player subjected to the greatest injustice of all was Jimmy Binks. Season after season Jimmy produced great performances behind the stumps. He was a superb wicket-keeper and a very good batsman. After Godfrey Evans he was far and away the best wicket-keeper in the country, but Jimmy was only chosen for England twice. To me this is scandalous. Jimmy was consistently very good but the selectors seemed to pick anybody over him – Roy Swetman of Surrey, Geoff Millman of Notts and Jim Parks of Sussex. They were all good wicket-keepers but to my mind nowhere near as good as Jimmy.

Those charged with running the game and selecting England teams invariably came from a wealthy background. They were former public school boys who went on to Oxford or Cambridge. Those who played for first-class counties did so without ever proving much. Cricket was top-heavy with such people, a hangover from the Victorian era. They had no idea about the modern game, no affinity or empathy with pros such as myself, and it is my firm belief that England would have won a lot more Tests had it not been for their influence in the game. They looked down on the pros and considered an amateur with a cricket blue from Oxford or Cambridge as a much superior choice when it came to selecting the England team.

Jim Sims, who played for England against Australia in 1936, was a miner but so talented at cricket that they took him on to the Lord's ground staff. In those days Lord's would send their ground staff to play for various teams on an ad hoc basis.

The ground staff were instructed to seek out the captain and report for duty, always remembering to call the skipper 'sir'. Jim used to locate the captain of the team he had been loaned to and say, 'Jim Sims, sir, Lord's ground staff.' Jim was nearly always asked to bat as a tail-ender and was only occasionally called upon to bowl. This went on for some time and Jim got fed up with it. One day he changed tack. He casually strolled up to the captain and said, 'Morning, sir. My name is Morton-Sims from Lord's, no less.'

The captain replied, 'Good man! Top stuff! How would you like to open the batting?'

Unbelievably, that sort of attitude was still prevalent in cricket throughout the fifties.

1958 ushered in the era of Ronnie Burnet as captain of Yorkshire. Ronnie had previously been the captain of the second XI and an amateur, but a decent and honest one, who only claimed his genuine expenses. Ronnie's appointment surprised many because he was thirty-nine years of age and had never played a first-class match. To be honest, as a cricketer he wasn't up to county standard, but he was a natural leader and tactically aware.

I played under Ronnie for the first time after I had missed a couple of county games due to a badly blistered left foot. The Yorkshire second XI were playing at Middlesbrough and I suggested this game would be a good opportunity for me to find out if I had recovered from the blisters in a match that had no real bearing. Bob Appleyard was making a comeback after injury and Brian Close was in the team too.

Right from the start Ronnie displayed his mettle as a captain. He asked Brian Close to open the batting and when Brian objected told him, 'It's a second XI game. You can do it, Brian. Secondly, I'm the captain and you either go in first or go back home.'

When our innings was over, Ronnie asked me to open the bowling. He told me to bowl only four overs to start with to see how the injured left foot stood up to it. A little later Bob Appleyard was bowling. I began to wonder what would happen when Ronnie tried to take him off. I didn't have to wonder for long. A few minutes later Ronnie said, 'Thanks Bob, take your sweater.' As I expected Bob kicked up about being replaced. Ronnie again asked Bob to take his sweater and again Bob protested.

'Put your sweater on and do as you're told!' commanded Ronnie then walked away leaving Bob completely nonplussed. It was from that moment that I thought Ronnie Burnet would make a good first-team captain and I supported him right from the start, although I knew we would have to do a bit of carrying.

Ronnie was appointed to put fire and discipline into the Yorkshire team and he accomplished that at a calculated cost. In August 1958 Johnnie Wardle, who had already been selected by England for the winter tour of Australia, was informed that he would be released by Yorkshire at the end of the season. The initial decision was given to Johnnie by the Yorkshire secretary, John Nash. However, when Johnnie asked to be omitted from the team to play Lancashire because he had written newspaper articles that were critical of some of his teammates, Ronnie Burnet told him to leave Yorkshire there and then and never return to the dressing room. The Yorkshire committee backed Ronnie and Johnnie subsequently left the club. Worse was to follow when the MCC then withdrew their invitation for Johnnie to go on the winter tour of Australia.

This affair damaged not only the prospects of the forthcoming winter tour, it also damaged the image of cricket in general. Though Johnnie was pictured in the press sitting behind a typewriter, I should imagine his articles that appeared in the *Daily Mail* that were critical of Ronnie Burnet and other Yorkshire players were almost certainly ghosted. That said, Johnnie would have had control over the content. Johnnie's mistake was simply that he was not a silent witness in what was often an uncomfortable atmosphere. I have to say he appeared quite philosophical about the whole thing. Apparently, when informed that he was not to tour Australia, Johnnie told the MCC secretary, Ronald Aird, 'It's my own fault and I asked for it.' It was and he did.

This was very much a time of transition at the club with new blood coming into the side. Bryan Stott, Ken Taylor and Doug Padgett as batsmen; wicket-keeper Jimmy Binks, Ray Illingworth and, of course, Ronnie Burnet were all awarded caps. Don Wilson was earmarked to replace Johnnie Wardle. All of which meant only Brian Close, Vic Wilson and myself remained from the side of 1950.

The summer of 1958 was not a good one for Yorkshire, nor for the weather. Almost a whole month was lost to rain. In six matches not even a first innings decision was reached and the weather was so bad at Hull for our game against Nottinghamshire, the third day was abandoned on the second!

Though the fixture list was disrupted, I still managed to take 106 wickets at an average of 13.33 and once again topped the club's bowling. Ronnie Burnet proved himself to be an astute captain. He encouraged me, praised me, was sensible about how often he called on me to bowl and I responded by giving him the best I had to offer – wickets and loyalty.

The weather was so wet that summer, most of the bowling in the Test series against New Zealand was given to the spinners. That said, I played in all five Tests. I was delighted to take 5 for 31 in the first Test at Edgbaston. At Lord's I made what the *Daily Herald* described as a 'sensational catch'. I anticipated a defensive back stroke from the Kiwi batsman D'Arcy, moved quickly up from square leg and, as the ball dropped like a dead bird from the bat to D'Arcy's feet, I threw myself forward and caught it with my hand on the batsman's boot. D'Arcy was so taken aback, he stood there trying to work out what had happened before finally walking. At the Oval I displayed a little cavalier batting when hitting the New Zealand leg-spinner for three sixes. I ended on 39 not out, which I believed to be a decent effort with the bat, seeing as I had been at the wicket for less than twenty minutes.

With so much new blood in the dressing room, though I was only twenty-seven, I felt like an old hand. My career was flying, I was picked for the tour of Australia. I was fit and strong, had developed into what teammates considered to be an excellent fielder, and was doing a bit with the bat. I knew my worth as a bowler to both club and country; what I didn't know was that I was about to enter a period of mature achievement, a period in my career that Brian Close describes as being 'Fred in his pomp'.

CHAPTER NINE

CAREER SUCCESS AND MARRIAGE FAILURE

AUSTRALIA HAD BECOME symbolic to me. Ever since I had been overlooked for the 1954–5 tour I felt my career could not be complete until I'd toured there. I regarded my selection for the team to tour under the captaincy of Peter May as being not only recognition of my prowess as a top-flight International fast bowler, but also as compensation.

In 1958 Australian cricket was embroiled in controversy, as the two great Australian bowlers Meckiff and Rorke had been accused of 'throwing'. Their unorthodox bowling actions led our tour managers to complain to Don Bradman, no less. I told the deputation their complaint was futile, that Don Bradman would simply tell them: 'And what of the action of the England bowlers Tony Lock and Peter Loader?'

I was told to shut up, that despite ten years' first-class experience I didn't know what I was talking about. The delegation were ushered in to see the great man. They put their case to Bradman, who promptly turned around and told the England tour management to 'first of all put their own house in order'. When they returned to our team hotel and informed everyone of Bradman's reaction I didn't say anything but believe I had a 'told you so' look on my face.

To be honest I thought the tour management did have a case, as I believed Meckiff's action was totally illegal and he should never have been allowed to play. Oddly, Meckiff wrote a book some years later in which he described me as 'a thrower', which to me demonstrated how much he knew about bowling. So there we were, two top International cricket teams, arguably the best in the world at the time, chucking the ball at each other. Just to make it more of a pantomime the Australian umpires demonstrated as much impartiality as a religious zealot. We just couldn't get favourable decisions and they no-balled England bowlers left, right and centre – me included!

The tour manager was F. R. Brown, with whom, prior to the tour, I'd had no acquaintance whatsoever. But that didn't stop Brown saying to me when first we met, 'Any trouble from you, Trueman, and you'll be on a slow boat home.' There were very few people in cricket I really disliked. There were a lot I had little time for, or thought little of, but not many I found abhorrent. F. R. Brown was one such person. In my opinion he was a snob, bad-mannered, ignorant and a bigot. Right from the moment we landed in Australia I was subjected to some gruelling physical strain as I was the team's workhorse and was made to bowl nearly all the time. After a week or so in Australia I contracted a mysterious back illness, which made me unavailable for the first Test. What brought it on was never discovered, but strangely I was to suffer from this illness on both my tours to Australia and both times I contracted the illness when in Brisbane . . .

F. R. Brown was very understanding. He told me, 'If you're going to be ill, you might as well go home,' which hurt more than the backache. Dual-sportsman Willie Watson had fallen and injured his leg on the boat journey out. He was hospital-ized in Ceylon and was then flown out to Australia, where he underwent an operation. Willie didn't play a match until we arrived in Brisbane, but F. R. Brown never suggested he might be packed off home. Brown was rude whenever he spoke to me and treated me with contempt. I bit my lip when con-fronted by him but did go and see skipper Peter May to complain about Brown's behaviour. Peter didn't say much, but to his credit went to see Brown. What was said I don't know, but for a time Brown gave me a wide berth, which suited me fine.

My mysterious back ailment cleared up when we reached Adelaide, which left me to wonder whether something in the Brisbane air disagreed with me. If that was the case it didn't disagree with me as much as F. W. Brown did. The back trouble cleared after I met an elderly lady there who told me to dump the tablets and medicine in the bin, collect a bag full of lemons fresh from the tree, squeeze them into a tumbler, add an equal amount of water, then drink it first thing in the morning. I was so desperate to be rid of the pain I was willing to try anything. I looked like old Father Time on the weather vane at Lord's as I headed for the nearest lemon tree. I filled a bag with lemons and followed the lady's instructions to the letter. Three days later I was bowling again.

I felt chipper, fit enough to play in the next match – a good decision, as I took 9 wickets, held a couple of catches and with the bat made 50 in thirty minutes. I thought I had done enough to be selected for the second Test in Melbourne, but the selectors had other ideas. Poor ideas, as it was to turn out. England were well beaten by 8 wickets. England were now two down in the series and they brought me back to try to help them out of the mire in Sydney.

I don't think I exaggerate in saying that as far as the Australian supporters were concerned I was the biggest attraction of the England team. Apart from my prowess as a fast bowler I think the Australian people warmed to me because in me they saw none of the characteristics they most dislike in the English. In addition to which, they liked my sense of humour and the fact that I would clown around in a game as and when circumstances allowed. I found the majority of Australian pitches that year not to my liking. They had little of the life Frank Tyson and Brian Statham had found and exploited three years previously. I found I had to bowl shorter than a full length, the ball didn't move as much in the air as it did in England, so I had to 'dig the ball in' to get pace and movement.

In my first over McDonald was dropped when it looked like a straightforward catch. Getting a wicket in my first over is always a great motivator, and seeing a decent chance put down annoyed me. The inadequately covered pitch was a help to the spinners but not to me. I bowled twenty-two overs for a return of 1 for 46. The spinners ruled the roost, but neither side could exert any real advantage over the other and game fizzled out into a draw.

The temperature for the state game against Victoria was 109 degrees in the shade. Fielding was jolly uncomfortable never mind bowling at pace. I reckon I shed a good few pounds when bowling thirteen eight-ball overs and taking 5 for 42. With Australia two up with one match drawn the destiny of the Ashes was at stake at the Adelaide Test. Jim Laker had picked up an injury, so England opted for all-out attack, the pace bowlers being Brian Statham, Frank Tyson and myself, backed by the medium-pace of Trevor Bailey and the spin – Australians would say 'the chucking' – of Tony Lock.

What life there was in the pitch soon evaporated – quite literally. It made for difficult bowling and Australia, particularly as one of the umpires consistently no-balled me for my front foot being just over the line. It was annoying, especially as this umpire seemed to allow Gordon Rorke to bowl with both his feet over the front line! Despite this, I was more than delighted with my return of 4 for 90 from thirty gruelling eight-ball overs. Frustratingly, though, the England batting simply wasn't up to the job. Between them Gordon Rorke and Richie Benaud sent a succession of England batsmen back to the pavilion. Australia won by 10 wickets and regained the Ashes.

I suffered, as did others, from appalling umpiring decisions when batting. Richie Benaud was bowling and I had it in my mind to swing the bat and hit him out of the ground if he pitched one up to me. Well Richie did but I was so keen to get at it that I hit the ground with my bat which released it from my grip. As my bat cart-wheeled away there was nothing I could do but stand and watch the ball come through and just miss my off-stump. My bat was a good two feet away when the ball came through to Australia's wicket-keeper, Wally Grout, who collected it, whipped off my bails and appealed for a stumping. The square leg umpire shook his head to indicate not out, but the other umpire at the bowler's end gave me out caught behind. It was unbelievable.

The press at home gave most of the England team a roasting; fortunately I was not included in that number. All the newspapers agreed I had emerged with my honour intact. I also had the distinction of taking my hundredth Test wicket in New Zealand, where England finally won a Test. It had been a very disappointing tour from our point of view. The majority of the players were uncomfortable out there, but I had much in common with both the Australian players and the supporters. I warmed to their down-to-earth attitude, and they to mine. One of the many things I learned on this tour was just how competitive Australian cricketers are. They were good shouters if not a little too cocky when the advantage in a game was with them. But it was their attitude when the chips were down for them that impressed me.

They seemed to be galvanized and collectively rise to the challenge. Again, that was something we had in common. I found that the only way to deal with Australian cricketers was to get stuck into them, like they always did with us. I found that underneath all their aggression and competitiveness there were 'bonzer' blokes with whom you could form long-lasting friendships. I made countless new friends during that tour. Norman O'Neill and I had many a battle on the pitch but we were to become the best of friends. Their supporters were no different. I was warned at the start of the tour that my aggressive demeanour on the pitch could get me into trouble with the fans. Especially those who inhabited the famous 'Hill' at Sydney, which, when riled, could make the riot scene out of *Prisoner Cell Block 'H'* seem like a Darby and Joan outing. I discovered to my delight that the supporters on the 'Hill' actually respected and admired an opposing player who gave as good as he got. Which I did. When I came up against the 'Hill' during the Sydney Test they gave me some stick, so I gave them some back.

They loved it. Just like the West Indies supporters, the Aussies love their cricket and are intent on making their trip to a match a damn good day out, bringing plenty of tinnies with them as well as a mouthful of jibes to be directed at opposing players. It was touching 100 degrees during the Sydney Test. When I was fielding on the boundary between overs one supporter on the 'Hill' held up a Fosters tinnie and shouted, 'Fred, you look in need of a beer, mate.' I shouted back that I could down the contents without it touching the side of my mouth. At the end of my next over I went across to Peter May and asked him if I could take the 'Hill' supporter up on his offer, just for a bit of a laugh. Peter laughed and gave me the OK, saying it would be good for public relations. When I returned to the boundary the supporter repeated his offer so I thanked him and took a swig of his tinnie. The whole of the 'Hill' roared with delight. When I finished bowling my next over I returned to the boundary to find about twenty tinnies lined up waiting for me in front of the fence. I had won the respect and admiration of the 'Hill', and from that moment on, they were great to me. I had plenty of verbal exchanges with Aussie supporters during the tour but they were always good-natured. I learned a lot on that tour not only about cricket but about how Australians view themselves.

The bigger the hat, the smaller the sheep farm.

The shorter the nickname, the more they warm to you.

Whether it is the opening of Parliament in Canberra, or a new fine art gallery in Sydney, there is no formal event in Australia that can't be improved by a sausage sizzle.

They will refer to their best friend as a 'total bastard', whereas their worst enemy is 'a bit of a bastard'.

When invited to a party the done thing is to take along a bottle of cheap red wine that slides down the throat like a rusty knife, then spend the evening drinking the host's tinnies. One should never feel self-conscious about doing that, as the host will expect it from you and will have catered for it.

When out in the territories the neon sign advertising the motel's pool will be slightly larger than pool itself.

The true mark of the esteem in which an Australian cricketer is held is not having a stand named after him, but a bar in the ground. Better still, a urinal. As in 'The Wally Grout Gents' in Sydney.

The benchmark of a man's masculinity is to erect a beach umbrella in the face of a strong south-easterly.

The wise person chooses a partner who is not only attractive to them, but also to midges and mosquitoes.

The 1959 season found me at the very top of my game. I was very popular with both the press and supporters, who liked it when I 'played to the gallery'. I had implicit self-belief, was always confident that I could take wickets. I feared no one and took to the field with a certain swagger, knowing that there were plenty of batsmen who feared me. When I squatted on my haunches, relaxed but poised, at short leg, with my cap at a jaunty angle, a blade of grass between my lips. I was relishing being who I was, what I was and where I was. And this was helped by Ronnie Burnet's captaincy

Prior to Ronnie assuming the captaincy, Yorkshire boasted arguably the finest collection of cricketing talent in the country but won absolutely nothing. Aside from the big names – Len Hutton, Johnnie Wardle and yours truly – there were those who couldn't get into the team, players whose talent was such they'd walk into the current Yorkshire team: John White-head; Jackie Firth, an excellent wicket-keeper who joined Leicestershire; Ken Smales, a wiley off-spinner who went to

Nottinghamshire; Freddie Jakeman, a very competent batsman. Norman Horner, Arnold Hamer and Geoffrey Keighley, all highly competent players, were also cornerstones of the second XI, who, when given the opportunity, played well in the first team.

I know people say cricket is a different game now, but I think this is only cosmetic. Coloured clothing, Team England, floodlit matches, the success of 'quickie' cricket are just some of the things that have changed cricket irrevocably in recent years. However, the way the game is actually played, getting runs and taking wickets, is in essence the same as it was in my day. I heard a Sky Sport presenter say today's bowlers are much fitter, stronger and faster than their predecessors. I have never heard such nonsense. I don't believe there is a current fast bowler around today who is quicker than I was in my prime. As for modern players being fitter and stronger, again nonsense. More often than not I would bowl in excess of 1,000 overs a season. There were many instances when I bowled long spells in searing heat. For example, once in Australia during an innings I bowled thirty-two eight-ball overs in a temperature in excess of 100 degrees. Towards the end of my spell the ball was like a rag doll's head. To do that one has to be fit and strong, I can tell you.

Leaving myself aside I wonder how many contemporary batsmen would be able to cope with Lindwall and Miller, Heine and Adcock, Frank Tyson or Brian Statham. Likewise, would some of the bowlers who have played for England in recent years be able to tie up the likes of Bobby Simpson, Norman O'Neill, Gary Sobers or Bill Lawry, to name but a few of the great batsmen around in my time?

Given all the internal turmoil the club had endured, Yorkshire were far from favourites to win the Championship in 1959. That summer our batting flourished, and was backed by excellent fielding and sustained bowling. I topped the bowling averages with 19.5 and took the most wickets with 140. I bowled over 1,000 overs, more than a quarter of which were maidens. I took 24 catches, scored 602 runs at an average of a little under 20. 1959 was a very good season for me, but more importantly it proved to be a glorious one for Yorkshire.

What Ronnie Burnet did was create a team around four established players: wicket-keeper Jimmy Binks; Brian Close, who had so much ability that if he had played regularly on good pitches could have just about scored a century every time he batted; Ray Illingworth, a truly great all-rounder; and myself, enjoying a fair amount of success in my career.

Ronnie Burnet instilled in the other members of the team a sense of what the game was all about and just what it meant to play for Yorkshire. Ronnie was a great motivator, a super leader and very good at man management. Above all, he made sure that no one regarded himself as greater than the team or of any more importance than any other player. Everyone played for everyone else. Ronnie had no time or place for prima donnas. At long last I was playing in a Yorkshire side that really was a team.

As the season progressed and we got better and better Ronnie would remind us that we had a destiny – to win the Championship. 'In years to come, when our playing days are over,' he once said, 'you will look back on what you knew to be the good times. Savour every minute of this season, lads, these are those good times.' Before we took to the pitch Ronnie would tell us 'Win, lose or draw, remember I am very proud of every one of you. Proud and privileged to be your captain. I said win, lose or draw – but if everyone of you simply does the job you are so capable of doing – we will win, and always win. Let's go – everyone as one!'

Well, when you heard such words as that, you took to the pitch pumped up and ready to get stuck in to the opposition. We were so galvanized, we would have died for each other. Cricket has much to do with individual skill, but it also has much to do with team effort. Teams win trophies, not collections of talented individuals. The success of Yorkshire in 1959 was very much a team effort, though, of course, the game of cricket being what it is, the onus fell on individuals at times. There were occasions when I and my fellow bowlers had to bowl a team out – we did it. There were occasions when we were chasing runs against the clock in order to win a match. I would join my teammates on the balcony as Doug Padgett or Brian Bolus danced down the wicket and went for the runs. We'd look at one another and smile – everyone was keeping their end up, doing their job in the name of the team. By the end of June we had beaten Nottinghamshire, Glamorgan, Warwickshire, Essex and Sussex. Doug Padgett had two centuries to his name while Ken Taylor, Bryan Stott, Brian Close, Ray Illingworth and a young colt by the name of Harold 'Dickie' Bird had one each.

In July we beat Derbyshire, Essex and Leicestershire, though lost to both Northamptonshire and Surrey. Surrey were once again mounting a serious challenge, having won seven consecutive Championships. Our form in August was a little indifferent, in that we beat Middlesex, Kent and Worcestershire but lost against Somerset and Gloucestershire. And so we went to Hove to play Sussex in our final game of the season with an outside chance of winning the County Championship should we beat the home side. Sussex gave no quarter. Their second innings dragged on interminably throughout the second day. When the last wicket eventually fell we had to make 215 in a hundred minutes to win the game.

It was then, I am sure, that Ronnie Burnet felt it had all been worth the considerable effort he had made. He'd put up with all manner of criticism when appointed captain, most notably that he did not have a first-class game to his name. There was the Johnnie Wardle affair and battles with other senior players who had since left the club. He was coming up to forty-one years of age and leading a team many of whom were little more than half his age. His role as captain had not been an easy one, but it all came right for him on the afternoon of 1 September 1959.

Ronnie was a little crestfallen at the time it had taken us to bowl out Sussex. He came into the dressing room, sat down and said, 'Well, lads, I thought we had a good chance of the Championship if we could win this one. But we've been set one hell of a task.' We all shared that thought.

'Don't you worry, skipper,' I said. 'We're going to win. There's nothing for us if we don't win, so let's set about rattling off 215.'

Doug Padgett nodded, reached into his bag and said, 'Give me that bat.' Bryan Stott was in a similarly determined mood. When Ian Thomson bowled the first ball of the innings, Bryan danced down the wicket and hit it straight back over Thomson's head for six. On the balcony we all exchanged the 'knowing' smile. We reached 50 in only twenty minutes. Bryan and Doug posted the 100 after forty-three minutes – and then they started batting a bit! They had been making tremendous progress up to this point but then really opened up the guns. We reached 150 in just over the hour mark.

Wickets started to fall as we took chances. Bryan Stott went for 96 and Doug Padgett for 79, the pair contributing the lion's share of the runs that afternoon. Those who followed Bryan and Doug also followed their example. After only ninety-five minutes we had our target of 215 and had won by 5 wickets. Bryan Stott and Doug Padgett contributed the majority of the runs, but afterwards no one thought of it that way. Everyone who batted contributed something and those who didn't go in suffered most! At one stage we were almost hoisted by our own petard. Brian Close was really giving it a go and at one point smashed the ball clean out of the ground. When such a thing happens in football they simply call for another ball. Not so in cricket. That ball had to be retrieved and, unlike football, there was no referee to halt the stopwatch and add the time it took to retrieve the ball on to the game. Brian scored six off that hit, but the five minutes or so it took to retrieve the ball and return it to the bowler's hand actually upped the ante.

I made a brief excursion into the middle. The first ball I hit for six. The second for four. The next ball we ran two. The ball after that a single. When I was again at the strike end I went for another big hit, missed and was stumped. When I came back up the pavilion steps one of the Sussex members quipped, 'Thirteen runs in five minutes? That's your trouble, Fred – too defensive when batting!'

Doug Padgett's innings I remember most of all. Doug made 79 and scored off every ball he received. You don't see that very often, not even in the new 'quickie' cricket! The Sussex skipper, Robin Marlar, set his field right back so that there were plenty of opportunities for singles and the occasional two and we took them. Bryan Stott ran so many singles and twos that, when he came into the dressing room, he was absolutely knackered, and spent five minutes with a cup of tea, sitting staring at the floor.

Given the years of dressing-room unrest and turmoil and the turnover in players, for us to win the Championship in Ronnie Burnet's second term as captain was a remarkable achievement. We had not been handed it on a plate, either. Every member of that side had really grafted. There were several games when we had to chase runs against the clock, culminating in the Augean task we were set at Hove. We showed great resolve, character, spirit, determination and not a little ability at cricket. It was the first time the club had won the Championship outright since 1946. What was of most importance to me was not what we had achieved, but how we had achieved it, the way Ronnie Burnet had galvanized a team in transition, the 'all for one and one for all' mentality we had all adopted.

I never felt the Yorkshire committee fully appreciated the renaissance that had taken place in the dressing room, nor the Herculean effort on the part of the players, a view enhanced when today I look back at the committee's message to the team in the annual report. It's a model of restraint: 'Your Committee heartily congratulates the team upon winning the Championship and upon the entertaining cricket played throughout the season, and feels that Mr Burnet's leadership played a great part in the Team's success.' They could say that again. And again and again.

On a personal level I received countless telegrams of congratulations, though one in particular both delighted and saddened me. It read: 'Best Wishes and Well Done – Johnnie.'

We celebrated our success at Hove, of course, but the champagne didn't flow as we had to travel to Scarborough that night, which was one dickens of a drive in pre-motorway Britain. The opportunity for the team to pay our tribute to Ronnie came at Scarborough. We had all piled in cars and driven in crocodile fashion up the north-east coast for the first game of the Scarborough Festival. We were playing the MCC – and Ronnie had been selected to play for the MCC.

'This isn't on,' we told him. 'Convey your apologies, do what you must, but you're not playing for the MCC. You have led this team to the Championship, we want you to lead the champions out to play in their next game.'

Vic Wilson, destined to be the club's first professional captain, took Ronnie's place in the MCC team, and Ronnie Burnet led his lads out at Scarborough. It was only right and proper that we should be behind him, because we had been right behind him from the day he was appointed as captain. Our game against the MCC was indicative of many of the games we'd played that season. We were set 260 to win in little over two hours and twenty minutes and we did it with twenty-five minutes and 7 wickets to spare.

I was selected for the 1959–60 England tour of the West Indies. Obviously I was happy, but I couldn't help but remember the unpleasantness of my last time there. Having said that, I was older, wiser and had gained a certain kudos in the game.

I was determined to steer clear of trouble and controversy. The tour turned out to be a good and happy one, not least because we had a good tour manager in Walter Robins.

Walter was a decent, fair-minded guy, the only MCC mandarin I had ever warmed to and got along with. He had a tremendous sense of humour and knew how to handle people when difficult situations arose, as they always do on tours. Walter had respect for all players and, as such, the players respected him.

There is not much privacy when you're on tour. With no home to retreat to, players live cheek by jowl with one another for months. Seeing the same seventeen faces every day at breakfast, lunch, dinner then over a drink in the hotel lounge bar at night can be a bit trying for everyone. There's friction, undercurrents; the pressure of restraining oneself day after day and the irritation of this gathers as the tour wears on. Invariably, the weather is sweltering, wives, partners and children are being missed, and there's always one player who is having a hard time of it where it matters most – out on the pitch.

Players become frustrated. Weary of the constant travel and living out of a suitcase. You stay in the best hotels, but after a time, one hotel looks just like another. There is fraught tension, occasionally tempers crack, and things are said that people don't really mean. Unless somebody in a position of authority has the nous to spot problems early and, just as importantly, the courage to deal with them properly and fairly, a tour can be a disaster. Walter Robins possessed that nous and courage, which made a welcome change. His tour management style played no small part in making the winter tour of 1959–60 one of the best I was ever involved in.

I was really on top form on this tour. It was not only a successful tour off the pitch but also on it, as we won the series, even though skipper Peter May took ill and had to hand the captaincy over to Colin Cowdrey. Colin was a superb batsman and one of the best slip fielders in the world, but I'm afraid my opinion of him as a captain didn't amount to much.

I took 37 wickets at an average of 23.86. I chipped in with 16 catches and batting in my normal position at number ten had an average of just under 14 – though we had the usual run-ins with the West Indian umpires. Umpires, like football referees, have a thankless task and are a strange breed. In Britain we have for many a decade boasted the best umpires in the world. In my experience as a player those in Australia could go either way. In India they were dreadful, but by far the worst I encountered where those in the West Indies. In one match I managed to find a damp patch on the pitch and made the ball rear up. It whacked one batsman on the glove and the catch was taken at short leg. But the umpire shook his head to indicate not out. When I protested he said the ball had hit the batsman's thigh pad.

'Thigh pad?' I queried. 'You don't normally find a thigh pad in front of a batsman's throat!'

Then I pointed to the batsman in question, who had taken his glove off and was rubbing his bruised hand. These were the days when just about every batsman would 'walk' if he got an edge – even when the umpire or opposing team were not aware of the fact. Australian players, however, would often stand if the edge was just the merest of a tickle in the hope of a not-out decision. For a batsman to remain at the crease when given out by an umpire, however, breaks the greatest unwritten law of the game.

The batsman I had rapped on the glove rubbed his hand, put his glove back on, casually surveyed the field and, casual as you like, prepared to bat on. This guy was so blasé that, with my very next delivery, I found the damp patch again and with some pace. The ball reared up, his reactions were too slow and it hit him square in the mouth. He had to be carried from the field and never returned to the crease. Colin Cowdrey was skipper that day and expressed his concern about what I'd done.

'Did you hit that man on purpose?' asked Colin.

'I never hit him,' I replied. 'The ball did.'

Although cowardice is no excuse, I did feel some sympathy for the West Indian umpires, who were occasionally in danger from some of the crowd. On our previous tour there had been a riot in the third Test at Georgetown. Some of the crowd were so incensed with one umpire, they followed him home and the police had to stand guard outside his house! We too witnessed a riot on this tour in Trinidad. The West Indians really love their cricket. It's their national game, they are very knowledgeable about it, and when they pay their hard-earned money to see a match they expect not only a full day's entertainment but some excitement too. The culture of the West Indian supporters in those days was to meet up prior to a game, enjoy a few 'Red Stripes', place a few bets, then set off for the game with a view to enjoying themselves seeing their team wipe the floor with the opposition.

They came to the Trinidad Test in their thousands. The ground was filled to capacity, and those locked out contrived to watch the game from any vantage point they could. They stood on the roofs of nearby buildings and even climbed the many trees that overlooked the stadium. As the game progressed and England took the upper hand the atmosphere changed from merely charged to volatile. A few beer bottles were thrown onto the pitch by unruly fans disgusted with their team's performance. It wasn't long before those odd beer bottles turned into a cascade of glass.

I was fielding near the boundary and became really concerned for my safety. But one fan called out to me, 'Don't you worry, Fred, we ain't gonna touch you, man. We want them umpires.' It became very ugly and there was no way the teams could continue playing. We left the field as calmly and as orderly as we could as the riot police streamed onto the pitch to rescue the umpires. Play was held up for quite some time but not enough to prevent England achieving another comfortable victory.

Yet again I was the workhorse of the team on tour. I deposited so much sweat in the dust of the pitch it could have created a decent damp patch to get the ball rearing. Only Ray Illingworth with his off-spin bowled more overs than me, but I finished as England's leading wicket-taker and set a record for the most wickets taken by an English bowler in the West Indies. My total career record of Test wickets at this stage stood at 149. I was immensely pleased with myself, because I had now passed Hedley Verity's record of 137. Hedley Verity was a name constantly mentioned in the pavilion at Headingley as being one of the greatest Yorkshire bowlers of all time. When I returned to the club following the winter, I heard a couple of committee members describing Hedley as the county's greatest ever Test bowler.

'Excuse me, gentlemen,' I said, 'sorry to interrupt your conversation, but I couldn't help but overhear what you were saying about Hedley Verity. Hedley was indeed a great bowler, but I've overhauled his record of Test wickets.'

'That's as maybe,' replied one committee man, 'but you must realize you are playing more Tests than Hedley Verity.'

'I beg your pardon yet again,' I said, 'but I have some knowledge of the history of cricket and that of this club in particular. In actual fact Hedley Verity had played in more Tests than me at that stage.'

The committee man in question just wouldn't have it. He disputed this fact, and what's more, neither he nor his colleague made any mention of my tally of Test wickets being any sort of achievement at all. It left me shaking my head. Even though I had 149 Test wickets, and had done more than my fair share to make Yorkshire a top county again, those two committee members would not admit that I was anywhere near as good a bowler as the old timers. In fact from the inference of their conversation I gained the impression that they didn't believe me to be a top-class bowler at all. That was Yorkshire cricket club in those days. Those who ran the club could make you feel unappreciated and miserable even when you were taking on and beating the best in the world.

My career as cricketer was at its height. Yorkshire retained the County Championship in some style in 1960. I was hailed as the best fast bowler in the world. I had achieved my dreams but I would not be allowed to fully appreciate or celebrate my success . . .

Though things could not have gone better for me career-wise, my home life – and particularly my relationship with Enid – was not good. At first I didn't realize it, but slowly it became apparent my marriage was breaking up. Looking back now, I feel there was an inevitability about it. The first five or so years of our marriage passed by happily. We were in love and like all couples we had defined our own type of love. I've learned from life that love can take many forms. There is the grand passion which is electric, stimulating and fulfilling. But that sort of love simply can't be all enduring all the time. There is also another type of love in a long-term relationship. Though it does not involve grand passion, it is stronger, in many ways more comforting. It's the companionable love in a relationship that does the ironing, gets the weekly shopping in, knows what clothes to buy for the children. A love which checks the car insurance and never forgets birthdays. Which remembers to answer letters, pay the window cleaner and which day the bin men will call when there is a Bank Holiday. It deals with dentists and doctors. Knows what day the children have to take their PE kit to school and when they are appearing in a school play or church festival. A love that provides a strong foundation to the flimsy multi-layered structure of day-to-day life. It's a perceptive and common-sense love that knows which picture should go where, what curtains go with the three-piece, what colour the bathroom should be painted. The love that decorates your dull facade, that delves into the toolbox and applies the nuts and bolts to keep yourself together.

This love is more important than the grand passion, but sometimes it isn't enough to keep two people together. Not when the mundane nature of that love conspires to change how one person feels about the other. Before I met her, Enid had enjoyed a full social life. She liked parties, having a fun time and was a very good dancer. For a time, while bringing up our young child, she had forsaken that lifestyle. But as the years went by and we had more children, as they got a little older she yearned to be out having fun again, to escape from the daily tasks of bringing up young children and dealing with a husband who spent too much time away from home. Enid wanted to get out and about at night when the opportunity allowed, to go dancing and partying. I, on the other hand, had no desire at all to go skipping round a dance floor or make small talk at parties with people I barely knew.

It wasn't that I was unsociable. I'm a very sociable person with, I have often been told, a very keen sense of humour. I liked a good time as much as the next person, but after a hard few days playing cricket preferred to relax at home before setting off again for another match. I was, however, mindful of the needs of Enid and worked hard to make our marriage a good one. I had been raised to believe in the virtues of family life and to regard marriage as a 'contract' for life. All the money I earned I did so for Enid, the children and our home. I never gambled, indulged in 'lads' nights out', took drugs, or spent money at night clubs. My only indulgence was a sports car – but I felt I needed fast transport. Living in Scarborough made life difficult for me as a husband and father even when I was playing in Yorkshire. For example, Sheffield is a hundred miles away from Scarborough, and such was the infrastructure of roads in the country at that time it took me two and a half hours to drive from Bramall Lane to my home. When Yorkshire were playing at one of the principal grounds in the county such as Sheffield, Leeds or Bradford, I would leave home at eight a.m. in order to arrive at around ten-thirty. Then, after a hard day bowling fast, I would drive back to Scarborough, arriving just in time to go to bed. It wasn't much of a lifestyle, but I put up with it willingly in the interests of marital happiness and the fact I didn't like to stay overnight in a hotel and be away from my family.

Looking back, how I managed to sustain this lifestyle for so long I don't know. I guess it must say something about my love of my family and my physical and mental strength that I managed a five-hour round trip and to bowl between twenty and thirty overs flat out all in the same day, day after day. And the six-month winter tours with England also placed a tremendous strain on the marriage. I don't think there are figures readily available for the number of divorces in the various sporting professions, but I should imagine the highest is that of cricketers. As Graham Thorpe and many others have found, there is no way you can be a husband and father at a distance of 12,000 miles, even speaking daily on the telephone. The situation regarding cricketers on an International tour and their families is now much better than it was in my day. Wives – and children – are now invited to accompany their husbands on a part of the tour. Winter tours are now organized in such a way they allow for England players to be flown home to be with their families for Christmas and New Year. And, of course, the world has shrunk in terms of travel from one country to another. In the past the England team travelled to Australia, New Zealand or India by boat. A winter tour could last six months as opposed to two or three months as is the case today.

A lot of people I met envied me for the fact that I spent the English winter on the other side of the world. They seemed to think I spent most of my time abroad lying at the side of a swimming pool or attending cocktail parties held in the open air on sultry nights. There was an element of that, but it was only small. Touring was really hard work. Fast bowling in high temperatures and humidities I found to be harder graft than working down a pit. I spent many a long evening alone in my hotel room reading books, fiddling with the air conditioning and wondering what Enid was up to at home and what my children were doing, all the time wishing that I was sitting alongside Enid on the sofa, in front of a crackling log fire, that we were enjoying a drink together and exchanging the news from our respective days.

There is also temptation when you are on tour. Cricketers are healthy, fit young guys, and when you are used to the joy of the physical side of a relationship, it is frustrating to go without sex for six months. You try not to think about it, but if a pretty young girl comes on to you, you can't help but think about it. I managed to control myself, but I knew plenty who did succumb to temptation. Though the gentleman players didn't have that worry: they enjoyed privileges that were denied us pros – including bringing their wives. Again, one rule for one, a different rule for another.

Enid never questioned my fidelity. There were plenty of things that did cause arguments, but that was never an issue. She understandably got uptight at not being able to live a reasonable life with me. That unrest eventually affected life when I was at home. All manner of things contrived to make her annoyed, sometimes, angry. Sometimes I felt I could never do anything right. The phone would ring often, and people were forever calling round to see me – me, not us. One thing that did anger her was that her name would often not be included on the invitations to parties and social functions. If the invitation didn't mention me by name only, invariably it read, 'Fred Trueman and Guest'.

It annoyed Enid and I can understand why. At one stage I refused to go anywhere unless she was officially included, and when given prior notice of an invitation would be at pains to tell whoever was issuing the invite, 'My wife's name is Enid by the way.' Another problem was my fame. When we did attend social functions or parties, people would talk to me and totally ignore her, or drag me off to meet someone else, leaving Enid with no one to talk to. No self-respecting woman is going to stand for that, especially as we spent so long apart, and so the rows started.

There were always people around when we needed to be on our own, enjoying quality time with one another. For example, I had been playing for England against the West Indies at Edgbaston and had broken another record when skittling them out. Enid came to meet me, full of affection and happiness for me. I always considered my success to be our success, I too wanted to savour the moment with just Enid. She arrived at the hotel expecting just me to be there, hoping we could go out for a meal together and celebrate. She couldn't get near because of the press and a crowd of well-wishers. When I came to meet her I was besieged. I could see her at the back of all these people.

I was in turmoil. Trying to say 'thank you' to the well-wishers while at the same time trying to force my way through their number to Enid. She lost her temper in front of everybody. I heard her shout, 'One day you'll come home without your bloody friends all hanging on your back.' Before I could reach her, she turned round and stormed out. I was upset and disappointed in her at the time, but I can now understand why she reacted in such a way.

This was not the only public example of her unhappiness. I was the subject of a BBC programme about my life, and in keeping with many programmes of the time this show was live. Naturally Enid was invited to take part and had a right go at me. In front of several million people she said how impossible it was to have a normal marriage and home life when married to Freddie Trueman. I didn't like what she said, but I have never held it against her. No woman could have coped with being my wife at that time. After Enid had said her piece the presenter tried to make light of it by telling the viewers, 'What you are seeing is how difficult it can be, being married to a star in sport.' What they were seeing was a marriage crumbling apart.

The arguments became more frequent. When Enid and I exchanged words there was sometimes direct anger, and when we weren't arguing, there was distended anger. She was so cross with me, or rather the effect my lifestyle was having on our relationship and family life, she would get on to me over something trivial, such as how I set the table for lunch. It wasn't Enid's fault we were breaking up, and, aside from the inadvertent pressure of my career, nor was it mine. You could well say it was the fault of us both and you may be right in thinking that, but I think we were victims of circumstance. If I'd had a normal nine 'til five job where I was at home much more, I would not have been happy either, because the fact that I was not achieving my goals in life would have been eating away at me. I felt I had been blessed with a talent and I wanted to pursue and explore it.

On occasions Enid and I would row, and when I'd had enough of rowing I'd storm out of the house and spend the night in my car. There was one notable occasion when I was playing against Australia at Headingley in 1961. On the Saturday afternoon I took 6 wickets for one run to put them all out. The press called it the finest piece of bowling ever to be seen in a Test. I sat there after the match, smoking my pipe and drinking a cup of tea with dozens of people from television, radio and the press queuing to interview me. When I left the ground there were so many autograph hunters and well-wishers it took me twenty minutes to reach my car. As I finally swung out of the car park, I wondered what all those people would have thought if they had known I'd spent the previous night sleeping on the back seat of my car in a Leeds car park with my overcoat for a blanket, following another sad and heated argument with Enid. On the morning of my success against the Australians I'd arrived at Headingley before anyone else so that I could shower, shave and change my clothing in order to make my outward appearance normal.

For some time my address was The Car, Yorkshire Dales. The fact I never rented a flat or booked into a hotel, I suppose, must say something about my state of mind at this time. Though fully aware that my marriage to Enid was effectively over, perhaps the fact that I had not rented a flat suggests I wasn't ready to let go. As I have previously said, I was brought up to respect family values, to consider marriage was for life. That my marriage was effectively over came as a great jolt to me and my state of mind, and deep down I was hanging on not so much to my marriage with Enid as to the values I held dear.

Eventually I came to terms with it all. It had been painful for Enid and it had been painful for me. People can only take so much inner pain. So one day, after another argument, I walked out intending that it would be final and booked into a hotel near Skipton, vowing to start my life all over again. But some weeks later I returned to the family home to see our daughter, Karen. When I walked in and set eyes on Enid, my stomach turned somersaults – I could see that she was expecting. At first I pretended I hadn't noticed. All manner of thoughts were cart-wheeling around in my head, all manner of emotions searing through my body. Eventually Enid said, 'I have something to tell you.'

I told her no words were necessary on her part because I knew. We talked and talked. The result of our talking was that I checked out of the hotel and moved back home. The love we felt for one another had waned, but there was just enough for us to decide we wanted to make another go of it.

Enid gave birth to twins Rebecca and Rodney. We did our best to make it all work, but it was a case of papering over not so much cracks as chasms. We bought another, bigger, house in Scarborough and tried hard to make life happy for us both, but the damage was irreparable. After a year or so, I realized our marriage was never going to work.

Enid and I were living out a lie. We weren't being true to one another and we weren't being true to ourselves. Yet we stuck it out for another six years. We'd take the children on holiday, or perhaps down to the local park of an afternoon. I'd see other couples on family outings and envied their joy and happiness. Outwardly we appeared to be a perfectly normal, happy family. But Enid and I were merely acting out our roles. As with all parents our love for our children was unconditional. We adored them. But Enid and I neither loved nor adored one another. Many was the time I felt, 'Why can't I have personal happiness as well as the fantastic success I'm enjoying as a cricketer?' There were times when I simply believed you couldn't have both, that life simply couldn't be that generous. I appreciated my success as a cricketer. I should have been celebrating it. My success should have made me joyous, but it never did, because of the pain inflicted upon me by my private life.

Looking back, I don't know how I managed to keep playing to the standard I did. The game has been a good friend to me but at no time more so than when I was going through the latter stages of my marriage to Enid. Cricket was my escape from the torture and pain.

Eventually I made the monumental decision to break with Enid for good. That was difficult enough, but not as difficult as the mechanics of the break-up itself. In many respects saying 'I want us to split up' is the easy part. Night after night I sat alone in hotels or the houses of close friends and cried like a child. I was convinced that life for me was finished. That there was nothing for me to look forward to. In truth I had very few close friends that I could open up to. Over the years, I'd made a concerted and successful effort to build a wall to keep people out.

I describe this as one long period in my life, not only to show the whole story, but also for you to realize the personal background to my career in cricket. When I left Enid, I was retired from cricket, so I no longer had the game to occupy my thoughts or provide me with an escape. The end of the sixties was a desperate period for me. My life was in crisis. The thought of living without the day-to-day contact with my children was unbearable. I was beside myself worrying about the effect the split would have on them. Not just at that present time or in the immediate future, but long term.

I wondered what they would think of me when they grew up. I had loved and respected my father and still do. I wanted them to love and respect me throughout their lives, but tortured myself wondering how this could be possible given the circumstances. Children have always got through to me. However, you never truly appreciate your feelings for children in general until you've had children of your own. I found I couldn't walk by a child who was crying without my heart going out to them.

Perhaps this is one of the reasons I have involved myself in raising countless thousands of pounds over the years for children's charities. This is one side to me which I normally keep quiet, but this book is my life story and my work for charity has played a key role in my life. My affiliation to children's charities was not through guilt I may have felt from my split with Enid. It began when I was a colt trying to make the grade at Yorkshire.

One of my coaches, Maurice Leyland, was full of ideas to encourage my career and made a habit of striking small bets with me. Maurice believed I could get a lot more runs with the bat and started wagering a pint that I wouldn't score a half-century one season. I have told you, I have never been a betting man, but a pint in those days was a matter of pence and as the bet was over a season I saw no harm in taking Maurice up on his offer. I won that bet and the following year he bet a packet of pipe tobacco and a pint that I couldn't score another fifty and take 10 wickets in a match. I won again. Next time he bet a stone of humbugs I wouldn't get a half-century and take 6 wickets in one innings, both in the same match. The first game we played that season was against Hampshire at Bradford, and I took 6 wickets very cheaply which left us chasing 114 for the bonus points. Johnnie Wardle was acting captain that day and he sent me in at number four with the instruction to 'have a go'. We needed 52 runs and I scored them all.

Our next match was at Harrogate, and when Maurice turned up he was carrying a bag containing a stone of humbugs. I don't know how but the press got to know about our little bet and worked up quite a story about it. That led to every sweet and toffee manufacturer in Yorkshire – and there were a lot of them – sending humbugs and other sweets with their compliments to the Harrogate ground. You could scarcely move in the dressing room for the things. There were humbugs and sweets in tins, boxes, jars, cartons – even a hundredweight sack. I gave some to my teammates to take home for their children, the office and ground staff helped themselves, but it still left countless tins, boxes, jars and the sack untouched.

I was at a loss as to what to do with all these sweets when one of the ground staff said there was a home for physically disabled children at nearby Killinghall and that the sweets might go down well with the children. I rang the matron and she said she would be glad to have them – on condition that I came along to present them. I loaded the sweets into my car and drove over that very day. What awaited me was an experience that has lived with me to this day.

The sight of these children tore at my heart. I walked about offering the sweets to these unfortunate children, when I came across a small boy who was encased in what to me appeared to be like a clothes horse made of tubular steel. If he wanted to move he had to grip one side and make it open to push one leg forward, then grip the other side of this framework to bring his other leg along. He walked up to me in this fashion and at first I was at a loss as to what to say. So I simply said, 'And how are you, son?'

He replied, 'I'm all right, thank you, Mr Trueman.'

Then I asked him if he was doing well.

'You bet,' he said. 'Next year I'm going to win the London to Brighton road race.'

That was too much for me. My eyes welled with tears. I patted him on the head.

'You do that,' I told him. 'I bet you could do anything if you put your mind to it . . .'

My words trailed away. I couldn't bring myself to talk any more. I couldn't stay any longer. The matron guided me out of the room and once outside my tears flowed. The matron told me that she understood. That experience marked me for life. I left that home swearing that if I did anything for charity then it would be for children, and made a solemn promise to myself that I would. If that little lad is still around I should like him to know that what he said to me that grey, wet afternoon so many years ago has helped raise not thousands but millions of pounds for children's charities.

A man often feels love the most when he is faced with the reality of losing the woman he loves. There was an element of this in my decision to finally split with Enid. But only an element, as I had by now resigned myself to the fact it was all over between us. When a couple in a long-term relationship misunderstand each other and misinterpret one another's actions, when, for whatever reason, they are unable to communicate their thoughts and feelings to one another on a daily basis, they are unable to successfully nurture each other and fulfil one another's needs. Basically, that's what happened between Enid and me. There is never a single reason for a break-up. There may be one reason in particular, but it is always joined by other, more minor things, the culmination of which renders the relationship irreparable.

Our divorce went through as quietly as possible for someone as well known as me. No other parties were involved. There was no fighting over tea spoons or who was entitled to what. Our marriage hadn't worked but Enid and I set out to try to make the divorce work. We were both perfectly reasonable about it. We'd both had our fill of arguments and pain and neither of us wanted any more.

I went to ground in the Yorkshire Dales, partly because I love the area, partly because living there I could avoid the press and everyone else. I found a house in an isolated spot, set within a wood on the fringe of the Dales, and set about trying to rebuild my life. Enid is a very kind and generous person who I could never fault as a mother to our children. For a good amount of the time we had together I loved her very much. Living alone in the Dales and without the day-to-day discipline and involvement of life as a cricketer to occupy me, this transitional period in my life was very difficult. The relief I felt at having been freed from a marriage that wasn't working was tempered by my regret that it hadn't worked. I was forty and believed I had little chance of starting all over again with someone else. I kept in touch with Enid. I had to, because I wanted to see the children as often as possible.

Splitting up with someone with whom you have had a long-term relationship is like a bereavement. There are processes one must go through. There are some days when you feel you are coping, that you're getting through it all remarkably well, only for these days to be followed by days when the pain racks your stomach so much you have to force yourself to eat a meal. I experienced so many days like that I shed pounds.

To heal the hurt in your heart you must feel it, but also recognize that it belongs to your past. Eventually I began to realize this. I didn't love Enid any more, but in a sense still loved her for the good times we'd had together. I never hated or even resented Enid. Far from it. I was just so terribly sad that things had not worked out between us and that our feelings for one another had changed. Though I could not possibly be aware of it at the time, this state of mind was to be my saving grace.

When I first took to the Dales I promised myself that I would never marry again. Never again develop a relationship with someone whereby I'd commit my heart and soul and in so doing make myself so vulnerable. You should never make promises like that to yourself. Along with the birth of my children, the best thing that was ever to happen to me in life was when I broke that promise.

I am not a great believer in fate. I believe in God. For a time I believed I could never meet anyone again with whom I could fall in love. But it happened. I don't know if it had to do with God or fate. All I know now is, Enid and I weren't meant to be. Someone else was meant for me – and I was meant for her.

Enid still lives in Scarborough. She never remarried and to the best of my knowledge has never taken up with anyone in a serious way. Though our love had died it was very important to me to put into a place a system of support for Enid and our children. My children have children of their own now, but my financial and, when required, emotional support for Enid has never wavered. My marriage to Enid did not work, but we did make the divorce work. Good endings make good beginnings.

CHAPTER TEN

TIME, GENTLEMEN, PLEASE

FORTUNATELY NONE OF the personal problems I encountered during the sixties, marital or otherwise, ever affected my performance on the field. There were times when the combined pressures of my marriage breaking down and constant hostility from the cricketing establishment sorely tested my spirit and resolve, but when I crossed the boundary rope there was only ever one thing occupying my mind – how to bowl out the opposition as quickly as possible.

Just as there were times when I felt I couldn't do anything right in the eyes of Enid, also there were times when I felt the same regarding the MCC. The harder I tried in matches, the more certain people in the cricketing establishment appeared to put me down. The more success I enjoyed, the more these people seemed to resent me. That's how I felt and I don't think it was a case of me having a chip on my shoulder. Countless players who were contemporaries of mine told me they thought the same.

There was an occasion when England were playing Australia at Headingley. Gubby Allen, an England selector, came down the nets, took out his handkerchief and put it down on the pitch at around a length.

'There you go Trueman,' he said, 'try and pitch the ball on that handkerchief. You're supposedly a good bowler, a good bowler would be able to do that time and again.'

A large crowd gathered to watch me endure this test. I couldn't understand why Gubby Allen was subjecting me to this and what he was hoping to achieve by it. Prior to a major International match he was subjecting one of the England players to an exercise in which he might fail? As it happened I didn't fail. I hit that handkerchief time and again but could have done without such pressure in front of a sizeable crowd of supporters before a Test match!

As if that wasn't bad enough, in front of the crowd of onlookers Allen commenced to tell me what I had to do to bowl out the Australians. If what he had said had been constructive, I would have taken it on board, but he was talking nonsense. It went in one ear and the other. I kept quiet because I had just got back into the England team and didn't want to be dropped yet again. I found the whole episode humiliating, but one person came to my aid. My old coach Bill Bowes witnessed what had gone on between Allen and me and said it all for me in his newspaper column the next day. Bill was not amused. Like me he couldn't understand the point of what Allen had done, other than to make me look small. In his newspaper article Bill pointed out that Gubby Allen had no right whatsoever to subject me to that kind of treatment. His final words I really appreciated. In making his point that I should not have been subjected to such an exercise, Bill wrote, 'particularly since he [Allen] never had any talent worth comparing to that of Freddie Trueman'.

I wasn't always able to keep silent and respectful during confrontations with members of the cricketing establishment. And, oddly enough, no matter how well I was playing following such an incident, invariably I would find myself dropped. There were numerous times when I'd be chatting to members of touring teams only to be told how astonished they were about the number of times I was dropped by England. The Australian bowler Neil Hawke once asked me why, so I told him, 'I believe it's to do with speaking my mind.'

Neil informed me an Australian player would never be dropped from the national team simply for speaking his mind, adding, 'If your selectors picked the England team purely on ability and form, you'd be a regular and getting on for half the current team wouldn't be in the side.'

Gubby Allen had another go at me a few days after I had passed the milestone of 200 Test wickets. I was practising in the nets at Lord's when he came up to me and asked why I took such a long run-up. He told me that when he was bowling for England, his run-up was only half that of mine and that he bowled just as quick as me.

'But how effective was your style?' I asked.

Allen asked me what I meant by this.

'Well, sir, with all due respect, I've studied Test match records over the years very carefully. Curiously, when it comes to taking wickets your name doesn't figure much.' I added that, whilst my name was listed as being among the four fastest bowlers of all time, his name was curiously absent.

He seemed rather upset at that fact and said, 'We can't tell you damn youngsters anything.'

I replied, 'That's not true, sir, but *you* certainly can't tell me anything about fast bowling.' Surprisingly, I was not dropped for the next England game!

Yorkshire began the 1960 season as reigning county champions, but without Ronnie Burnet. Ronnie had announced his retirement at the age of forty-one, believing the team needed a younger man. Ronnie's successor, Vic Wilson, the first professional captain of Yorkshire, was a wise appointment, one indicative of the changing nature of the game. Vic was a very tall, physically strong guy from Malton in the North Riding. The complexion of his face suggested a rude man of the open. He came from farming stock and looked the part. He was a very good, sometimes spectacular, left-hand batsman, especially when the ball didn't turn. His bravery and his huge hands – they were like shovels – made him a wonderful short-leg fieldsman. When the team heard of Vic's appointment as captain we were unanimous in our approval.

In each of the four seasons from 1959 to 1963 I bowled more than 1,000 overs. The most productive of the consecutive four-figure seasons was that of 1960. Despite the heartache of my private life, in terms of my career 1960 was a great year for me. I was the first player in the country to reach 100 wickets and ended the season with the grand total of 175, which was the highest tally of my career to date. What's more, those wickets cost only 13.98 runs a piece. I was living up to my nickname of 'Fiery Fred' and my efforts helped Yorkshire retain the Championship in Vic Wilson's first season of captaincy. This was some achievement as we contrived to win only one of eight games in July and consequently had some catching up to do. We did it, though we were helped by the fact that our closest competitors for the title, arch-rivals Lancashire, blew up during the run-in and failed to win any of their last six matches.

We had to beat Worcestershire at Harrogate in our last Championship game to retain the title. This game was touch and go throughout. A lot of time was lost to rain, the wicket was damaged and typically we found ourselves faced with another huge task. It is the mark of that Yorkshire side that, yet again, we rose to a big challenge to beat Worcestershire by 9 wickets. In addition to my success as a bowler I once more made a mockery of my position as a tail-end batsman, finishing the season with a batting average of 20.68, which included a top score of 69.

Vic Wilson proved himself a worthy successor to Ronnie Burnet. Vic handled me intelligently, using me at starts and restarts, asking me to take my sweater before I was tired and bringing me back when he felt my bowling was what was needed to penetrate. At times the procedure was varied, as at Taunton, when, in our penultimate county match, we were desperate for points to overhaul Lancashire. We had heard the weather forecast for the next few days and there was every likelihood of our last game against Worcestershire at Harrogate not going the distance or else being so affected by rain it would render a result impossible. It rained in Taunton and we didn't get the match under way until five p.m. on the first day. We were all out for 184, the damage in the main having been inflicted by that fine bowler and legend of Somerset cricket Bill 'Bowling' Alley. We hadn't made much of a total but I was determined to go out and bowl us to a first innings lead because we were desperate for bonus points. I bowled twenty-seven of the sixty overs possible and took 4 of the 5 Somerset wickets that fell – the other was a run-out – before the heavens opened and washed out the last day.

The county game I remember most from this year was our game against Lancashire at Old Trafford. As well as their traditional importance, the 'Roses' matches in 1960 were crucial to the outcome of the Championship. Our game against Lancashire in August drew 75,000 supporters over the three days. On each day Old Trafford was heaving with a mass of humanity and we were treated to the rare sight of the boundary rope being adjusted to accommodate more people around the perimeter of the pitch.

In those days a 'Roses' match took on all the fervour of a Liverpool–Everton 'derby' match in football and it was very much a 'private party', as the two clubs and their supporters turned their backs on the rest of cricket for three days and battled it out. A guy from Essex once found himself at a 'Roses' match and his indiscriminating applause finally brought instructions from both sets of supporters who told him, 'Hey! Keep out o' this. This has nowt to do with thee!'

Those who saw the grim, tight-lipped 'Roses' matches of the pre-war years will need no convincing about the truth of Emmott Robinson's terse summary of conversation on those occasions: 'We say "How do" int' morning and "Good neet" at t' close and in between all we say is "How's that?".'

The Second World War changed men and it changed their attitudes. After the war 'Roses' matches, like most other things, were different. The post-war matches brought together players and supporters who had spent long years serving alongside one another in Lancashire and Yorkshire regiments and it was difficult to recreate, never mind retain, the atmosphere of passionate rivalry between the two clubs that in the thirties bordered on hostility.

Nevertheless, the unique atmosphere of a 'Roses' match remained from the forties right through to the sixties. Gates were closed before eleven o'clock on the Saturday and more often than not on Monday as well. The players, while exchanging more in the way of conversation than simply 'How do' and 'Good neet', were, however, locked in combat from the moment the first ball was bowled. Personal rivalries were born and some of them stretched over the years and, in some cases, were taken to different counties when the respective players moved clubs.

In the mid-seventies, Leicestershire were playing Yorkshire at Bradford. Included in the Leicestershire side was Ken Higgs, not a native of Lancashire but a player who served the Red Rose county well for many a year and one who had experienced many a hostile 'Roses' match. And now he was bowling to an old adversary of his, Geoff Boycott.

Higgs caused a few playings and missings and suddenly he was transported. It was as if he was no longer wearing the leaping fox of the hunting shires on his shirt but the Red Rose of his former club. Higgs denounced Boycott with a tirade of language that would have embarrassed Bernard Manning. Boycott's reply was not exactly diplomatic either. The battle of words grew in intensity with every Higgs delivery, until umpire Don Oslear, in his first season on the county circuit, stepped in. Oslear spoke to Higgs. He then spoke to Boycott. It made not one iota of difference. Before Higgs delivered his next ball he issued a threat to Boycott. Boycott's reply was not essentially conciliatory. Following Higgs' delivery the two were at each other's throats again.

Don Oslear called a halt to proceedings and walked over to have a word with the Leicestershire captain – one Raymond Illingworth, himself a veteran of many a 'Roses' match. Oslear made it plain and simple to Ray that the swearing and threats between Higgs and Boycott had to stop – or else. Ray nodded and walked away. At the end of Higgs' over, Ray walked across to the other umpire, Cec Pepper, and said, 'Pep, do me a favour. Ask your mate over there not to interfere in private "Roses" battles.'

Earlier in the season Lancashire had triumphed over us, so we went to Old Trafford hell bent on turning the tables on them. The ground was full to capacity for each of the three days. Brian Statham and Ken Higgs did the damage. We were bowled out for 154 in the first innings.

Bob Barber and Alan Wharton reached an imposing 157 for Lancashire's second wicket before I got some reward for my efforts. I finished with 4 for 65 and Lancashire were all out for 226, a lead of 72. We batted marginally worse in our second innings and were bowled out for 149, with Brian Statham returning match figures of 9 for 66. It was the sort of situation which would have prompted many a county to make a token attempt to take wickets with their spearhead attack and then, as the situation became more hopeless, to introduce the more casual bowlers and concede victory. That was never us.

The Lancashire spinners had been amongst the wickets in our second innings and it would have been alien to all Yorkshire tradition to neglect our own spinners. So starting with spinners was certainly one of the tactics we discussed as we planned our strategy in the dressing room. Finally it was decided that to start with spinners carried too much of an element of risk and we decided upon a pace attack led by yours truly.

I was intent upon using every possible use of the lift that was in the pitch to give the Lancashire batsmen as much trouble as possible. As a team we had had to face some real tough tasks. Lancashire were a very good side, topping the county table at the time, and they only needed 78 to win. It's the mark of the confidence I had in myself and in my team-mates at that time that I thought, with their help, I could bowl Lancashire out for under 78. Realistically, we couldn't bowl them out, but we could hope to put them under pressure when they got behind the clock. Above all we wanted to prevent a Lancashire victory. That was the realist in me, the emotional side of me said, 'You can do it, Fred. You can bowl them out.'

My partner in attack was Mel Ryan, who had never won a regular place in the side and in fact only played a handful of matches each season. As such, his experience of bowling 'tight' at county standard was limited, but he bowled magnificently that day. Though Mel's fifteen overs cost 50 runs that wouldn't be considered particularly expensive in any other situation, he kept chipping in with wickets. At the other end I bowled a sixteen-over spell that I now consider as having been one of the best pieces of bowling in my entire career.

We set about the Lancashire batting in no uncertain terms. As the wickets went down, with their target of 78 getting ever closer by painful degrees, hopes began to rise on our side while panic set in on the other. No one in a packed Old Trafford left their seats. Just when I thought we could really do it, the Lancashire wicket-keeper, 'Chimp' Clayton, dashed my hopes. He had summoned 15 runs which were worth their weight in gold to his team, but he was at the non-striking end when the last ball was bowled at a quarter-past five. Lancashire were on 77 for eight – the scores level. A wicket would give us a valuable draw, a ball that didn't yield a run would give us a draw as well.

The field was distributed with painstaking care as I pre-pared to bowl the last delivery. The batsman was Jack Dyson, a dual-sportsman who also played football for Manchester City. We knew Jack wasn't particularly partial to my fast bowling, and it was apparent to me that he was all too acutely aware of the pressure that was on his shoulders. 'Chimp' Clayton stamped his feet at the bowler's end, no doubt wishing he had the strike.

Clayton was giving Dyson all manner of advice on what to do. There was a season's coaching in what he told Dyson for the sake of one ball. I took a deep intake of breath, gave Dyson a withering look before starting to walk back, and I think from that, he expected a bouncer.

That walk back was even longer than normal. I was going at a snail's pace because I was turning over in my mind what sort of delivery I should bowl. Finally I decided on that old standby, usually regarded as the classic delivery for such an occasion – a yorker. My mind was totally focused as I commenced my run-up, I could see in my mind's eye the bottom of the leg and middle-stump. It was as good a yorker as I have ever delivered but Dyson countered with the only possible effective answer. He shuffled forward, bat and pad close together, and somehow got an edge. It was an edge just thick enough to evade the diving Jimmy Binks and the ball joyously bounced on its way to the freedom of the fine-leg boundary.

As Disraeli once said, 'There are lies, damned lies and statistics.' The statistics in the 1960 Yorkshire handbook read: 'Yorkshire lost by two wickets at 5.15 p.m. on the third day.' It says nothing of the drama, the tension, the heartbreak, of one single delivery. My figures for that innings were sixteen overs, four maidens, 2 wickets for 28 runs. Though I only collected 2 wickets it was as good a spell of bowling as I ever produced, but I would have traded one or two more spectacular-looking Test analyses for a runs column that read 24 instead of 28! That was how important 'Roses' matches were back then – and that game in particular.

After the game I wound down by sitting in the dressing room and smoking my pipe. I was just about to have a shower when Brian Statham came in and said 'Bad luck, lads.' Brian came over and sat down next to me.

'Well, Fred, one of the best "Roses" matches I have ever seen. Certainly the best "Roses" match I've ever played in,' said Brian. 'And after that bowling performance by you and Mel Ryan, all I can say is, you didn't deserve to be on the losing side.'

We had lost the battle but our consolation was to be that we won the 'war' and retained the Championship at the expense of our closest rivals. It's odd, but the 'Roses mentality' lives with me still. Over forty years have passed since the 1960 season and when I look back on it now initially I think of it not as the season we retained the County Championship but as the time Lancashire recorded the 'double' over us.

When I think of 1960 now I can also readily recall taking 7 for 60 against Northamptonshire at Bramall Lane. It was a game that developed into a personal tussle of one-upmanship between Frank Tyson and me. Frank took 6 for 57 but I countered with 7 for 65 in Northamptonshire's second innings, giving me match figures of 14 for 125, which were the best of my career at that time. More importantly my bowling helped Yorkshire to a 6-wicket victory.

Just as important was our game against Surrey at the Oval. Surrey's domination of the Championship in the fifties did not sit well with Yorkshire folk. The fact that we had broken that domination was a great source of satisfaction to us. What's more, a Yorkshire victory at the Oval had become almost an emotional need. The Oval wicket was placid, and after I bowled Mickey Stewart for 12, Parsons and Fletcher held me up until almost lunchtime. I reduced my pace slightly in order to get more movement and it paid dividends. I tore down the Surrey innings to 123 and finished with figures of 7 for 43. Yorkshire declared on 434 for 4, thanks in the main to Brian Close, who hit a whirlwind 198, and Doug Padgett, who made a busy 177. Surrey offered sterner resistance in their second innings and made 312. I bowled thirty-six overs of real aggressive bowling and finished with figures of 7 for 82. In the process of winning the Championship we were also laying old ghosts to rest.

As my bowling had stepped up a gear, 1960 also saw me rather busy with the bat. Against Kent at Gravesend I hit five sixes and seven fours and against Leicestershire I halted a semi-collapse by scoring 52 in little over half an hour – a tally including four sixes and five fours. In our final match against Worcestershire, when we clinched the title, we were up against the clock and I feel I helped our cause somewhat by hitting five sixes and three fours when making a quick 56.

The summer of 1961 saw me take 155 wickets at an average of 19.35. Again I put up what I thought was a decent show with the bat. My season average was just under 20 with a top score of 80 not out. I believe I made a telling contribution to Yorkshire's seventeen Championship wins, which was a handsome tally, but not enough to win us the title. That went, to the surprise of many people, to Hampshire.

I played in four of the five Tests against the touring Australians. My performance in one Test prompted some newspapers to say I won the game almost single-handed. I took more wickets against Australia than any other bowler and only had one match when I didn't reach the lofty standards I had set for myself. That was in the fourth Test, and for the final Test at the Oval I was dropped! The fact that I was dropped, seemingly for producing a performance that most bowlers would have been satisfied with but that was not up to my usual high standards, hurt me. It once again reminded me that, though I was England's leading wicket-taker in the series, I was still not an automatic choice for the team.

Kent's Colin Cowdrey captained England in the first two Tests. The first Test at Edgbaston fizzled out into a draw. The second Test at Lord's was frustrating. Time and again when bowling Bill Lawry, Bill edged, played and missed but still survived. It was Napoleon who said, 'Give me my lucky generals.' Bill Lawry was Australia's 'lucky general', not only in the Lord's Test but throughout the series. Australia triumphed at Lord's. I took 6 wickets and Brian Statham 5, but Graham McKenzie and Alan Davidson ripped through what was fragile English batting. When Australia batted again needing only 71 to win, Brian and I displayed some of the mettle that had been lacking in our so-called specialist batsmen. At one stage we had Australia on 19 for 4, but we couldn't stop them winning by 5 wickets.

At Headingley Peter May assumed the captaincy for the first time since the second Test against the West Indies on the winter tour of 1958–9. Derbyshire's veteran Les Jackson was recalled to the England team for the first time in over twelve years, which prompted many a quip in the dressing room as to how the game had changed since the last time Les had played International cricket. As Les hovered, wondering where he should sit in the dressing room, the comments came: 'Sit down in the corner, Les, W. G. Grace isn't around any more,' 'You can tell how long it is since you last played for England, Les. Your National Insurance number is three,' 'How are you going to cope, Les, not having your old bowling partner Tom Richardson?' (Richardson played for England against Australia in 1912!)

Les took all the quips in good heart, but his recall after all those years wasn't quite a record. That eminent batsman George Gunn had a period of eighteen years between England appearances!

The Headingley pitch, with a number of whitish blotches, looked a strange one before the game even started. There was no bounce, pace or movement to it, which resulted in spinners on at both ends well before lunch.

Australia had lost three wickets when Les Jackson and I took the second new ball immediately after tea. Since the pitch had no pace, the experts present – and there are always plenty of them in a Headingley crowd – probably thought England should have stuck to the spinners. As soon as I picked up the first wicket – that of Norman O'Neill, who played too soon and edged an out-swinger into the hands of Colin Cowdrey – I felt a tremendous lift. I find it difficult to put into exact words the effect a first wicket had on me. Suffice it to say my confidence received a tremendous boost from being off the mark. The certain knowledge that it would not be a day when I would labour for no reward produced an edge to my bowling. I bowled with more verve and vivacity and, more often than not, a little more speed. I dropped one short to Neil Harvey, who turned the ball to leg, where my old room-mate Tony Lock took the speeding ball with hungry certainty. I missed a caught and bowled when Peter Burge hammered a delivery back at me. Though I got hand to the ball when diving at full length, I couldn't hold on to it.

The next over Les Jackson picked up the wicket of Peter Burge – caught in the gully. Simpson was the next to depart when I had him lbw. A similar fate then beset 'Tiger' Mackay off the bowling of Les Jackson. Australia were reeling and my tail was up. I bowled Richie Benaud then had Wally Grout caught at the wicket. All this happened in the space of an hour. Having been 183 for 2 at tea, Australia now found themselves on 208 for 9. The Aussie tail-enders Graham McKenzie and Alan Davidson did a bit of wagging before spinner David Allen had McKenzie caught at the wicket. Australia were all out for 237 and I had figures of 5 for 58. Naturally I was delighted with my performance, especially as a number of people believed the Headingley wicket would be of little help to me.

On a pitch from which the dust rose more sharply than the ball England made 299, which gave us a first innings lead of 62. When Australia batted again they were 13 for one when Peter May dropped Neil Harvey off my bowling. May then decided to use spin at one end and pace at the other before opting for spin at both ends.

I was itching to get back on as I felt I could make the breakthrough with a spell of off-cutters. Peter May, however, stuck with the spinners. It was originally only to allow the spinners to change ends that May recalled me to bowl, the instruction being I would bowl just the one over.

When I delivered the third ball of the over, Neil Harvey, batting with all his usual grace and aplomb, went to drive, but the stroke was too early. The ball didn't turn, it simply held up, and Ted Dexter at cover took the catch. I think that single delivery was the tipping moment in that game. It filled the Australians with misgivings and their earlier assuredness was not evident in the batsmen that followed. I perceived this more or less straight away and couldn't wait to get at them. I reduced my run-up a little but not my pace and aimed at the dust patches on and outside the right-hander's off-stump.

Norman O'Neill edged an in-swinger to Colin Cowdrey at short leg; I clean bowled Simpson. The wicket of Richie Benaud followed, when I bowled him through the gate with an acute off-cutter. Then 'Tiger' Mackay edged on to John Murray behind the stumps. I'd bowled twenty-seven deliveries and had taken 5 Australian wickets for no runs. Australia had collapsed from 99 for 2 to 109 for 8. I felt very proud when my England teammates stood aside and applauded me up the pavilion steps at tea with the cheers of the Headingley faithful ringing in my ears.

After Les Jackson bowled Wally Grout. I took the wicket of Alan Davidson to finish with figures of 6 for 30 and match figures of 11 for 88. England only needed 59 for victory and to square the series, which was accomplished without appreciable difficulty.

In praising England and our victory a number of news-papers singled out Peter May for specific praise on his return as skipper. Saying his decision to dispense with the spinners and call me on to bowl my off-cutters was, as the *Daily Sketch* put it, 'an inspired piece of captaincy'. In truth it was pure serendipity as far as Peter's captaincy was concerned. Yet for all my efforts, all the praise from the MCC mandarins was reserved for Peter May. I can't say that upset me, but it did disappoint me. I wondered what on earth I had to do to have an MCC selector simply say, 'Well done, Fred.'

Should an England bowler produce such a performance against Australia today – or any International side – he would be guaranteed his place in the Test team for some games to come. England lost the Old Trafford Test due, in the main, to ineffective batting when faced with Benaud and Simpson, but I was the player dropped for the final Test at the Oval.

At Old Trafford Les Jackson was replaced by Worcestershire's Jack Flavell. Apparently, when told he was not to figure in the next Test at Old Trafford, Les was informed that he was merely being 'rested'. Rested for a game that would determine the outcome of the Ashes? Les was given the assurance that his England career wasn't over, and to await a future call. To this day, he's still waiting for the phone to ring.

I greatly admired Les Jackson as a bowler and a man. He gave his all for Derbyshire and all for the equivalent of fifty quid a month. There was no secret to his success as a bowler other than his penchant for holding the ball in one position with the seam between the two main fingers and the thumb underneath. The only other Jackson trait was in his action, his arm being a little higher or lower in accordance with the circumstances. Having joined Derbyshire immediately after the Second World War, he continued to give sterling service until his retirement in 1963, holding all the main club records as a bowler. When he retired from cricket he went to work for the National Coal Board in Mansfield as a driver and eventually ended up working as the chauffeur to one of the directors of the NCB.

Les was a super bowler and a great servant of both Derbyshire and, when called upon every decade or so, England. Why he was never chosen more often for England is a mystery to me to this day. Quite simply, any number of bowlers

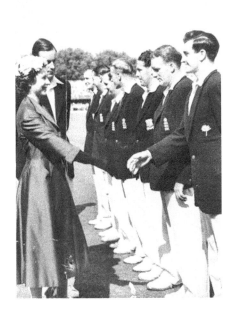

21. *Above, left.* I'm a patriot through and through and consider it a real honour that I have had the opportunity to meet Her Majesty the Queen on several occasions.

22. *Above, right.* With John Nash and Norman Yardley at Headingley.

23. *Below.* The team that retained the ashes in 1953. Skipper Len Hutton is seated centre front.

24. After taking my 300th Test wicket.

25. Posing for the *Sunday People*. The told me if I broke the record on the Saturday they could get an exclusive photo, and they'd send me a case of champagne. This is the exclusive photo and the champagne duly arrived!

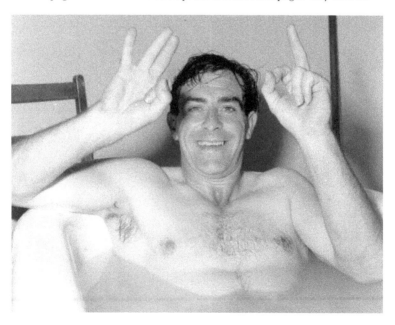

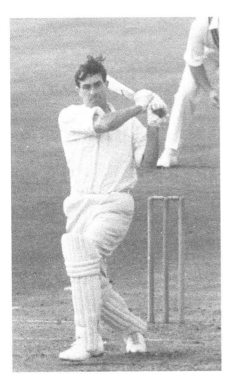

26. *Above, left.* I have never been described as an all-rounder, but for a supposed tail-ender I had a very respectable average.

27. *Above, right.* What I did best – bowling.

28. *Below.* Taking a catch in the slips during a Yorkshire practice session.

29. After beating the Aussies – as captain of Yorkshire I was especially proud. It also marked the time that I began to think of retiring.

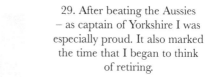

30. *Above*. With Enid after the birth of Karen.

31. *Right*. With Rodney and Rebecca in our Scarborough garden.

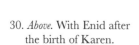

32. My first new career – as a stand-up.

33. And as an actor! I was honoured to be part of an episode of *Dad's Army*.

34. With Tom Graveney. I was delighted when Tom was appointed President of the MCC in 2004. The first former pro cricketer to be appointed to the position.

35. The *Test Match Special* team, not long before I was axed by the BBC. Seated front row to my right are Trevor Bailey and Christopher Martin-Jenkins. Back row, third from right, is 'The Bearded Wonder', *TMS* statistician Bill Frindal.

36. *Above. The Conversation Piece*, which hangs in the Long Room at Lords, the setting for the painting itself. Left to right: Godfrey Evans, Trevor Bailey, Peter May, Brian Statham, Denis Compton, Alec Bedser, Colin Cowdrey, me, Ted Dexter and Tom Graveney.

37. *Below, left.* With my hero, Harold Larwood, in Sydney, where he settled following his retirement from the game.

38. *Below, right.* With Raquel Welch at my daughter's wedding.

39. *Above.* After seeing the plight of disadvantaged children at a young age, I've tried whenever possible to help out. This was taken after a successful fund-raising effort for a local charity. Far left is Gordon Strachan and on my right is former Leeds and Great Britain Rugby League captain, Garry Schofield.

40. *Left.* A kiss from Veronica, the love of my life, after collecting my OBE, which I was given to believe by Denis Thatcher was awarded for my services to charity and not cricket.

41. *Below.* The box in which my mother kept all my press cuttings. I only recently rediscovered it and it's a treasure trove of old memories.

chosen ahead of him in the fifties were only half the bowler Les Jackson was.

The fact that I was dropped for the Oval Test further proved to me – if it needed proving – that the selectors had little clue about what they were doing. I'd taken 20 wickets in four Tests, and though I missed the Oval Test, still ended the series as England's leading wicket-taker. It wasn't the first knock-back the selectors had given me, and I knew it would be far from the last. I simply returned to Yorkshire and, in what was left of the season, did what I did best – took wickets.

At this point I was bowling so well, in county cricket I was not only highly effective but, on my day, virtually unplayable. I remember one game in 1961 against Leicestershire. I didn't open the bowling on the Saturday because I was feeling rather under the weather, having had two teeth removed at the dentist's earlier in the day. On Monday, however, I felt as right as rain – which fortunately there was none of. I took 7 for 45 and when Leicestershire batted again enjoyed figures of 5 for 13 in their second innings. Against Derbyshire at Bramall Lane – always a favourite venue of mine – I returned match figures of 11 for 123 and also had a score of 58 with the bat. I took 11 wickets in our game against Essex at Southend.

But such performances, and the fact that I was England's leading wicket-taker that summer, in the eyes of the selectors wasn't good enough to earn me a place for all five Tests.

Yorkshire's final match of the 1961 season was at Bournemouth against Hampshire, who had just clinched the Championship. Having won the title in each of the two previous seasons we set about Hampshire keen to prove that for all they were champions we were the better team. Yorkshire beat the champions without too much trouble. Ray Illingworth in particular covered himself in glory by taking 12 wickets in the match. I got a few and clinched a victory for Yorkshire when I moved smartly to run out Roy Marshall. In the dressing room after the game we could hear the Hampshire players celebrating their season of success. We had been into the Hampshire dressing room to offer our congratulations, but as we came out Doug Padgett turned and said, 'Let them celebrate the moment, because that title is only on loan. We'll win it again next season.' More true words have rarely been spoken.

Having wintered at home, I was keen to be playing cricket again and couldn't wait for the 1962 season to commence. In the event 1962 was to be another highly successful season for yours truly and, more importantly from my point of view, for Yorkshire.

1962 is particularly memorable as it was my benefit season at Yorkshire. All manner of sporting dinners, quizzes and social functions took place over the year and I chose Yorkshire's game against Surrey at Bramall Lane as my benefit match. I chose this particular match because Surrey were top-class opposition but mainly because Bramall Lane was where I really started out and was the nearest senior ground to Maltby. On the occasion of the game itself the only kindness not bestowed upon me came from the weather. The game was constantly the subject of delays due to bad light and rain and ended in a draw. To my great delight and eternal gratitude the Yorkshire public braved the somewhat inclement weather and healthy attendances were posted for all three days. In total my benefit fund raised £9,331. I was deeply touched by the generosity of my fellow Yorkshire folk. I felt the sum raised, which was only a couple of hundred pounds short of Len Hutton's record for a Yorkshire benefit, was indicative of their appreciation of my efforts over the years in the name of Yorkshire cricket.

Duty with England and other representative matches resulted in me playing in only twenty-three of Yorkshire's thirty-two County Championship matches. Make of this what you will, but of the nine games I missed, Yorkshire contrived to win but two. We were involved in an amazing match with the reigning champions, Hampshire, at Bradford. We batted first and failed to take command of the game due in the main to some inspired bowling from Derek Shackleton, who bowled throughout – thirty-one overs – to end with figures of 7 for 78. We restricted Hampshire to a first innings lead of just 14 and I was well pleased with my figures of 5 for 34. The game was no nip and tuck but once again swung in favour of Hampshire.

When I came into bat we were in dire straits at 70 for 6. The first ball I received from Derek Shackleton I hit over the football stand and out of the ground. My partner at the other end was Vic Wilson and between us we steadied the ship with a partnership of 67. We set Hampshire a total of 163, which given the quality of their batting they must have thought they were eminently capable of reaching with some to spare. At one point they were 156 for 5 and very much in the driving seat. But the 'never say die' attitude we had fostered in the dressing room then came to the fore. With Hampshire needing just 7 runs to win and 5 wickets in hand, the rallying call swept around the field. We bulled each other up, gritted our teeth, galvanized our collective spirit and embarked upon yet another Augean task. I had Jim Gray, who was on 78, caught behind by Jimmy Binks before Ray Illingworth and I cleaned up. Between us we took the remaining Hampshire wickets at the expense of just one run to give us an amazing 5-run victory. Creating a 'never say die' attitude within a team is one thing, but you have to possess the quality players to turn around what many would see as a hopeless situation. It was the mark of that Yorkshire side that not only did we have a tremendous collective spirit, but quality aplenty.

In 1962 I was honoured to be asked to captain the Players in the very last Gentlemen versus Players match. I had played in previous Gentlemen versus Players matches; one in particular stands out as it resulted in me being at loggerheads with Yorkshire. In the event the 1962 Gentlemen versus Players would also, albeit indirectly, result in me having a dispute with the club!

Matches between the Gentlemen and Players were deemed
to be first-class representative games and began in 1806. They
ended when amateur status was abolished after the 1962
season. The blazer brigade of Old Etonions and Oxbridge still
ran the game, but the composition of the players had changed
immeasurably over the years. The game had always had its
professionals, but by now the vast majority of those playing the
game were professionals and we were exerting out influence on
the game. Attitudes and policies were changing and not before
time.

Before Test matches became annual events, the Lord's
match between the Gentlemen and Players was the high point
of the English season. The teams were selected by the MCC
and even with the advent of annual Test matches, an invitation
to play was regarded as one of the game's highest honours –
and an opportunity to impress the selectors. For the record,
the Players had won sixty-eight of the 137 matches, the
Gentlemen forty-one, and twenty-eight had been drawn.

Though the kudos attached to this fixture was nothing like
it had been, it was still a highly enjoyable encounter, something
bolstered by the fee. Every professional selected for the Players
received a cheque for £56 plus expenses. The cheque was paid
by the MCC direct to the player's county and, as far as I was
concerned, there lay the rub.

After one of the previous Gentlemen versus Players
matches, I sat in the dressing room chatting to Lancashire's
Geoff Pullar and Brian Statham. In the course of our conversation I told Geoff and Brian that I was unlikely to play in
another Gentlemen versus Players game. They asked me why.
I informed them that the fee involved was simply not enough
and that I was financially better off playing for Yorkshire. As
soon as I said this I saw the surprise register on their faces and
knew something was up.

'Oh, I don't know,' said Brian. 'Fifty-six quid plus exes is
decent money in my book.' I was perplexed.

'Fifty-six quid? Where do you get that sum from?' I asked. 'We only get twenty-two pounds.'

'Where do you get the sum of twenty-two quid from, more the like,' said Brian.

Geoff and Brian both assured me that the fee for playing in this fixture was indeed £56 plus expenses. What's more, they told me this had been so for years.

I was furious. Someone at Yorkshire was not being fair and on the journey back to Leeds I made up my mind to find out who that 'someone' was.

On my arrival I made a beeline for the office of John Nash, the Yorkshire club secretary. John was a decent guy, someone I admired and respected, but he had some answering to do. Initial greetings over I cut to the quick when asked the reason for my visit.

'I've only been receiving £22 for playing in representative matches,' I told him. 'I've been informed that the actual fee paid by the MCC for my services is £56 plus expenses.'

'That's right,' said John.

'But it isn't bloody right, is it?' I said. 'I've been thirty-four pounds light for every representative game I've ever played at Lord's.'

'Everything has been conducted properly. Strictly by the book,' he said. This threw me. For a moment I thought there might be something I'd missed. An MCC ruling I didn't know about. So I went fishing.

'Everything done by the book?'

'Absolutely.'

That told me nothing.

'In accordance with . . .' I purposefully let my voice tail off.

'Strictly in accordance.'

I wondered if tearing my hair out would do any good.

'According to . . . you know?'

'The directive I was given. Yes.'

A little light was coming. It was far off and coming very

slowly. It was a very small light. About half a glow worm's worth.

'So you are deducting money from my fees in accordance with the directive you were given?'

'That's absolutely right, Fred.'

It dawned on me then that the rub of this matter had all to do with the Yorkshire club committee.

'So the decision to deduct money from my fees is an internal one?' I asked.

'The thing is, Fred,' opined John, 'what you don't seem to understand is this. When you are away playing representative matches someone has to take your place in the first XI. That player has to be paid. So his wage is taken out of your fee.'

'I'm not having this!' I said, in no uncertain fashion. 'The way that works, I'm paying his wages, not the club! You can stuff that for a game of soldiers. I'm not having it. It's not fair, nor is it reasonable. If this club plays a player it pays the player! I'm not paying other people's wages!'

Our conversation became somewhat heated. Rather than see it escalate into something unsavoury, I thanked John for his time and before bidding farewell informed him that as the situation now stood. I had no alternative but to refer the matter to the MCC themselves.

To the chagrin of my own beloved county club, the MCC came down on my side and ruled Yorkshire guilty of 'malpractice regarding the payment of professional fees'. To their credit the MCC also ruled that Yorkshire had not only to pay me the full fee of £56 for the match in question, but also instructed the club to pay me back all the money they had previously deducted from my fees. Though I received what I was entitled to, my stand in the name of fair play and justice only further served to add to my reputation as a troublemaker with some members of the Yorkshire committee.

When I captained the Players against the Gentlemen in 1962 there were rumours that it might be the last. However, the MCC committee was not scheduled to meet until November to discuss a recommendation from the Advisory County Cricket Committee that the distinction between amateurs and professionals be abolished.

At that November meeting the motion was carried by ten votes to seven. Given the traditional stance taken by the MCC, their decision surprised many, though economic circumstances would, I am sure, have eventually led to the demise of the amateur anyway – their expense accounts were often more of a financial burden to county clubs than a professional.

In 1962 fifty amateurs were playing in county cricket, twelve of them as captains. But in 1963 that number dropped by a third. Within three or so years there were no former amateurs at all in the first-class game. I was all for the abolition of amateurs. It meant there would be no more, 'sir' or 'call me Mister So and So'. No more 'fancy caps'. We were now all of the same cricketing flesh and blood, and no one was afforded privileges based on their status.

Of course there were those who lamented the passing of the gentlemen players and feared for the future of a game which was now the preserve of professionals. The cricket writer E. W. Swanton, for example, believed it was in the best interests of the game to have a balance between those who played the game for a living and those who did not. But in 1962, the professionals were by far in the majority, so there *was* no balance to speak of. If the influence of those fifty amateurs did create a balance, then their status in the game was too great for such a small number. At the time Swanton was also concerned that, with the abolition of amateurs, cricket would struggle to find future leaders, in my opinion a myopic view that was demeaning to pros. Swanton's was a typical establishment opinion that only former public schoolboys and Oxbridge graduates had the ability to lead, as far as I was concerned, a view that belonged to the First World War – and we all know what a tragic and disastrous hash our leaders made of that war. So where would cricket find its future leaders?

Well, at that time Yorkshire had not one but two players in the ranks who would prove themselves great captains – Ray Illingworth and Brian Close. Though I think it was right to abolish the distinction between amateurs and professionals, I am very much a traditionalist. Especially where cricket is concerned. When I first came into first-class cricket I did so knowing nothing except how to bowl fast. My years in the game stimulated a great and abiding affection for it and its traditions, its roots and history. So despite the distinctions between amateurs and professionals becoming blurred due to the changing economic and social climate, the fact that this particular fixture had been played at Lord's since 1806 was enough to make me cherish it. Having said this, my affection and respect for the traditions of this fixture were at odds with my deep sense of fair play and equal justice for all.

Leading a side at any time is a distinction; to lead one in the final game of a series with a pedigree like Gentlemen versus Players was a real honour. To be perfectly honest, the game itself didn't amount to much. It was rain-affected and eventually the elements had the final word as the Players chased a winning total that was well within our reach. The game ended in a draw, not the sort of note on which we would all have liked that series to end. I can't remember too much about the game itself, but I do recall one or two incidental matters that were indirectly connected with the occasion.

The Reverend David Sheppard was under consideration for a place in the England team due to tour Australia that winter. Ted Dexter of Sussex, the captain of the Gentlemen, had just emerged as the selectors' choice as England captain, just ahead of Kent's Colin Cowdrey and David Sheppard. Colin Cowdrey had been initially named as the captain of the Gentlemen, but had been admitted to hospital with a stomach problem while David Sheppard, on sabbatical from his work in an East End mission, had still to prove current form to the selectors. Sheppard scored 112 for the Gentlemen in the first innings before being caught and bowled by Freddie Titmus. In the second innings he made 34 before being once again a victim of Titmus. Sheppard was a good batsman, but it says much for the Quixotic policies of the MCC selection committee that he was chosen for the tour of Australia on the strength of the 112 he made for the Gentlemen against the Players.

Immediately after the game I took part in a television programme and it was getting on for ten p.m. before Phil Sharpe and I set off for Taunton, where Yorkshire were playing the following day. As one would expect on a Friday night in July, the road from London to the West Country was thick with traffic and our progress was painfully slow at times. To add to our problems, we took a wrong turn west of Sparkford and were well on our way to Exeter before we realized our mistake and turned the car around. Eventually we reached the team's hotel at around three a.m.

In those days many hotels didn't have an internal telephone system, so there were no early-morning alarm calls. Instead, you received an early call from a porter or maid knocking on your door. To request this you wrote your name, room number and the time you wished to be awoken on a board in reception. Phil and I did this, but nothing was going to plan.

In the event the room I was allotted was different to the one I had been originally assigned and for which I had requested the early morning 'knock'. Probably due to my tiredness I never noticed the difference in room numbers. Consequently no one came knocking on my door in the morning. Yorkshire had a strict policy about players turning up for matches in good time. Players had to be at the ground at least one hour before play was due to commence on the first day, and half an hour before play on the second and third days. Failure to comply with this would result in a player being dropped from the team.

Strict club rules do not make tired and heavy sleepers wake on time. Having received no early-morning knock, I continued sleeping. Phil Sharpe hung about in reception for me until twenty-past ten before asking reception what number room I was occupying. Of course the receptionist gave Phil the number of the room I had originally been allocated. Phil went up to that room, saw it was unoccupied and simply thought I had got up early and set off for the Taunton ground without him.

I eventually woke up, saw the time, jumped out of bed and showered and shaved in record time. I dashed off to the Taunton ground arriving just before eleven o'clock only to be told by skipper Vic Wilson that he had already announced the team and that I wasn't playing. Vic also informed me that during the pre-match press conference he had informed the press that I had been dropped for failing to report on time for the game.

I was very disappointed. I was especially disappointed to miss this particular match as Taunton had, for whatever reason, always been a happy hunting ground for me. In the event Yorkshire didn't take a single bonus point from the game, which ended in a draw. That result might have cost us the Championship, as things were very tight at the top of the table at the time. Phil Sharpe, on arriving at the Taunton ground, had told Vic Wilson that we had arrived extremely late the night before, but that he had not been able to find me in the hotel. As the 'deadline' approached, why Vic or a club official hadn't telephoned the hotel to ascertain my where-abouts, I don't know. A simple call could have averted the trouble. That I didn't receive such a call annoyed me. Perhaps the opportunity to discipline me was welcomed by some. Whatever, I found myself once again summoned before the club's disciplinary committee to explain myself. The committee informed me that if I was not chosen by England to play in the Trent Bridge Test, then I must rejoin the team on Tuesday night at Bristol for the game against Gloucestershire that formed the last of what we used to call our 'Western Tour'.

I greatly admired Vic Wilson and respected him as a captain, though I believe he created that situation. As I have previously stated, we had a tremendous team spirit and as players were willing to give our all for one another. Why didn't Vic 'bat' for me that morning? There was no need for him to announce the team at the time he did, before a quarter to eleven. Given my efforts on behalf of the club and my team-mates, I would have expected some effort to have been made to find out where I was before peremptorily dropping me from the team.

I was also annoyed with the stance taken by the Yorkshire disciplinary committee. I drive 400 miles to Leeds, then 400 miles back to Bristol, when it is only fifty miles from Taunton! How daft is that? The disciplinary committee comprised William Worsley (club president), Brian Sellars (chairman of the cricket committee) and John Nash (secretary). The committee had Vic Wilson's report to hand and I was asked if I had refused to report back to Bristol. I informed them that this was not an issue, as I had been selected to play for England at Trent Bridge on the occasion of Yorkshire's game with Gloucestershire. In the end the committee awarded me travel expenses for the journey I had made to Leeds from the West Country and the price of my lunch. They also told me my match fee for the Somerset game would be paid, as the committee believed I had been the subject of 'extenuating circumstances', inasmuch as the hotel had directed me to a different room and I had subsequently not received the early-morning call I had requested. I left that disciplinary committee meeting very pleased with the fact I had been vindicated, and not a little satisfied that I had stuffed someone who seemingly had been out to get me. Time, gentlemen, please!

CHAPTER ELEVEN

HOME AND AWAY

His Grace the Duke of Norfolk was appointed as manager of the England tour of Australia in the winter of 1962–3. His appointment astounded just about everyone connected with the game. He was a very pleasant man, a true gentleman and a real cricket enthusiast, but he had no track record or qualifications suited to the job to which he had been appointed. Perhaps his appointment as tour manager had a little to do with certain MCC mandarins wanting to further ingratiate themselves with members of the establishment. The Duke of Norfolk was very close to the Queen, often going racing with her and organizing many a ceremonial event. Maybe they were hopeful of an honour?

I had the sort of season in 1962 whereby the MCC had to pick me for the tour of Australia. I'd bowled 1,141 overs and taken 153 wickets at an average of 17.75 each. It had been a long, hard summer, and when I boarded the ship that was to take us to the other side of the world I was looking forward to a well-earned rest before facing the Aussies.

We were only a couple of days into the journey when it became apparent to me that I wasn't going to be allowed to have that rest. Ted Dexter informed the players that Gordon Pirie, who had run in the Olympics for Great Britain, was among the passengers, and he had offered to supervise daily training for all players. All I wanted to do was sit in a deckchair and recharge my batteries until we got to the nets in Perth. There would be light training, that I expected. Also a couple of one-day matches along the way. But regimented daily training routines? I wasn't up for that.

To me Gordon Pirie was one of those athletes Britain produced by the number in those days – very good at coming second or third. One of the first things Gordon told me was that I should stop eating steak and go on a diet of salad, fruit and nuts. Apparently he knew a man in the Arctic who kept to such a diet and was still chasing reindeer at the age of ninety-five. I told him he'd find there were very few, if any, reindeer in Australia and even if there were some, I had no desire whatsoever to chase them. I was only interested in chasing Australian batsmen – back to the pavilion – and I needed steaks to do that.

I attended the first regimented training session. Gordon Pirie had us running up and down the decks of the ship, which is the worst thing a fast bowler can do, as it tightens the calf muscles. He also told me that he could devise some exercises especially for me that would strengthen my legs. The very legs which had just seen me safely through over 1,000 overs! He started going on about what this regimented training had done for him only for me to jump in on his conversation.

'Have you ever run against a guy called Vladimir Kuts?' I asked.

Pirie told me he had.

'Yes,' I replied, 'and if I remember correct, Kuts was on his lap of honour before you crossed the finishing line. So if that's what your regimented training does for you, then you can count me out. I'm at the top of my profession. I aim to stay there for as long as possible.'

If the man had been able to point to an Olympic gold medal my attitude to him and his training methods might have been different. He wasn't best pleased with my attitude, and as I concluded my final session with him said as much.

'Can you swim?' I asked.

'Yes,' he replied.

'And a good job too,' I said. 'You've got every chance of

doing plenty of swimming. There's a whole lot of ocean out there, and that's where you'll be if you keep bothering me.'

Ted Dexter was still very much taken with the man and his methods and tried to convince the team to follow Pirie's instructions. I went to see Alec Bedser, the assistant manager on the tour, and a man who knew something about bowling, to explain the damage pounding around the deck could do to me. Alec was in agreement with me and told me to forget about attending Pirie's training sessions. I already had.

After that little confrontation the voyage turned out to be the best I ever experienced when on tour. We had a great time socially, which helped gel the players and improve team spirit. I set about organizing a calypso band to play at one of the ship's fancy dress parties and the Marylebone Calypso Club was born. The band consisted of Ken Barrington, Ted Dexter, Ray Illingworth, Colin Cowdrey, Tom Graveney and myself. We got together to rehearse some of the calypso songs we had learned when on tour in the West Indies, often adding our own lyrics. I fronted the group, telling a few jokes and stories and introducing the songs:

> There's this man
> Peter May is his name,
> Surrey his club and
> cricket his game.
> May may in May
> play his opening shot,
> May may do well
> May may do not,
> It all depends
> on this you see,
> how May may cope
> with FST!

It was hardly the sort of stuff that would threaten the songwriting careers of the emerging Lennon and McCartney but it went down a storm at the ship's party and we were awarded first prize. The ship's captain was so delighted that he added half a dozen bottles of champagne to our prize. The following day we clubbed together to buy some brandy and cases of beer and invited lots of people we had become friendly with to a party in my cabin. My room was crammed full of people and I was up in a corner behind a makeshift bar trying to mix champagne and brandy cocktails when Tom Graveney squeezed past the bodies and told me to stand aside.

'Leave all this to me,' Tom said, 'I know how to do all this.' He did. Tom turned out to be as good as any barman at making champagne cocktails, even down to the sugar frosting on the rims of the glasses. We had a great night, it was all good clean fun, but I must admit I suffered a little the next day. I'd drunk so much brandy and champagne it was a wonder I didn't wake up speaking French.

We disembarked in Bombay, from where we flew to Ceylon for two one-day matches. I bowled reasonably well, particularly in the second match, taking 5 for 22. I don't think I'd have bettered those figures had I subjected myself to Gordon Pirie's training methods. On the contrary, I don't think I'd have done as well, as I am certain I would have ended up with problematic calves. From Ceylon we journeyed to Australia, where it was all to go wrong both on and off the field.

The very first press conference was overloaded with questions about whether the Duke of Norfolk's horses would be seen on the Australian race tracks. I couldn't believe it. We were there to contest the Ashes, and there was our tour manager talking about horse racing and whether the jockey Scobie Breasley was to fly out and ride for him. Then Ted Dexter's wife arrived in Australia. Ted's wife was a looker and a model. She is a very lovely lady, but on hearing of her arrival, when Ted faced the press, the majority of questions posed were about his wife. Would she be modelling whilst in Australia? What would she be wearing? What did she think

about Australian haute couture? Do Australian fashion design-
ers match up to those of London and Paris? That's all very
well in its own right, but these questions were being asked
during an England cricket team press conference!

On top of all this we were besieged by clergymen eager
to meet the Reverend David Sheppard. I have always been
a believer and am very active in my local church, but I have
to say that on an International cricket tour I found it quite
unnerving to see so many men of the cloth around the dressing
rooms, nets and hotels. In no time at all the news in the press
concerning the England team centred on where the Duke of
Norfolk's horses were running, what Mrs Dexter was wearing
and where David Sheppard would be sermonizing.

I became extremely fed up with it all. We were the England
cricket team there to contest the Ashes, and so I was forthright
when it was my turn to attend a press conference. A sports
writer from the *Sydney Herald* asked me what I thought about
the tour up to then. I told him I was rather confused, in that
I didn't know whether we were supposed to be playing under
Jockey Club rules, for Dexter Enterprises or engaged on a
missionary hunt. The journalists ran with the story and it
appeared in the newspapers as a leading sports story. I found
myself in trouble with the MCC again.

Self-appraisal is no guarantee of merit, but few would argue
with the fact that as far as the Australians were concerned I
proved to be the most popular member of the touring party.
I received all manner of invitations to endorse products and
speak at dinners. I was angered when the MCC barred me
from endorsing commercial products and making appearances
at sporting dinners. I objected strenuously because I had
grafted hard to reach the top of my profession and become
famous enough for companies to want to pay for using my
name. As far as I was concerned it was a legitimate part of
my living and the MCC had no right to deny me the opportunities that were coming my way.

This was an era when there was no way of making decent money from cricket alone, even at International level. As a key member of the England team my full fee for the entire tour was in the region of £250. Some members of the MCC suggested that should they allow me to endorse products and speak at dinners, I should pay the proceeds into the players' pool. Apparently Ted Dexter had been paid a few quid for writing newspaper articles and had done the same.

I rejected this idea outright. None of the other members of the team were likely to be asked to advertise anything, except maybe dog collars, so I rejected this suggestion. The response of the MCC was, given my stance, they would not allow me to speak at dinners or endorse products. I reckon that ruling cost me well over £2,000. As one MCC official put it, 'Your failure to comply with our directive means the players' pool will only amount to a matter of pounds when it could be in excess of well over £2,000.'

'Yes sir,' I said, 'and who would have contributed the lion's share? Me. I'm devoted to our cause and I'm a team player through and through, But for you to expect me to go out and work for the benefit of others, when others are not working to the benefit of me, I find unacceptable.'

That 1962–3 tour of Australia was, like that of 1958–9, a great disappointment to those who took part and those English supporters who watched it. The Duke of Norfolk was not up to the job of tour manager for the entire tour. S. C. Griffith was asked to take the place of the Duke, while he returned to England to attend to 'private matters'.

I don't think I performed better on that tour than I did in the Melbourne Test. In searing heat I took 3 for 83 and 5 for 62. There was some fine batting from Colin Cowdrey and Ted Dexter. David Sheppard overcame the ignominy of a first-innings duck to make a century in the second and England enjoyed their only Test victory of the Australian part of the tour. I must have bowled particularly well because the Australian press were full of praise for my performance, albeit grudging on the part of some newspapers. David Sheppard described my series of stints from the bottom end as 'the finest sustained and accurate fast bowling I have ever seen'. Back home the English press reserved all the plaudits for David Sheppard. I was particularly galled by this. This was typical. No matter how well I performed certain elements of the English press rarely gave me credit. Brian Statham once remarked, 'I don't know what you have to do to impress them, Fred. In the eyes of press I'm unlucky not to have taken more wickets, but when you beat the bat for no reward they accuse you of inaccuracy.'

There was another moment of irritation in Melbourne. Along with my teammates I attended a Saturday night party at the house of some local government official. Bill Johnston, the Australian medium-pace bowler, was among the guests and we spent most of the evening together talking cricket. We got on extremely well and a few days later Bill came to see me at the team hotel. He did not look happy. He told me there was a story circulating around the city that we'd had a big argument at the party and ended up throwing punches at each other. He wanted to know where this story had come from. I allayed his concern and explained that scurrilous stories about me were ten a penny back home and he had simply been the victim, along with myself of course, of yet another ridiculous gossip tale.

'Yeah, guess that's it,' said Bill. 'I've heard plenty of stories about you, Fred. Guess it's a case of many hoping the tree may be felled so that they can gather chips by its fall.'

As I say, the Melbourne Test was the only Test England won in Australia. That we didn't build on that victory, in my opinion was because from then on a lot of tactical mistakes were made. Some of them vital mistakes. I liked Ted Dexter a lot. He was a very good batsman with a wonderfully fluid style, he was a fine fielder, but to my mind he was no captain of

England. Ted extolled more theories than Charles Darwin, but lacked the experience and tactical nous to carry them through. Ted had come straight from university into a relatively mediocre Sussex team. If a team lacks quality and ability, there will be no one to nurture and develop a potential captain. Playing in a bad side you pick up bad habits. If there is no captain of real quality to teach a player for several years by example and experience, how is it suddenly possible for him to acquire the acumen required to captain an International team? It was unbelievable. The Australians would never have made that mistake.

In the days before the Sydney test I was flown up to that great city ahead of the rest of the team in order to take a good look at the wicket and form an opinion. The Sydney pitch usually favoured fast bowling, but on this occasion the wicket was totally bare. So I reported back saying that it was my considered opinion that we should play an extra spin bowler. Fred Titmus backed my opinion and when he got back in the dressing room he turned to Ray Illingworth and David Allen and said, 'Get your fingers loose, boys, because one of you two will be playing for certain.' Ted Dexter looked at the pitch and was of a different mind. Ted told Len Coldwell, Brian Statham and me that we had bowled so well at Melbourne that none of us could be dropped. I told him that the Melbourne Test had nothing to do with this one, that we were here to try to win the Ashes.

'It's horses for courses, skipper,' I told him. 'It's madness to go with three pace bowlers on that pitch. One of us has to be dropped if we are to stand a chance of winning. I'm loyal to my country, drop me if you like, you can always put yourself on as a third seamer if need be.'

Ted discussed the matter with the selectors and the decision was to ignore my advice, and play Len, Brian and myself. It was a farce. The pitch didn't have a blade of grass on it and I was reduced to bowling off-cutters, but I couldn't pitch them slow enough to have much effect. At the other end Freddie Titmus had a field day. Fred caused all manner problems for the Aussies with his spin, while Ray Illingworth and David Allen could only watch on in frustration from the pavilion in their civvies. If either Ray or David had played they would have given invaluable support to Freddie Titmus, and I feel England would have won the Sydney Test. In the event we lost.

My frustration was compounded at Adelaide. There it was obvious we needed a three-man pace attack, but the selectors dropped Len Coldwell as a result of him labouring in vain at Sydney, and played an extra spinner! Even with that handicap we might have won had it not been for poor fielding. A number of chances were dropped, three off my bowling. David Sheppard was the main culprit and after another dropped chance I said, out of sheer frustration, 'The only time your hands are together is on a Sunday.' These catastrophic mistakes meant that the Adelaide Test was drawn, the series was tied, so the Aussies retained the Ashes. It was heartbreaking stuff.

Again I suffered from back trouble when in Brisbane. I went to see a specialist, who diagnosed a displaced bone at the base of the spine. The specialist thought he'd discovered such a serious congenital spinal weakness that I should be sent home to undergo surgery and might never bowl again. As you can imagine, I was horrified to hear this. When the news of this reached the press at home, a journalist paid a call on my parents to ascertain their reaction to my dreadful news. Dad's reaction was typical.

'It's bloody daft,' he said. He was proved right. Once I left Brisbane the back problem disappeared and thankfully to this day has never returned.

With 20 wickets at 26.05 I was second only to David Allen in the bowling averages for that five-match Test series. In first-class matches of the complete tour I took more wickets than any other bowler and only Fred Titmus with his spin bowled more overs than me. Though I was very disappointed with the tactics we had deployed and the fact that mistakes had, in my opinion, cost us the Ashes, I was very happy with my own efforts. Extremely happy, actually, because when we moved on to New Zealand I created a new record.

Lancaster Park, Christchurch, in New Zealand is a multi-functional stadium. In its time it has staged cricket and football, but primarily it is a rugby stadium. As such it is not always easy to get the real feeling of Test cricket on a ground built specifically for another sport. Lancaster Park lacks the essential charm of a cricket ground and is more utilitarian than aesthetically pleasing. Curiously the backdrop to this stadium is both breathtaking and vulgar. Beyond one stand are the beautiful Port Hills, while beyond another is a functional though hideous gasworks.

In the previous Test at Wellington I had enjoyed a 5-wicket haul that took me within one wicket of Brian Statham's record of 241. So at Christchurch the home crowd were aware that I was close to making cricketing history. The bars emptied, the crowd swelled, and you sensed the high level of expectation that was in the air – particularly when I had Bill Playle caught by Ken Barrington. As so often happens, that level of excitement and expectation became the subject of sod's law. Could I get the one wicket I needed? Could I hell as like. Graham Dowling and Barry Sinclair added another 80 runs for New Zealand before I was to feel a happy feller. It always seems the more you beat the bat without getting an edge, the more the batsman contrives to play and miss. This is especially so when you are desperate for a wicket. I sensed the home crowd were eager for me to get that wicket too. Every time Dowling or Sinclair played and missed a chorus of 'aaahs' rang around the ground. To me it appeared that next to a New Zealand century or victory over England, they seemed to want to see a new cricket world record set up before their very eyes.

In bowling to Dowling and Sinclair I tried every kind of delivery in the repertoire. If they got a nick, it didn't go to hand. If they didn't get a nick, the ball passed the stumps by a cat's whisker. I simply kept plugging away, determined I wouldn't be beaten. Eventually I dropped one short to Barry Sinclair. He went back for the pull shot. The ball reared up and quick. He stepped too far back and onto his wicket. It was Test wicket number 243 for me and the record was mine. As my teammates walked towards me to confer their congratulations, I felt happiness, joy, pride and relief all at the same moment. It was a very strange sensation, one my mind and heart had never felt before.

When I had at last taken the crucial wicket, sod's law kicked into action again. I sent the wickets tumbling and ended the match with a 9-wicket haul which elevated me to the magical figure of 250 Test wickets. Back at the team hotel I received a deluge of telegrams. They came from the county clubs in England, cricket supporters of all hues, fellow players, film stars, TV and show-business personalities, politicians and from cricket federations and associations from all around the world. But to my great sadness and disappointment only one English first-class county did not send a telegram of congratulations to me – Yorkshire. I felt very hurt at that. Everyone in the world of cricket recognized I had reached a milestone in Test cricket except the officials of the club I was devoted to and loved. I had given my all for Yorkshire, but the more success I achieved, the more certain members of the Yorkshire committee appeared to resent me. When I eventually returned to Leeds, the Yorkshire president, Sir William Worsley, offered his congratulations to me when we met at a pre-season lunch where the players traditionally get together with club officials.

'I'm sorry I wasn't there to see it, Fred, but I was in Hong Kong, visiting my daughter at the time,' Sir William informed me.

'Yes, sir, I am aware of that fact,' I said, 'which is probably the reason why I received no congratulations from my own county.'

He stared at me.

'What are you saying, Fred?'

I explained that I had received telegrams of congratulations from every English county but Yorkshire. At first he couldn't believe what I was saying was true.

'But why no telegram of congratulations on such an auspicious occasion for a Yorkshire player?' he asked.

'I think by way of your opening conversation you may well have answered that question,' I ventured.' I can only assume it was because you were in Hong Kong.'

I later took the matter up with the Yorkshire secretary, John Nash. John informed me that no telegrams of congratulation can be sent out from headquarters unless the president was there to pay for them!

'What about phone calls?' I asked.

John then said, 'If you'll excuse me, Fred. I have just got my eye on someone who I really must talk to on a matter of club business.'

Happily, there is another side to this story. Two days after I created the new record for Test wickets, the England party attended a dinner given by the New Zealand Board of Control, at the time their equivalent of the MCC. The New Zealand captain, John Reid, gave an after-dinner speech during which he produced a ball. It was the ball I had been using when I took my 243rd wicket. It had been mounted and inscribed and there and then John called me up and presented it to me. Everyone in the room took to their feet and applauded wildly. Then suddenly I was quite overcome.

As I stood there looking out across the packed dining room at all those people standing and applauding. I couldn't help but wonder why, when others seemed to appreciate my qualities as a man and a cricketer, my own beloved club never did.

I have since returned to New Zealand on many occasions.

Sometimes just for a holiday with the love of my life, Veronica. Sometimes combining a holiday with a series of after-dinner and theatre appearances. On such occasions I was able to do the sightseeing there is never time to do when touring as a cricketer. I have many happy memories of New Zealand and its people. But my abiding memory is that of Barry Sinclair and that Test at Lancaster Park, Christchurch. It's a funny thing, when you go on tour as a cricketer you think you are there to win Tests. You are. But as the years pass by, you come to realize you were also there to create your memories.

Memories of that 1962–3 winter tour? Stopping off at Aden (in what is now Yemen) and attending a function held by a local sheikh. On being told the sheikh had 198 wives, replying, 'Does he know that with another two he could have a new ball?'

As my friendship with His Grace the Duke of Norfolk blossomed, His Grace saying to me, 'Call me Dukie, Fred.'

In Sydney being asked by a reporter what did I think of 'our bridge'. 'Your bridge?' I replied. 'Our bridge more the like. It was built by a Yorkshire firm – Dorman and Long – the supervising engineers were from Yorkshire and you still haven't paid for it yet!'

My good pal Brian Statham being told by a typically forthright young Australian lady, 'There are two things that worry me about you, Mr Statham. The way you bowl, and the bulge you always have in your pants.' And Brian replying: 'I wouldn't worry, lass. You're not likely to come into contact with either.'

At a dinner the Australia batsman Norman O'Neill saying to me, 'Fred, come and sit alongside me. I don't feel comfortable to have you opposite me even at a dinner table.'

Ken Barrington being interviewed by an Aussie radio cub reporter. The young reporter asking Ken, 'Ken, the series is finally balanced. Both teams have one win to their names. Do you feel that, given those circumstances, the fact that the series is delicately balanced and could go either way, it's anybody's game and we know that. So with all to play for, and the destiny of the Ashes up for grabs, do you feel, given your personal performances to date, which have been sterling without, and I say this with due respect, ever being startling, by that I mean, for all you have batted well, you still, by your own standards, perhaps have not produced the form you may have hoped to produce, do you, all things considered, hope or believe you are capable of producing a big innings – and by that I mean at telling total – a century maybe, perhaps more? Or at least a score that is getting near to a ton? Do you feel you are capable of producing an innings that will tilt the series in England's favour? And by that I mean, England going on, with the benefit of your run-making, be it a century or thereabouts, to clinch the series? That is, beat Australia and seize the initiative which may allow your team, given your side's performances in the remaining Tests hold up, allow England to take back the Ashes, which Australia currently retain? In name only of course, as tradition dictates that the urn containing the ashes of the burned stumps of the very first Test match between England and Australia should always remain at Lord's.'

Ken's reply was characteristic of his wicked wit: 'Sorry, could you repeat the question?'

That I am able to reproduce that cub reporter's question and Ken's reply verbatim, I am indebted to radio producer Les Woollam, whose personal archive of radio recordings from around the world contains many such gems.

I was now thirty-two years old, an age many considered to be on the wrong side for a top-class International fast bowler. I felt, however, I still had a few years left at the very top. No one had taken more wickets than me on the tour of Australia and New Zealand – proof enough that I still had much to offer. For all the set-backs and lack of credit, my enthusiasm for cricket remained undiminished. I sensed that amongst my fellow England players I had gained more genuine respect on this tour than on any before. I was still at pains to curse a non-trier or an edger and, more importantly, I still possessed my speed as a bowler. My thirst for success was unquenchable, I wanted to bowl out more and more batsmen.

As I started the 1963 season I was filled with the burning ambition that I hadn't felt since first arriving at Headingley for winter nets all those years ago. To me it seemed that all down the years I had played second fiddle to somebody. That I was 'there', but never quite there in comparison to someone else. Of my 'school' Brian Close was the first to get his Yorkshire cap, first to play for England. Brian Statham had been the first to beat Alec Bedser's world record of Test wickets. I was forever being told that when it came to bowling I was very fast, but that on his day Frank Tyson was faster than me.

When people asked, 'All right, Fred?' I'd reply, 'Yes, I'm all right, thank you.' I was, but deep down in my heart I wasn't happy. Regarding the trials and tribulation of my marriage to Enid, I coped as best I could. I yearned to be happy in my personal life. Like anyone else I had needs I wanted to fulfil. I had much love to give and needed my love reciprocated. It wasn't happening with Enid, yet at this point in my life, I couldn't let her go. So it was a matter of coping, accepting I had a marriage that had its problems and just get on with it. No marriage is perfect. For a time I simply accepted that Enid and I had more problems than most. It was as if I had to be content with second best even in my personal life.

As I have said, I never let the turmoil of my private life affect my cricket. In 1963 I felt I had the opportunity to, at long last, not play second fiddle to anyone. That season I didn't just have the chance to beat everyone, I had my sights set on something which everyone had considered impossible – a world record of 300 Test wickets.

That summer the West Indies were the tourists and I couldn't wait to get at them. At this point in my career I had perfected a new, shortened run-up of twelve paces, instead of nineteen, and it proved highly effective. I found I could make the ball move away that little bit later, and when conditions were conducive to my bowling the results were devastating. That season I took 129 wickets for Yorkshire at an average of 15.5. I took 5 wickets in a match on ten occasions, and five times took 10 wickets in a match. I also scored my first ever first-class century and finished the season with a first-class batting average of 22.37.

The series against the West Indies was a humdinger and the Test at Lord's was the tightest match of all. The outcome of a fiercely contested game hung on the last over. The West Indies needed one wicket to win, whereas England needed just 8 runs for victory. In the event the game ended in a draw, but every newspaper agreed it was the most nail-biting draw in the history of English Test cricket.

In Wes Hall and Charlie Griffith the West Indies boasted an express spearhead attack of fast bowlers. Wes was one of the greatest fast bowlers of all time, with a superbly fluid and flowing action. His lightning-fast bowling was a fire that illuminated cricket, not one that destroyed its beauty. Tall, wide-shouldered and narrow-hipped, he came hurtling towards the crease like the thoroughbred athlete he was. He flowed into a classically high action and a gloriously smooth follow-through. All this incorporated the timing, balance and rhythm required to propel the ball at a pace to alarm even the bravest of batsmen.

Charlie Griffith was more idiosyncratic. Most of the England team knew Charlie Griffith from the 1959–60 tour, where he came across as being a run-of-the-mill fast bowler, coming off a short run-up. Wes was the quicker, it was not for nothing that he entitled his autobiography *Pace With Fire*.

In tandem they epitomized fast bowling at its fiercest in the first half of the sixties. Wes subsequently became an MP in

Barbados, was appointed Minister of Tourism and Sport for the island and also proved himself a more than capable manager of West Indies teams.

When the West Indies played Yorkshire at Middlesbrough, Doug Padgett and Jackie Hampshire asked me how quick Charlie Griffith was. I told them I had been up against him a number of times and he was just medium-fast, and I couldn't understand why he'd begun to knock down wickets right, left and centre. Yorkshire won the toss, elected to bat, and somewhat later Ray Illingworth came to me and said, 'Fred, you had better come and see this. You're not going to believe it.' I went out on to the balcony of the home team dressing room and saw Charlie Griffith coming off a new, thirty-five-yard run-up and bowling bullets. Except that it wasn't a smooth, fluid run-up like that of Wes Hall, more of a waddle. He hit both Doug and Jackie, and they came off the Middlesbrough pitch saying he was the fastest thing thing they had ever seen. 'And that run-up,' said Jackie, 'if he went any further back he'd been in Sunderland!' Our resolve and quality as a team came to the fore in that match. Yorkshire beat the West Indies despite Griffith, but England didn't fare as well.

The first Test at Old Trafford was a disappointment. The wicket had nothing to offer fast bowlers and I was disappointed to only add 2 wickets to my total. Charlie Griffith didn't fare as well, only managing one, whilst Brian Statham on his home ground saw the ball hit in the general direction of every other Lancashire ground for no reward at all. The West Indies were fortunate enough to get us batting on a turning wicket and their spinners, in particular Lance Gibbs, won the Test for them. For the Lord's test Brian Statham was replaced by Derek Shackleton of Hampshire. Derek was after Alan Moss's record. He was thirty-eight and it had been eleven years since he had last been selected for England. As Ken Barrington said at the time, 'They'll be calling on Alec Bedser next.'

Ted Dexter won the toss, but rain delayed the start of the

game. When we eventually got under way I bowled the first over to Conrad Hunte. It was somewhat of a ropey over from my point of view, but I soon got in the groove, using every patch of greenness in the pitch. I was moving the ball about so much in the air and off the pitch the West Indies batsmen uncharacteristically shut up shop. The batsmen got edges but the ball either didn't go to hand or else the chance was dropped. Come lunch the West Indies hadn't lost a wicket but had only posted 47 runs on the scoreboard. Ted Dexter's tactical plan simply seemed to be one of containment while hoping I made the breakthrough. Derek Shackleton and I bowled seventy-two overs between us on the first day. At the close the West Indies were 245 for 6 and I had taken 5 of those wickets. It had been a very hot and humid day that made my out-swinger 'go' late, and I pumped so much sweat it darkened my shirt. At the end of play my teammates stood to one side and applauded me into the pavilion. When I reached the dressing room I happened to glance into the mirror. The face I saw was a stranger to me. It was haggard, drained and sheeny grey with exhaustion.

The West Indies made 301 all out and I finished with figures of 6 for 100 from getting on for fifty overs. In England's first innings Ted Dexter did what he was really good at – batting. Ken Barrington and Fred Titmus chipped in with good performances to make a total of 297 – only 4 runs behind on the first innings. On Saturday the gates at Lord's were closed twenty minutes before the start of play. Conrad Hunte pulled for a six in my first over, which only served to make me more determined to stamp my mark on the game. I gave it my all, along with invaluable support from Derek Shackleton and David Allen, and the West Indies found themselves at 104 for 5. I fired ball after ball through Gary Sobers, but a century from Basil Butcher with sterling support from Frank Worrell steadied the West Indies' innings.

On Monday Derek Shackleton and I set out in determined mood. In less than half an hour between us we took the last 5 wickets for the cost of only 15 runs. Our bowling figures read as follows:

	O	M	R	W
Trueman	26	9	52	5
Shackleton	34	14	72	4

My analysis was the best of any pace bowler in that Test, which was most satisfying. England, having been set 234 to win, reached 116 for 3 on the fourth day when bad light stopped play. In actual fact we were effectively four wickets down, as Colin Cowdrey had broken his arm as the result of a demon ball from Wes Hall that had reared up in the twilight.

Rain and bad light caused further interruptions to play, and come the close England needed 8 runs off the last over for victory. Derek Shackleton and David Allen were at the crease. Derek swung at Wes Hall's first ball and connected with nothing but fresh air. He pushed Hall's second delivery away and they scrambled a single. David Allen glanced the third delivery for another single. With David Allen backing up so much he nearly reached the strike end before the ball, Derek kissed the fourth and was run out.

The injured Colin Cowdrey came to the crease with the crowd strangely hushed amidst the high drama. Hall's final two deliveries were slide-rule straight. David Allen played back to the first and forward to the second. And the most tense and dramatic Test match in living memory ended in a draw. But what a draw!

The West Indies were some team. Of *Wisden*'s five Cricketers of the Year in 1963, four were tourists: Gary Sobers, Conrad Hunte, Charlie Griffith and Rohan Kanhai. The fifth was my Yorkshire teammate and now captain Brian Close, who had been battered black and blue by some fearsome West Indies bowling at Lord's.

For the Edgbaston Test another of my Yorkshire team-mates was selected for England duty. Phil Sharpe's selection prompted some snide suggestions in the press that he must be the first player to get a Test place purely by virtue of his ability as a fielder. If the people who wrote that tosh had had a word with me I would have been able to suggest to them a list of players who went on England tours abroad who could neither bat, bowl nor field to anywhere near International level. Phil Sharpe was one of the best slip-fielders in the world – one of the best of all time. He played in twelve Tests and averaged 46.23 with the bat. So I believe we can regard his exquisite slip-fielding as something of a bonus.

There had been a lot of rain prior to the Edgbaston Test and Gary Sobers provided more trouble for our batsmen than either Hall or Griffith. England made 216, a disappointing total and indicative of the fact that there would be a lot of hard work ahead. England only called on the services of four bowlers, and one of those, Tony Lock, only delivered two overs of spin. In addition to myself the other bowlers were my opening partner Derek Shackleton and Ted Dexter. I finished with figures of 5 for 75 from twenty-six overs, which, given the circumstances, pleased me. In our second innings Phil Sharpe answered his critics with 85 not out. On the last morning Tony Lock gave his bat some air, hitting a whirlwind 56 and Ted Dexter set the West Indies to score 309 to win, or, more to the point as far as I was concerned, gave me four hours and forty minutes to try to bowl them out.

England began well. We removed both openers cheaply, but when Rohan Kanhai took root at the crease our hopes of victory dissipated. Kanhai received sterling support from Basil Butcher and Joe Solomon, and we began to look anxiously at the clock, especially as Gary Sobers and Frank Worrell were still to come. It was at this juncture that I noticed that Derek Shackleton, who was a master of swing and seam at a very medium pace, seemed to be coming off the pitch faster than I was. That got me thinking. I recalled a game at Lord's when I'd seen Frank Tyson bowling in harness with David Smith of Gloucestershire, a bowler of much less pace than Tyson but one who could move the ball around. On this occasion, however, Smith was quicker off the pitch than Tyson. It seemed like an optical illusion at the time, but I had seen it more than once on various tracks, and this looked like one of them.

I decided to opt for a shorter run, which I was beginning to use with more frequency. I used the seam and it worked a treat. Suddenly the West Indies batsmen were more than just rattled, they went to pieces. In four overs I took the last six West Indies' wickets for 4 runs, and they came from a lucky edge off the bat of Lance Gibbs. Less than an hour after lunch it was all over. We had defeated the West Indies by 217 runs and I now had another best-in-Tests analysis of 12 for 119. I delivered over 15,000 balls in Test matches altogether, and undoubtedly the best of them came during the first innings at Edgbaston.

Gary Sobers, like many other sublime left-hand batsmen, was not always fully aware of the location of his off-stump when a right-handed bowler was coming in over the wicket and going wide of the crease. This was something I often did when the opportunity arose. With the ball coming across at a wide angle, the wicket-keeper took the place usually occupied by first slip and it was possible to deploy an extra gully. The extra gully was advantageous when a left-handed batsman drove a ball which, to him, appeared to be well wide of the off-stump. The slightest misjudgement, or a little movement, could easily result in an outside edge to the extra fielder in the gully. This is the tactic I employed when up against Gary Sobers in the Edgbaston Test. Gary is one of the greatest cricketers ever to have graced the game, certainly the greatest all-rounder. He has a great cricketing brain and his thought processes are lightning quick. He knew what I was up to in an instant, so engaged me in a battle of wits. I knew he knew, so reasoned that he would take some positive action to try to dominate the situation.

I directed my next delivery across him from wide of my crease, and Gary decided, at that moment, to apply discretion. Convinced the ball was travelling wide, he shouldered his arms to let the delivery pass. If the ball were to carry along its normal line it would, in all probability, have passed six inches wide of the off-stump, as Gary expected. But I had engineered this delivery to break at the last moment and rip out his off- and middle-stumps. I can see Gary now. For a few seconds he stared at the remaining stump in utter disbelief, then raised his eyes to the heavens. At the other end I heard two voices speak almost simultaneously.

'I don't believe what I just seen,' said the West Indies skipper Frank Worrell.

'What a ball!' exclaimed the umpire.

Afterwards, Gary and Frank came up to me and demanded, 'Fred, that was some ball. How do you bowl a ball like that, man?'

'You've gotta be joking, boys,' I told them. 'If I tell you that, you'll be working on how to play it and looking for it next time. Sorry, guys . . .'

All these years on, I think it safe enough to tell everybody. I always remember something Maurice Leyland once told me when I had bowled one in the nets which had come back from leg to off. I looked a bit puzzled, and when Maurice asked me if I knew what I'd just done, I confessed that I didn't. Maurice walked up to me and patted me on the shoulder. 'You can do it, Fred,' he said. 'You can bowl a ball like that naturally. Never try and find out how you can do it, just do it. Because if you don't know, the batsman has no chance of knowing.'

Scratch the surface of any bowler, especially a fast bowler, and you'll find a batsman trying to get out. I didn't like to bat, I loved it. Don Wilson and I seemed to contribute something extra in entertainment value to the end of a Yorkshire innings. That said, batting was somewhat of a two-edged sword for me. I liked to bat but never wanted my runs to take up too much time, because I knew not long after I was out, I'd be bowling, which is probably the reason why I always 'gave it a real go' when I had a bat in my hands. As Don Wilson used to say of my batting, 'up like a rocket and down like a stick'. That suited me, as I wanted to be as fresh and rested as possible for the natural part of my game.

Over the years, from being the rawest of number elevens, I gradually began to develop my batting technique. If you have anything at all about you as a bowler, you learn about batting from the great batsmen you encounter. In looking for their weaknesses you inevitably learn to appreciate their strengths when observing their technique at such close quarters. I learned not to bowl bouncers at certain batsmen, which ones were weak when playing around the off-stump, which ones hated a leg-stump yorker and so on. I learned and never stopped learning.

Come 1963 I had fifteen years of first-class cricket experience stored away in my mental card-index system. When batting, I would occasionally attempt a shot that was the speciality of some top-class batsman I had recently been trying to dismiss. Most people expected me to score most of my runs in the area between mid-wicket and long on, and if anyone pitched up a half-volley that is where runs for me would come from. But I was also confident enough to attempt various other shots, for example the classic cover drive.

The Yorkshire president, Sir William Worsley, told me that he had sufficient confidence in my ability as a batsman that he believed I would one day score a first-class century. 'When that day happens, Fred,' he told me, 'there'll be a cheque in the post to you the very same day.' All the same, it isn't easy to score a century when you regularly bat at number nine or ten. Simply because of the lack of time – even if you are batting well, batting well, because you are in the lower order, eventually you will run out of partners. I always remember a young player called David Smith. He was given a trial by Derbyshire and was selected to play in their first pre-season practice game against Cheshire of the Minor Counties League. Before the match David was full of himself. He dashed out of the pavilion and excitedly told relatives who had come along to see him play, 'The skipper says that if I make a century today, they'll play me in the first team!' He returned to the dressing room his heart overflowing with hope, only to see the team sheet pinned up and that he was batting at number ten. They have never been known for taking unnecessary risks at Derbyshire!

I had made fifties and sixties, even posted scores in the eighties. These knocks had delighted me, but up until 1963 the one knock that I really wanted had always eluded me – a century. Brian Close had assumed the Yorkshire captaincy and our game against Northamptonshire at Northampton on 4 May was Brian's first County Championship match as skipper. Though Brian had captained Yorkshire against both Oxford and Cambridge Universities, naturally he wanted to get off to a flyer when skippering the club in a county game for the first time. Instead, it was Northamptonshire who enjoyed a flying start to the season.

Our innings seemed to be in ruins in less than two hours. Bryan Stott and Phil Sharpe both only made 4. Geoff Boycott and Ray Illingworth only just made it to double figures and Doug Padgett made 18. With Brian Close playing a captain's innings, we were 106 for 5 when I came to the crease. I'd been promoted in the batting order due to injuries. Brian had said to me, 'Sorry, Fred, but you're going to have to bat at number seven.' Perhaps, subconsciously, I was thinking my big chance had arrived at last. I told Brian, 'It's all right, I'll do my best.' Brian responded by saying, 'You'll bloody well have to!' In the Yorkshire dressing room technical matters of that nature were always discussed with such understanding, diplomacy and grace, the most common response to a delicate situation being, 'We don't play this game for bloody fun, thou knowest!' You'll bloody well have to . . .'

So there we were, five wickets down against a Northamptonshire attack that was, with all due respect, not the best in the world. Brian Close was determined and resolute. As always he had complete confidence in his own ability to turn the situation around, his only worry being getting somebody to stay out there with him while he did it. Brian was really going some, displaying his immense, though all too rarely seen, talent as a batsman. He had no fears or doubts at all, except for the guy at the other end, and I was determined that he would not have to worry about me. Though we have always been the best of friends, there was always a keen, friendly rivalry between Brian and me. I think he believed at times that he could use a new ball better than me, and there were certainly occasions when I told him, 'There are times when I could bat better than you with a blindfold on, mate' – and believed that to be true!

This, however, was not one of those times. Brian was banging. We passed the 200 mark, a revival in the making, and I found myself passing 50. Then I played a loose shot. The ball came off the edge of my bat and I was almost on the point of walking when I saw Northamptonshire's wicket-keeper, Keith Andrew, uncharacteristically put down the catch. I turned to look down the track in some relief and found Brian Close's face six inches from mine.

'Right, that's a let-off,' he said through gritted teeth. 'Now get your bloody head down; we still need a lot of runs.'

I was a fast bowler promoted to number seven. The team had endured a dreadful start and I'd made over 50. That Brian still wasn't satisfied with my performance was not only the mark of the man, but indicative of the drive, fight and motivation that existed amongst the players in that Yorkshire team. I thought to myself, 'What do I have to do to impress you, Brian?'

'I know what you're thinking,' he shouted to me from the non-strike end. 'You're thinking, "What do I have to do to impress him?" The answer to that is, "Get your bloody head down!"'

So I got my head down.

Brian Close and I went on to add 166 for that eighth wicket. Brian made 161 and I hit 104 – my first century in first-class cricket. That was on Saturday. On Monday morning I opened my mail at home. There was an envelope bearing the Yorkshire club crest. When I opened it, it contained a cheque for £10 from Sir William Worsley.

Yorkshire retained the Championship that summer and to put the icing on the cake I made another century – for England. I had been chosen to play for England against Young England at the Scarborough Festival on 4 September. I reached 100 not out – and this was batting at number nine. I have always got on well with the people of Scarborough, and they were most appreciative of my efforts with the bat. Especially when a young England bowler, Richard Hutton of Yorkshire, the son of Len, took the second new ball and bowled me a bouncer. I attempted a hook – not a stroke at which I was particularly adept – managed to get a top edge and the ball skied over the wicket-keeper's head and dropped just short of being a six. Richard Hutton delivered himself of an unsolicited testimonial the type of which would not have best pleased the chaplain of Repton School but which had me grinning like a Cheshire cat.

'In case you're thinking of bowling me a bouncer again, young man. Let me remind you,' I informed him, 'at some point you will be facing my bowling.'

I had to wait almost two years before I made my second first-class century, and to my delight it was again at Scarborough. One month earlier I had played in my sixty-seventh and final Test for England against New Zealand at Lord's. At the time, whether I fully realized that game against New

Zealand was going to be my last for England, I don't know. Given my age and the fact I was a fast bowler, I thought it would be difficult at thirty-four to be selected again as a number one strike bowler, but as ever I lived in hope. My third first-class century was gained at the expense of Northumberland in a game at Jesmond. The fact that as a number one strike bowler and tail-end batsman I managed to score three centuries during my career is a source of some pride to me. But my proudest day was to occur in the season of 1964, and against Australia at that . . .

CHAPTER TWELVE

THE FINAL BOW

1963 WAS A GREAT season for me. I finished top of the Test, first-class and Yorkshire bowling averages. I scored two centuries and was the leading taker of Test wickets in the world. It was, however, not enough for me. I had my sights set on what many had once thought to be impossible – a new world record of 300 Test wickets.

Australia were the tourists in 1964 and after the third Test, at Headingley, I needed just three more to become the first ever bowler to claim 300 Test victims. I was very confident of getting them at the next Test at Old Trafford, but was hit by a bombshell. When the selectors announced the England team for Manchester, I had been dropped!

Though initially bitterly disappointed to have been excluded for the Old Trafford Test, in the event it was a good one for me to miss. The pitch turned out to be a real batting wicket. The England spearhead attack of Fred Rumsey (Somerset) and John Price (Middlesex) toiled and laboured while Australia's Bobby Simpson helped himself to a triple-century. The Old Trafford Test turned out to be a monumental display of batting gluttony with 1,281 runs scored and only 19 wickets taken. My replacement, Fred Rumsey, learned about Test wickets the hard way and did not survive to the Oval. To my great satisfaction I was recalled to face Australia in the last Test of the series.

England had another poor innings of 182. We were really up against it. I didn't think skipper Ted Dexter knew how to prevent the Aussies running away with the game. Australia were slowly grinding out the runs that put them in an unassailable position. Before lunch on the Saturday, I think Ted Dexter was getting pretty desperate as he cast about for an idea of what to do next. The look on Ted's face I had seen before, a sort of vacant, glazed expression. Eventually his eye fell on Peter Parfitt. I sensed Ted was going to ask him to produce what Peter imaginatively referred to as being, his 'version of off-spin'.

When his playing days were over, Peter was invited to join a Lord's committee to investigate players' suspect bowling actions. On hearing Peter had been appointed to the Lord's 'chucking' committee, Richard Hutton told Peter, 'Parf, what on earth are you doing on a committee that's examining dodgy bowling actions? It's like having Hitler preside at the Nuremberg Trials!' It's an anecdote Peter himself loves to recall. But many a true word is spoken in jest.

As Ted Dexter approached Peter, I seized the initiative from him. I walked up to Ted and said, 'Skipper, give me that ball!' I just about snatched the ball from Ted's grasp. He was so taken aback that I had put myself on to bowl, he never said anything and let me get on with it. I decided to bowl off my shortened run, cutting the ball rather than swinging it, at something less than my normal pace. It paid dividends in no time at all. I managed to get one to nip back and bowled Ian Redpath. The next man in was 'Garth' McKenzie and I got him first ball, caught in the slips by Colin Cowdrey.

I felt my forehead tickling as the adrenalin pumped around my body. I was not only on a hat-trick against the Australians, I was also on for the world record of 300 Test wickets. The Oval came alive. Apparently high up in the top of the Oval pavilion there was a sudden scramble in the Australian dressing room. As Ian Redpath and Tom Vievers had ground inexorably on, the Australian dressing room had taken on a very relaxed atmosphere. A card school had been in operation and those who had chosen not to play cards had been consulting the *Sporting Life* for the most likely means of improving their personal finances and injecting some excitement into the day. There had been no urgency in the Australian ranks. The Poms were being sorted and a first-innings lead of at least 200 was a distinct possibility. Suddenly my two consecutive wickets had turned the game on its head and Neil Hawke was all fingers and thumbs as he raced to get his pads and gloves on. Neil left that dressing room at some pace, descended the stairs two at a time and eventually emerged at the top of the pavilion steps just in time to meet me walking up them. It was lunch.

I had to sit through forty minutes of agony and agonizing. I sipped a cup of tea, nibbled at a sandwich but my stomach was up and down like a ride at Alton Towers. On the floor above, Neil Hawke was occupied by his own thoughts. He later told me that he was thinking, 'Well, I suppose this is my best chance to get into the record books. Few will recall my exploits as Test cricketer. But I'll always be remembered as being the player who was Fred Trueman's 300th Test victim. I guess I'm going to be remembered for all time.'

That, incidentally, is a typical Hawke thought. He was in fact a seriously good International bowler but a very modest player. Neil was so self-effacing I used to joke that, should he ever sit down and write his autobiography, he'd probably only mention himself twice. Neil and I were good friends. Our friendship started during England's tour of Australia in 1962–3. We simply seemed to get on with one another. After games we would find ourselves chatting while we shared a few tinnies and I found Neil to be a really warm guy who possessed many qualities I admired. One evening I rang him at the Australian's team hotel and said, 'Nat King Cole is in concert tonight. I've been lucky enough to get my hands on four tickets. Brian Statham, Geoff Pullar and myself are going. Would you like to come along?'

Neil replied, 'The taxi's pulling up now, mate'. So the four of us went along to see the legendary Nat King Cole and were spellbound by his sublime, silky voice. After the concert the four of us took off to a restaurant and over dinner talked about cricket and music. Years later Neil Hawke said to me, 'D'ya know – when I heard the news that Nat King Cole had died, I sat down and thought about that bonzer night when the four of us went to see him in concert. Great days.'

'Strangely enough, Neil, that's just what I did too,' I informed him. Later our friendship deepened when he came to live in the North of England for several years, flourished in business and displayed his prowess as a golfer by getting his handicap down to scratch. He became a member of the Nelson Golf Club and as captain helped put that club on the golfing map.

As far as I was concerned the lunch interval seemed interminably long. Eventually, however, we were all coming down the pavilion steps and I walked out to face my destiny. The Oval was packed, but you wouldn't have known it. When I began my run-up ready to deliver my 'hat-trick' ball, the Oval was as quiet as a minister's study. However, my delivery swept harmlessly past Neil Hawke's off-stump. There was a collective 'aaah' from the crowd, followed by what sounded like 15,000 bicycle tyres deflating simultaneously. The world record was not to be, at least not on a 'hat-trick' ball.

Australia added 16 runs, with Neil Hawke making 14 of those. Just when he appeared to have got his eye in, I made a delivery move away at the last moment. Neil went fishing and edged the ball to Colin Cowdrey at first slip – my 300th Test wicket and a new world record. The Oval erupted. Neil was the first man to congratulate me; he was followed by my England teammates, who all warmly shook my hand and patted me on the back. I didn't run up to Neil and snarl at him or wave a clenched fist triumphantly in the air as I see some players do nowadays when picking up a wicket. There were no high-fives. No gestures towards the Australian dressing-room balcony. I simply smiled to myself and let forth a sigh of deep contentment. I felt very proud, yet as I took the congratulations of the crowd and my teammates, at the same time deeply humbled. As Neil began his walk back to the pavilion, he said, 'Hey, Fred! Me and the boys be all right for champagne tonight then?'

'Too right you will,' I replied. 'See you all after the game. Drinks on me.'

It was a great moment, one that will be committed to my memory for as long as I live. The West Indian spinner Lance Gibbs eventually passed my final tally of 307 Test wickets and his record has since been broken several times. However, no one can ever take it from me that I was the first bowler to reach 300. A lot of sweat and toil had gone into achieving the world record; there were blood and tears too.

All I can say is – they weren't mine!

Just as in 1953 success for me at the Oval had been tinged with the sadness of the death of my grandmother, on the same ground I received another body blow. That season I took 100 first-class county wickets at an average of 21.94. I took 17 wickets against the Australians in four Tests. In first-class matches I averaged 17.0 with the bat. The new world record of Test wickets was mine, but at the Oval, when the selectors announced the England squad for the forthcoming winter tour of South Africa, I wasn't included. I thought, 'Thank you very much.'

My non-inclusion in the touring squad was to me inexplicable. I was gutted and again felt very harshly treated. Instead of touring with England, I signed up to the Rothman's Cavaliers for a tour of the West Indies. While touring the West Indies I kept up to speed on events from South Africa. When I read the news of the fifth Test in Port Elizabeth I nearly choked on a Red Stripe. John Price of Middlesex had broken down and Somerset's Ken Palmer, who was in South Africa on a coaching engagement, had been called up to play for

England, opening the bowling with Ian Thomson of Sussex. I thought to myself, 'With all due respect, Ken Palmer and Ian Thomson forming the England spearhead attack? Do me a favour!' Ken and Ian were both good lads. Good honest county bowlers. But International bowlers? Never in a million years were they that standard. Once again I was left to ponder on just what I had to do to be called up to the England team.

All these years on, as I now reflect, I often think of what might and should have been. There is no bitterness and resentment in me. I am far too happy and contented ever to feel that.

My bowling was made up of more than simply an action which enabled me to bowl fast for twenty seasons. My style of bowling also owed much to the many hours I had spent studying the great bowlers of my day and the past. Likewise, there was more to my bowling than the studied looks and chilling words I offered to batsmen. My bowling was a combination of all these things, and I feel I would have been a lesser bowler without just one of those characteristics.

On the occasion of my 300th Test wicket, although there was no official congratulatory telegram from my club, one committee member did send me one privately. Eventually Headingley did mark the occasion by presenting me with a silver tea service. I was presented with this by Sir William Worsley at the annual Yorkshire lunch. As Sir William handed the tea service, he said, 'Just a moment, Fred. May I just look at something?' I handed the tea service back to him. On examining it more closely Sir William pointed out to me that it had not been inscribed.

'That is no good,' he said, 'no good at all. How the dickens will anyone in the future know why this was presented?'

Sir William informed me that he would make arrangements for a fitting message to be inscribed. I had the mildly embarrassing situation of having been called up to receive a presentation and of returning to my seat empty-handed, much to the amusement of Closey, Ray Illingworth and my other teammates. Over two months later I happened to be in the Headingley club office when a committee member said to me, 'Oh, Fred. That's your tea service over there.'

'Oh, right, thank you,' I replied, and collected it as I left the office. That committee! They really knew how to make a player feel he was appreciated!

In the summer of 1965 both New Zealand and South Africa toured, with England playing three Tests against each team. I was recalled by England against New Zealand, played in two Tests and took 6 wickets. That made my grand total of Test victims 307. I really believed there were more to come. But that was it. I never played for England again. I was dropped from the second half of the series against South Africa because the tourists played a dodge, and the England selectors went for it hook, line and sinker.

That summer I took 127 first-class wickets at an average of 14.25. I was in good form and good nick. However, a South African player told me his guys had conned the MCC selectors. Eddie Barlow told me that during a cocktail party at Lord's, some of the South African players had told some MCC selectors that, having played against both me and Brian Statham, they thought we'd had our day and were over the hill. May I remind you, 127 first-class wickets this particular season.

What the South Africans had pulled was in fact an old Aussie trick to get the MCC to play what the Australians referred to as 'patsies' rather than a player they felt would cause them trouble. The most famous instance was that of Doug Wright. When talking to MCC selectors Don Bradman would wax lyrical about the merits of Doug Wright, who, he told the selectors, was the finest spin bowler he'd come across, and that just the sight of his name on the team sheet had Australians worried. The selectors kept picking Doug against Australia, and Don Bradman kept knocking double-centuries off him!

An MCC official told me the reason that I'd not been picked was because they considered me too old, though interestingly, on the tour of South Africa, the selectors had taken Sussex's Ian Thomson, who was three years older than me. The South Africans really had pulled the wool over the eyes of the England selectors . . .

During the three seasons up to and including 1968, we completed a hat-trick of County Championships, and in those years I had the honour of captaining Yorkshire several times – usually because Brian Close was unavailable through injury, often after having been hit when fielding a few centimetres from a batsman! Brian has an outstanding cricket brain. As a player he never stopped thinking about cricket and talking about technique and tactics. He, however, wasn't the only member of that Yorkshire team to possess such knowledge and enthusiasm. The committee believed both Ray Illingworth and I to be good enough for the job, and in the absence of Brian Close, both Ray and I had the honour of leading out the team.

Over these three seasons of consecutive Championship success for Yorkshire, in cricketing terms I grew old gracefully – though I was still eminently capable of splaying wickets and blasting batsmen with a few well-chosen words. In 1966, the first of Yorkshire's three consecutive Championships, I took 111 wickets at an average of 21.46. The following season I took 75 wickets at 21.46, and in 1968 my haul was 66 wickets at 20.83, though in the latter season I missed a number of matches due to injury.

In that final season I could still be 'Fiery Fred'. Against Leicestershire at Bramall Lane I took 6 for 20 in the second innings. Of those wickets, one had been yorked; another bowled by a late in-swinger; another caught from an off-cutter; from a slower delivery I made the batsman play too soon; and the final wicket came as a result of the batsman edging an out-swinger. What you might call varied bowling.

In the Yorkshire team that day was Richard Hutton, son of Len, who possessed a ready and sarcastic wit.

'You must have bowled the lot today, Fred,' said Richard, tongue in cheek. 'Inners, outers, yorkers, slowers. Tell me, Fred, have you ever bowled a straight ball?'

'Aye, I tried that once, against Peter Marner,' I informed him. 'It went straight through him like a stream of piss and flattened all three stumps!'

I thought to myself, 'Aye, that's told you, you precocious young scamp.' I liked Richard really. He was forever winding me up, but I took it all in good heart. I simply put it down to the fact that he'd never had the benefit of a proper education. He went to Cambridge.

Memories abound from that hat-trick of Championships. I remember, in 1966, routing the middle of the West Indies innings, taking more wickets in that innings than either Wes Hall or Charlie Griffith did in the whole match. That season I also took 4 wickets for 7 runs in the 'Roses' match and finished with first-innings figures of 5 for 18. Against Derbyshire I burst through in the old manner taking 3 top-order wickets that left our opponents on 19 for 4. I took 3 for 15 when Derbyshire batted again and the 43 I made with the bat was the highest individual score of the game. Towards the end of the season, I took 8 for 35 in one innings against Essex, which set up a must-win match against Kent.

Rain shortened the play. We batted first and made the modest total of 210. When Kent batted I made an early breakthrough, taking the crucial wickets of Mike Denness and Colin Cowdrey to leave our opponents on 9 for 3. I then mopped up the Kent tail end to finish with figures of 4 for 25. But disaster loomed. In no time at all we were reeling at 62 for 7. I made 18 out of 27 for the eighth and ninth wickets. When Kent batted I bowled Mike Denness for a duck and carried on giving it my all. We won that match by 24 runs in the extra half-hour – and with it the County Championship.

In 1967 I bowled short stints to maintain my considerable pace. I came across any number of sluggish wickets that summer, but still found I could startle a batsman with a bit of fire. My Yorkshire teammates recognized this and were forever offering encouragement. But in truth I could no longer bowl at the pace I once did for the period of time I once did. The judicious use of me as a bowler by Brian Close or Ray Illingworth, however, enabled me to bowl at top speed.

In 1967 Yorkshire played a very strong MCC team. At one point we had them at 23 for 7 and I had helped myself to four wickets. In our first Championship match of that season I took 5 for 39 against Glamorgan. I followed that with 3 for 20 against Kent, and then 3 for 25 against Worcestershire. Finally, in the University match at Fenner's I took 5 for 39 against Cambridge – statistics that suggest the MCC selectors had been wrong to think me too old. I couldn't bowl the long spells I once did, but in short bursts I knew I could still do a job for Yorkshire. In May 1968, however, I received a bombshell. I reported to Middlesbrough ready to play against Warwickshire, only to discover I had been left out of the team and that Chris Old had taken my place. I was named as twelfth man. I was shell-shocked, but what really hurt was the manner in which the news was delivered to me – by Alan Smith, the Warwick-shire captain!

Brian Close later admitted that he hadn't the heart to tell me himself. When Brian and I did discuss the matter I let him know exactly what I thought about his decision before buckling down to my duties as twelfth man.

That incident, coupled with the fact I had begun to resort to fast to medium-fast deliveries, forced me to consider retire-ment, even though I was still quicker than a lot of the bowlers who were defined as fast. I was down in the dumps, especially as I was overdue a benefit by the club and there was every likelihood of me not being given one. Brian Close had had his second, but the committee informed me they had already chosen a beneficiary for 1968 and that it wasn't me!

I found it all very disheartening. To make matters worse, when Brian Close heard that I had been refused a benefit, he urged the committee to present me with a cheque for £1,000 in recognition of my twenty years of sterling service. The committee refused. Blocking my second benefit was unforgivable. I was very popular with Yorkshire supporters and people of the county in general. I'm sure that had I been awarded the benefit I was entitled to, it would have smashed all records. Yet again I felt very badly done to by the Yorkshire committee.

Despite this disappointment, the 1968 season also provided me with some great moments. I was very proud to be a member of the team that accomplished the hat-trick of Championships. But towards the end of the season I enjoyed one of the highlights of my career. I captained Yorkshire against Australia at Bramall Lane.

Even with the absence of the injured Brian Close, we still had a very strong team and Australia paid us the compliment of turning out what was nigh-on their first choice – including Bill Lawry, Ian Redpath, Doug Walters, Ian Chappell, Graham McKenzie and 'Jackie' Gleeson. Australia were some team, but we reckoned we were a match for any International touring side, and as captain I was aiming at nothing short of victory. I won the toss and decided to bat. The match was played in warm, occasionally muggy weather which was an advantage to the bowlers, but I had every confidence we would post a decent total. My confidence was not misplaced. The lowest score amongst the first five to bat was 33. Geoff Boycott, Phil Sharpe and Doug Padgett batted superbly, taking us to 271 for 4.

When Australia took the second new ball an hour or so before the close of play, I was a tad disappointed to see that the Aussie skipper, Bill Lawry, had placed both a third man and a deep fine leg. As a captain Bill erred on the side of caution to the point of being negative. I felt at this stage of the game if he set an attacking field he had a reasonable chance of getting us out before stumps were pulled. That said, an attacking field would provide us with the opportunity of making a few quick runs and I could then think about a declaration. We batted through to close of play and into the second morning.

Before play began I walked past Bill as he was practising in the nets.

'I take it, you've declared,' Bill ventured.

'No,' I replied, 'we'll bat on.'

I wanted us to get a score of around 350 and then have a go at bowling them out twice. I felt that was possible, as I had had a good look at the wicket and knew it would turn as the game progressed. I was out in the middle with Ray Illingworth when, with the score at 355 for 9, I issued the declaration. That gave us about half an hour before lunch to have a go at Australia and, as it was only thirty minutes or so, it meant the shine would still be on the ball after lunch.

Things started to go our way. Our fielding was top class. I don't think there has ever been anything quite like that Yorkshire side when we were going all-out to win. They were really up for it, and the combination of our superb fielding and good bowling saw us get Australia out for 148.

At the end of the Australian innings the Bramall Lane groundsman asked me which roller I wanted and I suggested he should address that question to Bill Lawry. Then, to make sure there was no misunderstanding, I called into the Aussie dressing room and said to Bill, 'Will you bat again, Bill, please?'

I had to make sure, as two years earlier a cock-up had occurred when Yorkshire had played India at Bramall Lane. I was skippering the side that day and was enforcing the follow-on. I thought a signal to the Indian captain, the Nawab of Pataudi, would be all that was needed to convey my intention.

'Noob' misunderstood and thought the signal indicated I wanted his side to take the field. After an interval of ten minutes both teams found themselves coming down the steps of the pavilion side by side! It was a right cock-up and the crowd had a right good laugh at our expense, though both teams saw the funny side too.

As I've said, Australia had a very strong side out, but I wasn't lying when I said to the lads, 'We can win this. Let's be up for it and get stuck into them!' The tourists had a lot of quality, not the least of which came in the form of Bill Lawry. Bill was a fine player with a magnificent defence. As a batsman he was supremely confident of his own ability. So much so one felt he could bat right through an innings unless something out of the ordinary happened. I had every confidence that we could keep knocking down wickets at the other end, but felt Bill was going to be the problem, one to hold us up as went all-out for victory.

It was that scamp Richard Hutton who sent us on our way. Richard produced a quite magnificent delivery to Bill Lawry. It started just outside the off-stump and looked to all intents and purposes a long half-volley. It turned out to be a magnificent yorker which swung late and crashed into the base of the leg-stump. Lawry b. Hutton 0. We were on our way, and a packed Bramall Lane knew it.

The sky on the third morning was battleship-grey and threatening rain. I was becoming anxious that for all our efforts to win the game, it might be the weather that won the day. As the light deteriorated I asked Ray Illingworth to bowl from one end and brought Geoffrey Boycott on at the other in order to forestall any appeals against the light, as the Aussies would have done if Richard Hutton or myself had been bowling.

A breeze blew the rain clouds over and when the light improved I thanked Ray and Geoffrey for their efforts and brought on Richard Hutton and myself to bowl. Richard took the wicket of Ian Redpath, who moved across so far to an in-swinger he was lbw. What followed was the main stand of the innings between Walters and Sheahan. I tried to put the pressure on the pair of them by engaging a close field but they made 50 together in an hour. At that time I'd taken a breather but brought myself back and bowled at a speed that belied my thirty-seven years. First I ripped out Sheahan's middle-stump, then I pitched one fractionally short of a length to Doug Walters, straight enough to compel a stroke. The ball flew down to gully and into the welcoming hands of Ray Illingworth. With the scent of an historic victory in the air, the crowds poured into Bramall Lane. We didn't disappoint them. Ray Illingworth did the bulk of the damage and I finished it all off by removing Graham McKenzie. The match was won at half-past three which, earlier in the day, was the time I had predicted it would be. Not since 1902 had Yorkshire beaten Australia, and we beat them handsomely – by an innings and 60 runs.

It was a superb performance by a superb Yorkshire team. Some fine catches were held and none dropped. I recall in Australia's first innings getting the wicket of Ian Redpath. I was bowling at something like my old speed, Redpath tried to glance me, and wicket-keeper Jimmy Binks executed the most amazing catch, hurling himself through the air to take the ball with one hand.

The champagne flowed that night, I can tell you, and we knew that the whole of Yorkshire celebrated with us. Every member of that team was only too aware of the responsibility and honour that rested with them when they crossed that white line. We knew we were heirs to a great legacy. When we played for Yorkshire we were not just playing for the club and ourselves but for all the people of Yorkshire, whether they be interested in cricket or not. It was something we accepted with pride as well as gratitude.

I think it can be reasonably said that in that Yorkshire team there were more top names than there have been since.

But there were no stars, the team was the star performer. Peter Stringer, a regular in the second XI, played in that game against Australia. He received the same match fee as I did, his captain and someone who had played in sixty-seven Tests for England. I wouldn't have had it any other way. If anyone in that side had shown even the slightest indication that he was developing a prima donna complex, either Brian Close, Ray Illingworth, Jimmy Binks or myself would have sorted it at once. No one was bigger than the team.

After our victory against Australia I took stock. I was coming up to thirty-eight, no longer the Fiery Fred of my pomp, but still able to bowl quick. I had just captained Yorkshire in a convincing win over Australia and the team were on course for a third successive Championship. With all that going for me, it seemed like an opportune time to bow out, while still at the top. I had seen the Yorkshire committee deal cynically, sometimes cruelly, with players who had given the club sterling service, and I didn't want that to happen to me.

I didn't reveal that I had made the decision to retire to anyone. Brian Statham announced his retirement soon after I'd decided, and I thought I'd see how he fared. When Brian walked out for his last match at Old Trafford it was an overwhelmingly emotional moment. I knew myself well. I knew I wouldn't be able cope with such a display of emotion. In truth I am a sensitive guy and I knew myself well enough to know that this sort of occasion and outpouring of emotion would reduce me to tears, and I wasn't going to allow that to happen. At least not in public and before the massed ranks of the media. So I made up my mind to go quietly and without a big send-off. In the event it was the best thing to go, not least because it confounded those who had never warmed to me and who predicted that I would go around every ground playing to the crowd for applause and well wishes. I announced my retirement well after the end of the 1968 cricket season.

There was no big farewell and parting was, indeed, such sweet sorrow.

I wrote a polite letter to the club, expressing my gratitude for the opportunity of having been a Yorkshire player for twenty years. I then rang the club president, Sir William Worsley, and requested a meeting. He said, 'It must be important, Fred. Come round now, if it suits you.' I drove to his house and when we were seated came straight to the point of my visit.

He said, 'Oh no, Fred. Don't do that. You can go on for years and you are probably one of the best fast-medium bowlers in the world.'

I told him I was sorry and handed him the letter. He read it, appeared deeply moved by the tenor of what I had written but said that he couldn't accept it.

'We are holding a meeting next week,' he informed me, 'and there is every likelihood you will be offered the captaincy.'

This came as a bombshell to me. You have to be a Yorkshireman to fully comprehend what the position of county captain really means. It's more coveted than the captaincy of England! When I got over the shock I told Sir William that if someone had only hinted about the merest possibility of this accolade I would have been delighted to carry on playing for another couple of years. However, I had given the matter of my retirement much considered thought and my mind was set.

'Besides,' I told him, 'I have announced my retirement in my column in the *Sunday People*. It will be public tomorrow morning.'

He asked me to telephone the *People* there and then to ask them to spike the story. I explained it was too late. The early editions would be already coming off the presses.

On leaving Sir William's house I drove over to see Brian Sellars. I was torn. I still felt my decision to retire was the right one, but I was gutted that I had missed the opportunity to captain Yorkshire. I gave Brian Sellars my letter. He invited me to sit down and poured us a drink. At one point during our conversation Brain said something that puzzled me. He told me that, inadvertently perhaps, I had helped the Yorkshire committee out of a difficult situation. He didn't elaborate, so I was left to mull over what he meant. On the drive home I wondered if the Yorkshire committee had plans to sack Brian Close from the captaincy and offer him the option of either playing under me or moving to another county.

Given Yorkshire had recently won their third successive County Championship under Brian's captaincy, one might be given to thinking that there was no way on earth the committee would want Brian out. But here we are talking of the Yorkshire committee, a body of people not exactly known to display loyalty to players, an administration not known for always making the right decisions. Also, there was the matter of Brian himself.

Without doubt Brian Close was a brilliant captain. But if he left himself open to criticism, it was over his attitude to young players. Brian was loath to give youth a chance at Yorkshire and believed that young players should have to fight their way into the team as he and I had done. Brian and I disagreed on the matter of young players. Yorkshire had a great team, but with one or two exceptions, we were all of a similar age. I could see in the not too distant future a point when wholesale changes would have to be made within a short period of time; changes that would be detrimental to the long-term success of the club.

I tried to persuade Brian to introduce young players one at a time. That way I felt the metamorphosis of the team would be gradual. I used to say to Brian, 'By playing one of the youngsters, he'll gain experience and learn. He'll contribute something, so if we have to carry one lad, so be it. This team is good enough to do that. It's better to blood youngsters gradually. If you don't do that, there will come a point when most of the established lads will retire around the same time.

Then the team will be comprised of mainly young, inexperienced players.'

Brian was stubborn and unyielding. He just kept on saying, 'Youngsters will have to fight for a place and will only play when they can contribute on a level that all the others do.'

In the years that were to follow, my fears were realized. In a few years, Yorkshire found themselves with a relatively young and inexperienced team, which led directly to a dismal run of failure. If I had taken over as captain I think I might have prevented that.

To begin with, I would have done everything in my power to persuade Ray Illingworth to stay. All Ray wanted was a two-year contract to provide some security for himself and his family. Given his talent and the sterling service he had given the club for so many years, I didn't think that much to ask. But the Yorkshire committee in their wisdom turned down Ray's request. Ray moved to Leicestershire, where he enjoyed phenomenal success. Under his captaincy Leicestershire underwent a renaissance. They won trophies and Ray became captain of England and under his guidance won back the Ashes in Australia. Ray was one of the best all-rounders in the world but, significantly, never became a regular in the England team until he was thirty-six and no longer at Yorkshire.

By and large a cricketer will be in his prime at around twenty-eight to thirty years of age. But in order to reach his prime, he must have been playing first-class cricket for some six to seven years. If young players had been gradually introduced into the team they would have gained invaluable experience which, in time, would have helped them develop into top-class players, and the future success of the club would have been assured. In the event, what lay ahead was a very barren and tragic period for the county.

The trouble was not only on the pitch. The supporters and ordinary club members refused to take a back seat and not voice their concern and opinions. An influential group banded together, formed an action committee and locked horns with the club's hierarchy. Jack Mewies, a solicitor, was one of the main protagonists. The in-fighting was unbelievable and the blood-letting considerable.

At the time I was writing for the *Sunday People* and found myself covering one of those meetings. At one point, when relaying the club's position, Brian Sellars took me by saying how pleased he was to see me there. He went on to say that the committee had never realized just what a good captain I was and how much I had done for the young players at the club. This statement caused all manner of ructions. People took to their feet and started to shout him down. The atmosphere became very hostile and I heard one supporter shout, 'So why didn't you make Fred Trueman captain then?' Brian didn't reply. I don't suppose he was in any position to reveal that the committee had intended to do just that.

Having announced my retirement I had some career statistics to contemplate. There were 2,304 wickets. No other fast bowler in the history of the game had reached that total. I had bowled over 20,000 overs – a phenomenal number for a fast bowler. There were 307 Test wickets at an average of 4.5 wickets a match. I was supposedly a tail-end batsman, but my batting average in Test matches was 21.57 and 18.29 in all cricket. All in all I scored some 9,000 runs, including three centuries. There was also my fielding: 438 catches, most of them at my favoured position of short leg.

But it is not just the statistics that place the story of my career in some perspective. I was a fast bowler who often bowled to an attacking field, more often than not without a third man or long leg, so that any ball that edged through the slips or the short legs, because of the pace of my delivery, often ran away to the boundary for 4.

When my contract at Yorkshire expired in November 1968, the committee decided they must mark the occasion with a farewell gesture. Since they owed me a benefit I secretly hoped they might be generous this time and bequeath me that honour. No such luck. They decided it would be more fitting to present me with a farewell gift. I was asked to inform them of the gift of my choosing. I chose a Charles II silver cruet set which I had seen in a shop and was informed that would be in keeping.

Considering I had given twenty years' sterling service to the club, what followed I found unbelievable. I was informed that the silver cruet set had been purchased at a cost of £220 and unfortunately the committee had set a limit of 100 guineas for my farewell gift. I was asked to pay the balance, which, given I had not been granted the benefit I was entitled to, I felt was particularly mean and crass of the committee.

There was no ceremony. No drinks in the committee room prior to being officially presented with the gift. A committee man simply handed it over to me one day when I was at Headingley. When I got home and took the cruet set out of the box, I discovered they'd not had it inscribed.

My career at Yorkshire was over. There was no welcome for me at Headingley any more. The following summer I called into the office to ask if I could have a couple of complimentary tickets for the Test match. One of the ticket administrators informed me, 'Complimentary tickets are only available to players,' adding: 'You don't play for the club now. What makes you think you are entitled to complimentaries?' I told her that sixty-seven Tests and 307 International wickets seemed a fair reason.

She replied, 'If I can arrange two tickets, what would you like me to do with them.' I told her and walked out.

Whenever I turned up at Old Trafford, Edgbaston, Trent Bridge or the Oval people would go out of their way to make me welcome. Not so at Headingley, because there it was clear I wasn't really welcome. However, I am a Yorkshireman through and through, and despite the cold reception I still followed the progress of the team with keen interest.

Cricket was the game I loved. In some respects, playing the game had moulded a part of my character. It had served to instil in me a sense of fair play, self-discipline and had been a catalyst to self-motivation. I had loved not just playing the game but also the camaraderie of my teammates. I had warmed to our sense of togetherness, rose to the battles we faced as a team. I enjoyed the dressing-room banter, the comic asides, the ribbing and the deep friendships I had formed. But now my playing days were over I wondered how I would cope without all that.

Cricket was one of the two great loves in my life. As when making the decision to split from a former lover, the actual decision is easier than the mechanics of the split. I wondered what effect not having the daily impetus of being involved in the game would have on me. Some players find the adjustment hard. Their lives have become accustomed to the daily discipline that cricket gives. For some, once their playing days are over, there is a vacuum in their lives which they find difficult to fill. Following their retirement from the game I had known some players become depressed and even try to find solace in drink. I assume their depression was the result of them believing the halcyon days of their life were over, that life had little to offer them any more and that all to come would be an anti-climax.

I never felt that. I was a little anxious at the fact I was now entering an unknown period in my life, but confident I had enough about me to embark upon a new career, whatever that might be. The decision was right because I felt I wouldn't miss playing cricket too much. What I would miss was taking wickets. That gave me the sort of buzz I knew I would never encounter again in life. But I was confident and optimistic that there would be other things in life that would stimulate me. A different buzz to taking wickets, but a buzz all the same.

When I announced my retirement from the game a life ended. I knew I was about to enter a very transitional period in my life, not only career-wise, but also at home. My marriage to Enid was drawing towards its end. I knew I had to move on. Career-wise I didn't foresee too many problems. I had been writing for the *Sunday People* in one way or another since 1957. I had numerous people and organizations who wanted me to speak at dinners, endorse products or make personal appearances. I had been approached by Yorkshire Television, who wanted to discuss certain ideas they had for me to appear on programmes they had slated for future broadcast. I knew I wasn't going to starve. I would have a new career sorted and soon.

What I had to sort out was my marriage to Enid. I was still plagued by the thought of the effect a split would have on the children. I toiled with the idea of simply accepting the marriage for being what it was and get by like that, rather than be without my children. The thought of the children without their mum and dad together under one roof filled me with deep pain. My decision to retire from cricket had been for me a monumental one. But I was now turning over in my head the biggest decision I would ever have to make in life.

CHAPTER THIRTEEN

MOVING ON

ONE OF THE FIRST opportunities to come my way was that of stand-up comedian. Sometime in 1969 I happened to be in a club in the north-east listening to a comedian. His jokes were so old they could have received telegrams from the Queen. It was not just his material that was poor, his delivery was edgy and had all the timing of an old cooker clock. Later that evening I asked the owner of the club what he was paying the man for the week-long engagement. He told me and my jaw dropped. I said something along the lines of 'I could do stand-up better than him'. One of the club's management said, 'Fred, do you *really* think you could do a week up here in front of a crowd like this?'

I have always found challenges hard to refuse, so I put a bold face on and said, 'Absolutely. I'm your man.' Someone then bet me I couldn't do it. That was it for me.

I approached the Lipthorpe brothers, who owned the Fiesta nightclubs in Sheffield and Stockton-on-Tees, and they agreed to book me as a stand-up for a week. The Lipthorpe brothers were very creative and always thought of some gimmick to grab the attention of the audience immediately, and the idea they came up with for my entrance was no exception. On stage they erected a paper screen onto which was projected a film of me bowling. The film was taken from the viewpoint of a batsman, so I was seen advancing on my run-up. When I was in the process of delivering the ball my image filled the whole of the screen. At which point, I jumped through the paper screen to make my entrance. On the first night the audience nearly jumped out of their skins when I came crashing through the screen!

Most of the material I used was of my own making and I found I had a knack for gags and funny anecdotes. I went down so well with audiences the Lipthorpe brothers booked me for another week, then another. I did the stand-up for nigh-on six weeks in total before I realized that, much though I enjoyed it, there were other things I would much rather be doing in life.

Life? Now that was beginning to change for me – and how. The most wonderful thing that would ever happen to me, which would bring me great happiness, was unfolding at this time and gathering momentum. In the telling of this, I must backtrack to 1966.

In the mid-sixties I played football for a team called the Yorkshire All Stars. We played friendly games, usually on a Sunday afternoon, to raise funds for various charities. All the players gave their services free and in addition to raising considerable sums for worthy causes, we enjoyed the games, which invariably evolved into a social occasion afterwards. The Yorkshire All Stars played local amateur and semi-professional teams as well as other representative sides such as the Show Biz All Stars, who I also turned out for on several occasions. We had a decent side. In addition to myself the team contained Brian Close and Ray Illingworth; the former athlete Derek Ibbotson; the Australian rugby league player Arthur Clewes; Mr Bond himself, Sean Connery; Jimmy Hill; the singer Ronnie Hilton; and occasionally the pop singer turned star of stage and screen musicals Tommy Steele.

After one such game at Keighley, I approached my car and noticed a young woman leaning against it. She was chatting to some people, but as I approached she stood upright. We struck up conversation. She knew who I was, but I didn't know her. She told me her name was Veronica. There was something about her that sparked something inside me. As we talked I could feel an indefinable chemistry between us. We connected, but it was more than that. I hung on her every word. Everything she said was important to me. She was bright, witty, happy and she conveyed those qualities to me in such a way I suddenly felt energized.

I was filled with hope and optimism. I went fishing for information, as one does when attracted to a woman. I asked what she did in life. My heart sank when she informed me she ran a pub with her husband, and another couple who were close friends of theirs. On the face of it I would have thought the conversation would have petered out there and then. There would be social niceties, before a polite withdrawal and farewell – for good. But the signals I was receiving and, I suppose, emitting myself gave me hope that the door was not shut. Veronica told me that she and her husband kept the Swan pub in Addingham. She invited me to call in one day. But it was the way she said this that excited me. It wasn't just a throwaway invitation. She said it in such a way I believed she really did want to see me again.

As I drove home from Keighley my stomach was doing cartwheels and my heart was racing. My mind was full of thoughts of Veronica. She was beautiful, easy-going, fun and fun to be with. Life is short, but, due to our respective circumstances, there seemed no way for a relationship between Veronica and me to develop. But I have always relished a challenge. What's more, whenever there was something I really wanted in life, I was always ready to be patient, to work at it. To think of long-term goals. I didn't know how or even if I could develop a relationship with this stunning woman who had bowled me over. But I knew I was going to try.

A week or so later I found myself in the Swan. I told Veronica I'd been driving through the area and decided to call in and say 'hello'. She, of course, knew the real reason for my appearance. She visibly brightened when she saw me. Her smile was genuine, there was a sparkle in her eyes. That did it for me. I knew we had something going between us.

In the ensuing years Veronica and I got to know each other so very well. Initially we were confidants. Sounding boards for each other to discuss the trials and tribulations of our respective marriages. One of the things that Veronica said she liked in me was that I was a good listener. When a woman talks to a man about a problem, invariably the man will listen for a short time before trying to offer a solution. Most men see themselves as problem-solvers. I didn't have the answers to many of the problems in Veronica's marriage, so I simply offered a sympathetic ear. I talked to her about my marriage to Enid. I found she was objective and wise. I was comforted by her understanding, her sensitivity and her emotional empathy. As time passed we talked of what sort of relationship we had.

Due to our respective circumstances we referred to it as a deep and meaningful friendship. Of course, it was more than that. We talked of having a friendship as we defined it, with no lids or boundaries. Should anything happen between us, then it would be natural and because we both wanted it to happen. The inevitable did happen. Eventually Veronica and I were more than simply very good friends.

Throughout the late sixties we met with increasing regularity and I had no doubt whatsoever that I had met the love of my life. We were both gloriously happy, yet at the same time, deeply unhappy in our respective marriages and that we couldn't be together as one all the time. Something had to give.

I needed someone to accept me for the way I am. Someone to trust me and depend on me for what I could provide. Someone who not so much admired me for what I had done in life, but for what I was trying to do. Someone with whom I could share a deep and meaningful love but also friendship and companionship. Someone who gave me the opportunity to fulfil her needs. That someone was Veronica.

Matters came to a head in 1970. I had been living on my own for some time, though I was still married to Enid. Veronica left her husband and initially set up home with her two children, Sheena and Patrick. She had no financial resources to speak of, so I gave her some money to buy the basics and I went out and bought them a three-piece suite and one or two other items of furniture. We quickly decided that a home of her own was not what we wanted. Veronica and I wanted to be together and we set about house-hunting together.

We came across a large stone-built bungalow with extensive gardens, set within a wood near Gargrave. We fell in love with the house straight away, though the gardens were overgrown and the house itself needed some work. I was earning £3,500 a year from writing my column for the *Sunday People*, that in itself would see us all right, though I was confident of securing more work elsewhere in the media. I used my savings to put a deposit down on the house, the mortgage went through without a hitch and to our great delight and happiness, Veronica and I at last had a home of our own.

The gardens had not been attended to for some time. What had once been lawns was an overgrown, jumbled mess of saplings, brambles and weeds; the apple trees were so laden with fruit the branches were almost touching the ground. I borrowed an agricultural mower and set about restoring the gardens to their former glory. That was some job.

It was four weeks of daily work before I reduced the gardens to lawn level and got rid of the vast amount of garden waste. There was still much work to do, but I didn't mind one little bit, because I was helping create a home for Veronica and me. Which is what I desired more than anything else in the world.

I realized that all the years of unfulfilled love with Enid were not, as I had thought for much of the time, a negative part of my life, but a positive one, as I had actually been preparing myself to be attracted to the woman who was right for me. My positive outlook was all down to Veronica and the love we shared. We were not only supportive of one another's physical needs for security and survival, but also supportive of each other's emotional, intellectual and spiritual needs. I had never achieved that depth of relationship with Enid. My hurt had healed because I recognized it belonged to the past, which enabled me to move on and share my life with Veronica. Enid and I were divorced in 1971. Veronica's divorce came through in 1973. When Veronica and I bought our home near Gargrave, we were there to build a new future together and to create our memories.

Veronica was the bedrock to my existence but also to my career. She gave me pertinent advice, was never wrong in her judgement of people and business matters, and I came to reply on her totally. She handled my diary for me and appreciated my true worth. Following my stint as a stand-up comedian, I began to speak at a lot of dinners. I was charging £30, but having heard me speak Veronica put my price up to £50. I couldn't believe that anyone would pay that amount of money to hear me speak. I was wrong.

We received even more requests for my after-dinner speaking. When Veronica put my price up to £75, then later £100, again I voiced my concern that no one would pay such an amount. Veronica assured me they would. 'Don't undervalue yourself,' she once told me, '£100 is excellent value. People will willingly pay it to have you speak at their dinners.' As always, Veronica was proved right. We were flooded with requests for me to speak at dinners.

My new career outside cricket began to diversify, and I didn't think life could get any better for me. But it would. I received a telephone call from Lawrie Higgins, a producer at Yorkshire Television. What resulted from our subsequent meetings was a TV series, hosted by yours truly, entitled *Sometimes You Win*. The premise of the series was simple enough. I would interview a celebrity who loved sport, and talk about their career in show business. I'd then ask them to predict the draws from Saturday's fixtures – in short, marking the card for pools punters. No one took the suggestions seriously, it was all a bit of fun and a vehicle for what was ostensibly a chat programme.

I was comfortable working to camera and though a little nervous to begin with, soon settled into my role of interviewer. The series was only broadcast in the Yorkshire region, but we had some big name guests. Amongst them Tom Jones, Engelbert Humperdinck, Jimmy Tarbuck and jazz musician Terry Lightfoot.

I have always endeavoured to have an open mind and have taken an interest in a wide range of subjects. Seemingly, this was recognized by another producer at Yorkshire Television. Barry Cockcroft asked me to host a series entitled *One-man Business*. The series was very much as the title suggests. I travelled around Yorkshire talking to people who ran their own businesses, many of which were dying trades. The sheer variety of one-man businesses never ceased to fascinate and amaze me. I talked to a blacksmith, an artist, a piano teacher, a thatcher and one man who ran a small quarry all by himself. The vast majority of viewers were, like me, not aware of the variety of one-man businesses that existed in the county. Yorkshire was introduced to itself and a simple idea proved a hugely popular hit.

The colloquial theme was continued when I was invited to a host yet another Yorkshire TV series, entitled *Yorkshire Spakes*. Once again this series involved me travelling around the county meeting everyday folk and talking about their life and work. I remember visiting Robin Hood's Bay, where I met a group of lobster fishermen. I was amazed to discover the lobstermen had a thriving little export business. The lobsters of Robin Hood's Bay are of a particularly fine quality and the vast majority of lobsters caught were packed live and immediately shipped by air to France, where they were prized by top restaurants. It was during the flight to France that I discovered that, while in the air, the lobsters would emit a high-pitched melodic hum, almost as if they were singing. Nobody knew how or why the lobsters did this. It was just one of the many curious aspects to people's work I encountered during the two series of *Yorkshire Spakes*. The series I have mentioned were only broadcast in the Yorkshire region, but I was soon to get my big break in television with another series that was taken on by the ITV network.

The idea of *Indoor League* came about during a discussion over lunch with Yorkshire TV executive Donald Batherstock. Donald had this great idea of getting people from pubs and working men's clubs to compete against one another on television. Donald wanted to afford 'ordinary' people the opportunity to appear on television by virtue of their skills. Initially Donald saw *Indoor League* as simply another regional programme. He placed adverts in local newspapers and flyers in pubs and clubs inviting teams to appear in the series. The response was overwhelming. We received thousands of applications from teams, some of whom played indoor sports we never knew existed. We had darts, dominoes, snooker and pool teams by the dozen, but also teams of skittle players, arm wrestlers and table football players. You name it, if the sport was played indoors in Yorkshire we featured it during the series.

The series hit the ground running and went from success to success. The ratings soared and it wasn't long before *Indoor League* went network on ITV. I hosted the programme for six years and enjoyed it immensely. It really felt like I was carving a new career for myself in broadcasting. *Indoor League* was fun to do, but I did have a couple of gripes concerning what I was asked to do. The first involved my prop. When introducing items I was always seen resting at a bar with a pint of beer near to hand. In truth I was drinking very little at this time, especially beer. To be seen throughout the nation always with a pint in hand was unrepresentative of me, but I went along with it, as the producers felt it was in keeping with the culture of the series.

My other gripe, albeit another small one, was the catch-phrase I was asked to deliver at the end of each programme – 'I'll see thee!' There is nothing wrong with local accents, indeed people should be proud of them, but I don't talk like that! It just wasn't me. I was also concerned that it portrayed a rather stereotypical view of Yorkshire people. Again, the producers persuaded me that the catchphrase was in keeping with the context of the series, so I went along with it. I was never comfortable saying it, yet all these years later people come up to me, talk about *Indoor League* and on leaving proudly say 'I'll see thee!'

Indoor League was good to me. I was propelled from regional broadcaster to being a household name. *Indoor League* allowed me another dimension and popularized me with sections of society other than devotees of cricket. But my transition from regional to national programming did not affect me personally. The way I saw it, I was still looking into a camera and to me every camera looks alike. That I was now addressing a much larger audience never affected me. I was aware of it, of course, but as you never receive immediate feedback when broadcast-ing on television I was, at the time, unaware of my growing popularity.

As the ratings continued to grow – and ever more people started shouting my catchphrase at me – I slowly came to terms with the fact that I really did have a new career. Though I applied myself in a professional manner to this new career as a TV host, I was never too serious or precious about my role. I was ever mindful that television, like cricket, can be notori-ously fickle. One day you are the flavour of the month, not so the next. So I just enjoyed 'the moment' but always had something else to fall back on should my popularity suddenly wane.

I never feared that my cricketing career would be forgotten

as the popularity of *Indoor League* grew. As far as I was concerned, they were two different worlds, populated by two entirely different audiences. What I had achieved in cricket would be there in the record books for all future generations to see. Television programmes, irrespective of their popularity, have a limited shelf life. In time they pass into the memory until the day comes when we forget everything. Then they are gone for ever. Not so achievements in cricket.

In many respects *Indoor League* turned me into a 'professional' Yorkshireman. I didn't exactly warm to this, but it was never a problem with me, as I didn't believe it to be demeaning to the fine folk of Yorkshire, and still don't. This was the seventies and many working people were making their mark in television and doing so while proudly extolling their roots. 'Can any good come from Nazareth?' the Bible asks. The notion that something worthwhile could come from the provinces was a mark of popular culture in the seventies. Television was opening its doors to 'the people'. In some ways *Indoor League* and other shows were making television more accessible to the masses. Something we take for granted today.

My career in broadcasting was not limited to television. In the early seventies I was invited to appear on BBC Radio's *Test Match Special* to offer comment and analysis of England's Test series against Pakistan. I must have done something right, because I was later asked to become a permanent member of the *TMS* team. BBC Radio had intermittently broadcast commentary of England's Test matches since the thirties, sometimes on the Light Programme (now Radio 2) and the Home Service (Radio 4). In 1957 BBC Radio found a home for cricket commentary on the Third Programme (Radio 3). *Test Match Special* was born, and, as the *Radio Times* of the day proudly boasted, 'You will not miss a ball, we will broadcast them all.'

TMS was already an established institution when I joined the team in the seventies. The programme had an eclectic mix of commentators and characters. John Arlott was the poet; Brian Johnston the mischief-maker who, like Peter Pan, had never grown up. There was the cerebral Don Mosey, the objective Trevor Bailey and yours truly. Also on *TMS* at various times were E. W. Swanton – one of the old school of cricket, who provided excellent close-of-play summaries – Rex Alston, Ken Ablack, Tony Lewis and, later in the seventies, Henry Blofeld and Christopher Martin-Jenkins.

Though he was irreverent and not to all tastes, there is little doubt that the popularity of *TMS* really took off in the seventies following the arrival of Brian Johnston. He brought with him jokes and japes and, of course, a plethora of cakes, baked for the team by well-wishers throughout the country. Brian attracted a new audience to *TMS* and in so doing to the erudite talents of John Arlott.

No matter what events were unfolding on or off the pitch, John would describe them with lyricism and poetry in the measured tones of a warm Hampshire accent. In 1975, during an England–Australia Test at Lord's, John had enjoyed a good lunch with his publisher and was in a particularly relaxed mood, when suddenly there was a commotion from the Tavern area of the ground. Trevor Bailey was the first to spot the reason for uproar, a streaker, which Trevor, for reasons known only to himself, referred to as a 'freaker'. A term immediately adopted by John, who broke from describing the cricket to relate to listeners the other event that was unfolding on the pitch, making the transition with consummate ease.

'We have a freaker,' said John. 'Not very shapely – and it is masculine. And I would think he has seen the last of the cricket for the day which, for him, is to his detriment and loss, as a dramatic match is beginning to unfold. The police are mustered; so are the cameramen and Greg Chappell. The interloper is being embraced by a blond policeman and this may be his last public appearance, but what a splendid one.

'He's now being marched down in the final exhibition past

at least 8,000 people in the Mound Stand, some of whom, perhaps, have never seen anything quite like this before. And so he disappears to await his fate at the hands of London's finest, with the score at 147 for 3.'

Unruffled, untroubled, unbelievably cool. Never at a loss to find the right words to describe a situation for those who could not see it. It was the mark of John Arlott. Many of John's descriptive phrases have passed into both broadcasting and cricket legend.

'Umpire Fagg, his face like Walt Disney's idea of what a grandfather should look like.'

On a characteristically long and dogged innings from Geoffrey Boycott: 'No man is an island, but he has batted as though he was a particularly long peninsula.'

'Dennis Lillee begins his run-up; black hair lounging on his shoulders like an anaesthetized cocker spaniel.'

'Brian Congdon remains at the crease to frustrate England, like some lingering, unloved guest at a party.'

'His [Tony Greig's] performance has held the England innings together as the shell does an egg.'

'The West Indies total, 687 for 8 declared. Richards, a masterful innings of 291. He set the tone. His attitude, contagious, like the gladness of a happy child.'

'Lloyd continually offered encouragement and instructions to his players in the field. His voice came in gusts, like linnets in the pauses of the wind.'

'The actress Charlotte Rampling is in the crowd. Charlotte Rampling. Her name to me, suggestive of an active verb.'

John was very proud of the fact that he wrote for the *Guardian* on two topics: cricket and wine. He was a great wine lover and his knowledge of his subject was second to none. I remember once visiting his home in Hampshire and being slack-jawed at the sight of his enormous wine cellar. John had recently been out for lunch with his bank manager. The bank had presented John with a bottle of a particularly fine wine which at the time cost in the region of £60 a bottle. John was delighted to have received such a vintage bottle of wine and was gushing in his praise of the bank, saying it was indeed a rare vintage that any wine connoisseur would be delighted to have as part of their collection. His son popped down to the cellar and when he returned had a surprise for his father. He told John that he already possessed about twenty bottles of the very same vintage. John simply had no idea what was down there.

When John moved to the Channel Islands he sold his cellar. The newspapers reported he received in the region of £100,000 for the sale of his wine. When I remarked that this was a tidy sum that would see him comfortable in his latter years, he blithely replied, 'Well, yes, not bad. Considering I kept all the best to myself. I'm having it shipped out to my new home.'

John's health began to deteriorate following the death of his son. As parents we expect our children to outlive us; when they don't it must be a monstrous and monumental emotional blow. John never came to terms with his great loss and, in my opinion, blamed himself. It was coming up to Christmas and John had telephoned his son asking if he could visit him. It was while journeying to John's home that his son was tragically killed in an accident. As he often said to me, 'If I hadn't made that call. If I hadn't asked him to come over. He'd be with us now.'

After the accident, John seemed to drink more than normal, and his health began to deteriorate. During one edition of *TMS* John and I were in the commentary box together. He was asking me for my summary of the play to date. As I was talking I noticed John's eyelids slowly close. His head dropped forward and his chin rested on chest. One arm fell loose at his side. I was convinced he'd died right in front of me and live on air. There was a very brief hiatus in my summary, just a second or two, before I gathered myself together and carried on broadcasting. My mind was in a whirl. While trying to stay 'on mike' and offer an objective summary of the play, I was reaching forward trying to feel for a pulse, then placing my hand in front of John's mouth in an attempt to feel any breathing. I really did think he'd gone and frantically tried to catch someone's attention. Fortunately Don Mosey appeared on the scene, immediately realized what had happened and took over from me on the microphone while members of the production team attended to John and called for medical help. John had blacked out. Whether it was some sort of stroke I don't know. What I do know is, he did the same thing on me during a Test at Old Trafford.

Brian Johnston always considered himself very lucky to be able to commentate on the game he truly loved, though sometimes I think he felt somewhat uncomfortable at the fact that something that was after all 'a game' played such an important and intrinsic role in his life. As he often said, 'I have spent much of my life and earned a decent living to boot, simply by talking endlessly about a bit of wood hitting a little bit of leather.' It was a strange way for Brian to describe the game he loved and was so devoted to.

In 1970 BBC Television decided they needed a more 'professional' approach to their cricket commentary. No more jokes, puns, no more human interest camera shots of dozing spectators in the members' enclosure at Lord's. Brian's time was up in television, but television's loss was radio's gain. The conditions in which the *TMS* team work are often cramped and hot. One would think this would give rise to niggles, but it never did, mainly because Brian created a wonderfully amiable atmosphere with his jokes and japes. Quite often Brian would read out letters sent in from listeners and use these as the catalyst to on-air conversation between the team members. I remember one such conversation quite well. It was typically surreal, typically Johnners.

'FST, if you were stark naked out in a snowstorm what animal would you like to be?' he asked.

I could see a joke coming, so played the straight man for him. 'I dunno, Johnners,' I replied, 'let's have it.'

'A little otter,' he replied with great glee.

'Who was the ice-cream man in the Bible, FST?'

'Can't rightly recall.'

'Walls of Jericho.'

'That's as maybe,' I replied, 'but what about Lyons of Judah?'

Johnners clapped his hands together with delight. An hour later he was still chuckling to himself. Simple jokes and plays on words never failed to delight Johnners. During one Test match he referred to a piece in the *Daily Telegraph* that said eating too many curries could be bad for your health. For a bit of fun I said, 'That's true. I know of a chap who ate five curries a day, every day, and he's ended up in hospital.'

'Goodness gracious,' said Johnners going for it hook, line and sinker. 'How is he?'

'He's in a korma,' I replied. He was so delighted with that little joke, when we came off air he told it with childlike enthusiasm to everyone he met in the ground.

I last saw Brian in 1994. I was in London and had called in to Lord's to buy some Christmas cards. On leaving I bumped into Johnners and we passed the time of day and wished one another the compliments of the season. On returning home I mentioned to Veronica that I had met Brian, that we had talked about the possibility of doing a theatre together, but I had been taken aback by the fact he looked tired and drawn. Not long after, I was sitting at home one morning when I received a telephone call from a promoter of sporting lunches. The promoter asked if I could get down to Bristol for lunchtime. I told him there was no way I could drive to Bristol in that time. He then asked if I could fly down and that he'd meet all expenses. I asked him what this was all about. His reply rocked me on my feet. 'It's Brian Johnston. He was due to speak for me at a luncheon today. He's been taken gravely ill. I think it's a heart attack.' Brian died at the age of eighty-one. One newspaper described him as 'the greatest natural broadcaster of them all'. I think you would find few who would argue with that.

Trevor Bailey was nicknamed by Johnners as 'The Boil'. This had nothing at all to do with any ailment and physical characteristic of Trevor's; rather it was a a throwback to his days as a footballer with Walthamstow Avenue when supporters would call out, 'Give the bawl to Boiley, mate.' Trevor won his blue at Cambridge University for soccer and played top amateur football for some years. He won an FA Amateur Cup winner's medal with Walthamstow in 1952, playing in front of a 100,000 crowd at Wembley, but cricket was his first love. He was a true all-rounder, as he proved in his sixty-one Tests for England, being a quality fast-medium bowler and a doughty, often obdurate batsman. Trevor played for Essex from 1947 until 1967, so our respective careers were almost parallel. He achieved the double of 1,000 runs and 100 wickets on eight occasions, and in 1959 became the first player since 1937 to take 100 wickets and score 2,000 runs in a season. He was a highly competitive opponent, a good teammate and I enjoyed immensely the time we spent together working on *Test Match Special*, where his summaries were always precise, objective and so descriptive you could almost smell the bat oil.

To be a part of *TMS* was to be a part of a very special team, a very different team to the one I had known as a player with Yorkshire and England. The *TMS* commentary box was the pokiest box on the Test circuit, so small I used to joke that when it was opened up in the morning, you had to take the key out of the door to step inside.

Yet that pokey box was a little oasis of fair play, often lyrical and poetic language, mind-boggling facts and statistics and surreal humour. Should there be guests, there was often not enough room for us all to be seated, so the broadcast would continue with some seated, some standing, with the door propped open to allow air to circulate courtesy of large Dundee cake or similar gift from a listener. Such Heath Robinson circumstances engendered a great camaraderie amongst the commentary team. There were no prima donnas because everyone had to rough it – even John Arlott.

One of the most popular aspects of *TMS* was the on-going conversation between the team that drifted in and out of the actual commentary. For many listeners it was as if they had joined a group of knowledgeable and humorous friends for a chat. The 'cricket talk' was so popular we actually received letters from listeners saying they liked it when it rained, because they preferred to hear us chatting about cricket and recalling anecdotes of past characters in the game.

We were all different. We had our own idiosyncratic ways, our own style, yet somehow we produced a chemistry that was appealing to listeners. I was a totally different type of person to Brian Johnston, in turn the pair of us were different to John Arlott. But we all fitted in and all got on famously with one another. What bonded us was our love of cricket. Working on *TMS* was great fun, both 'on' and 'off' air. The years I spent working on *TMS* were the happiest time of my life in the media. *TMS* had a great team, both on air and behind the scenes.

There was a well-known Yorkshire character who Brian Johnston would often invite into the commentary box to offer his opinion on the game in question. After one such visit this well-known character enquired if his contribution to the programme had been all right. Brian said it had been fine but remarked that the guy hadn't been his usual effervescent and ebullient self.

'I know,' he remarked off-microphone, 'I've got problems with the three Ms.'

'The three Ms? What are they?' asked Brian.

'The missus, the maid and the mortgage,' said my fellow Yorkshireman, 'they're all overdue.'

Everybody was convulsed with laughter, which I am sure puzzled the millions of listeners not privy to our off-mike conversation.

On one occasion at Headingley in the seventies, Trevor was socializing in the committee room when he suddenly realized he should be on air delivering the lunchtime summary of play. He literally ran out of the committee room, down the stairs two at a time, then up the steps to the commentary box and slumped into his seat. Peter Baxter handed over to him, but Trevor was so out of breath he couldn't speak and just sat there wheezing. They faded him out. Eventually, on the same day in 2001, the BBC faded us both out – for good.

We had seen it coming. I remember Don Mosey once saying to me when I had been deliberating on how long I might continue to be a member of the *TMS* team, 'Fred, as long as I am around, you'll be OK. When I go, start to make plans. They'll get rid of you.'

This seemed to be the case when the *TMS* producer called a meeting to discuss the future of the programme and we weren't invited. As I said to Trevor, 'We'd better start making plans.' I was in Spain when I received the dreaded telephone call from BBC Radio's Head of Sport – which, as it was routed through my phone in England, I had to pay for!

'I don't know how to speak to a sporting icon,' he said before giving me the news. When he'd finished I sat out on the balcony reflecting on the end of an era. Trevor Bailey was disappointed the BBC didn't allow us one more programme together where we could have ended by thanking the *TMS* listeners, the back-room team and bade a respectful and dignified farewell. But it was not to be. One day we were on air as part of the *TMS* team; when the next series got under way, we weren't. One BBC person explained, when referring to the exit of Trevor and me, '*TMS* is looking to attract a younger audience of radio listeners to cricket.' With Trevor and I replaced, I can't imagine too many young people switched over to *TMS* from Trevor Nelson on Radio 1!

After so many years of loyal service to *TMS* I felt a little badly done to. Things must change, of course they must, but to the best of my knowledge not one *TMS* listener had ever complained to the BBC that I had become staid or that my contribution to TMS was not what it had been previously. On the contrary, right up until my last broadcast I was still receiving letters saying how much people enjoyed my contributions to the programme.

Cricket is a game of opinions and not all listeners agreed with the comments I made, but not one suggested I was past my prime. In fact, I am led to believe that the BBC received a considerable post that disagreed with their decision.

I never felt my contribution and loyalty to Yorkshire cricket club was fully appreciated by those charged with running the club, and likewise I think my contribution to *TMS* was not appreciated by the new hierarchy in BBC Radio. After so many years of being a part of the *TMS* team, I was not even afforded the decency of a meeting to discuss my future, or lack of it, with the programme. I think it's a shame, but I'll leave it up to you to decide whether *TMS* has improved, or whether it is even on a par with the *TMS* we all once knew . . .

In 2003 I attended Trevor Bailey's eightieth birthday party. He was on top form and was, of course, the perfect gentleman. It is the mark of the man that many of the great and good of cricket – as well as a number of true legends – turned up to help him celebrate. For all he achieved in cricket with Essex and England, Trevor's most exciting moment in the game came when he was a schoolboy. I relate this story because in many ways it sums up Trevor Bailey the man, that is, a highly talented cricketer but one who is modest of his achievements and a man who enjoys the simple pleasures of life.

In 1938 Trevor was a fourteen-year-old schoolboy playing for Dulwich College Colts. For various reasons the college first XI were down on numbers and Trevor was selected to play. The college cricket team was pinned up on a notice board and all the boys who had been awarded college colours appeared with their initials before the surnames. The last name on the list was Bailey, T. E., as he had yet to be awarded his cricket colours.

Trevor was so excited that he had been chosen for the first XI, he asked several times to be excused from lessons so he could go to the toilet. He would then race down to the notice board and gaze at the team that had been pinned up. He performed so well against Bedford School, he retained his place in the first XI for the next game and for the rest of that summer. Dulwich College won all their remaining games, which hadn't happened for over fifty years.

At the end of the season the captain of the college cricket team received a letter saying, 'Dear Captain, congratulations on a superb performance.' The letter contained five guineas (£5.25), which was a handsome amount in 1937. As the success of the college cricket team had been a team effort, the captain used the money to take the lads into the West End, where they had dinner in a restaurant before attending a show at the London Palladium. Trevor has never forgotten the thrill and excitement of playing for his school first XI at the age of fourteen, nor the night out in the West End. It was the first time he had ever seen a show and the occasion made him feel very grown up. Trevor loves telling that story, but often omits to mention the most striking part.

On one occasion after he had related the tale I asked who had sent the brief note of congratulations and the five guineas.

'Oh, it was from an old boy of the college,' Trevor informed me, 'P. G. Wodehouse.'

As I have said, Trevor Bailey is a very modest man, always keen to underplay his achievements and experiences.

I gained plenty of experience in television throughout the seventies. *Indoor League* gave me national exposure and was very popular with viewers, but I received a surprise while attending a television dinner in Birmingham. It was some sort of awards event and I was very warmly received by those gathered, as was the former footballer and World Cup winner Bobby Charlton. I was sitting next to Bobby and we remarked how kindly the audience had been towards us when all of a sudden the room erupted. At first I was nonplussed but then realized that the standing ovation was for a small, genteel lady who had walked on stage. I didn't have a clue who she was and to the best of my knowledge neither did Bobby Charlton. The woman stood before the microphone but couldn't say anything for three or four minutes as the audience were on their feet applauding and cheering her. Somewhat embarrassed at not knowing who this apparent star was, I asked one of my fellow diners.

'You mean to say you don't know who she is?' he replied incredulously. 'Man alive, that's Amy Turtle from *Crossroads*.'

I was none the wiser. At the time we didn't receive *Crossroads* on Yorkshire TV, as it had yet to go fully network. The audience were in raptures at the sight of this Amy Turtle; I was simply bemused. Some time later Yorkshire TV did take up *Crossroads* and I couldn't wait to see it and discover for myself what all the fuss had been about.

When I eventually watched *Crossroads* I was left even more bemused. I thought it was dreadful. How that audience had been so moved by the appearance of Amy Turtle was beyond my ken. The only thing I found moving about *Crossroads* was the scenery.

Some years later, I was asked by a reporter if it was true I had been auditioned for *Crossroads*. It wasn't true, just another ridiculous tale that gets attached to my name.

'Absolutely,' I fibbed, 'but I didn't get the part because I kept remembering my lines.'

One of the great bonuses to me of appearing on television was when I was asked to appear in an episode of *Dad's Army*. To me *Dad's Army* is one of the all-time great sit-coms of British television. The writers and creators, Jimmy Perry and David Croft, knew their subject and created their characters with confidence, precision and affection. Rarely has there been a comedy series with so many strong parts for so many of the cast. And what a cast! It was like a 'Who's Who' of British comedy and theatre of yesteryear, with the exception, of course, of Ian Lavender, who was on his way up in the business. *Dad's Army* was a very British pleasure, depicting a simple, fresh and innocent Britain that did once exist. Yet within the world of *Dad's Army* were so many truths about human behaviour: Captain Mainwaring's resentment of the upbringing and connections of his sergeant and assistant at the bank, Mr Wilson; how Britain often muddled through the war Heath Robinson like, yet with great courage. It was accessible and humane, touching and very funny, because it was true. The mark of its success and brilliance is that it has matured with age. An undisputed classic in the pantheon of British television comedy.

The episode I was invited to appear in was called 'The Test' and was first broadcast in 1970. The story involved Air Warden Hodges challenging Mainwaring's Walmington-on-Sea platoon to a cricket match. Of course, Mainwaring selects himself as captain of the Platoon team and proceeds to give plenty of advice on batting at a practice session to his men, until the time comes for him to put his theory into practice, and he is bowled first ball by Private Pike. That was the script and, credit to Ian Lavender as Pike, when they shot the scene, he did bowl Arthur Lowe first ball.

I played the part of the ringer in Hodges' team, cricket pro Ernie Egan, who unfortunately strains his shoulder before Hodges can get one over on Captain Mainwaring. I really enjoyed taking part in *Dad's Army* and to this day the fact I appeared in an episode of one of the all-time great classic comedy series is a matter of some satisfaction. Having been involved in the series, albeit for one episode, I got to know the cast and I realized something unique about *Dad's Army*: the cast became the characters they portrayed, and the characters became them. Perhaps that was the key to the great and enduring success of this superb comedy series.

One of the most enduring employments I enjoyed was that of a columnist for the *People*. In the main I wrote about cricket, but would also dabble in football. Reporting on a match is not as straightforward as you might think. You spend a good proportion of the game on the telephone. Just before the match starts, you ring through the team news, then after twenty minutes file so many words on the progress of the game and give a longer report at half time. The process is repeated in the second half. After the game I'd go down to the manager's office to get some quotes, dictate those over the phone and invariably have to write another report geared to the edition that was for the area where the away team was situated. It was hectic at times. Often I would be on the telephone filing a progress report when a goal would be scored. You had to be multi-skilled to keep an eye on the game while also talking down.

It was, however, my weekly column with the *People* from which I derived most satisfaction. I had a completely free hand to say what I liked, and though my opinions upset one or two people, the general feedback was good. Readers liked the fact that I didn't sit on the fence when talking about cricket. I told it how I saw it and on my many visits to county grounds I found people were at pains to say how much they agreed with what I had to say about the game.

Typically, the one ground where I was never made to feel warmly welcome was Headingley. After the ticket debacle, I rarely paid a visit to Headingley, but when I did it was almost always because of *Test Match Special*. On one such visit I drove up to the gates that led to the official car park only to be stopped by the gateman, who asked what I wanted. I politely asked him to open the gates so I could park.

'You can't park here,' I was told. 'You don't play here any more.' I pointed out that other employees of *TMS* had gained access to the car park and asked why I wasn't allowed in. The gateman repeated his reason – 'You don't play here any more' – and we engaged in a debate that lasted for a few minutes.

Meanwhile, behind me a lengthy queue of cars had formed, all impatiently waiting for access to the car park. The queue of cars was causing congestion in the side street and it wasn't long before a policeman arrived. On speaking to the gateman and me and having determined the reason for the hold-up, the policeman ordered the gateman to open the gates. The gateman attempted to hold his ground, but the policeman was having none of it.

'Traffic is snarling up and it's down to you,' the policeman said with some assertion. 'Now, open these gates and let Mr Trueman in!'

Reluctantly the gateman did as he was bid. Now, whether word got back to Headingley's hierarchy about this incident, or whether someone in authority at the club witnessed the event, I don't know. What I do know is, that gateman was never seen working at Headingley again.

I could have referred to such incidents in my column in the *People*, but I never did. Only now, all these years later, do I feel it proper to do so. I wrote about the state of the game, gave my opinions on the performances of the England team and individual players. In so doing, I would also like to think my knowledge of bowling and technique carried some weight. Not just with the readers of my column, but amongst fellow cricketers as well.

In 1975 I was approached by that great Australian fast bowler Dennis Lillee. Dennis told me something I already knew: he was having a problem with his run-up and bowling action. I told him I could help, and what's more, it would take no more than fifteen minutes to sort him out. I had noticed that Dennis's bowling had been suffering because he was setting off on his run-up too quickly and his left arm and left shoulder were dropping too early. I pointed this out to Dennis, telling him that should he begin his run-up at gentler pace, then slightly delay the descent of both his left arm and shoulder, he would be back to his fluid and fearsome best.

Dennis adhered to my advice in the nets and sure enough, his problem was solved. The following day he went out and got everything right. He bowled superbly well – against England, I'm afraid. One absolutely perfect delivery beat John Edrich all ends up and ripped his middle-stump from the ground. As he walked back to his run-up marker, Dennis glanced up to the radio commentary box and caught sight of me. A big grin on his face, he raised a thumb and nodded his head. Questions were asked as to why Dennis Lillee had done this, and I received all manner of letters and telegrams asking me what the hell I was doing offering bowling advice to Australians and, of all people, Dennis Lillee. I filed them all under 'B' for bin.

Trevor Bailey, however, had a different view. He told *TMS* listeners it was a great pity that some of the prima donnas of current English cricket didn't have the sense to seek my advice about bowling. As Trevor concluded, 'In life we judge ourselves by what we feel we are capable of doing. In cricket people should be judged by what they have achieved and done. Sadly, that is rarely the case.'

Chris Old, who was in his pomp with Yorkshire and England in the late seventies and early eighties, was another bowler who often sought my advice, and I was only too pleased to help him in any way I could. He once told me that by acting on my advice he began to get much closer to the stumps in his delivery stride, improving his strike rate. Chris was a very good fast bowler and also a useful tail-end batsman, as he proved during England's historic Test victory over Australia at Head-ingley in 1981. Ian Botham quite rightly took the plaudits for his marvellous 149 not out in England's second innings, but I'm sure Ian would be the first to acknowledge the sterling support he received from Graham Dilley (56) and Chris Old. In making 29 Chris shared a ninth-wicket partnership of 67 with Ian Botham, a partnership which proved invaluable to England when Bob Willis wreaked havoc the next day, his 8 for 43 helping England win a Test they'd seemed destined to lose.

Even today I'm always ready to coach or offer advice to anybody from International cricketers to schoolchildren – because I feel an obligation to do so. In spite of the treatment meted out to me from certain quarters, I harbour no bitterness and know I owe the game a great deal. By helping young players, be they colts or schoolchildren, I see that as an opportunity to give something back to cricket for all it gave to me. I only wish there were more opportunities to pass on my experience and knowledge of the game.

Throughout the seventies, eighties and nineties I continued to work in the media while establishing myself as an after-dinner speaker. I also embarked on a number of theatre tours, which I am pleased to say played to packed houses. Away from my new and varied line of work I relaxed by becoming increasingly interested in rural matters. I have studied birds and their habits for as long as I can remember. My home, situated by a wood at the foot of rolling hills near Skipton, is in a superb location for studying birds and wildlife in general. In the garden pheasants visit my lawns most days. Other regular visitors are bullfinches, robins, goldfinches, wrens, great spotted and green woodpeckers, tree creepers, nuthatches, blue tits, coal tits, pied wagtails, and should there be a rare visitor, such as a bunting, I call out to Veronica and she will join me at the window to observe the behaviour of the 'stranger'.

I put out bird feed on a daily basis and many birds have

become so accustomed to my presence they are almost tame. I had one cock robin that used to come and tap on the window with his beak every morning for his breakfast! At night I have seen various species of owl, including barn owl, brown owl and screech owl. Herons are also regular visitors. I see them flapping sedately across the valley and have also spotted dippers and kingfishers on streams near Skipton. At one time I was very keen on shooting and received regular invitations to join parties on the splendid grouse moors of Yorkshire. However, attitudes change over the years, and for a long time now I have preferred to observe birds in their natural habitat rather than blow them out of the sky.

In the seventies and eighties there were attempts to persuade me to enter politics, including firm invitations to stand as a Conservative candidate. I politely declined. I have helped raise funds for the Conservative Party by offering my services as an after-dinner speaker but that's as far as my political involvement goes. Politics is too underhand a business for me. In my opinion there are too many politicians who are there to further their own careers rather than help others and society in general. They may not have started out that way, but that is the way they end up. And that is why a career in politics was never for me.

One of the great satisfactions of my life was that my dad lived to witness my entire career in cricket. He never changed one iota in all the time I knew him and refused to move out of the old family home in Maltby even when I suggested buying a modern bungalow for him and Mum, which I knew would offer them a superior quality of life and be more manageable than the old home. I knew he was very proud of me, although he never showed it, and so too were my former workmates at Maltby Main pit. Whenever I secured a good haul of wickets they used to write my match figures on a board and put it in front of the cage so Dad could see how I was doing the moment he came up from the coal face. It is little things like that that I shall always remember. They made me feel proud, yet at the same time, very humble. My dad, as I previously said, never wanted me to work down the pit. He hated mining from start to finish. He always said he would retire the day he was sixty-five and he did.

It was a Thursday, he came home from the pit for the last time, stripped off his working clothes and burnt them in the back yard. Dad remained a major influence in my life until the day he died, though his influence continued well beyond that. Many was the time I went back to Maltby with problems and we would sit in front of the fire and talk them over. He was a very sensible and knowledgeable man and so easy to talk to there was nothing I felt I could not discuss with him. He worried when I wasn't doing as well as I should, and got angry when I was wrongly accused of something or unfairly dropped. At such times his advice to me was always the same: 'Don't worry son, they'll want you before you'll want them.'

Sometimes he would give me a rollicking if he thought I was being thoughtless, particularly with regard to my batting. It offended his cricketing principles to see me go in, swing the bat and take what he saw as unnecessary risks. I used to tell him I couldn't be expected to bowl fast all day then bat like an opener. He would concede I had a point, but would always tell me to get my head down and bat properly because it would improve my chances of Test place. He was, of course, right.

During his retirement he spent a lot of time in the garden and came regularly to see me play. On the day I retired I went home with him. Over a cup of tea I said, 'Well, that's it, Dad. I'm finished.' He was sitting in the same place where, twenty years earlier, I had given him my first Yorkshire cap. I could see he was deeply moved. For a minute or so he said nothing, he simply stared into his tea cup. Then he looked at me and said, 'Well, I've been very fortunate, son. So very fortunate indeed. I was there to see you start playing cricket and I have lived to see your marvellous career to the finish. I can die happy now. And I'll never watch Yorkshire again.'

He never did. He died two years later at the age of seventy-eight. Mother died some years later. Despite all my efforts to persuade her to move from the old Maltby home, she never did.

I have remained close to my brothers and sisters, Arthur, Phyllis, Flo, John, Dennis and Helen. But there is one family mystery that has puzzled me to this day. I had another sister called Stella. When I was nine, Stella married a nice guy whose name was Chester Taylor. I can still recall their wedding day. Chester was a maintenance fitter working with the safety equipment at Maltby Main and following their marriage, he and Stella went to live in a colliery-owned house at Stainton, where I was born. Stella was very much in love with Chester and he with her. He worshipped her and would do anything for her. A year or so after their marriage and before they had any children, Stella took ill. Her condition deteriorated and, sadly, Stella died. As you can imagine, the whole family was devastated. Chester was numbed and seemed to be occupying another world on the day of the funeral. Following Stella's funeral everyone assembled back at the house in Stainton.

Eventually we bade our farewells, and as we departed I looked back. Chester was standing in the back garden gazing into the distance. I noticed his shoulders were jerking up and down. I was only nine and so very saddened at the untimely death of Stella, but I also felt great sadness for Chester. The one great love of his life had been taken from him before they had had any real time to enjoy life together. That was the last time I, or any of my family, saw Chester. The day after the funeral he simply disappeared. The family made enquiries as to his whereabouts but found no trace of him whatsoever. No one heard from Chester for many, many years. Then a few years ago I decided to make one last effort to find him. I knew

Chester had worked in mining and chanced that he might have continued to work in that industry. I contacted the National Coal Board and they informed me they would do whatever they could to help me in my quest to locate him. A few months after my initial enquiry I received a letter from the Coal Board saying Chester was living in sheltered accomodation in Scotland. He was long-since retired but I got in touch with him and invited him to visit Veronica and me. He stayed a few days and he told me how he had been so heartbroken he simply couldn't face up to life in the Maltby area and had packed his bags and headed for Scotland to 'start his life all over again'.

Chester told me that he had followed my career and, though he had never been to see me play, he was very proud of what I had achived. He returned to Scotland and though Veronica and I always sent a card at Christmas we never heard from him again. A few yeas ago, one Christmas Eve a policeman turned up on our doorstep. The policeman said he had some bad news for me. Chester had fallen down the stair in his apartment, fractured his skull and died. A fortnight later I received a bill for the expenses of his funeral which I duly paid. Why the bill came to me and who sent it I have no idea but I met that expense as Chester was, however briefly, 'family'. Stella and Chester were very much in love, all these years on it still saddens me that they never fulfilled the love they shared for one another.

Thankfully I have been far more fortunate. Better than good. My marriage to Veronica was the making of me. We have now been together for over thirty years and our loving relationship has just got better with the passing of the years. Veronica is my best friend as well as my wife and I am devoted to her. Whenever I receive invitations to travel abroad, to speak at dinners and appear in theatres, I always insist that Veronica comes too. I still provide support for Enid, and Veronica approves of this. One thing I learned from my first marriage is the time you spend in any relationship is not a loss if you learn from it and end it in a positive way. I embarked upon my relationship with Veronica in a very positive state of mind, keen to appreciate every moment we spent together, to never take anything in our relationship for granted and see every day as being very special. Every day has been, and, God willing, will continue that way.

CHAPTER FOURTEEN

20/20 AND ALL THAT

In 1989 I HAD the honour of being awarded an OBE. I was, of course, very proud to receive such a prestigious award, though I was led to believe that it was awarded for my services to charity, rather than cricket. That intimation was made by Denis Thatcher. When Margaret, the then Prime Minister, informed him of the honour, he suggested to his wife that I was worthy of a higher honour for my services to cricket. Margaret said there was nothing she could do to alter the situation, as the decision had not been hers. She felt it was not her place to interfere, or attempt to influence the system of honours.

I felt very humble when I attended Buckingham Palace. I am a patriot through and through and a great supporter and loyal servant of Her Majesty the Queen. Amongst her many other qualities, Her Majesty is a gracious and affable lady, who possesses a keen sense of humour.

I had the honour of meeting the Queen again in 2002 when I was invited to attend the 'British Achievers Luncheon'. The occasion was to mark the fiftieth year since Her Majesty's succession to the throne and was attended by people whose career achievements were considered of some benefit to this great nation of ours. On arrival I was ushered into a room where I was greeted by the Duke of Edinburgh. After enjoying a conversation with the Duke, I chatted to two good friends, rugby league legend Martin Offiah and the former British and European heavyweight champion Henry Cooper. As we chatted I was suddenly aware of an excited buzz in the room. Unbeknown to me, Her Majesty had entered from a side room and was making her way to the dining hall. As she crossed the room she glanced in my direction, paused for a moment, then came over to me and said, 'Oh, I haven't seen you in such a long time. How are you Mr Trueman?' We talked and I was left feeling so proud and pleased at the fact Her Majesty had recognized my face and singled me out for conversation. It is a moment I shall never forget and delighted me as much as the auspicious occasion itself.

Less auspicious was the phone call I received from new sports editor of the *People* the year before – ironically not long after my departure from *Test Match Special*. I had been writing for the *People* for forty-three years and realized I'd had a better run than most. I was and still am very grateful for my time at the *People* and to the many readers who read my column and took the time to write to me. But when the call came, it was a shock and I was left feeling quite down.

I had an inkling that something was up when the cricket season got under way and I was not asked to write about it. Having been a mainstay of the *People* for over four decades, I assumed someone would ring soon to ask me to file copy. When I did receive a call from the new sports editor, it was to thank me for my contribution to the newspaper over the years. During the course of that conversation I asked the sports editor why he'd waited so long to ring me; after all, the cricket season was now well under way. He said that he'd been 'meaning to ring me for some weeks but with one thing and another, other matters had taken precedence'. It was answer of sorts. As I had written for his newspaper for over forty years (I should imagine I had started before he was born), I felt he might have had the good grace – and the professionalism – not to have kept me in limbo for so many weeks. That said, I reckon it took that long for him to pluck up the courage to make the call. When I put down the phone, I was mindful of the words of Euripides: 'The faint-hearted do not count in battle, they are there, but not in it.'

I have to say I was disappointed that my employment with both *Test Match Special* and the *People* ended more or less at the same time. But given the longevity of both employments, I could have no complaints and certainly felt no bitterness. It wasn't as if my career has ground to a halt; on the contrary, I am as busy as ever. Fortunately I am in great demand as an after-dinner speaker both here and abroad. I appear on television and radio as and when invited. Such invitations are not always to do with cricket.

As everyone knows, I am somewhat of a raconteur and have a wealth of funny stories, not only about cricket, but celebrities I have made friends with during my life, people such as actors Trevor Howard, Errol Flynn, David Niven and Arthur Lowe. I was surprised to discover Errol Flynn was a keen cricket fan and often played for the Hollywood Ex-Pats team, which was mainly made up of British actors, writers and technicians. As Flynn said, 'How can I not be interested in a sport that gives me the opportunity to bowl a maiden over.'

Trevor Howard and I were very good friends. Trevor loved his cricket and when not filming would often fly to wherever England were playing to offer his support. In the early sixties England were touring Australia, which coincided with the filming of *The Key*, a movie Trevor was starring in. After one of the Test matches, a steward approached me and said that an English gentleman wondered if I had a few minutes to chat with him. Not wanting to rebuff a fellow Englishman so many miles from home, I asked the steward to usher the man into the dressing room. It was Trevor Howard.

We sat talking cricket for some minutes when the steward reappeared citing a similar request. I asked Trevor if he had any objections. Trevor said 'of course not', so I asked the steward to show the man in. The man in question turned out to be that great comedy actor Terry-Thomas. A few minutes later the same steward appeared and asked if I would speak to yet another Englishman. 'The more the merrier,' I replied. I sat slack-jawed when the next guest entered the dressing room. It was John Mills.

The four of us had a wonderful conversation about cricket for about half an hour. I didn't want to end our conversation but I was still in my whites and rather conscious that after a hard day's bowling I might not be smelling of violets. I asked Trevor, John and Terry if they would excuse me for a few minutes whilst I showered. Freshened up, I returned to the dressing room.

'Feel better for that?' asked Terry.

'Not really,' I replied in my finest Terry-Thomas impression. 'What a rotten shower!'

Trevor and Terry invited me to a party that evening, where I met the Australian actress Anne Baxter, who came across as being a real lady. Later I also managed to strike up a friendship with a Hollywood star.

It's funny how you gain an impression of someone purely from the roles they play on the screen. Ernest Borgnine had always struck me as being very macho and slightly manic. In reality, however, he was a very warm, friendly and jovial guy. What began as a casual conversation with Ernest at that party was to develop into a lasting friendship. Ernest didn't know much about cricket, but that mattered not one iota. We found plenty of other topics of conversation that were of mutual interest – not least of all movies. For all his fame Ernest Borgnine was a very down-to-earth guy, which is why I think we got on so well. He saw Hollywood for what it is – as he once said, 'It's an asylum run by the inmates.'

With my great collection of stories I occasionally receive invitations to appear on chat programmes, and as I am a believer and regular church-goer, religious programmes too. As the former footballer Jimmy Greaves kindly wrote in his 2003 autobiography *Greavsie*, 'No one has more funny anecdotes and stories than Freddie Trueman. He's a natural for TV chat programmes and why he isn't invited to appear on them more often is a mystery to me.'

Occasionally I wish I was starting my cricket career now, because with the standard of county cricket being what it is, I think I would be twice as successful. The game and the way it is played has changed irrevocably over the years. It has changed from a side-on to chest-on game, and most of the batsmen I see today seem to jump about like a cat on a hot tin roof before the bowler has even released the ball. As for the bowlers themselves, rarely nowadays do you see a side-on bowler, which I think is a great pity, as side-on is the only way you can bowl an out-swinger, the most effective ball of the lot.

I shake my head in wonder when I see contemporary batsmen moving before the ball is delivered. I assume that is how they are coached these days, but moving early gives the bowler an enormous advantage. I was always taught to make your play a fraction of a second after the ball is released. Len Hutton was a master of that. I bowled to such legendary batsmen as Gary Sobers, Peter May, Colin Cowdrey, Neil Harvey, Denis Compton, Tom Graveney, Clive Lloyd, Frank Worrell, Everton Weekes, Rohan Khanai and Keith Miller, and not one of them moved before I delivered the ball.

If I were bowling today I wouldn't have to bowl at the leg-stump to turn a batsman round, because the vast majority of them are already there. Which means the batsman's first line of defence has gone. If I were twenty-eight again and playing today, I would bowl leg and middle, move the ball away and stand a good chance of hitting the off-stump as well as finding an edge. With the standard of English cricket today, if the ball was swinging, I know I would be knocking down wickets like ten-pins.

Cricket still has its loyal following, but generally speaking it does not enjoy the high profile it once did. Should you walk down any high street in the country, stop fifty people and ask them to name the current England cricket captain, I should imagine no more than half a dozen would know his name. Yet this country is supposed to uphold sport as a major cultural force in our society. In 2000 Surrey conducted a survey asking a cross-section of Londoners what the Oval meant to them. The Oval is part of the social history and fabric of the capital, the ground that was graced by Jack Hobbs, Alec Bedser, Peter May, Jim Laker, Tony Lock, Ken Barrington and latterly Alec Stewart. The vast majority of people surveyed could only think of the tube station.

Cricket has become marginal to the lives of many people. The game's administrators realized this and hence, one assumes, they came up with the idea of 20/20, or 'quickie' cricket as some refer to it. 20/20 cricket is still in its infancy and early indications are that it has proved popular with bedrock cricket fans and has also attracted a new generation of youngsters into county grounds. For all of its positives, I am not a fan of 20/20. It may popularize the game, but I feel it is to its detriment in the long run. I can't see how such short-lived games will help develop young cricketers to the optimum standard.

In an attempt to make cricket more appealing the game's administrators have also introduced day/night games and coloured clothing and given county day sides American-style suffixes such as Sharks and Dynamos. All well and good, but it appears to me that the administrators have attended to the peripheries while ignoring the root cause of the decline of English cricket.

Attendances at county matches are dreadful. The gate receipts from one 20/20 game at Headingley in 2003 exceeded the total gate receipts for all of Yorkshire's county matches – and Yorkshire are one of the better-supported teams. In itself that is indicative of the initial success of 20/20, but it speaks volumes about the appeal of county cricket.

The counties and the England and Wales Cricket Board

appear to want different things. The counties would like a busy domestic programme of 20/20 and day/nighters, whilst the EWCB seem to believe the answer to the ills of the game is strong England Test and one-day teams. It is not hard to see why county cricket matches nowadays play to only a handful of spectators. What pass as today's top players are tied to Team England and to International cricket for the best part of the season, which often means England players play only two or three games a season for their club. Little wonder people do not want to attend county games when the 'stars' are rarely, if ever, on duty.

Cricket has diminished as a sport in many urban areas. In the age of the cult celebrity what can it offer young people today? Not great players, that's for sure. With all due respect, English cricket has not had a player to capture the imagination of the public or empty the bars at grounds since Ian Botham.

Dickie Bird is much loved. As a character he is amiable, a tad eccentric, but ostensibly unremarkable. Dickie's auto-biography sold phenomenally well and I am delighted for him. On one hand, you may view the great success of Dickie's autobiography as being the measure of the love and affection people have for him. On the other, it could be seen as a barometer of the state of English cricket and its lack of great players over the past fifteen years or so. Essentially, Dickie's book filled a void, and good for him. Only Ian Botham's autobiography in 1994 stands out from the other cricket books of the time. Until Dickie's came along in 1997, all cricketing books were banal and written by banal players.

England struggled to win a Test series for over a decade and have not won a series against Australia since 1987. The players who represented England in that time were no great shakes when it came to top International cricket. Some who played for England during this era would have struggled to make their country side in the fifties and sixties. Of that I have no doubts whatsoever.

Youngsters still play cricket today, but not in the numbers and the way they once did. County clubs and league clubs have in recent years made great strides to attract more young-sters to cricket and should be applauded for that. But the dearth of suitably qualified coaches and the lack of land are millstones around the neck of young cricketers. School teachers give up their free time to run school cricket teams and do their best to teach technique. At the end of the day, however, most are not suitably qualified to coach. It would be an enormous benefit to cricket if a National Coaching School with regional centres and bases in every city and town was set up. I was fortunate as a boy to have teachers who encouraged me in my cricket and who did their best to help me develop as an individual. But it wasn't until I came under the influence and tuition of great old pros such as Cyril Turner and Bill Bowes that I began to flourish and discover what cricket was all about. I didn't even know how to hold the ball properly, never mind bowl to any effect, until Cyril Turner showed me how.

Cricket's real problems lie in the first-class game. In 2003 there were instances of counties paying twenty-eight-year-old players to play second XI cricket. Quite simply, with the standard of county cricket being as poor as it is, if these guys haven't made the grade by their mid-twenties, what on earth are they doing still contracted to county sides?

As I have said, 20/20 cricket is not for me. Apart from the reasons I have previously given, I just find it too gimmicky. I hear a lot of people cast aspersions upon the burgeoning corporate entertainment in cricket. More often than not I am told the majority of those who patronize corporate hospitality boxes and tents are not fans of cricket. I see nothing wrong with corporate hospitality in any shape or form. Indeed, if it were not for that, the game would die. As for the argument that many of those who patronize corporate events are not true cricket fans, one could say the same about many of those who attend 20/20 matches. In the final analysis, does it matter?

Cricket needs to attract a new audience and if just a percentage of those who, for whatever reason, find themselves at a cricket match for the first time take a liking to the sport and want to come again, then that's a positive for the game. Besides which, corporate hospitality and 20/20 do generate much-needed revenue for cricket.

I feel the general standard of county cricket is poor and our Test cricket not much better. I like Michael Vaughan, he is a very personable guy. His laid-back attitude could be misinterpreted by some as a sign that he lacks commitment, but nothing could be further from the truth. He gives it his all when leading either Yorkshire or England and has demonstrated he has all the hallmarks of being a very good captain. I wish I could offer similar plaudits for all of his England teammates, but I can't. A good many of those who have represented England over the past fifteen years or so have been journeymen cricketers and nothing more. Their lack of ability, technique and questionable application apart, I have, at times, been appalled by their attitude both on and off the pitch. The snarling, the high-fives and goading of the batsman when a wicket is taken has changed the game of cricket from an entertainment into a conflict. When I played Test cricket, players' application and motivation could not be faulted, but there were many laughs to be had during a game. How many times do you see contemporary Test cricketers, or county cricketers for that matter, having a laugh between themselves out on the pitch?

The general attitude of some of today's players leaves much to be desired to my mind. A couple of year ago I had the good fortune to accompany that great Australian bowler of the 1940s Sam Loxton to a charity match at home of Sir Paul Getty. At the end of the day's play I introduced Sam to a player who had recently 'retired' from Test cricket. During the course of our conversation Sam asked the recently retired England player, 'What's all this with wearing helmets these days?'

I expected the erstwhile England player to be gracious and

diplomatic, perhaps saying something on the lines of, 'Well, we have to wear them. That's the rules. Society is very litigious nowadays and those charged with running the game are worried if someone is injured they might take out an action.'

Instead, the former England man replied, somewhat snidely, 'I know what you are going to tell me. "I never wore a helmet when I played cricket in *my day*!"'

To which Sam replied, 'Never wore a helmet when I played cricket? I never wore a helmet at Tobruk!'

Unless the EWCB and the counties act as one and introduce positive and practical measures to regenerate the game, I can see the day when a number of county teams will opt to go part-time. I wouldn't like to see that happen, but I think it is a distinct possibility. It's been said that for county cricket to survive and prosper we need fewer full-time professional teams. But rather than having fewer professional clubs I would like to see more professional clubs, more professionally run. Club cricket is fine, but time and again it has proved to be a less than effective nursery for the professional game. Those youngsters who do come through invariably become swiftly sucked into a structure that cultivates mediocrity. The purpose of club cricket is partly to nourish the professional game. In recent years, however, how many cricketers who have made any sort of mark in the professional game began their careers in club cricket? The answer to that is precious few. Club cricket has for years failed in what should be one of its prime aims – to nurture fresh young talent for the professional game. The Central Lancashire League was once a hotbed of emerging talent. To the best of my knowledge, in recent years the only player to emerge from that league has been Chris Schofield, a young leg-spinner who joined Lancashire from Littleborough. In citing the Central Lancashire League I am not singling that league out. The story is much the same whichever league you refer to, in the north or south of the country.

Before the letters flood in, let me say many league clubs

boast anything up to a dozen qualified coaches and field several teams at junior level, both boys and girls. That is marvellous, but this cannot hide the fact that quality players are not coming through in the numbers they once did. The problem league clubs and English cricket in general has is developing all that promise into something substantial.

The majority of those who do sign for county teams either fail to make the grade or simply become 'ordinary' players. In order to address the problem some county clubs have instigated their own initiatives. In recent years, Leicestershire have established a scholarship programme with a local school and Loughborough University whereby they sponsor a player on an annual basis. This initiative runs in tandem with any joint project which the club runs with the county board, an organization that is separate from the club. The two bodies provide a six-figure sum on an annual basis to fund top-quality coaching in schools throughout Leicestershire.

Leicestershire are to be applauded for their efforts, but their initiative has yet to be adopted by other county clubs. The new media centre at the Oval is state-of-the-art architecture and technology. Many see the Oval's media centre as being symbolic of the regeneration that is taking place in cricket. It is a marvellous facility for the media, but could the millions of pounds that were spent in its design and construction have not been better spent? Such money could have funded a National Coaching School with regional bases. Some of that money could have been given to county clubs to fund local initiatives such as the one at Leicestershire. Instead, we have a state-of-the-art media centre which houses the world's media for one Test match per year at the Oval. True, it is used by the media who report on Surrey county games, but when one considers the millions of pounds spent on the it, is it really cost effective? And what sense is there in spending that kind of money when the domestic game lacks great players and characters and has increasingly become marginalized?

English cricket is devoid of great characters. Aside from Andrew Flintoff, the rest appear to me to be dull as ditchwater. I have previously mentioned the likes of Ray Illingworth, Ted Dexter, Tom Graveney (once referred to as 'Mr Gravy' by the Queen when Her Majesty was presented to the England team during tea at Lord's), Denis Compton and Ken Barrington as being just a few of the great and colourful characters who energized the game of cricket in my day. One of the greatest characters I ever had the privilege to know was my teammate Brian Close.

Brian has enjoyed a colourful and controversial life. As a red-blooded Yorkshireman, he is steadfast in his opinions. Ask him about the state and standard of English cricket today, the Beckhams or George W. Bush and you will receive not only his views on the subject but have them imprinted on your chest by a finger that jabs to and fro like a woodpecker suffering from an overdose of caffeine.

I've known Brian since we were kids in the Yorkshire council team, and realized then that his greatest strength could also be his one weakness – his total belief in his own infallibility. In one particular game when Brian was captaining Somerset, he wasn't batting too well, whereas at the other end, his teammate Peter Roebuck was building a tidy score. At the end of an over when Brian had played and missed a number of deliveries, he wandered down to the middle of the pitch to do a little gardening and with a jerk of his head indicated Peter Roebuck should join him. 'It's got me beat,' said Brian. 'It's unplayable at my end, but they're bowling bloody rubbish to you.'

At times Brian could make Walter Mitty seem a modest realist, but what a cricketer! Once during a game at Arundel, the home of the Duke of Norfolk, Brian scrubbed about for half an hour before being dismissed for two. The next man in lofted the very next delivery high and handsome over the boundary for six and into a nearby lake. 'What a pillock,' announced Brian. 'I could have done that but I didn't want to lose the ball!' On another occasion, Brian was once dismissed for a duck only to come into the dressing room and tell everyone, 'Bloody umpire! He gave me the wrong guard!'

Brian is renowned for his bravery. He'd stand as near to a batsman as he could and when circumstances deemed it necessary, was not averse to telling the batsman how poorly he was playing, or what he might expect in the way of a delivery from me. There were instances when Brian would continually talk to a batsman. Worcestershire's Derek Richardson was once subjected to such a stream of banter from Brian. When Derek was eventually removed, a Worcestershire member who had missed the dismissal asked him, 'How were you out?'

'Bowled Trueman, talked Close,' replied Derek.

Any number of Brian quotes have passed into the folklore of Yorkshire cricket. Having been awarded a second benefit year, on seeing the queues forming outside the ground for his chosen benefit match, Brian said, 'When I see a crowd like this at my benefit match, it brings a lump to my wallet.'

Brian was completely obsessed with cricket. He could talk about it endlessly. He would talk about its relation to other sports, its relation to life, to society, to trouser fluff. When captain of Yorkshire, if an idea came to him about the technique of a certain player, he would ring that player to talk about it irrespective of the time of day. Having had an idea as to why Tony Nicholson was having problems with his bowling delivery, Brian rang Tony at two a.m. A bleary-eyed Tony answered the phone and on hearing it was Brian wanting to discuss his bowling said, 'Skipper, do you know what time it is?'

Unabashed, Brian turned to his wife Vivienne and said, 'Vivienne, Tony wants to know what time it is, clock's on your side.'

His last Test innings was when he had been recalled by England, twenty-seven years after his first appearance. He was forty-five and facing the might of the 1976 West Indian pace attack. He was an excellent tactician was Brian, he chose to play Michael Holding and Wayne Roberts with his chest and arms rather than his bat and for a time was as unmovable as a rock in a raging sea. The following morning just about every newspaper carried photographs of Brian naked from the waist up. His torso was like the Kandinsky painting *Concentric Circles*. Helmets and body armour? Brian wouldn't have been seen dead in them, but such was his approach to batting and close fielding I often wonder why we never saw him dead without them.

He still feels a sense of injustice at having the England captaincy taken away from him over alleged time-wasting in a county match. Can you imagine the furore in the tabloids should that happen today? After a long and glorious career with Yorkshire he was, in the end, treated very badly by the club (so nothing new there then). Brian was with Yorkshire for twenty-two years and his reward for his application and loyalty was the sack.

The committee, I feel, trumped up reasons for getting rid of Brian. Brian Sellars accused him of having insulted the president of Lancashire CCC, W. H. Lister. Lister had come into the dressing room following a Lancashire victory at Old Trafford which crowned them champions of the Sunday League. Lister was thrilled his side had won that day. Brian, not knowing who this chap was, said, 'They were bloody lucky.' Somehow that comment got back to Brian Sellars and his colleagues on the Yorkshire committee. According to Closey, the committee used this inadvertent comment, along with his dislike of one-day cricket, as their excuse for sacking him. We don't always share the same opinions, especially about cricket. But I share his view that one-day cricket limits ability – so you can imagine what he thinks of 20/20!

He joined Somerset, where he enjoyed considerable success as captain between 1972 and 1977. If Somerset can be said to have been Brian's swansong, he enjoyed the benefit of having marvellous accompanists in Ian Botham and Viv Richards. Brian didn't change one iota while at Somerset. He was still as brave as a lion and still maintained implicit belief in his own ability. As Ian Botham recalls, once during a Gillette Cup match against Leicestershire following an injury to the Somerset wicket-keeper, Brian took over behind the stumps – but refused to wear the gloves.

I am often bewildered at the penchant of the game's administrators to tinker with the rules of the game. At the risk of sounding like a spokesman for the 'union of bowlers' I fear such tinkering will in the end reduce bowlers to little more than delivery men whose prime purpose is to provide cannon fodder for batsmen.

The odds are loaded in favour of batsmen nowadays. One of my bugbears is covered wickets. In my day as a player one of the advantages England had when playing teams from the southern hemisphere was our uncovered wickets. We were used to playing on such wickets; the likes of Australia, West Indies, South Africa and India were not. Of course, we conceded that advantage when on tour, but now, when we opt for covered wickets at home, we provide batsmen with the best possible batting conditions.

The lbw law was changed and forced bowlers to bowl on one side of the wicket if they were to stand any chance of a dismissal. A law which precluded any chance of a decision should the batsman manage to move an inch outside the off-stump when hit on the pad. The restriction of the number of fielders that can be deployed in a leg trap is also to the detriment of the bowler. As for one-day cricket, the laws virtually compel bowlers to place the ball where it is most convenient for the batsman. The laws of one-day cricket also deny the bowler the opportunity to place his field in such a way that it restricts the inevitable run-making.

It appears to me that those who have tinkered with the

rules of the game have done so in the belief that the public only want to see runs being scored. What the administrators don't seem to realize is cricket is supposed to be an equal contest between bat and ball, but the dice are now loaded against bowlers.

So we now have a situation in English cricket whereby a team can make 400–500 runs, or an individual player a double-century, simply by batting adequately. When his run-making earns him an England contract and he finds himself up against top-class International players, people then wonder why he struggles to make a real impact.

The history of cricket is one of great batsmanship, but also the technique and power of fast bowling unsettling even great players and wresting the initiative from such batsmen. Not any more it isn't. The game's administrators have contrived to change the rules in favour of batsmen because they believe what will put bums on seats is runs and plenty of them. And we wonder why English cricket doesn't produce the great bowlers it once did . . .

The terminology of cricket has also changed over the years. Many of the terms I knew now seem to have a totally different meaning. Time for a little levity, I think. Here are what some common cricketing terms appear to mean now.

Fielding restrictions – the laws that make a captain place fielders in positions where he doesn't want them.
20/20 – ironically, lack of vision on the part of game's administrators.
Leg-break bowler – twelfth man.
Maiden over – unattainable quest in 20/20.
Full toss – journeyman bowler's attempt at a yorker.
Spearhead bowling attack – three or four bowlers hell bent on defending.
Day/nighter – one-day game, the starting time of which has been changed from when most people are at work in

the morning to when most people are at work in the
late afternoon.

All-rounder – player who is average at more things than the
average player.

Central contract – piece of paper that ensures a player is a
county player in name only.

Opening batsman – most likely winner of Man of the Match
award.

World Cup Final – Australia versus somebody else.

Required run rate – a figure per over which the upper-order
batsmen have set their own lower-order batsmen in
order to gain victory.

Slower ball – this used to be a delivery bowled at a much
reduced pace than previous deliveries and bowled at
the end of an over to surprise a batsman. Now the
norm.

Spinner – slow medium-pacer with short run-up.

Nat West Trophy – Gone West Trophy.

Genuine fast bowler – medium-fast.

High-fives – opportunity when wicket is taken for third man
to get himself on TV.

One of the game's true characters – wears an earring.

Loyal county player – never been approached by another
county.

Reduced target – a modernism of cricket whereby statistical
superiority can be achieved through practical inferiority.

Has been offered the light – but will never see it.

County membership – whereby supporters fork out £300 a
season to see their team perform devoid of its best
players.

Having said all this, cricket is still for me the greatest
game in the world. Only English cricket has been sadly lacking great players – and for some years now. But that's not
to say great players are not around today. They are, but they

play for other countries such as Australia, Pakistan, India, South Africa and, in the case of Brian Lara, the West Indies.

We live in the era when cult celebrity status is bestowed upon people whose image outweighs their talent. Football is a prime example of this, but in an attempt to make the game more appealing to the general public it is happening in cricket too. I recently heard Phil Tufnell being referred to on television as 'a legend of English cricket'. I nearly fell off my chair laughing. W. G. Grace, Jack Hobbs, Harold Larwood, Len Hutton, Jim Laker, Frank Tyson, Ray Illingworth, Geoffrey Boycott, Colin Cowdrey and, of course, Ian Botham are some of the legends of English cricket. But by no stretch of the imagination could Phil Tufnell ever be categorized thus. After 11 September I wondered how the media could ever again be obsessed with 'cult celebrities' who have a modicum of talent, in some cases no discernible talent at all, and who never have anything meaningful to say for themselves. But today the cult of the celebrity appears to be as strong as ever it was, which both bewilders and saddens me. It used to be that fame was what you earned for being extremely good at what you did. Nowadays fame has little to do with talent and more to do with how many times your picture appears in newspapers or how frequently you appear on television.

I am in my seventies now but still fit, active and working hard – and God willing long may that continue. I play golf regularly and to a decent standard, though of course not to the standard I aspire to! In a celebrity tournament in 2003 I hit my first hole-in-one. I'm happy to say that I won that tournament playing against guys, some of whom were considerably younger than me. I don't smoke and, other than the occasional glass of wine when Veronica and I sit down to a meal, I don't drink. Yet I still hear stories about me speaking at dinners and consuming endless pints of beer! And as the many people who have heard me speak at dinners or seen my theatre show will testify, I don't swear.

Having reached my seventies, to my delight I have discovered a number of benefits of being that age. No one expects
you to run – anywhere. There is little left to learn the hard
way. You can live without alcohol – but not without glasses.
My joints are more accurate meteorologists than Michael Fish
and Suzanne Charlton. In a hostage situation I would be likely
to be the first to be released. I don't have to slow down for
speed cameras . . .

I am still a great lover of sport and follow most sports
avidly. I was delighted when the England rugby team won the
World Cup. Martin Johnson is one of the greatest team
captains of all time in my book. A leader who led from the
front and inspired those around him to greater things. Though
I am absolutely delighted at the victory of Clive Woodward's
men, the fact that it has been thirty-six years since England last
won a major world championship makes a mockery of the
belief held by many that we are a great sporting nation. We do
love sport, but there is simply not the infrastructure, funding,
facilities and necessary talent to nurture and develop what
talent exists to produce true world champions. The England
rugby team has been an oasis in what has been a barren desert
for British sport and I sincerely hope English rugby can achieve
what will be as difficult a task as winning the World Cup –
that is, building on that success.

Looking back on my career in cricket both as a player and
broadcaster I am very grateful for all the good times I enjoyed
and the great friends I made. Paul Getty Junior and I were
particularly good friends. Paul loved his cricket, and though he
never made it public, put a lot of money into the game,
particularly at grass-roots level where he was very keen to
encourage youngsters to take up the game. I have never ceased
to be amazed by the kindness and generosity of people.

I was once in Australia attending a function at the residence
of the then Prime Minister Robert Menzies. Mr Menzies took
to the floor to speak and at the end of his speech bowled me

over. He made mention of the fact that I was visiting his country and was in attendance at the occasion. He then went on to say, quite rightly, that it was my birthday that day and asked me to join him on the podium to accept a presentation to mark the day. I was both flabbergasted and delighted that the Prime Minister of Australia knew that it was my birthday and wanted to present me with, as he said, 'a small gift by way of a token to the respect in which I was held by the Australian people'. I felt very humble indeed as I listened to Mr Menzies' generous words before accepting his kind gift of a beautiful inscribed tankard. The Japanese have a saying, 'little fish are sweet', and the birthday gift bestowed on me by Robert Menzies on behalf of the Australian people was indeed a very sweet moment for me.

Thankfully I have enjoyed many such sweet moments. Creating a world record when taking my 300th Test wicket. Winning seven County Championships outright with Yorkshire when winning the County Championship really meant something. My sixty-seven Tests for England. However, for me the most pleasing and satisfying thing about my career in cricket was the great and lasting friendships I made.

To this day I hold the Duke of Norfolk, Sir Paul Getty, Robert Menzies and Sir William Worsley in high esteem and consider myself very fortunate indeed to have known such wonderful gentlemen as good friends. The most satisfying and enduring friendships I made through cricket were with my Yorkshire teammates such as Brian Close, Ray Illingworth, Doug Padgett, Jack Hampshire, Ken Taylor, Bob Platt, Don Wilson, Peter Parfitt, Jimmy Binks, Phil Sharpe and Geoffrey Boycott. When you go through what we went through to win games and championships, you get to know your teammates more than as just good friends – you know each other as men. Cricket, like other team sports, bares the character of individuals. You get to see and know the mental as well as the physical strengths of one another. You find out how you and your teammates react and behave when the pressure is really on. When the odds are stacked against you and the team is galvanized and sets out to achieve what many consider to be an impossible task, such a situation reveals the true self and you see your teammates as they really are. The bond between players is very strong, which is why we have all remained the best of friends after all these years and why, when we do get together, there is a very special atmosphere in the room.

Some might find it surprising that I included Geoffrey Boycott in that number. Geoff and I have often been at loggerheads, particularly in the seventies, when there was a lot of in-fighting at Yorkshire and Geoff led a group that took control of the club. I was totally opposed to Geoff at that time and what he did, but life is too short to bear grudges, besides which, I never had a grudge against Geoff, merely a difference of opinion with him. I have also had differences of opinion with Brian Close, Ray Illingworth and others, but that does not mean to say we are not good friends. The in-fighting that took place at Yorkshire is water under the bridge. Life has moved on and so have Geoff and I. He is a welcome visitor in my home, and when the news broke of his illness, I was one of the first people to ring him up and convey my sincere wishes for his healthy recovery and to let him know that if there was anything Veronica and I could do, he only had to pick up his telephone and ring.

I am very happy and content in life. I still watch a lot of cricket, though when watching on television I do so with the sound turned down. I do so because I find a number of commentators who have no experience whatsoever of playing cricket at a decent level, never mind International level, talk a lot of drivel. Such commentators are not unique to television these days, they are also to be heard on the radio. I was once taken to task by one such commentator on the matter of fast bowling. In short, his ideas were totally different to mine. At one point I said to him, 'What do you know about fast bowling anyway? You never played cricket at any decent level.'

His response was to say, 'May I remind you I played for Cambridge University against both the Army and the RAF.'

To which my reply was, 'As I was saying . . .'

I have two great loves in life. First and foremost is my wife Veronica. The best moment in my life was the day I met her. I cannot imagine what my life would have been like had Veronica not entered it. She is everything to me and for over thirty years has made me blissfully happy. The other love in my life is cricket. I have expressed my opinions on the game past and present. There is much about cricket today that I don't like, but I still love the game.

I am an avid reader of books, but every book I have read that deals with love is either about love blossoming, or love ending. Rarely does one read about enduring love. I would like to think that this is such a book. For in telling the story of my life to date, I have told you the way it was; in so doing revealing my enduring love for Veronica and the game of cricket which, in their respective ways, have made me who I am – The real Fred Trueman, who, having read my story, you will now know.

Epilogue

I BEGAN THIS BOOK by mentioning a slightly fractious encounter with the Duke of Norfolk, and how we later became friends. Not only did he enrich the game of cricket, he also allowed me to gain an insight into the very highest echelons of society – yet another reason that cricket remains a great game. The Duke of Norfolk was not only a brilliant organizer and champion of cricket, he also made professionals feel an integral part of that high society. He was a wonderful character, and his wealth of stories meant he was fantastic company. My favourite of these concerns Sir Winston Churchill.

It was very close to the end of the great man's life, and Churchill was by now bedridden and seriously ill. The Duke of Norfolk had been called back from a winter tour of Australia to help make arrangements for Sir Winston's funeral. On his return, the duke paid a visit to Churchill. According to the duke, he arrived at Churchill's bedside whilst Sir Winston was sleeping. Eventually Churchill opened his eyes and on seeing the Duke of Norfolk engaged him in conversation.

'Ah, Norfolk,' muttered Sir Winston. 'I know why you are here.'

'I am here to ask after your well being, Sir Winston,' said the duke, 'hoping that your recovery will be a speedy one.'

'Ah, I know the real reason for your presence,' said Sir Winston. 'You are charged with overseeing the arrangements for my funeral. Tell me, Norfolk, will Her Majesty the Queen be in attendance?'

'In the event of your passing, Sir Winston, as and when that may eventually be, I should say yes, Her Majesty the Queen will attend your funeral. As head of state, Her Majesty will see it as a matter of duty, as well as wanting to pay due respect to your good self,' replied the duke with characteristic diplomacy in the light of such a sensitive matter.

'And will arrangements be made for the president of the United States to attend my funeral?' asked Sir Winston.

'In the event of your passing, Sir Winston, as and when that may eventually be, yes, as leader of the most powerful nation in the world, the president of the United States will be in attendance at your funeral,' the Duke replied.

Sir Winston gave a slow nod of his head to indicate his satisfaction. For a few seconds there was an uneasy silence as Sir Winston gathered the strength to continue the conversation.

'And tell me, Norfolk. Will de Gaulle be there?'

'In the event of your passing, as and when that may eventually be, on the occasion of your funeral, in his capacity as president of France, Charles de Gaulle will be present, Sir Winston,' the duke confirmed.

Again, there was a moment of uneasy silence before Churchill spoke again.

'Should that be so,' said Sir Winston, suddenly finding strength in his voice, 'will you make the necessary arrangements for my cortège to leave from Waterloo station?'

Of the establishment figures involved in cricket in my time as a player, the Duke of Norfolk was an exception. He made a telling contribution to the game, whilst many of the old Etonians and Oxbridge set, in my opinion, contributed next to nothing. Modern-day cricket for me is a curate's egg. As previously stated I do not agree with many of the changes to have taken place in the game, but some have indeed been for the good of cricket. Thankfully, the establishment figures – the vast majority of whom didn't have a clue about the game – have been eased out of the game. However, modern cricket still seems devoid of behind-the-scenes people of the Duke of Norfolk's calibre.

But of course it's not all doom and gloom. In June 2004 I was absolutely delighted to learn that my old pal Tom Graveney had been appointed president of the MCC. It was an appointment that met with my wholehearted approval, and one that must have had some of the old lords and earls who once ruled cricket spinning in their graves. Tom became the first 'commoner', the first former professional cricketer, to be appointed to what is still the most prestigious and highly rated position in English cricket. When I heard the news of his appointment, I was left with the feeling that the wheel had now turned full circle.

Tom was one of the premier batsmen of the post-war generation. He played in seventy-nine Tests between 1951 and 1969 and if the selectors had had anything about them should have played in far more. One selector, justifying this position, said it was because Tom was 'casual and lacking in purpose'. This is a batsman who scored 4,882 Test runs at an average of 44.38, including eleven centuries and a top score of 258. In First Class cricket between 1948 and 1972, Tom notched 47,793 runs, incorporating 122 centuries, at an average of 44.92. I don't know about you, but to me that doesn't sound like the career of a batsman 'lacking in purpose'.

Tom delighted in the batsman's art. So much so that spectators quickly caught his mood and joined him in his enjoyment. He was the first player of the post-war years to make 100 First Class centuries and at all times was a delight to watch. His upright, elegant batting and superb technique could master just about every type of bowling. He played for Gloucestershire from 1948 to 1960 but after losing the captaincy left to join Worcestershire. Some believed his best days with the bat were behind him, but the truth was he was in his pomp at New Road. And yet for all his prowess Tom was only ever in and out of the England team. He captained England once, against Australia in 1968, but in the early to mid-sixties often found himself out of favour with the selectors.

He was recalled to play for England against the West Indies in 1966 when he was approaching forty years of age. He belied his age by scoring two centuries and 96 against what was a fiery and formidable pace attack, and remained an automatic choice for England until 1969 when once again he was treated shabbily by the selectors.

Tom was selected to play for England but informed the selectors that his benefit match with Worcestershire fell on the rest day (the Sunday) of the Test. As many people had purchased tickets for his benefit game, Tom informed the selectors that he was obliged to play. So on a day when his England colleagues were resting or enjoying a round of golf, Tom duly played in his benefit. For his trouble, Tom was suspended by the selectors for three Tests. Tom was never to play for England again. A sad and undeserved finale to his International career.

Now Tom is President of the MCC. He can call the tune, and knowing him, it will be a sweet one. In his role as president he will, I am sure, display much common sense, objectivity and fairness to all – the mark of him as a man. I should imagine Tom will also bring much humour to the position, and whatever tasks he sets about doing what he will not convey is a 'lack of purpose'!

I am delighted for Tom. He knows that should he ever need any help or advice from me, all he has to do is pick up the phone. I never thought I would live to see the day when a former pro was appointed to such an exalted position in the game. That I have done fills me with pride and instils in me the belief that there is much to be said for the modern game after all.

CAREER STATISTICS

ALL FIRST-CLASS MATCHES: BOWLING AND FIELDING

10 Wickets in a Match (25)

for Yorkshire

v Derbyshire	10	for	90	at	Bradford	1957
	11	for	123	at	Sheffield	1961
v Essex	11	for	94	at	Southend	1961
	10	for	67	at	Bradford	1966
v Gloucestershire	11	for	101	at	Huddersfield	1955
	10	for	65	at	Bradford	1963
v Hampshire	12	for	62	at	Portsmouth	1960
v Kent	10	for	136	at	Scarborough	1953
v Leicestershire	12	for	58	at	Sheffield	1961
v Northamptonshire	14	for	125	at	Sheffield	1960
v Nottinghamshire	11	for	94	at	Sheffield	1951
	10	for	94	at	Scarborough	1955
	10	for	142	at	Worksop	1962
v Surrey	14	for	123	at	The Oval	1960
v Sussex	13	for	77	at	Hove	1965
v Warwickshire	10	for	73	at	Bradford	1960
	10	for	36	at	Birmingham	1963
v Cambridge Univ.	11	for	75	at	Cambridge	1957
v Oxford Univ.	10	for	32	at	Oxford	1955
v West Indies	10	for	81	at	Middlesbrough	1963

for England

v Australia	11	for	88	at	Leeds	1961
v West Indies	11	for	152	at	Lord's	1963
	12	for	119	at	Birmingham	1963

for MCC

v Otago	13	for	79	at	Dunedin	1958–59
v Otago Invitation XI	11	for	83	at	Dunedin	1962–63

8 Wickets in a Match (10)

for Yorkshire

v	Essex	8	for	37	at	Bradford	1966
v	Gloucestershire	8	for	45	at	Bradford	1963
v	Kent	8	for	28	at	Dover	1954
v	Nottinghamshire	8	for	68	at	Sheffield	1951
		8	for	53	at	Nottingham	1951
		8	for	84	at	Worksop	1962
v	Sussex	8	for	36	at	Hove	1965
v	Minor Counties	8	for	70	at	Lord's	1949

for England

v	India	8	for	31	at	Manchester	1952

for MCC

v	Otago	8	for	45	at	Dunedin	1958–59

Hat Tricks (4)

for Yorkshire

v	Nottinghamshire	at	Nottingham	1951
		at	Scarborough	1955
		at	Bradford	1963
v	MCC	at	Lord's	1958

How He Took His 2304 Wickets

Caught	1115	48.4%
Bowled	899	39.1%
lbw	273	11.8%
Hit wicket	17	0.7%

ALL FIRST-CLASS MATCHES: BATTING

							How out				
Season	Mtchs	In	NO	R	HS	Av	c	b	lbw	st	ro
1949	8	6	2	12	10	3.00	2	2	–	–	–
1950	14	15	9	23	4*	3.83	3	2	–	1	–
1951	30	24	7	114	25	6.70	3	8	1	5	–
1952	9	4	3	40	23*	40.00	–	1	–	–	–
1953	15	16	2	131	34	9.35	–	10	1	2	1
1953–54 WI	8	9	3	81	20	13.50	2	3	1	–	–
1954	33	35	5	270	50*	9.00	10	18	–	–	2
1955	31	38	8	391	74	13.03	14	13	2	–	1
1956	31	30	3	358	58	13.25	9	15	1	2	–
1956–57 IND	2	4	2	96	46*	48.00	1	–	–	1	–
1957	32	41	14	405	63	15.00	8	12	2	3	2
1958	30	35	7	453	61	16.17	15	12	1	–	–
1958–59 ANZ	17	21	2	312	53	16.42	10	5	3	1	–
1959	30	40	9	602	54	19.41	14	10	4	2	1
1959–60 WI	10	13	2	153	37	13.90	6	3	2	–	–
1960	32	40	5	577	69	16.48	20	10	4	–	1
1960–61 SA	4	5	1	139	59	34.75	2	2	–	–	–
1961	34	48	6	809	80*	19.26	26	14	2	–	–
1962	33	42	4	840	63	22.10	20	10	7	1	–
1962–63 ANZ	12	14	–	194	38	13.85	11	3	–	–	–
1963	27	41	6	783	104	22.37	26	6	1	–	2
1963–64 WI	2	2	–	28	28	14.00	–	1	–	1	–
1964	31	39	4	595	77	17.00	19	12	3	–	1
1964–65 WI	3	2	–	24	23	12.00	2	–	–	–	–
1965	30	39	2	636	101	17.18	14	16	7	–	–
1966	33	43	4	448	43	11.48	26	7	4	1	1
1967	31	33	5	342	34	12.21	19	6	3	–	–
1967–68 IND	1	2	–	42	33	21.00	–	1	–	1	–
1968	29	30	5	296	45	11.84	13	6	4	–	2
1969	1	2	–	37	26	18.50	1	–	–	1	–
Total	**603**	**713**	**120**	**9231**	**–**	**15.56**	**296**	**208**	**53**	**22**	**14**

All First-Class Matches for Yorkshire

| | | | | | | | | How out | | |
Mtchs	In	NO	R	HS	Av	c	b	lbw	st	ro
459	533	81	6852	104	15.15	226	157	42	14	13

County Championship Matches

| | | | | | | | | How out | | |
Mtchs	In	NO	R	HS	Av	c	b	lbw	st	ro
381	448	65	5928	104	15.47	190	134	34	12	13

Centuries (3)

for Yorkshire

v Middlesex	101	at	Scarborough	1965
v Northhamptonshire	104	at	Northampton	1963

for an England XI

v Young England XI	100*	at	Scarborough	1963

Fifties (26)

for Yorkshire

v Derbyshire	58	at	Sheffield	1961
v Essex	54	at	Colchester	1959
v Gloucestershire	50*	at	Bristol	1954
	58	at	Sheffield	1956
	61	at	Bristol	1958
	77	at	Sheffield	1964

Fifties (continued)

v	Hampshire	58*	at	Bradford	1958
		53	at	Bournemouth	1958
		51*	at	Bournemouth	1961
		55	at	Middlesbrough	1965
v	Kent	69	at	Gravesend	1960
v	Lancashire	54*	at	Sheffield	1961
v	Leicestershire	74	at	Leicester	1955
		52	at	Leeds	1960
v	Middlesex	54	at	Lord's	1964
v	Somerset	63	at	Leeds	1957
v	Surrey	50	at	Bradford	1964
v	Warwickshire	57	at	Harrogate	1964
v	Worcestershire	56	at	Harrogate	1960
v	New Zealand	60	at	Bradford	1965
v	West Indies	55	at	Middlesbrough	1963

for T. N. Pearce's XI

v	Australia	80*	at	Scarborough	1961
v	West Indies	50	at	Scarborough	1963

for Players

v	Gentlemen	63	at	Lord's	1962

for MCC

v	Combined XI	53	at	Perth	1958–59

for Commonwealth XI

v	Transvaal	59	at	Johannesburg	1960–61

Century Partnerships (7)

v Leicestershire	133	for the 8th wkt with R. Illingworth at Leicester, 1955 (FT 74; RI 61)
	102	for the 6th wkt with K. Taylor at Sheffield, 1961 (FT 43; KT 159)
v Middlesex	147	for the 8th wkt with J. G. P. Chadwick at Scarborough, 1965 (FT 101; JC 59)

Century Partnerships (continued)

v Northhamptonshire	166	for the 6th wkt with D. B. Close at Northampton, 1963 (FT 104; DBC 161)
v Somerset	116	for the 8th wkt with R. Illingworth at Leeds, 1957 (FT 63; RI 97)
v Cambridge Univ.	114	for the 6th wkt with D. B. Close at Cambridge, 1963 (FT 49; DBC 86)

for an England XI

v Young England XI	120*	for the 8th wkt with T. E. Bailey at Scarborough, 1963 (FT 100*; TEB 44*)

Most Runs Off One Six-ball Over

26 (440666) off D. Shackleton, Yorkshire v Hampshire, Middlesbrough, 1965. (Subsequently, in the second innings, Yorkshire were all out for 23, which is their lowest total in any first-class match.)

How His 593 Completed Innings Ended

Caught	296	49.9%
Bowled	208	35.1%
lbw	53	8.9%
Stumped	22	3.7%
Run out	14	2.4%

TEST MATCHES: BOWLING AND FIELDING

Season		Test	O	M	R	W	Av	5 W in In	10 W in Mtch	Ct
1952	IND	4	119.4	25	386	29	13.31	2	–	1
1953	AUS	1	26.3	4	90	4	22.50	–	–	2
1953–54	WI	3	133.2	27	420	9	46.66	–	–	–
1955	SA	1	35.0	4	112	2	56.00	–	–	–
1956	AUS	2	75.0	13	184	9	20.44	1	–	4
1957	WI	5	173.3	34	455	22	20.68	1	–	7
1958	NZ	5	131.5	44	256	15	17.06	1	–	6
1958–59	AUS	3	87.0 †	11	276	9	30.66	–	–	3
1958–59	NZ	2	44.5	17	105	5	21.00	–	–	4
1959	IND	5	177.4	53	401	24	16.70	–	–	5
1959–60	WI	5	220.3	62	549	21	26.14	1	–	6
1960	SA	5	180.3	31	508	25	20.32	1	–	4
1961	AUS	4	164.4	21	529	20	26.45	2	1	2
1962	PAK	4	164.5	37	439	22	19.95	1	–	6
1962–63	AUS	5	158.3 †	9	521	20	26.05	1	–	–
1962–63	NZ	2	88.0	29	164	14	11.71	1	–	–
1963	WI	5	236.4	53	594	34	17.47	4	2	3
1964	AUS	4	133.3	25	399	17	23.47	1	–	3
1965	NZ	2	96.3	23	237	6	39.50	–	–	1
			245.3†							
Total		**67**	**2202.3**	**522**	**6625**	**307**	**21.57**	**17**	**3**	**64**

How He Took His 307 Test Wickets

Caught	161	52.4%
Bowled	104	33.9%
lbw	39	12.7%
Hit wicket	3	1.0%

10 Wickets in a Test Match (3)

v Australia	11 for	88	(5 for 58, 6 for 30)	at	Leeds	1961
v West Indies	12 for	119	(5 for 75, 7 for 44)	at	Birmingham	1963
	11 for	152	(6 for 100, 5 for 52)	at	Lord's	1963

7 Wickets in a Test Innings (3)

	O	M	R	W			
v India	8.4	2	31	8	at	Manchester	1952
v New Zealand	30.2	9	75	7	at	Christchurch	1962–63
v West Indies	14.3	2	44	7	at	Birmingham	1963

Test Match Bowling Against Each Country

	Mtchs	O	M	R	W	Av	5 W in In	10 W in Mtch	Ct
v Australia		245.3 †							
	19	399.4	83	1999	79	25.30	5	1	21
v India	9	297.2	78	787	53	14.84	2	–	6
v New Zealand	11	361.1	113	762	40	19.05	2	–	11
v Pakistan	4	164.5	37	439	22	19.95	1	–	6
v South Africa	6	215.3	35	620	27	22.96	1	–	4
v West Indies	18	764.0	176	2018	86	23.46	6	2	16
		245.3 †							
Total	**67**	**2202.3**	**522**	**6625**	**307**	**21.57**	**17**	**3**	**64**

Test Match Bowling in England

	Mtchs	O	M	R	W	Av	5 W in In	10 W in Mtch	Ct
v Australia	11	399.4	63	1202	50	24.04	4	1	11
v India	9	297.2	78	787	53	14.84	2	–	6
v New Zealand	7	228.2	67	493	21	23.47	1	–	7
v Pakistan	4	164.5	37	439	22	19.95	1	–	6
v South Africa	6	215.3	35	620	27	22.96	1	–	4
v West Indies	10	410.1	87	1049	56	18.73	5	2	10
Total	**47**	**1715.5**	**367**	**4590**	**229**	**20.04**	**14**	**3**	**44**

Test Match Bowling Overseas

	Mtchs	O	M	R	W	Av	5 W in In	10 W in Mtch	Ct
v Australia	8	245.3†	20	797	29	27.48	1	–	10
v New Zealand	4	132.5	46	269	19	14.15	1	–	4
v West Indies	8	353.5	89	969	30	32.3	1	–	6
Total	**20**	245.3† **486.4**	**155**	**2035**	**78**	**26.08**	**3**	**–**	**20**

TEST MATCHES: BATTING

Season		Mtchs	In	NO	R	HS	Av
1952	IND	4	2	1	17	17	17.00
1953	AUST	1	1	–	10	10	10.00
1953–54	WI	3	4	1	38	19	12.66
1955	SA	1	2	2	8	6*	–
1956	AUST	2	3	–	9	7	3.00
1957	WI	5	4	3	89	36*	89.00
1958	NZ	5	4	1	52	39*§	17.33
1958–59	AUST	3	6	–	75	36	12.50
1958–59	NZ	2	2	1	42	21*	42.00
1959	IND	5	6	–	61	28	10.16
1959–60	WI	5	8	2	86	37	14.33
1960	SA	5	8	1	99	25	14.14
1961	AUST	4	6	–	60	25	10.00
1962	PAK	4	2	–	49	29	24.50
1962–63	AUST	5	7	–	142	38	20.28
1962–63	NZ	2	2	–	14	11	7.00
1963	WI	5	10	1	82	29*	9.11
1964	AUST	4	6	1	42	12*	8.40
1965	NZ	2	2	–	6	3	3.00
Total		**67**	**85**	**14**	**981**	**–**	**13.81**

Test Match Batting Against Each Country

	Mtchs	In	NO	R	HS	Av
v Australia	19	29	1	338	38	12.07
v India	9	8	1	78	28	11.14
v New Zealand	11	10	2	114	39*§	14.25
v Pakistan	4	2		49	29	24.50
v South Africa	6	10	3	107	25	15.28
v West Indies	18	26	7	295	37	15.52

§ Highest score: at The Oval, 1958, in 25 minutes, including 3 sixes off A. M. Moir

COUNTY CHAMPIONSHIP MATCHES:
BOWLING AND FIELDING

		Mtchs	O	M	R	W	Av	5 W in In	10 W in Mtch	Ct
v	Derbyshire	24	755.2	178	1850	108	17.12	7	2	17
v	Essex	20	591.4	120	1492	96	15.54	7	2	9
v	Glamorgan	17	371.1	100	858	54	15.88	4	–	13
v	Gloucestershire	23	528.0	122	1331	91	14.62	5	2	22
v	Hampshire	22	603.5	174	1331	91	14.62	6	1	20
v	Kent	20	491.1	92	1265	82	15.42	3	1	10
v	Lancashire	35	977.5	226	2307	128	18.02	8	–	18
v	Leicestershire	22	593.2	131	1536	88	17.45	6	1	18
v	Middlesex	28	754.5	159	2037	89	22.88	2	–	20
v	North'shire	18	548.3	133	1372	65	21.1	4	1	22
v	Nott'shire	29	786.4	190	1826	131	13.93	10	3	22
v	Somerset	25	676.4	165	1572	108	14.55	3	–	22
v	Surrey	32	910.0	222	2272	107	21.23	5	1	28
v	Sussex	21	602.4	146	1557	79	19.7	4	1	12
v	Warwickshire	24	654.1	183	1542	109	14.14	7	2	11
v	Worcestershire	21	507.3	122	1193	62	19.24	2	–	14
	Total	**381**	**10353.2**	**2463**	**25341**	**1488**	**17.03**	**83**	**17**	**278**

How He Took His 1488
County Championship Wickets

Caught	716	48.1%
Bowled	585	39.3%
lbw	178	12.0%
Hit wicket	9	0.6%

COUNTY CHAMPIONSHIP MATCHES:
BATTING

		Mtchs	*In*	*NO*	*R*	*HS*	*Av*
v	Derbyshire	24	27	4	338	58	14.69
v	Essex	20	21	4	288	54	16.94
v	Glamorgan	17	20	–	180	37	9.00
v	Gloucestershire	23	29	3	488	77	18.76
v	Hampshire	22	31	5	573	58 *	22.03
v	Kent	20	21	–	264	69	12.57
v	Lancashire	35	38	11	400	54 *	14.81
v	Leicestershire	22	25	2	417	74	18.13
v	Middlesex	28	35	2	555	101	16.81
v	North'shire	18	23	3	396	104	19.80
v	Nott'shire	29	26	7	266	34 *	14.00
v	Somerset	25	27	3	372	63	15.50
v	Surrey	32	44	3	434	50	10.58
v	Sussex	21	26	5	362	43	17.23
v	Warwickshire	24	29	6	266	57	11.56
v	Worcestershire	21	26	7	329	56	17.31
	Total	**381**	**448**	**65**	**5928**	**–**	**15.47**

How His 383 County Championship
Innings Ended (Dismissals)

Caught	190	48.1%
Bowled	134	39.3%
lbw	34	8.9%
Stumped	12	3.1%
Run out	13	3.4%

GROUNDS

Matches Played on Yorkshire Grounds

	Mtchs	In	NO	R	HS	Av	O	M	R	W	Av	5 W in In	10 W in Mtch	Ct
Bradford	58	70	11	890	60	15.08	1376.4	324	3367	213	15.80	12	4	53
Harrogate	12	11	1	248	57	24.80	295.1	94	619	44	14.06	3	–	8
Huddersfield	5	6	2	25	12	6.25	162.2	33	432	32	13.50	2	1	4
Hull	20	23	2	182	39	8.66	550.2	129	1280	80	16.00	2	–	10
Leeds	48	57	11	679	63	14.76	1324.1	311	3368	181	18.60	8	1	46
Middlesbrough	12	16	1	325	55	21.66	303.3	74	696	54	12.88	4	1	10
Scarborough	61	77	22	1142	101	20.76	1425.4	267	4097	203	20.18	9	2	43
Sheffield	53	53	8	806	77	17.91	1560.3	356	3954	225	17.57	17	4	45
Total	**269**	**313**	**58**	**4297**	**–**	**16.85**	**6998.2**	**1588**	**17813**	**1032**	**17.26**	**57**	**13**	**219**

Other Grounds in England Where He Appeared in 6 or More Matches

	Mtchs	In	NO	R	HS	Av	O	M	R	W	Av	5 W in In	10 W in Mtch	Ct
Birmingham	18	20	5	161	29*	10.73	568.4	126	1580	79	20.00	6	2	9
Bournemouth	6	11	2	222	53	24.66	136.4	37	331	16	20.68	1	—	6
Bristol	9	10	2	143	61	17.87	180.4	37	479	28	17.10	—	—	5
Cambridge	12	11	2	167	49	18.55	283.2	87	629	45	13.97	2	1	7
Chesterfield	9	10	1	92	48	10.22	281.5	62	682	28	24.35	—	—	4
Hove	10	12	3	113	34	12.55	337.2	86	850	46	18.47	4	1	2
Leicester	12	15	2	223	74	17.15	304.2	61	770	36	21.38	2	—	10
Lord's	50	62	9	737	63	13.90	1488.2	324	4108	191	21.50	9	1	24
Manchester	25	32	9	286	40*	12.43	741.0	161	1854	83	22.33	3	—	15
Northampton	8	10	2	255	104	31.87	249.2	58	637	23	27.69	1	—	8
Nottingham	16	13	2	116	31	10.54	518.2	127	1232	77	16.00	5	—	14
Oxford	9	6	1	56	23	11.20	263.5	91	482	50	9.64	3	1	4
Taunton	8	8	1	114	42	16.28	208.0	55	453	28	16.17	—	—	4
The Oval	28	38	2	367	45	10.19	777.2	186	1851	103	17.97	6	1	28
Worcester	9	13	3	144	43	14.40	254.0	59	606	25	24.24	—	—	2

Overall Summary by Grounds

	Mtchs	In	NO	R	HS	Av	O	M	R	W	Av	5 W in In	10 W in Mtch	Ct
In Yorkshire	269	313	58	4297	101	16.85	6998.2	1588	17813	1032	17.26	57	13	219
Others in England	275	328	52	3865	104	14.00	7758.1	1832	19497	1045	18.65	56	10	170
All in England	544	641	110	8162	104	15.37	14756.3	3420	37310	2077	17.96	113	23	389
In Australia	21	27	1	445	53	17.11	494.4†	49	1596	67	23.82	3	–	19
In India	3	6	2	138	46*	34.50	79.0	11	262	9	29.11	–	–	1
In New Zealand	8	8	1	61	21*	8.71	221.4	66	491	45	10.91	5	2	6
In South Africa	4	5	1	139	59	34.75	114.4	16	326	22	14.81	1	–	2
In West Indies	23	26	5	286	37	13.61	790.4	197	2169	84	25.82	4	–	21
							494.4†							
Total	**603**	**713**	**120**	**9231**	–	**15.56**	**15962.3**	**3759**	**42154**	**2304**	**18.29**	**126**	**25**	**438**

AS CAPTAIN

	Mtchs	Won	Lost	Drawn
1962	2	1	–	1
1965	3	2	–	1
1966	2	1	1	–
1967	16	9	2	5
1968	7	4	1	2
1969	1	1	–	–
Total	**31**	**18**	**4**	**9**
		58.1%	**12.9%**	**29.0%**

ONE-DAY CRICKET

Gilette Cup (for Yorkshire 1963–68)

Mtchs	In	NO	R	HS	Av	O	M	R	W	Av	Ct
11	9	1	127	28	15.87	119.2	15	348	21	16.56	5

His best Gillette Cup performance was against Somerset at Taunton in 1965 – 10.2 overs, 4 maidens, 15 runs, 6 wickets – and this earned him the 'Man of the Match' award.

John Player League (for Derbyshire 1972)

Mtchs	In	NO	R	HS	Av	O	M	R	W	Av	Ct
6	4	1	28	10*	9.33	45	3	159	7	22.71	–

INDEX

OTHER PAN BOOKS
AVAILABLE FROM PAN MACMILLAN

ANDY GRAY
GRAY MATTERS   0 330 43199 4   £7.99

PIERLUIGI COLLINA
THE RULES OF THE GAME   0 330 41872 6   £6.99

BOBBY ROBSON
MY AUTOBIOGRAPHY   0 330 36985 7   £6.99

DAVID REMNICK
KING OF THE WORLD   0 330 37189 4   £7.99

All Pan Macmillan titles can be ordered from our website,
www.panmacmillan.com, or from your local bookshop
and are also available by post from:

Bookpost, PO Box 29, Douglas, Isle of Man IM99 1BQ
Credit cards accepted. For details:
Telephone: +44 (0)1624 677237
Fax: +44 (0)1624 670923
E-mail: bookshop@enterprise.net
www.bookpost.co.uk

Free postage and packing in the United Kingdom

Prices shown above were correct at the time of going to press.
Pan Macmillan reserve the right to show new retail prices on covers
which may differ from those previously advertised in the text
or elsewhere.

www.ingramcontent.com/pod-product-compliance
Ingram Content Group UK Ltd.
Pitfield, Milton Keynes, MK11 3LW, UK
UKHW040641280225
455688UK00002B/52